ROCKY BOYER'S WAR

ROCKY BOYER'S WAR

AN UNVARNISHED HISTORY OF THE AIR BLITZ THAT WON THE WAR IN THE SOUTHWEST PACIFIC

Allen D. Boyer

NAVAL INSTITUTE PRESS
Annapolis, Maryland

This book has been brought to publication with the generous assistance of Marguerite and Gerry Lenfest.

Naval Institute Press
291 Wood Road
Annapolis, MD 21402

Library of Congress Cataloging-in-Publication Data is available.
ISBN: 978-1-68247-096-1 (hardcover)
ISBN: 978-1-68247-097-8 (eBook)

Maps created by Beth Robertson, Mapping Specialists Ltd.

♾ Print editions meet the requirements of ANSI/NISO z39.48-1992 (Permanence of Paper).
Printed in the United States of America.

25 24 23 22 21 20 19 18 17   9 8 7 6 5 4 3 2 1
First printing

To Margaret Anne Boyer

Contents

Illustrations

Photos

Maps

Author's Note

This book follows and draws on a diary kept by Lt. Roscoe A. Boyer, my father, during his service in the Southwest Pacific. This diary is currently in my possession. The book reflects my father's own experiences and readings of events—his opinions and recollections. To frame or expand on what he wrote, I have used other material, primary sources where possible: unit histories, Missing Air Crew Reports, service newspapers, stateside newspapers, and commanders' memoirs. Sometimes I have verified what he reported, other times clarified or corrected it; but my father speaks in his own voice. His assessment of events he witnessed and people he encountered is unflinching (and at times unflattering), and his observations are presented as he recorded them during his time in the Pacific. Spelling and usage have been modernized and standardized. My father wrote grammatically and spelled well, but he constantly used abbreviations, frequently printed whole entries in block capitals, never indented a line or broke for a paragraph, and sometimes wrote as carelessly as some people type.

Writing seventy years ago, in the middle of a war, my father wrote of the enemy as Nips or Japs, offensive slurs. This was the language of the military in which he served; it has not been changed. He himself did not use those terms with mockery or contempt. He considered that the Japanese fought with courage and intelligence, and if he armed warplanes that flew against them, there were times when he thought he might die at their hands.

The only people to whom my father ever applied a disrespectful epithet were West Point graduates. Ring-knockers, he called them, after their customary way of calling a meeting to order.

INTRODUCTION

A War and a Diary

Half an hour before midnight, the first Japanese shell exploded overhead. It was a star shell, a sudden smear of blinding white light against the black night sky, and the scorching glare lit up the airfield. The bomb craters in the runway. The tanks of aviation gas, drained dry. The gray smoke above the fire in the bomb dump. The control tower and the banged-up bomber and the burning wreck of the fighter plane. The brass shell-casings fired off by the antiaircraft guns. And on the tarmac, a scattering of silhouettes and shadows: the handful of Fifth Air Force men and the empty bomb trolleys they were wheeling back into cover.

They were the airmen of the 71st Tactical Reconnaissance Group. "Reconnaissance" meant that they flew patrols looking for the Japanese. "Tactical" meant that if they found the Japanese, they bombed and strafed them. This evening, things were spun around: the Japanese had moved first and gotten too close. For once, the airmen knew exactly where the Japanese were. What they did not know was whether they could stop the Japanese warships before the Japanese found the range and brought their guns to bear on the airfield.

All that evening, in the dark, they had worked to arm the planes. They had sent out every bomber and fighter-bomber that could fly, carrying every bomb they could find and find fuses for. Not all of their planes had come back and some that did had been shot full of holes. None of that had made a difference.

For three long hours now they had watched the Japanese warships come south along the coast toward them. They had seen searchlights and ripples of flame and sometimes a swarm of firefly lights in the darkness. The firefly lights were their own bombers' running lights, and the ripples of flame were enemy antiaircraft guns, shooting at the bombers. No matter what their planes had done, the Japanese ships were still coming south.

They were in the Philippines, on the island of Mindoro. It was 1944, a hot dry evening, the day after Christmas.

Since the year began, they had fought their way north—from New Guinea to the Philippines, two thousand miles of mountains, jungle, islands, and oceans. In the Fifth Air Force, they had been the artillery for Douglas MacArthur's army, and sometimes the tank corps too. The airfields had been the front line. They had made rough landings in valleys where airfields could be built, flown in squadrons of warplanes while the Japanese were still being cleared out, and moved the front line forward. They had sidestepped entire Japanese armies and cut them off and left them behind, sitting on empty islands. They thought MacArthur was an ass, but he hadn't made many mistakes and he hadn't gotten them slaughtered on beachheads.

Mindoro was close to the Japanese and far from help—this time, MacArthur might have made a mistake. They were three hundred miles from the Sixth Army divisions on Leyte, farther still from any friendly air base, nowhere near any Navy fleet. They would have to handle, by themselves, whatever the Japanese threw at them. At their last base Japanese paratroopers had landed on the runway, shouting "Banzai!" and firing submachine guns. That recollection was on everyone's mind. Tonight the radio section was talking about a convoy of enemy troopships. One bomber pilot had seen landing barges alongside the destroyers. Against paratroopers with submachine guns all they had would be their pistols, and against the Japanese cruisers their bombers didn't seem to have done much good. If the Japanese warships were firing star shells now, they would be firing high explosive shells next.

⑨

That night on Mindoro, Rocky Boyer—1st Lt. Roscoe A. Boyer—was one of the officers loading the bombs. He was my father. Rocky was twenty-five then. In his young life he had been a farm boy, a college boy, a draftee, and a sergeant, and now he was communications officer for the 110th Tactical Reconnaissance Squadron. The next day, out of the officers in his tent, he would be the only man left alive.

In the Southwest Pacific during the war, no one was supposed to keep a diary. At reunions, after the war, when they found out that Rocky had done that, other men from his old squadron looked again at him, sharply. They knew that Rocky had kept their radios working. They had heard that he had been a college professor after the war, and retired as a full colonel. They had to think about what he might have said.

They had been on troopships with Rocky and flown over the same mountains that he had. They knew the same places, Moresby and Nadzab and Biak and where servicemen went on leave in Sydney. They had stood around in the same blacked-out tropical midnights, waiting for the sirens or gunshots that would sound the all clear. They had had the same friends whose planes hadn't come back. They had shot the breeze together and listened to Radio Tokyo and griped about Colonel Hutchison and rejoiced when retribution overtook Colonel Brownfield. They had gone to church with him, and Rocky might know what had happened that time when the chaplain wrote to MacArthur. Rocky had stolen a jeep for them. He was the officer they sent to buy beer because he was the officer who didn't drink. That night at Mindoro, when the Japanese ships shelled them, Rocky had driven to the airfield in the blackout and helped Smitty and Jensen load up the P-40s.

Rocky kept his diary during a year that took him from a Mississippi training base to New Guinea and from New Guinea to the Philippines, the Southwest Pacific air war of 1944. Of that brilliant and hard-fought campaign, an American blitzkrieg led by planes instead of tanks, Rocky told a narrative in counterpoint. He tried out titles—*The Prelude to Battle*, or *Behind the Lines*—but his tone was never grandiloquent. Once he remarked that he had been a lieutenant when he kept the diary, and that he had probably thought that anyone with a higher rank was a scoundrel. He agreed with what Bill Mauldin said, that every soldier wanted to write a book exposing the Army after the war.

The story is wrapped around three battles and a scandal, but it is not the Pacific War of the standard histories. The pilots Rocky knew did not dogfight with Zeros; they shot it out with Japanese antiaircraft gunners. They strafed Japanese aircraft and freighters and had their own warplanes burned to cinders. They died in bad weather, and when their engines cut out on them, and when they buzzed the airstrip. They had staff officers who got drunk and cut loose with pistols. They heard rumors and read newspapers, and they played office politics in the base HQ. They wanted to be promoted and they wanted to go home. This is their story of the air war.

1

FROM SUGAR CREEK TO SALINAS

The story was front-page news. Roosevelt's peacetime draft had taken hold of its first Franklin College graduate. On commencement afternoon, the *Franklin Evening Star* announced:

> It'll be a short jump from campus life to army life for Roscoe Boyer of Frankfort, Franklin College graduate and athlete.
>
> Boyer graduates at 4 o'clock this afternoon and is scheduled to report to his draft board in Frankfort at 8 o'clock Tuesday morning for induction into the U.S. Army for a year of training.
>
> A veteran football player, Boyer saw action on the Grizzly squad for three years. He had planned to enter the teaching profession upon graduation. His field is mathematics and he had taught a semester at Masonic Home high school as a practice instructor.
>
> Boyer has accepted his fate in good humor and plans to continue his hobby of sketching and drawing while in the army.[1]

In fact, Rocky felt no good humor. The draft and the Army hung over his life for long years. The Army would ship him back and forth across the continent; the Fifth Air Force would send him halfway around the world. It would be five years before he taught high school math again. It would be six years before he married the girl who watched him walk across the stage for his diploma.

⑤

Rocky Boyer was born in March 1919 in Sugar Creek Township, Clinton County, forty miles north of Indianapolis. The road to the city ran past Vonnegut's Hardware.

Clinton County was farmland then and it is farmland now, huge square fields of corn and soybeans and hogs looking back at you through the fence. The Boyer family had raised corn and taught school there since the land was cleared. Rocky's father was Van Roscoe Boyer. Rocky's mother was Laura Hester Wright, from Washington, Indiana. Her father was a truck farmer, a stocky little man who grew vegetables for the markets in St. Louis and Chicago and worked hard enough to send to college his daughter as well as his son.

Laura was a petite auburn-haired girl, pretty, who painted and made jewelry. Van was tall and broad-shouldered, with a pointed sense of humor. He had turned down a newspaper job to stay on and run the farm. It was not easy. Van got his crops in each year and taught high school history and Sunday school. Laura painted with watercolors, which were cheaper than oils, and joined ladies' societies. They handled what farming threw at them, but the effort left them angry; they could be tense and bitter. Van was a Democrat in a Republican county and blamed the politicians because the road past his house was gravel, not asphalt. Laura had illnesses that she did not talk about.

Rocky played high school basketball. Outside school, he raised show calves, bringing home ribbons from as far afield as Cleveland. Hybrid corn was being introduced, and the seed companies offered money for prize seed corn. Rocky spent long afternoons in the corncrib, choosing the ten most perfect ears of Reid's Yellow Dent field corn. For that he won a prize as well.[2]

Rocky went to Franklin College. He majored in mathematics and helped start the science club. He lived in the Sigma Alpha Epsilon house and paid his way through school by doing chores in the SAE kitchen. He played guard for the Franklin Grizzlies' football team. Rocky was strong—to water the livestock, he had worked a pump handle hundreds of times a night, every night for years—but he did not have the massive frame of a lineman. In the fall of 1940, when she was a Franklin College freshman, Margaret Anne Dillard first heard Rocky's name when the cheerleaders called for a cheer when he was being carried off the field.

Margaret Anne was from southern Indiana's Orange County—from the county seat of Paoli, with its sawmills and limestone quarries, not the spa towns of French Lick and West Baden. She was a bright, pretty young woman with long dark hair and expressive eyes. She was an English major, an officer of Pi Beta Phi, and editor-in-chief of the Franklin student newspaper. The first movie they went to had a quick gag about a dog and a fire hydrant; he laughed at it and then apologized. They walked back to campus along the middle of the street, something she had never done before. She liked the way he laughed and the way he walked. They went out again, often, to the Nook on campus, where you could buy 5 cent ice cream cones.

Rocky's senior year at Franklin began in September 1940. That same month, Congress passed the Selective Service Act. It soon was clear that Rocky would be called up. The draft board allowed him six months' deferment, enough to finish college.

ⓢ

On June 10, 1941, the day he was inducted, Rocky began keeping a journal. "My first day out in this cold cruel world," he began. "Yes, the draft got me—and how!"[3]

The crowd that gathered at the armory was perhaps one of the most cheerless masses that I have ever witnessed. All the mothers, fathers, in-laws, sweethearts, were there. My mother never let go a tear, she is too much of a lady, thank God.

On the bus down, there were twenty-four of us. No comments were made at first, except that we were on a one-way bus, and the cynical expressions upon the boys' faces were obvious. The undertaking seemed to be taken as a challenge. Most of the men were chain smokers, but perhaps that tension will work off—at least I hope so.

This evening I wrote my parents and Margaret Anne a card. Never before in my life have I desired to see a girl—any girl—one that would maybe turn and speak. Margaret Anne—she's swell—and if I could only see her or maybe talk—well, it's best that I should forget her anyway.[4]

In his postcard to Margaret Anne, Rocky objected, "I am in the Army now although I cannot recognize my mother across the street."[5] Rocky had bad eyes without his glasses, but the Army and his draft board did not care about that.

By the weekend, Rocky was on a train to Camp Wolters, Texas, west of Dallas. Rocky wrote that he had peeled potatoes across the state of Missouri. At Camp Wolters, the food improved, and the company was more congenial.

The fellows in my battalion can do something besides talk about getting drunk, dice, cards, and lewd women. These fellows write in all their spare time and buy newspapers galore. When the fellows do talk it is about some current events or some paramount problems. The secondary schools of Indiana are well represented by fellows from Wabash, DePauw, Ball State, Goshen, Franklin, Purdue is here, while IU is not here, also Indiana Central is forgotten.[6]

Among the recruits, Rocky met Jews for the first time, and liked them. (Before, he had seen Jews only from a distance, in the stockyards, *schochetim* slaughtering steers in accordance with kosher law—"little rabbis," farmers called them, quizzically but respectfully.) A Jewish draftee taught Rocky how to play chess, a favor he never forgot.

Over the summer, it became clear that draftees would see much more of the war than a year of training.[7] On this point, Rocky had sour conjectures.

> As usual England will have someone else fight their war and as usual Franklin D. Roosevelt is looking after a few already rich men's interest in Europe and will send our youths over to Europe. . . . 75% of the fellows here will attempt to run away if the present bill passes.
>
> Nearly all of these letters are written during a ten minute "break" which we get every hour. During these intervals the men usually relax on their cots and curse Roosevelt, which I hope that another Boyer never votes for again. He broke his word once and he'll do it again.[8]

This was unexpected; Rocky had been a staunch Democrat. His only lapse had been to attend Wendell Willkie's huge hometown rally at Elwood, Indiana, holding his younger sister Anndora on his shoulders. Van read Rocky's letters and said something about his son deserting and going off to join the Russians. But Rocky's tone was shifting. His morale was better.

> Our company is permanently organized. Our latest plans are to contact a few sororities at Texas Christian and exchange—well, anything. We have several fraternity men within our group. We have sent form letters to three different sororities. We plan to exchange several social affairs, since we have Saturday afternoon and Sunday off.[9]

Four years of being an SAE had left their mark. However downtrodden, Rocky was ready to plan a set of fraternity mixers. But he made fewer self-pitying perorations; he began making sententious pronouncements. Increasingly, he was humorous.

> Last night, I went to see a moving picture, *Penny Serenade*, in which an earthquake lasted for more than a minute. However in history there have been only two quakes that lasted more than a minute—one in 1923, I think in Japan, and the other when a South Sea island blew up.
>
> This morning the articles of war were read to us— all one hundred and ten of them.[10]

The Army shuttled Rocky to Fort Custer in Michigan, back to Fort Leonard Wood, then to Fort Carson in Colorado. Whenever the barracks failed inspection, the men ran the belt line—a gauntlet between two long lines of fellow soldiers, every man whipping at each runner with the sharp buckle of a GI belt. Rocky got tired of running the belt line because the latrine had failed inspection. He spent an evening cleaning the toilets and the sinks, the sergeant noticed the difference and asked who had done it, and Rocky was promoted to private first class. Soon he made sergeant. One night, the first sergeant in his outfit got drunk and wrecked a jeep; he was busted and Rocky moved up. He had his own clerk and driver now. The division was shipping out when an application that

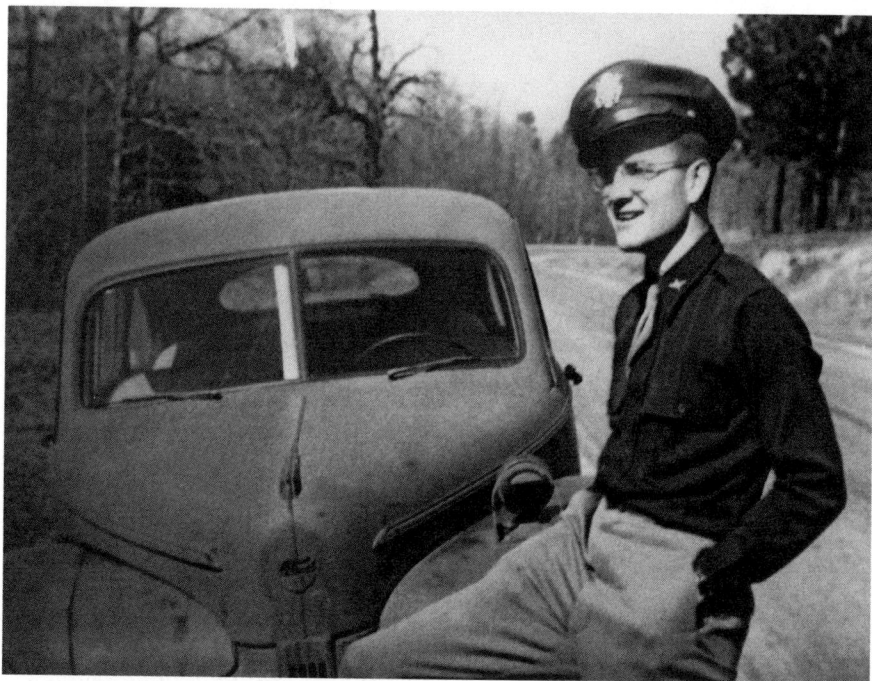

In May 1943, the 71st
Tactical Reconnaissance
Group moved from Louisiana
to its final training base,
Laurel Army Airfield in
Mississippi. This snapshot
of Rocky was taken during
a roadside halt. Collection
of the author

Margaret Anne Dillard in
1941. By 1943 she was
wearing Rocky's fraternity
pin and he spoke of her as
"my future wife." During
the drive to Laurel, he typed
her a love letter on radio
truck equipment. Collection
of the author

Rocky had filed earlier was accepted. He became an Air Corps cadet at Scott Field, in Illinois, which boasted that it produced the best damned radio operators in the world. In November 1942, Rocky was mustered out as a sergeant and commissioned as a second lieutenant. He was assigned to Salinas, outside San Francisco, where the 71st Observation Group (as it was known at the time) was flying antisubmarine patrols. He came home to Indiana once, in May 1943, when the Group moved east to Louisiana. He saw Margaret Anne at Franklin and gave her his SAE pin.

Later that month, the 71st Group's headquarters moved from Shreveport to Laurel, Mississippi. Rocky was in charge of the convoy. From his mobile headquarters, he sent Margaret Anne a letter.

Where am I? In the back end of a bouncing radio truck and we just passed Camp Shelby, Miss. These little silent Coronas come in handy on such conditions as this for it enables one to write no matter how rough the road might be. By the way I have on a pair of ear phones and am listening to music. This is fun, writing you, seeing the country, all I need is an ice cream cone and a blue eyed girl on my right, one on my left always cramps my style if I had one.

What shall we talk about, college profs, or radio, or you, time out for popcorn, we got it at Ellisville. And finally I can return the favor. Here are two grains for you.

Almost time to stop and attempt to contact the 17th Sq radio station which is standing by for us at Laurel.

See you later this afternoon, darling.

Rocky

Margaret Anne kept the letter and envelope, with the jokes and the fondness, and two flattened-out kernels of popcorn.

2

SHIPPING OUT

At Laurel Army Airfield, in September 1943, security was tightening. Gates were being locked now, guards posted, unit insignia being snipped off uniforms. At night in the barracks, first sergeants were making random bed checks.

Col. William Sams, commanding officer of the 71st Tactical Reconnaissance Group, had started the lectures in July. Do not discuss your planes, he had warned his airmen. Do not discuss supplies, inspections, or morale. In particular, do not disclose any changes of station. "If you receive personal visits, letters, telegrams, or phone calls at the new destination, this fact will be considered prima facie evidence that you have told someone the destination, and you will be court-martialed but being sentenced won't keep you from going overseas unless you are shot. It might cost you your life from drowning. *Your family or friends must not come to see you.*"[1]

The Group's move overseas had begun six months before, in a conversation no one in the Group had shared. Across a desk in Washington, a general had asked his president for aircraft.

Face to face with Franklin Delano Roosevelt was George Kenney, commander of the Fifth Air Force—senior airman in the

Southwest Pacific, where he was running the air war for Douglas MacArthur. Kenney was a short, energetic man—a scrappy terrier of a general. Never at a loss for words, always ready with figures and arguments, he was a debater born wrong, or perhaps a world-class public relations man. He knew he was fighting the Japanese on a shoestring, while bombers and troops poured into Europe.

Kenney had a story to tell his president: the story of the Battle of the Bismarck Sea, how his pilots had strafed, bombed, and sunk all fourteen ships in a convoy of Japanese troopships. Roosevelt asked if Kenney were getting more warplanes. Kenney said no. Then Kenney made a joke to make a pitch: the president had made so many other commitments that there were no planes left for his Fifth Air Force. "The President laughed and said he guessed he'd have to look into the matter," Kenney wrote. "I got a hunch that I was going to get some airplanes."[2]

Kenney's hunch was right. Before he left Washington, the Joint Chiefs of Staff promised him airplanes. They did not offer him the planes he wanted, B-24 Liberators and P-38 Lightnings; the Army was buying B-17 Flying Fortresses and P-51 Mustangs, because that was what the Eighth Air Force in England wanted. The Joint Chiefs promised Kenney three groups of bombers and two groups of fighters—provided that he would take planes that no other theater wanted and find crews for them among the men he already had. Then, for a bonus, the Joint Chiefs offered Kenney one further unit: four squadrons' worth of aircraft, packaged together in an observation group.[3]

No war is fought like clockwork, but the president's words had something of that effect: they set men in motion across the continent, gradually but inexorably. The 71st Observation Group became the 71st Tactical Reconnaissance Group. The Group headed east, from Louisiana to Mississippi, from Esler Army Airfield to Laurel Army Airfield—flight crews in their bombers, mechanics in jeeps, and a young lieutenant in a bouncing radio truck, listening to the radio and typing a love letter.

This portion of a 71st Tactical Reconnaissance Group photograph shows officers of the headquarters section: Col. William Columbus Sams (seated at left), Chaplain Charles F. Smith (standing at left), and Lt. Roscoe Allen Boyer (the young officer standing at right).
71st TRG; collection of the author

In September Rocky opened a new notebook. He was twenty-four now; he had been in the service for three long summers. He had shed his draftee's self-pity (mostly), but he still indulged a sense of melodrama. "FINDER," he printed, "This is the diary of Lt. Boyer, Roscoe A. 0-856663 A.C., Rural Route 3, Frankfort, Ind. U.S.A." Then he skipped a line and wrote out a title, in block capitals: "THE PRELUDE TO BATTLE." He dated it in careful block letters: "September 8, 1943."

"We'll sail from San Francisco. The combat crew members will leave from Hamilton Field. We'll carry both winter and summer uniforms (that means we're going to India or China for they told me troops going to the islands are taking only suntans). Also we're not taking any heavy tents and that's a good sign. They thought we would receive our orders to move around October 3. And for God's sake, Boyer, don't tell a damn person." Thus spoke Lieutenant Melvin Beck during our very confidential conversation in our radio truck following his plane trip to Barksdale Field, Shreveport, Louisiana.[4]

Rocky was not the only officer to begin a diary. Another airman in the Group would ask, a year later, as a joke and reminiscence: "How many guys started diaries that never finished them?" The colonel would be keeping a diary; so too a flight surgeon, and a clutch of eager young men with lieutenant's bars and pilot's wings, and a mechanic of steady industry and few words. No diarist seemed to have parsed the Army regulation that diaries be collected periodically and stored in rear areas, nor the recent *Field Artillery Journal* article that urged that soldiers might keep diaries restricted to individual routine life. There was as yet no sign that anyone in the 71st Group might write what Bill Mauldin said every soldier wanted to write, "a book exposin' the Army after the war."[5]

〽

There were double guards at the base gates, and the Mississippi Highway Patrol had been alerted to watch the roads outside. Mail was now posted in each squadron's orderly room, where officers could keep an eye on it, not through the base post office. No civilians were to be admitted to the base, except those employed there. The days, however, were hot as well as long, and morale demanded that certain exceptions be made. "An officer from each building where there is a Coca-Cola dispensing unit should contact Lt. Thannum at the Post Exchange relative to the servicing of the unit."[6]

Before calisthenics, Major Smith, our intelligence officer, and I discussed the personal items we should take overseas. Can openers, a year's supply of soap (the kind that will float—who knows, we may be washing in rivers), handkerchiefs, razor blades, preference of shaving soap over shaving cream because the latter may be broken and damage other articles, books (a few we are carrying are the *Decameron* of Boccaccio, the Bible, *Leaves of Grass*, collection of short stories, poetry, dictionary and a few contemporary plays), sport shoes, swimming trunks, toilet paper, perhaps a few rubbers to be used not only "for the prevention of disease," but also to cover flashlights, batteries, etc., toothbrushes, heavy paper for the sleeping bag, diary, sewing kit, ink, camera film and a large knife. Of course we'll think of many other things as time goes by.[7]

The week ahead would be spent hiking: five miles Monday, seven and a half miles Tuesday, ten miles Wednesday, twelve miles Thursday, and fifteen miles on Friday—all followed by regular parade on Saturday. The hikes were facts, but there was a metaphor behind them: the men of the 71st Group now could see that they were headed overseas.

Had our first five-mile hike. Fifty percent of the men developed blisters. Their discipline was poor—some smoked in ranks, waved their arms, commented about passing civilians. Much to everyone's surprise, the colonel went along.

Major William Tennille of the 17th Bomb Squadron paced his men over the five mile route without a break in one hour and ten minutes. The Major has been wearing house slippers ever since.[8]

Next day, the pace was slower. The cadence dropped from 120 beats per minute to 110 beats, falling away from the official Army quick-step. The sore-footed airmen saw other signs that reason was creeping into the process.

> Had our seven and one-half mile hike today. The colonel went again and after the march took his staff car to check the mileage. Undoubtedly he thought as did the rest of us that it was nearer nine miles than seven. Rumored the colonel called off the hikes for Wednesday.[9]

If the men were surprised to see Colonel Sams hiking with them, they did not yet know him well. A commanding officer, ex officio, is called "the old man." Sams seemed even older to some of his flyers. He was thirty-seven years old, people said he had medical conditions, and he was a career man from the spit-and-polish Regular Army. When anyone asked about promotions, Sams pointed out the long years he himself had spent as a lieutenant.[10] Sams had a wife and children and he husbanded his men and planes. But Sams was also the sort of officer whose energy and élan American soldiers describe by borrowing foreign terms. In the Lafayette Escadrille, they would have called him *un beau sabreur*; in more recent wars they would have labeled him gung ho. Sams had waited seventeen years to fly warplanes in combat and was not going to miss his chance.

As for Major Tennille—there was something to take seriously in the rumor Rocky heard. Bill Tennille was wearing slippers because his feet were blistered. With his fast-paced forced march, Tennille had shown that he had a passion for speed, that he would share without flinching his men's tasks and pains, and that he was eager to drive too hard. He was the sort of officer, all this suggested, who would order a charge and then rush in at its head.

The 82nd Squadron, which flew fighter planes, was taking orders from a different species of commander, Maj. Donald M. Gordon. Months before, at DeRidder Army Air Field in Louisiana,

Gordon had begun to earn his men's contempt. He had chewed them out for blowing out tires when they landed their P-39s and told them he would show them how it was done. He took up his own plane and landed flawlessly. Then, while taxiing, he carelessly flipped the wrong switch and, instead of retracting his flaps, folded up his airplane's wheels. It was a common mistake, but it was a fool mistake and Gordon picked this moment to make it. The whole squadron watched and heard the screeching, propeller-bending crash. They sent a jeep out to pick up Gordon. The flyers then sat by in a group, no man among them saying a word, while the major walked through them back to his quarters.[11]

By September 24, the 71st Group was packed for wherever they were bound. Rocky had tried to add to the assortment of items he was taking overseas: "I tried to get a girl to get a bottle of ink in town for me—but not my luck—must be losing my grip," he wrote.[12]

They had been packing in the rain, and a master sergeant said they would have enough water to last a month whenever they opened the waterproof boxes. The 110th Squadron was being split off; someone said Gen. George Kenney had seen them on maneuvers and didn't want them in his air force. Everyone had spent two days loading railroad flatcars and waiting for a switch engine, and that night the tension broke.

> Last night 80% of the officers were drunk. The evening started with gambling: poker, rummy, blackjack and craps and ended with a football game in the officers' club. Most of the glasses were broken and no fights resulted but about two this morning we were awakened by three officers driving a jeep across the boardwalks between trees and through the small ditches.
>
> Left Laurel at 4:30 p.m. The train consisted of 10 coaches, two boxcars serving as baggage and one baggage

car converted into a GI kitchen. Personnel included HQ and 82nd Fighter Squadron. The 17th Bomb Squadron was supposed to follow us immediately. The train turned east at the gate so it looks like the East Coast. The newspaper headlines say "12 Ships Sunk."[13]

By breakfast-time they reached Atlanta; on the third day, they reached Camp Patrick Henry, outside Newport News. Here Rocky first heard, officially, where they were headed: "some island north of Australia."[14]

〽

The officers of the 71st Group had spent two years preparing for combat. They had seen the end of the beginning of the war. They had watched the Japanese overrun the Pacific, and then be stopped: by the United States Navy at Midway, by the Marines on Guadalcanal, and by Douglas MacArthur in New Guinea. What lay ahead could be read in the headlines of the newspapers they bought on their way eastward, for not every story was about ships being sunk. That week, the banner headlines thundered about Italy and Corsica and Mark Clark's Fifth Army and Nazis burning the city of Naples. Doughty British flyers had put Germany under an aerial siege. Europe came first and would continue to come first. News from other theaters made the front page, too, but in shorter stories and smaller type. The Allies had taken Finschhafen and raided Rabaul. MacArthur might have a rival supremo in Mountbatten. (News stories about Mountbatten may have been why the Group heard so many rumors about going to China.) And from the Southwest Pacific, a wire story reported an advance by airmen and infantry: "Australians landed by big American transport planes have seized Kaiapit, 60 miles north of newly-captured Lae, New Guinea. The transports swept down on a grassy field last Saturday night and Sunday, disgorging Australians who repulsed enemy counterattacks and drove the Japanese out of the immediate area."[15]

At Camp Patrick Henry, waiting to sail, they spent eight days. Officers were housed in the post Bachelor Officer Quarters. The post had a chapel, paneled in dark wood, with chimes donated by the Firestone family. Rocky went to three services there. So did other servicemen: the chapel was so small or so popular that every seat in its pews was taken. Other officers found different ways to pass time. The senior officers went out on Saturday night—the colonel, the intelligence officer, and the flight surgeon together. It did not end well. They "returned to the BOQ at 0415 and woke most everyone," Rocky recorded. "Major Smith had a cut on his head and blood was quite noticeable on the board walk in front of the BOQ."[16]

On October 5, finally, they boarded the USS *General John S. Pope*. The *Pope* was a new Army troopship, fast enough to sail without a convoy.

Rocky's stateroom was crowded with officers. One was Chaplain Smith—Lt. Frederick C. Smith, a Southern Baptist preacher. Rocky was used to talking with preachers, and wrote down what the chaplain confided: that the senior officers should stop chasing nurses, that some men due to ship out had suddenly declared to him that they were homosexuals, and that only two Jews were left in the Group. Smith was the oldest man in the stateroom, probably the tallest, trained at the Southern Baptist seminary in Louisville and the Army chaplains' school at Harvard. Rocky thought that Chaplain Smith was changing during the trip. "Often wonder why he tells some of those shady stories. Is it his true nature, or is he trying to impress us with his sophistication, or doesn't he know any better, or is he attempting to become one of us?"[17]

The other officers in the stateroom were all young lieutenants. Rocky offered a set of sketch portraits:

> Lieutenant Gilbert, West Pointer, impressed me by his deep friendliness. Lieutenant Dixon is another West Pointer. Quiet, complacent, affable. Lieutenant Alexander

is never wrong and is all for Alexander, and thus a true Californian. Lieutenant Foster knows but never tries to impress. Lieutenant Mosher of the 17th Squadron is strictly a student of books. Lieutenant Foss attempts to be a brain on all subjects. Lieutenant Tate is quiet, a Texan, and a very fine man. Lieutenant Parks, of Marion, Indiana, perhaps has more brains, master of many sciences, knows hundreds of cowboy songs, and is unconscious of his entertainment. Lieutenant Wilkey, a typical Missouri Mule. Very practical, brains galore. Has been a man about the world—and will have the last word in any argument. Hates the Army.[18]

Willard Gilbert and Lyndall Tate would retire as colonels (as would Rocky Boyer). Charles Foss and Donald Alexander would transfer out. Chaplain Smith would expose a scandal that it took two generals to bury. Bob Foster was weather officer and wore a harried look. Ralph Wilkey was a handsome young man with upswept coal-black hair, a rockabilly guitarist before the term was coined. George "Butch" Dixon looked self-confident, even smug, which perhaps explains what happened later. Of Lawrence Lundberg, Rocky said nothing, but Lundberg would earn the Distinguished Flying Cross, twice, on two afternoons twelve years apart, giving his life the second time. Hugh Mosher would be dead before summer.

Officers were crowded into staterooms, but enlisted men were packed into compartments down below the waterline: four hundred men in an area eighty feet long, sixty-five feet wide, less than nine feet high, jammed with tiers of bunks. Officers had mattresses and sheets, enlisted men slept on canvas. Officers were assigned "compartment duty," watching over enlisted men; some officers talked about wearing pistols when they went below. The trip was not comfortable but it was not eventful.

Most of the activity aboard ship can be classified under racking up time (sleeping), gambling, reading, sitting, and being sick. There's a regulation stating that no drinking will take place aboard ship and there has been none. As for gambling, yesterday it was reported that one officer won $475. Two or three days ago one enlisted man said a Marine had won four thousand in a craps game in the latrine.[19]

Colonel Sams sat on the boxing tournament steering committee, with four chaplains and two Navy doctors. (Chaplains on troopships were advised to bring six pairs of boxing gloves, two punching bags, and two medicine balls.)[20] The tournament filled out the pages of *The Crow's Nest*, the ship's journal, in an issue that featured advice on Australia, a plea to return books to the ship's library, and "Hymn Sing Big Success."[21]

Rocky and the other lieutenants talked about "the female situation in our unknown theatre. They all agreed the American soldiers would not rape women as the Japs however there will be isolated instances. And the reason—the U.S. soldier prides himself in his ability in means of seduction. They also agreed (except the chaplain) those black women will become whiter every day."[22]

In four days they reached the Panama Canal. Two days after leaving the Canal, they crossed the equator. Six days later, in the South Pacific, they neared the line on the map that marked the eastern border of the war zone.

Before noon it was reported throughout the ship that a naval radio operator was listening to a Tokyo news broadcast and heard that our ship by its actual name, USS *General John Pope*, was sunk just outside the Panama Canal six days ago. Could it be that we are dead—already![23]

Panama was now four thousand miles behind them; Australia was more than four thousand miles ahead. In that blank quadrant of ocean, Rocky recorded a dream.

> Woke and felt very tired for during the night I dreamt I met Norman Vandivier again in the SAE House and as customary his hand grip was crushing. By doing likewise it exhausted me. Now my arms are sore and ache. Norman has been missing since Midway.[24]

At Franklin College, Norman Vandivier had been a senior when Rocky was a freshman. At Midway, flying a Dauntless SBD dive-bomber, Vandivier was one of the aviators who attacked the Japanese fleet carrier *Kaga*. He was awarded the Navy Cross posthumously. After bombing the *Kaga*, on his way home to the *Enterprise*, Vandivier ditched his plane, with a last transmission reporting he was out of fuel.

Rocky never talked about dreams, and this was the only time he ever wrote about one. He was fond of mathematics, not the supernatural. But that space of empty waves was a place that a ghost might haunt, or where a man's dreaming mind could turn to a friend who had gone before him to war. The war was weighing upon Rocky, and his dream marked it. As he headed for combat, he was grappling with its ghosts.

🌀

At the end of the ocean, another week away, lay Australia. On October 28, the *General John S. Pope* dropped anchor off Brisbane. Rocky and everyone else expected to go ashore the next day and ate breakfast early.

> Traveled up bay, passed flat islands into a river not more two thousand feet wide. Found the town of Brisbane to be neat and colorful, built on low regular hills. The residential district comes to the rocky bottomed river and for a mile women waved to us. Women—ah.

Our boat was turned around in river and we docked at approximately 0900. Then came the news we would not debark.[25]

Chaplain Smith was allowed ashore—no one else. He brought back three newspapers, two songbooks, a pineapple, apples, pears, bananas, and three pints of ice cream.

The ministry of a good chaplain was practical. The Army chaplain's manual stressed the importance of the following qualifications: "typist, musician (vocal or instrumental), experience as a printer or publicity man, sign painter, stereopticon or moving picture operator."[26] On the voyage out, Chaplain Smith had lugged aboard his organ, hymnals, violin, and typewriter; he had played piano in the officers' lounge; he had stuck up for lower-grade NCOs when first sergeants tried to turn them out of quarters that they envied. From this point, Chaplain Smith's ministry would be summed up in lists: rosters of men for whom he arranged outings, schedules of clubs and lectures that he organized, journals and snacks that he obtained for the airmen in his charge.

Rumors were rife: if the Group wasn't going ashore, they must be headed even farther afield: to Sydney, to India, to Persia. But when they moved on, it was to Milne Bay, the Allied port at the eastern tip of New Guinea. They started taking Atabrine, the pill that turned skin yellow and was said to cause impotence and represented the American answer to malaria.

At least they could mail letters home now. Rocky sent four letters to his parents, six to Margaret Anne. With Lieutenant Scott, he was assigned to censor enlisted men's mail. The enlisted men seemed tense. "There was a definite lack of humor in all the letters I censored," Rocky wrote. "The most common comment was 'Please don't worry; I love you.' 'It will be a long time before I return' ran a close second."[27]

Rocky went out on deck that night with his friend Bob Foliart, another lieutenant. For the first time, they marked the energy with which the American forces moved across the New Guinea landscape.

> What appeared to be another jungle coast line this after-
> noon was a mass of lights tonight. Amphibious jeeps and
> trucks were in the water and it seemed a bit strange to
> see automobile headlights out on the water. Searchlight
> batteries were in operation. . . . These ships departing
> from here to the combat fields are landing barges and
> Liberty Ships. There is a hospital ship and a large hospi-
> tal (80 nurses) here. Seven-day leaves are granted after
> six months in area. Perhaps on paper only.[28]

Already there were hints of how hard it was for a man to find his way back stateside. A captain who came on board to brief them had been overseas for twenty-two months.

They transferred to a Dutch ship, the SS *Van Heutsz*—less comfortable than the *John S. Pope*, for her power was unreliable, her plumbing was crude, and she had been built to carry coolie labor.[29] On November 6, they finally went ashore. They marched for a mile, through mud, under palm trees, to their first campsite. They kicked at land crabs, ants, and centipedes, and (Rocky and Major Smith had guessed right) washed in a river. The day after that, suddenly, they moved to Port Moresby.

> We woke, ate our canned rations. I ate my cereal dry so
> as not to dirty my mess kit. We cleared the area of coco-
> nut logs and raked rocks so to form walks. At 1100 the
> chaplain, Lieutenant Unger and I went to the small creek
> to wash our clothes. . . . After washing one uniform and
> one pair of coveralls, I walked out to midstream and sat
> down. Immediately, First Sergeant Williams appeared,
> yelling, "All 71st men out. We are moving." The chaplain,
> a slow fat Southerner, bitched a little.

We rushed to the area to learn we were leaving in one hour. At 1300 we had our equipment in trucks, climbed in, and headed off to the airport (we hoped). . . . Along the beach we saw three Jap landing barges with holes 3' in diameter and one large ship on its side. The road was narrow in places and one truck got stuck. . . . We took off at 1430. First we went due west over a very large lake but had to make a 180° turn because of a storm and reached the sea below. Along the coast were beautiful beaches, jungles one minute and grass areas another. We saw a few coconut groves and three native villages built on stilts.

We landed at one of the seven landing strips at 1545. There were B-24s galore. We unloaded the plane. Yes, we officers did it all ourselves. Time flew. We rode and rode—over gravel roads past what looked to me huge ant hills. Finally there was a halt. Told dinner was waiting for all. And our dream came true—we had steaks. The Fifth Bomber Command placed us in a native constructed enlisted men's recreation hall and furnished miscellaneous mosquito bars, blankets and folding cots. Sleep came in spite of the water coming through the coconut leaves.[30]

The trip had confirmed the hierarchy of rank, in which officers lived above enlisted men, relied on their labor, and read their mail. Rocky and the other airmen had seen the energy of the war, the headlights that lit the New Guinea darkness, and the bombers galore in the Port Moresby revetments. They had been mired in the mud of the tropics and been lifted out of it by American air power. They had seen the detritus of war by land and sea, and been warned of the hazards of the air. The prelude to battle— Rocky had thought shipping out would be that. Even yet, the journey from Laurel to Port Moresby might not be that; but what they had seen might be summed up as an overture.

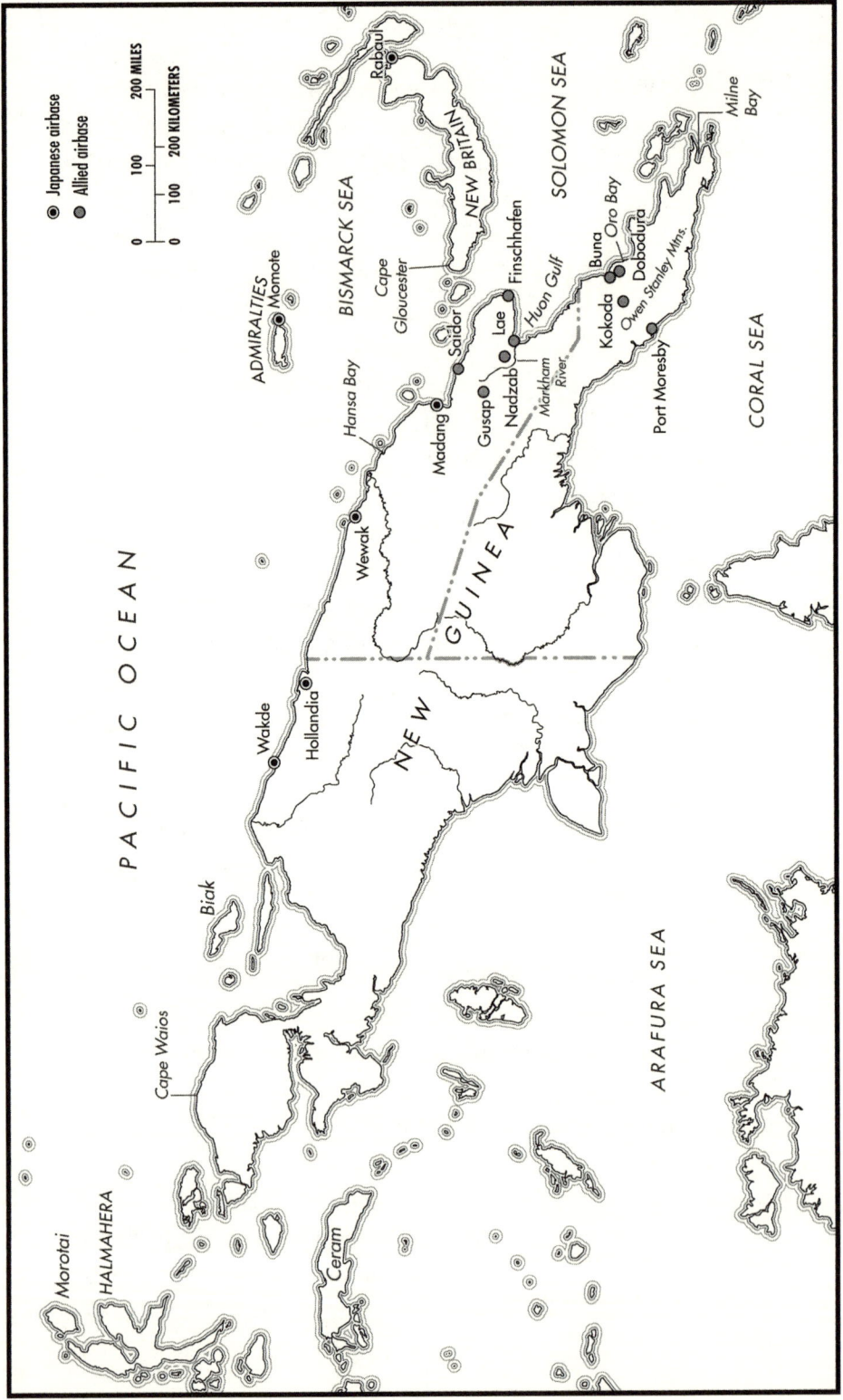

MAP 1. *New Guinea*

3

AN ISLAND NORTH
OF AUSTRALIA

An island north of Australia, where Rocky had heard that the Group was headed, meant New Guinea. So did the rumor that George Kenney would be the Air Corps theater commander, for New Guinea was where Kenney was fighting Douglas MacArthur's air war.

New Guinea was in the Southwest Pacific. In that antipodean part of the world there were two separate theaters of war—divided by a line as clear as the equator, as E. J. Kahn noted. "The South Pacific, to clear this matter up, is an area that includes Guadalcanal. . . . It is commanded by Admiral Halsey. The Southwest Pacific, consisting of Australia, New Guinea, and various other islands, belongs to General MacArthur."[1]

As the 71st Group unpacked barracks bags, its airmen were heading for what an experienced newspaperman called the toughest fighting in the world. The United States Army advised its soldiers: "New Guinea is a primitive, hard country and a new world to men from overseas. You go there to fight a dangerous enemy, the Japanese. But they are not the only enemy. The country itself will fight you with all its forces—its mountains, swamps and forests, its heat and rain, its snakes, crocodiles, scorpions and lice, above all with its mosquitoes and its invisible army of disease germs."[2]

New Guinea is the second-largest island on the planet. The mountains that run down its centerline rank with the Rockies and the Andes as a dangerous cordillera: "The main island, shaped like a rearing dragon and lying just under the equator, has a spine of mountains 1,000 miles long. At the western end, snowcapped peaks rise to more than 16,000 feet. At the eastern end, the tallest soar between 13,000 and 14,000 feet, and are clothed almost to their summits in dense rain forests. From this mighty backbone of ranges, row upon row of razorbacks extend like herringbones, with roaring torrents in every canyon between them and everlasting rainclouds on every crest."[3]

New Guinea was a green hell, said men who served there.[4] The Army's official history of the early fighting in New Guinea spelled out why:

> The Japanese could scarcely have chosen a more dismal place in which to conduct a campaign. The rainfall at many points in the peninsula is torrential. It often runs as high as 150, 200, and even 300 inches per year, and, during the rainy season, daily falls of eight or ten inches are not uncommon. The terrain, as varied as it is difficult, is a military nightmare. Towering saw-toothed mountains, densely covered by mountain forest and rain forest, alternate with flat malarial, coastal areas. . . . The mountains are drained by turbulent rivers and creeks, which become slow and sluggish as they reach the sea. Along the streams, the fringes of the forest become interwoven from ground to treetop level with vines and creepers to form an almost solid mat of vegetation which has to be cut by the machete or the bolo before progress is possible.[5]

In the lowlands, rivers, swamps, and mangrove swamps dominate. Among these are broad swathes of grass, as tall as a man—
kunai in Pidgin, or kogon grass, blady grass, *kurukuru*, or Japanese
bloodgrass. There are impassable rivers, the largest being the
Sepik. Allied officers and infantrymen loathed the river: "In its
course of some 700 miles it spread into seemingly limitless
swamps, flowed deeply through a main channel a quarter of a
mile or more wide in places, and bore with it masses of debris and
floating islands of tangled grass and scrub. Crocodiles infested it,
and hordes of mosquitoes bred there."[6]

The western half of New Guinea was Dutch, part of the Netherlands East Indies. The eastern half, in 1884, had been divided by
Queen Victoria and Kaiser Wilhelm I. The Germans claimed the
part of the island north of the mountains, which became Kaiser
Wilhelm Land, and the large islands offshore, which they renamed
the Bismarck Archipelago. The British claimed the southeastern
quarter of the island, which they called Papua. In 1906 the Australians assumed control of Papua; in 1914 Australian forces captured the German settlements and the German colonial capital
of Rabaul. After the war, the German possessions were given to
Australia as a mandate. The island of New Pomerania became
New Britain, and New Mecklenburg became New Ireland.

Less than half of New Guinea was "under control." That meant
little—only that a head tax was paid, tribal wars were no longer
fought, and colonial officers administered justice. The rest of New
Guinea was only "under influence," or, beyond that, merely "pen-
etrated by patrols." There were approximately 4,500 Europeans in
the Mandated Territory, approximately 1,500 Europeans in Papua.
The tribes native to the island numbered some 1.8 million people.[7]

The New Guinea Territory continued to be governed from
Rabaul, offshore on New Britain. Rabaul could boast a crosshatch-
ing of streets beside a magnificent deep-water harbor. Its prewar
population counted 850 Europeans, 1,000 Chinese, and 4,000
Melanesians.[8] Papua, a poorer colony, was governed from a

sleepier town, Port Moresby. In 1940 Moresby had a population of a thousand whites. Another thousand or so people worked in Moresby by day. They were Motuans, from the villages in the area, and were required to leave the white town after dusk.[9]

On the east coast, along the hundreds of miles of beaches and jungle, settlements were few. At Finschhafen there was a German mission. At Salamaua there was a harbor, with a customs house, stores, banks, and pub. At Lae, there was a good airfield; Amelia Earhart had taken off from there in 1938, on her last flight. The airport had been built to serve the up-country gold-mining district, and a town had grown up around it: a dozen stores, a hotel and club, a hundred young white men, a few white women, sixty-odd Chinese. Thirty years before, the people of Lae had welcomed the German missionaries; they themselves ran the mission school now, and they had built a church for their congregation of seven hundred souls.[10]

Farther north along the coast was the port of Madang, which Chancellor Otto von Bismarck's empire builders had also laid out. At Madang had been built a jail, hospital, quarantine station, copra warehouse, and cricket ground; there were thirty Europeans and a miniature Chinatown. The 71st Group would know Madang well—the harbor, the plantations around it, and the deadly anti-aircraft guns that the Japanese put in place there.[11]

The air war in New Guinea would not be fought above the jungle. A close look at the background of most wartime aerial photos shows that the landscape is not the random unshaped canopy of a jungle: the palm trees that form such a dense mat are usually planted in neat rows. They are the trees of hundreds of coconut plantations—white outposts along the coast. Madang was surrounded by plantations; so were Lae and Alexishafen and Finschhafen, and the coast all the way north past Hansa Bay, points connected by the Old German Road. The 82nd and 110th Squadrons flew missions to Erima Plantation, Yalau Plantation, Awar Plantation, Potsdam Plantation—to Ulugan Plantation, too, where more than one pilot died. From the meat of the coconuts grown on these plantations, when it was dried and shipped out as copra, came the coconut oil used in soaps made by Lever Brothers and Procter & Gamble.

In New Guinea, Western consumer culture had shaped the landscape where the war was fought—just as it had built the Italian pastures and vineyards where troops battled, and Normandy, where armies shot at each other through the hedgerows that divided French fields. The Allied base at Milne Bay was built in a plantation, just as air bases back home were laid out on pastureland. An American pilot remembered that at Milne Bay, the trees were "set in a checkerboard pattern that looked like a giant cornfield. We were told that our government paid Lever Brothers seventy-five dollars for every tree destroyed."[12]

🌀

In early 1942, the Japanese moved south with phenomenal speed. Within weeks after Pearl Harbor, they dispatched a fleet to deal with the solitary battalion of Australian troops that had been sent to Rabaul. On January 21, Japanese warplanes struck the tiny white settlements of the New Guinea coast, bombing and strafing. Colonial rule collapsed and the white population fled.[13] Within two months after Pearl Harbor—while American troops were encircled on Bataan, and British troops were being outfought at Singapore—only one Allied base remained above the Australian continent: Port Moresby.

The Japanese had opened the war by taking control of strategic islands. In December 1941, a handful of Japanese landings cut the established air routes between the United States and Australia. Before the war, the few planes that crossed the Pacific had gone from California to Hawaii to Midway Island and Wake Island, then on via Guam to Manila or Port Moresby. After the Japanese captured Wake and Guam, American military transportation officers mapped out a new route to the Pacific theater: from Hawaii south to Christmas Atoll, west to Canton, south to Samoa, then straight west for three days, via Fiji and New Caledonia to Brisbane. The route posed so many risks that the Army sent bombers to the Pacific by flying them across South America, Africa, and India—until the Japanese captured the Netherlands East Indies and cut off the northern approach to Australia.[14]

Port Moresby was fought for because it had an airfield, and because its capture would perfect Japanese control of the Southwest Pacific. The Imperial Japanese Navy wanted to protect its base at Truk. That meant capturing Rabaul, the nearest established port. To protect Rabaul, in turn, it was desirable to capture Port Moresby. The Japanese fully understood the threat that land-based aircraft posed to naval forces.

> In Allied hands Port Moresby could soon become a major thorn in the Japanese side. Allied heavy bombers could roam as far north as Truk. . . . But in Japanese hands Port Moresby could become the base for air operations against northern Australia and deep into the Coral Sea; Rabaul and Tulagi would thereby be covered in the one direction from which an enemy counterattack might materialize. Moreover, once in Japanese hands Port Moresby would complete the air ferry route from Singapore and the Philippines via the Indies and New Guinea to Rabaul. Thus the Japanese . . . would have a mesh of mutually supporting air bases that could be used to concentrate overwhelming numbers of land-based aircraft against any Allied naval force.[15]

Guadalcanal, likewise, was fought for because it was air-base terrain. The Imperial Japanese Navy had never planned to fight a decisive battle at the end of a supply line stretched south into the Solomons; nor did the United States Navy plan to send its precious carriers and cruisers into those waters, so far from home and still so distant from Australia. Rather, the Japanese had landed on

Guadalcanal to build a final air base—to protect Rabaul's south-eastern approaches and threaten the shipping routes between Australia and the United States. From Guadalcanal, Japanese bombers could have covered the Coral Sea with an air blockade. Kawanishi flying boats could have scouted even farther afield, even as far as the safe southern course that the *John S. Pope* had steered.

֍

The first Japanese air raid on Port Moresby came on February 3, 1942.[16] By the time the Japanese ceased raiding, eighteen months later, Moresby had been bombed or strafed more than a hundred times.[17] *Guinea Gold*, the Australian military newspaper published there, was called the war's most-bombed newspaper.

During the early months of 1942, the situation at Port Moresby was bleak. Osmar White recalled that he and his fellow war correspondents could write of Australians defying the Japanese bombers, but they could not tell the whole truth. The story they could not tell was one of desperation and cheerless improvisation. "We could not write: The strength, equipment, training and leadership of the New Guinea Force is inadequate. . . . It is enervated by tropical diseases and it is badly fed, overworked, discouraged and very nearly hopeless. It is without reserves or air support. If the Japanese come, organized defense will not last more than 48 hours."[18]

At first, the Japanese air raids came daily. There were no Allied fighter planes at Moresby, and only one small battery of antiaircraft guns. The Japanese bombers stayed high, or the Zeros strafed the town at building height, and it was weeks before the gunners actually shot down a Japanese plane. In March 1942, the Royal Australian Air Force (RAAF) flew in a squadron of P-40 fighters to defend the town. The P-40s were outclassed by the Zeros, but the pilots flew until all of their planes were shot down or wrecked.

At the end of April, just when the RAAF could fight no longer, the Eighth Pursuit Group of the United States Army Air Force arrived with two squadrons of P-39 Airacobras. GI engineers came ashore with them: two black units, the first American ground troops to reach New Guinea, the 96th Engineering Battalion (Colored) and the 576th Engineer Company. Veteran Australian units began to arrive, shipped home from the Middle East. The Allied situation at Port Moresby remained difficult, but no longer did it seem desperate.

⑤

As well as sending air raids, the Japanese twice began campaigns to capture Port Moresby. In March 1942, a Japanese naval task force landed troops at Lae and Salamaua. American carrier planes struck the landing ships and damaged them so badly that the Japanese did not press on to land more troops at Moresby. In May, during the Battle of the Coral Sea, while the huge Japanese fleet carriers *Shokaku* and *Zuikaku* fought it out with the American fleet carriers *Yorktown* and *Lexington*, Japanese losses once more saved Port Moresby. American dive-bombers and torpedo planes sank the Japanese carrier *Shoho*, the flagship of a second Japanese invasion fleet that had hooked around the eastern tip of New Guinea, heading for the beaches at Moresby. Deprived of their air cover, the destroyers and transports of this landing force turned back to Rabaul.[19]

In July 1942, the Japanese moved southward a third time—a move that would result in two huge battles. The Japanese shipped construction troops southward along the Solomon Islands, hundreds of miles, to Guadalcanal. At the same time, they landed 3,500 combat troops at Buna, on the east coast of New Guinea, less than 120 miles by air from Moresby. This landing force, with its engineers, bearers, and packhorses, set off for Port Moresby across the mountains. This path they chose, the Kokoda Track, would carry for Australians the same associations that other nations give to Thermopylae and Stalingrad.

The Kokoda Track was a footpath that crossed numberless mountain ridges, sometimes narrowing down to a trail less than three feet wide. Along this rough terrain, in tropical downpours, the Japanese doggedly fought their way, encircling and overrunning Australian forces. By mid-September, the emperor's troops were exhausted and sickened, but they were only twenty-five miles from Port Moresby, so close that they could see the ocean beyond the port. Here they were supposed to hold, while reinforcements arrived. At this point, the forward troops were recalled—ordered to fall back on the coast. A second Japanese landing in New Guinea, at Milne Bay, had failed. At Guadalcanal the fighting had intensified: the Japanese Imperial Army staff had committed to that island the infantrymen and warplanes meant to support the Kokoda expedition.[20]

When the Japanese fell back from the Kokoda Track, they dug in at Buna, where they had come ashore. They fought from bunkers made from thick coconut logs, overgrown with grass or jungle vines. The Japanese had fortified the high ground—which meant, in the marshy terrain at Buna, that the Japanese held all the terrain that was not actually covered with muck or standing water. The Australian Ninth Division came down in pursuit from the mountains, and a fresh American unit, the 32nd Division, was brought into action, ferried by air from northern Australia to Port Moresby. The Americans opened a new front on the east coast of New Guinea. Some of the new American regiments followed a tortuous trail across the mountains—but other Allied troops, in a striking advance, were flown directly to the combat zone. Engineers found a landing field site near Buna, at Wanigela Mission, and an advance guard hacked out in the kunai grass a strip on which transport planes could land. Kenney then rushed in a battalion of Australian infantry to defend the place and a hundred American engineers to build a longer airstrip, and began flying in soldiers and munitions.[21]

At Buna, a squadron of Zeros was flying from a prewar grass airfield at the old mission. Fifth Air Force warplanes caught the Zeros on the ground, strafed them, and cratered the runway.[22]

With air superiority gained, the Allies were able not only to fly in supplies by air but to send munitions northward along the coast. The Fifth Air Force took on a decisive role. "Its transports moved whole regiments and brigades to the front. In addition to evacuating some 6,000 Australians and American sick and wounded, it had flown out other regiments and brigades that were returning to Moresby for rest and rehabilitation. It had delivered 2,450 tons of rations, equipment, and ammunition to the troops at the front. . . . [T]he attack could not have been sustained without the airlift."[23]

Lt. Gen. Robert Eichelberger, the American commander at Buna, declared, "Both Australian and American ground forces would have perished without 'George Kenney's Air.'"[24]

Slowly but consistently, the Allied troops fought their way along the trails to the coast. In late January 1943, Japanese commanders ordered Buna to be evacuated, and those Imperial soldiers who did not die fighting slipped away into the jungle. A few weeks later, the Japanese recognized that they had lost Guadalcanal as well and sent in destroyers to draw off the soldiers who still were fighting there.

At Port Moresby, Japanese air raids dwindled and finally ceased. On the tracks that led inland from the harbor, the black engineers bulldozed and leveled new airfields: Three Mile Strip, Five Mile Strip, Seven Mile Strip, Twelve Mile Strip, Fourteen Mile Strip, and distant Seventeen Mile Strip. Like lines of fortifications, the new airdromes surrounded the camps of the garrison.

"We had more men than the Jap," George Kenney brusquely wrote. "We owned the air over New Guinea. We were bombing and machine-gunning his troops and burning up his supplies. We could supply by air, while the Nip had to run an air blockade with his vessels every time he wanted another bag of rice, another round of ammunition, or another Jap soldier to replace his losses."[25]

The Fifth Air Force had won the first phase of the air war: its bases were now secure, and it dominated the air above the Allied advance. Kenney's men had moved on to the air blockade—and already Kenney and MacArthur were outlining the next phase of the air war: a drive northward, island by island, toward the Philippines.

To understand the challenge that Kenney and the Fifth Air Force faced—to appreciate the scope of the islands and oceans across which Rocky and the rest of the 71st Group would fight their way—transpose the map of the theater onto the map of the United States.[26]

Conjecture that Port Moresby is at Pensacola. The Japanese naval citadel of Rabaul is five hundred miles to the northeast, at Charlotte. The Japanese army base at Wewak is 475 miles north— if Moresby is at Pensacola, Wewak is at Nashville. The Japanese headquarters at Hollandia is 650 miles northwest of Pensacola, at Oklahoma City. The island of Biak, from which MacArthur's forces would leap to the Philippines, is in the Oklahoma Panhandle.

If these Japanese strongholds seem remote, the bases upon which the Fifth Air Force had to rely were even more distant. With Moresby at Pensacola, Guadalcanal is in Cuba, Brisbane is in Nicaragua, and Darwin is near Acapulco. From Port Moresby to Sydney is 1,695 miles, the distance from Pensacola to the coast of Venezuela.

When its squadrons moved forward to Nadzab, in late 1943 and early 1944, the Fifth Air Force moved north 190 miles (from Pensacola to Columbus, Georgia). This was an opening move; MacArthur and Kenney were planning longer, bolder strokes. From Port Moresby to the Philippines—to Tacloban in Leyte Province, where American forces would land in October 1944—is more than 2,000 miles. This is the distance from Pensacola to Edmonton on the Canadian prairie. From Port Moresby to Manila is 2,400 miles, the distance from Pensacola to the Pacific coast above Vancouver.

4

THE AIR BLITZ WAR

The war in New Guinea, after the Japanese were stopped on the Kokoda Track and defeated at Buna, became a war of airmen and engineers.[1] Fifth Air Force chief George Kenney cast off old doctrine, rigged planes and trained men for new missions, and brought attack aviation to the fore. The Fifth Air Force's squadrons broke the power of the Japanese—sank convoys, wrecked airfields, blockaded garrisons. Under commanders who scouted ahead of the Allied lines, driven by engineers who worked under Japanese fire, the Fifth Air Force went on the offensive. The march of its airfields spearheaded the Allied advance.

As the Buna offensive was gathering, in October 1942, George Kenney wrote a long letter of advice to Gen. Hap Arnold, commander of Army Air Forces. Kenney began by forcefully declaring the independence of his aerial forces—that air power had taken the place of traditional arms.

> Tanks and heavy artillery can be reserved for the battlefields of Europe and Africa. They have no place in jungle warfare. The artillery in this theatre flies, the light mortar

and machine guns, the rifle, tommygun, grenade and knife are the weapons carried by men who fly to war, jump in parachutes, are carried in gliders and who land from air transports on ground which air engineers have prepared. These engineers have landed also by parachute and by glider, with airborne bulldozers, jeeps and light engineer tools . . . the whole operation preceded and accompanied by bombers and fighters.[2]

Kenney did not stop with proclaiming air power's equality with artillery and armor. He connected these observations with a strategic thesis adapted to the geography of the Southwest Pacific.

In the Pacific theatre we have a number of islands garrisoned by small forces. These islands are nothing more or less than aerodromes or aerodrome areas from which modern fire-power is launched. Sometimes they are true islands like Wake or Midway, sometimes they are localities on large land masses. Port Moresby, Lae and Buna are all on the island of New Guinea, but the only practicable way to get from one to the other is by air or by water: they are all islands as far as warfare is concerned. Each is garrisoned by a small force and each can be taken by a small force once local air control is secured. Every time one of these islands is taken, the rear is better secured and the emplacements for the flying artillery are advanced closer and closer to Japan itself.[3]

If "islands" were to be seized, if airfield sites were to be fought for, Kenney proposed to seize them.

Consciously, sharply, Kenney was breaking with prewar doctrine. Before the war, when engineers and air force commanders pondered the construction of airfields, they thought in defensive terms. The model they followed was the model of fortification, à la the Maginot Line. Air bases were located to protect cities or other strategic objectives. They were constructed to blend into the landscape, camouflaged as farms ideally, with hangars disguised as barns and barracks as farmhouses, so that they would be hard for the enemy to identify and destroy. The airfields from which the Royal Air Force fought the Battle of Britain had been built on these lines.[4] So had the Luftwaffe airfield at Tempelhof, constructed to resemble a Berlin housing project. In the East Indies, on the eve of war, the Dutch had built the secret airdrome of Ngoro, almost perfectly disguised among a landscape of cane fields and rice paddies—with dummy ditches that crisscrossed the runways, and meandering dummy roads. American pilots found themselves baffled, unable to spot their landing place, even as a Dutch biplane led them in for the final approach.[5]

These concepts were static, and Kenney rejected them. In the early days of the war, Kenney had called for creating an "Air Blitz Unit," a formation of planes and ground forces that would leapfrog across enemy lines, moving forward to surprise and outflank the enemy—a unit "entirely dependent upon air transportation and radio-telephone communications," with "no ground line, no highway, nor railroad, and no typewriter."[6] In short, Kenney proposed an air war of ground maneuver, to move his warplanes forward with the agility of Heinz Guderian's panzers.

Kenney also stepped away from high-altitude bombing, the tactic favored by advocates of strategic bombing. Kenney favored attack aviation and skip-bombing. As Kenney saw it, attack aviation meant low-level strikes behind the enemy front line—against depots, supply trains, columns of reinforcement.[7] In skip-bombing, a warplane attacked at masthead height—bore down on a ship with all guns blazing, dropping its payload at the last minute, so that the bombs skipped across the water into the vessel.[8] The B-17 and the B-24, lumbering, heavy four-engine bombers, lacked the maneuverability for these tactics. Attack aviation and skip-bombing became the role of the B-25 medium bomber. To beat down antiaircraft fire, Kenney's armorers packed extra .50-caliber machine guns, up to eight of them, in pods around the nose of each B-25.

⑤

Kenney envisioned building forward airfields as a matter of moving from island to island, and MacArthur and his staff were thinking along the same lines. At the same time that Kenney was calling for air blitz warfare, MacArthur's headquarters circulated an appreciation on "Defensive and Offensive Possibilities." This envisioned defeating Japan by a campaign that would work north through New Guinea and the Philippines. It foresaw both a war for air bases and MacArthur's strategy of bypassing Japanese garrisons:

> New Guinea as a whole is of little value except to provide a very limited number of airdromes from which further operations can be initiated to clear out hostile forces in New Britain, New Ireland, and the Admiralty Islands and to acquire the airdromes in those localities for the purpose of controlling the sea. . . . It is not necessary that all terrain along the line of operations be occupied. On the contrary [the offensive] consists of a number of jumps for the purpose of securing and holding airdromes from which our aviation can operate offensively.[9]

Kenney's "air blitz" strategy was of a piece with this perspective. MacArthur's staff talked of fighting a war for air bases. Kenney saw pushing forward air bases as a means of fighting the war.

In late 1942, when he airlifted the 32nd Division to New Guinea and flew battalions to the front at Buna, Kenney first won MacArthur's endorsement of air power. In March 1943, Kenney proved his point again. In the Battle of the Bismarck Sea, his bombers and strafing planes sank a Japanese convoy carrying a fresh division to Lae—infantrymen and artillery with which the Japanese would have renewed the ground war in New Guinea. "A convoy of this magnitude [Thomas Griffith has written] represented a very severe threat to MacArthur's hopes of continuing his advance toward the Philippines. With Australian and American ground troops worn out by the fighting near Buna and Gona and only limited naval force available, the only way to stop the Japanese from consolidating their position in New Guinea was through air power."[10]

Only Kenney's airmen could have stopped this Japanese offensive, and only Kenney's airmen did. Over two days, the Fifth Air Force, sending in waves of B-25 strafers alongside RAAF Beaufighters, sank every troopship in the convoy.[11]

MacArthur approved the victory with a proclamation of Olympian eloquence. The destruction of the Japanese convoy, he wrote, "cannot fail to go down in history as one of the most complete and annihilating combats of all time."[12] This put the seal on Kenney's favor with his commander. George Johnston wrote:

> It was Kenney who showed MacArthur how to make air power the decisive element in his operations. . . . When the Papuan campaign was in its final stages MacArthur was in his headquarters, towering over the diminutive, chunky Kenney. Someone asked the General if he was convinced that air power could win the war. He threw his arm affectionately around Kenney's shoulder and said, with a smile, "This little feller has given me a new and pretty powerful brandy. I like the stuff. It does me good. And I'm going to keep right on taking it!"[13]

The Southwest Pacific became a war in which air forces did what ground and naval forces did, and naval and ground forces fought to support the air forces. Historians have confirmed what Johnston saw in wartime. "MacArthur's principal strike weapon was to be his air force," Peter Dean has written. "The ascendency of Allied air power . . . gave the Allies control of the sea. This control of the sea gave MacArthur the ability to occupy more islands and use them as airbases to dominate more of the sea. Thus, 'command of the air gave command of the sea which gave initiative and control of the ground,' providing a clear logistics edge to the Allied forces as well as 'unparalleled strategic mobility.' "[14]

At Rabaul there were Zeros from the Imperial Japanese Navy, but Kenney did not face these alone. Other American forces confronted Rabaul, from Navy carriers and bases in the Solomon Islands. More of a threat to the Fifth Air Force was the Japanese base at Wewak, where the Japanese Fourth Air Army had begun a buildup. Rabaul was a more formidable citadel; Wewak posed a more immediate danger.

The Japanese airfields at Wewak were within range of American heavy bombers, but still too distant for Kenney's fighter aircraft to reach. Kenney could not risk sending bombers to Wewak without fighter cover. To provide fighter cover, Kenney moved his air force forward. In the plains and valleys of New Guinea, he looked for islands that he could isolate and capture.

In the western watershed of the Markham River, in the rough country west of Lae, Kenney's engineers found a site where an airdrome might be built, outside the village of Tsili Tsili. As at Wanigela Mission, Kenney rushed in American engineers and Australian troops. (Kenney preferred to use Australian infantry. They fought well, liked American rations, and didn't mind taking orders from an air force commander—the Australian Seventh Division soon started calling itself the Seventh Airborne.) By early August 1943, this frontline base, Marilinan Airfield, was able to serve as an advanced fighter-drome—a base to refuel P-38s so that they could fly with the bombers the rest of the way to Wewak. Kenney now could plan a full-scale attack on the Japanese Fourth Air Army.

Kenney's strategy was basically counterpunching. He hoped to draw an armada of Japanese planes to Wewak, as the Japanese massed for an assault on his forces—then to get his planes in the air first and catch the Japanese on the ground. In mid-August, Kenney judged the time was right. Reconnaissance photos showed that the four airfields at Wewak had been crowded with fighters and bombers, 225 aircraft. Kenney succeeded in launching the first strike—landing it at the last and most devastating moment. On August 17, 1943, at dawn, the Fifth Air Force caught the Japanese on the ground:

> Coming in over the tops of the palm trees, [the B-25 crews] saw a sight to gladden the heart of a strafer. The Jap bombers, sixty of them, were lined up on either side of the runway with their engines turning over, flying crews on board, and groups of ground crewmen standing by each airplane. . . . The B-25 formation swept over the field like a giant scythe. The double line of Jap bombers was on fire almost immediately from the rain of fifty-caliber incendiaries pouring from over 200 machine guns, antiaircraft defenses were smothered, drums of gasoline by the side of the runways blazed up, and Jap flying crews and ground personnel melted away in the path of our gunfire, in the crackle of a thousand parafrag bombs, and the explosions of their own bomb-laden aircraft. We hit them just in time. Another five minutes and the whole Jap force would have been in the air on the way to take us out.[15]

In two days of attacks, the Fifth Air Force devastated the Japanese squadrons at Wewak. After these air raids, the Japanese Fourth Air Army was unable to interfere as Allied troops moved up the New Guinea coast.

⑤

At the end of August, two weeks after the Fifth Air Force had devastated Wewak, the Allies seized the lower Markham Valley. The Australian Ninth Division landed at Lae, while the American 503rd Parachute Infantry Regiment jumped into the kunai grass plain at Nadzab, thirty miles inland. Within days, an airfield had been built at Nadzab. Following up, still in September, the Fifth Air Force moved the Allied front line forward yet again. "The Markham and Ramu Valleys . . . were like a giant corridor some 115 miles long running from southeast to northwest," the Australian official history observes. "From end to end of the river corridor towering mountains rose on the north and south. The valley itself was flat and kunai-clad and most suitable for airfields." The Fifth Air Force drove north along the Markham and the Ramu like a tank army.[16]

The Air Corps officer who led this advance was a youthful colonel who had finished the air base at Marilinan, David William Hutchison. Hutchison was a reconnaissance man. He was called "Photo Hutch" to distinguish him from fighter-plane commander Col. Donald Hutchinson (who was called "Fighter Hutch"). The sobriquets were ironic, for Photo Hutch would prove as pugnacious as Fighter Hutch.

In mid-September, after the Australians recaptured Lae, Hutchison checked out an L-4 Cub observation plane, stowed a carbine in the cockpit, found an engineering officer who would fly with him, and flew up the Markham Valley to a village at Kaiapit, sixty-five miles away. They saw no Japanese. Hutchison circled a level strip of ground from which the kunai grass had been burned off when the villagers were hunting wild pigs. Hutchison and the engineer landed, surveyed and staked out a landing-strip, and flew back to Lae.[17]

Hutchison radioed Port Moresby, where George Kenney was at ADVON. ADVON was the "advanced echelon" of the Fifth Air Force, the forward headquarters from which Maj. Gen. Ennis Whitehead ran the day-to-day air war. Hutchison outlined what he had done. He volunteered, if a battalion of Australian troops could be found, to finish the base at Kaiapit and put down other airfields at Gusap and Dumpu. Kenney and Whitehead showed the radio message to MacArthur, who said that if an officer had the gall to fly an observation plane up the Markham Valley, he deserved the chance to help take it.

Thirteen transport planes arrived early next morning, with a company of Australian infantry. They flew to Kaiapit, made rough landings on the strip that Hutchison had marked off, and secured a perimeter. Hutchison himself flew two round-trips the first day, flying in rations and ammunition and flying out Australian wounded. Other planes in Hutchison's makeshift fleet flew in two thousand more Australian soldiers, with material for an offensive: jeeps, anti-tank guns, quick-firing 25-pounder field guns, ammunition, and rations. Hutchison now had eighteen C-47s to move the troops and four P-39s to fly cover. The planes made five round-trips each day, sometimes more, moving like clockwork, Air Force historians wrote, "with a sort of time-table precision that was the sum of all the air hauls that had preceded this one." In two weeks and one day, only one day behind Hutchison's promised schedule, Gusap and Dumpu were in Allied hands.[18]

Hutchison had done exactly what he had volunteered to do. Following his lead, the Fifth Air Force and Australian Seventh Airborne had moved upcountry along the Markham, in an unbroken series of short smashes, more than a hundred miles. For this initiative, Hutchison received the Silver Star and (from his Australian brothers-in-arms) the Distinguished Service Order. These were honors to let the papers know about, back home in Mineral Point, Wisconsin. They marked ambition and success for a man who had once been rated mediocre.

ᢙ

In the autumn of 1943, while the *John S. Pope* was streaming across the Pacific, the Fifth Air Force and the United States Navy launched a series of air strikes against Rabaul. The Fifth Air Force attacked Rabaul on October 12, October 18, October 23, October 24, October 25, October 29, and November 2. The first raid brought together more than 300 Allied warplanes, including 107 B-25s and 117 P-38s, one of the largest strikes in the Southwest Pacific. The final raid was the "toughest fight the Fifth Air Force encountered in the whole war," the Fifth Air Force's chief acknowledged.[19] It threw 75 B-25s and 75 P-38s against the Japanese defenses. Kenney had expected 50 to 60 Japanese fighters; as many as 150 took off to meet the American planes. On November 5, the Fifth Air Force cooperated with a raid by Adm. William Halsey's carriers. After that, Kenney's men launched follow-up raids, and scrubbed others due to bad weather, while the Navy completed the destruction of Japanese air strength at Rabaul.[20]

As 1943 drew to a close, while Kenney had seized the initiative, the Japanese had resolved to throw in new resources. An Imperial conference had determined to build 40,000 warplanes in the next year and to construct more than a hundred new air bases in the nation's new "absolute defense zone"—western New Guinea, the Moluccas, Celebes, and other islands between Australia and the Philippines. The Japanese still had a formidable air fleet: a hundred warplanes at Wewak, hundreds more in the Netherlands East Indies (including Hollandia, halfway up the coast of New Guinea, where the Japanese had amassed a huge depot and were building three airdromes).[21] Against these forces, the air war remained to be won.

The Allies moved against Japan on two fronts, by sea and by land. The United States Navy fought its way west across the Central Pacific—capturing Kwajalein, Saipan, Guam, and Peleliu—while MacArthur's forces fought their way north along the coast of New Guinea to the Philippines. In the end, William Manchester has written, "The two drives in the Pacific became mutually supporting, each of them protecting the other's flank: [Admiral] Nimitz, for example, diverted enemy sea power which would

otherwise have pounced on MacArthur from the east. Their strategies differed—MacArthur's was to move land-based bombers
forward in successive bounds to achieve local air superiority,
while Nimitz's was predicated on carrier air power protecting
amphibious landings on key islands, which then became stepping-
stones—but that was because they were dealing with different
landscapes and seascapes."[22]

During 1944 the Fifth Air Force would win the air war in the
Southwest Pacific—would drive across the Japanese defense zone
to the Philippines, more than two thousand miles. George Kenney
had mapped out that plan of campaign; David Hutchison would
lead in building the airfields that drove the campaign forward.
It would be a brilliantly successful campaign, and a hard-fought
one. In the fighting for two islands—Biak in the Schoutens, and
Mindoro in the Philippines—the Japanese would resist with deadly,
unexpected force. In those sudden, savage encounters, it would
be the 71st Tactical Reconnaissance Group that fought back.

5

PORT MORESBY

Before the war, Port Moresby had been an unknown anchorage at the end of the world. Making fun of its remoteness, E. J. Kahn joked for his friends in Manhattan that Moresby reminded him of Scarsdale. The black soldiers who landed there had the same impression; they remarked that Moresby was a long way from East St. Louis. In the first year of the Pacific War, the town had become a bombed-out place. "Moresby is a dry, dusty, dirty town," Kahn wrote, "consisting of a few houses, hotels, warehouses, and docks squatting on a hill that rises from a curving harbor. Most of the buildings are made of wood and many of them, today, are rather splintered."[1]

When the 71st Group arrived, the Japanese air raids at Port Moresby had ceased. But the end of Japanese raiding had done nothing to diminish the greatest risk of air warfare: the New Guinea weather. Osmar White saw keenly how the physical landscape of Port Moresby swept up into the fantastic panorama of the sky.

> Bright kurukuru grass, four to seven feet high, grew down to the runway. Near the strip of road that served the field,

the grass was powdered by grayish-white dust. Low gum trees with broad, soft leaves were growing out on the rolling hills as far as the eye could see. Away to the north a high, inky-blue range of mountains, the Owen-Stanleys, was topped by the cumulus cloud that will always, for me, be the epitome of the New Guinea scene. In that land, whenever the sun shines and whenever one looks at mountains, there are always battlements of cloud tipped by light and shadowed in purple.[2]

For airmen, these battlements of cloud were the most dangerous element of the New Guinea climate. The storm fronts of New Guinea were constant and unpredictable; the weather could close in on a plane without warning. Often the storm fronts could not be flown around and could not be flown above, and any cloud could hide a mountain.

৯

At this point, the squadrons of the Group remained scattered across the Pacific. While the 82nd Squadron was sailing from Virginia, the 110th Squadron had backtracked across the continent to Camp Stoneman, on a muddy arm of San Francisco Bay. The squadron sailed in a converted freighter, reaching Brisbane in early December.

The air crews of the 17th Squadron, although they flew to New Guinea, were in transit as well. They had stayed on in Laurel then moved to Savannah, where they received their B-25s. From Savannah they went to Sacramento. They stripped the planes and flew thirteen hours westward to Hawaii. There they rested, for weeks, while their planes were modified for the long flight west. From Hickam Field, they hopped 1,300 miles south to Christmas Atoll. They would fly from that barren sandspit to the equally barren sandspit of Canton Island, then on to the bulldozers, Quonset huts, and bustle of Samoa and Fiji. They would arrive in January.[3]

In Port Moresby, the headquarters section was orienting itself on the new terrain. The men taught themselves the layout of the Allied camps, and—this took longer—were working out their place within the Fifth Air Force.

> Colonel Sams told us he had griped about the circumstances which we had gone through just as we had all done but he wanted us to stop. . . . The colonel, Major League, and I took a trip over to camp in attempt to locate a new campsite nearer the Fifth Air Force HQ. The colonel doesn't care to move primarily because there's one objective in such a move and because of overcrowded mess halls, dirty latrines, poor showers, and absence of electrical power. Later he called on the Fifth Air Force chief of staff, who told him to return at five p.m. We also called on the Air Force signal officer, Lieutenant Colonel Croxton, who was in Australia for X-ray treatments, and his assistant Captain Stump did not enlighten us on our future operations. Evidently we will perform short reconnaissance missions for task forces.[4]

The talk in the Moresby barbershop was that the Group would go to Dobodura. The barber said Dobodura was a pretty fair place. At Milne Bay, on the other hand, laundry wouldn't dry on the line.

As they talked to veterans—or heard the gossip in the barbershop—the Group gained a new appreciation for what the New Guinea air war actually involved. No longer did it mean scrambling P-40s and P-39s to defend Port Moresby. Rocky wrote:

> As far as I can ascertain from men who have been here since the very beginning, only a few Jap patrols ever came on this side of the Owen Stanley Mountains. However,

Port Moresby and Darwin were bombed repeatedly. On one bombing, the Japs sent over three recon ships and off went our fighters who followed the Japs out over the sea, and meanwhile in came the Jap bombers. One lone P-40 went up to act as an interceptor—shot down a plane or two—and this pilot was later fined by Group HQ for intercepting enemy planes over an airdrome.

The largest raid was 106 planes. Everything dates around this raid, if you were here when the raid took place, you're a veteran, if you arrived later, you're a recruit.[5]

Now there were few Zeros in the air, and the New Guinea air war had become a struggle with Japanese antiaircraft gunners. "All the pilots have great respect for those men in England mainly because of the great belts of anti-aircraft fire through which they must fly, whereas here ack-ack fire is only encountered near the targets," Rocky reported. "The men here have the greatest respect for the Japs. Too many men are being shot down because they believe they can fly through antiaircraft fire."[6]

For the Group and its squadrons, Rocky would have to plan and install telephones and a switchboard for Group HQ and the squadrons, and get the line strung for this telephone system. Then there were the teletypes—more delicate machines to maintain. He knew he would have to ask about getting wire and linemen, for the Group had no telephone wire of its own. He would have to retrieve the radio gear that the Group had packed up, back in Laurel, and work out a radio net to ensure that messages received on the high frequency (HF) radio truck at Group HQ could be relayed to the very high frequency (VHF) radios used by Fifth Air Force warplanes. Beyond that, he had to ensure that the Group's radio system meshed with the other Allied radio networks in the theater.

The colonel said Major Baker would arrive in Milne Bay within the next day or so and our equipment will be flown over. Our SCR-299Cs which are mounted in trucks will not be sent and instead we'll be issued a set which can be airborne. It is fortunate that Major Baker is accompanying the equipment for most of the time the Service of Supplies unloads equipment off the boats regardless of for whom the equipment is intended, and it (SOS) reissues. I hope my safe is in good condition because it has all my camera equipment—and Major League's too.[7]

In later wars, the military would work to ensure its various computer systems were compatible. In 1943 the radio problems that Rocky had to solve involved frequency and range. He sketched a plan for a communications grid—straightforward, schematic, zigzag lines of control running from Group HQ to the squadrons' B-25s and P-39s—duplicate links from Fifth Air Force to the squadrons, if Fifth Air Force should want that. In the meantime he turned to assignments from Lieutenant Gilbert, preparing a memo on what navigational aids the Group's flyers could count on.

Mail had arrived, "41 V-Mail letters from Margaret Anne, my future wife."[8] A V-Mail was a letter form produced by the American military for servicemen, a small single sheet that could be read by a censor, then folded over to make its own envelope. Many servicemen still preferred sheets of stationery and airmail envelopes, but any man would welcome scores of love letters.

Rocky began calling on Fifth Air Force signal officers and looked over their communications setups, and saved the letters to reread that night. "Captain Meyerhein said we could write home and only say we are on an island in the southwest Pacific," Rocky recorded. "We could not mention our previous means of travel nor places seen. The captain must write very dull letters."[9]

> No one seems sure what we intend to do. The colonel
> said, "It seems they (Fifth Air Force) are attempting to
> plan operations, install means of communications, and
> move troops. All at one time." And then he smiled know-
> ing what may happen.
>
> The colonel is very ill but he is one of these individu-
> als who will not consult a doctor. He wants to fly against
> the Japs. He wonders why our B-25s have not arrived. We
> wonder too.[10]

Colonel Sams was exasperated. He had commanded three squadrons in Laurel, scores of warplanes and hundreds of men; now he was in charge of none. He could not tell when his group's equipment would arrive, where the airplanes were, what had happened to Major Tennille and the 17th Squadron. "Arrived Moresby by air on the 7th," he wrote. "Got the brush-off all around on the 8th, 9th, 10th. Went to Dobodura by air 11th returned 12th. Went to Ahioma the 13th; saw Gordon and Harris and returned the 14th."[11]

By the middle of November, they had almost settled in at Port Moresby. "Captain Meyerhein reports that we may state we are in New Guinea in our letters."[12] The rumors had featured more detail. The men could frame a discussion of what sort of reconnaissance they might be assigned to and with what units they might be working. Characters began to appear.

> No one knew why we are here but it finally became
> known that a certain colonel, an old reconnaissance
> man, sold the idea of combined reconnaissance to
> General Kenney. At the present the Bomber Command
> has charge of all long-range reconnaissance. There is a
> photo squadron (F-4s and F-5s) for ground support but
> no one is familiar with actual ground support. There
> has been little in this sector.

As for our Group, it is rumored we will become a wing and have Colonel Sams as deputy commander. General Kenney was supposed to come up from Brisbane this morning to form this unit. Meanwhile we'll remain attached to the Fifth Bomber Command. The colonel and Major Smith went on a combat mission early this morning—their first.

The colonel said the squadrons would be stationed over the mountains but has never said exactly where we'll go.[13]

The combat mission on which Colonel Sams and Major Smith flew was a bombing raid to support the Australian Ninth Division at Sattelberg. The planes returned early.

Here's the dope on yesterday's raid. Colonel Rogers took out 54 bombers fully loaded out on mission. After being out about 1¾ hrs they must have encountered foul weather as they turned around and dropped all their bombs (cost, around $2,000,000) into the ocean, because the planes could not land loaded with 1000 pound bombs. Come to think about it, this raid which never got there cost more than Clinton County contributed in the second War Loan drive. The cost of bombs is approximately four dollars per pound. The colonel made one statement about the raid, "We did make a nice pattern in the sea."

Sams made a sardonic comment; Rocky expanded on it. They could see already that not every mission ended in victory or death.

§

Women were so rare that men counted and studied the ones who appeared: one nurse with a dog, another nurse on a major's arm, twenty nurses in slacks and white blouses at an officers' club dance, eight girls at a special-services show ("the jokes lacked punch but the music was good").[14] Women could often be seen, from a distance, at the Fifth Bomber Command.

> At 2030 this evening seven Aussie girls in uniform (maybe Red Cross) arrived at the club to spend the evening socially. Drinks were passed around. A few of the rankest of the rank monopolized the young girls and we of low rank merely looked on. Their uniforms were a bit unusual because their legs were covered by leggings. Skirts unusually long for this day and age—leggings as far as you could see. Most of the nurses wear slacks when off-duty and come on their dates to the club. It takes at least a captain to rate a nurse.[15]

Mail was a barometer of morale. Servicemen were better contented when they received mail and were able to send it. Enlisted men resented that their officers read their mail (particularly because some officers gossiped about what they read).[16] Officers resented their own mail being opened, particularly when souvenirs of New Guinea—such as they were—were removed. "Lieutenant Scott said the clothing sent home by officers was fumigated in the Hawaii Islands and some time ago there was a great rumpus over articles being removed from the packages. No feathers may be sent to the States. It is also believed that no grass skirts may be sent."[17]

The mail bore the brunt of broader complaints. With letters from home delayed, with the frustrations and uncertainty that the Group was facing in Port Moresby, Rocky took a small, resentful act of rebellion against the military postal system.

> Went into Port Moresby this afternoon to mail most of my woolen clothing home. . . . Took my clothes to the censor who removed all my cadet issue shirts and said

I couldn't send them home. After he put his stamp on the box, I took it downstairs to mail but before doing so, opened the box and stuck in the shirts.

Did not receive mail which increases the total of times with no mail to nine. Wonder if Margaret Anne will try air mail. Sent three letters home, one by air, one V-Mail and one regular, all asking Mother to send Margaret Anne orchids for Christmas and also check on the mail service. The last letter I received was post-marked September 26th.[18]

Behavior can be expression. Disobeying authority can be a rebel's way of asserting control. When Rocky stuffed his wool shirts into the package, in defiance of the censor's stamp, he was getting back something of his own against the Army, in both senses of the term. The wool shirts could do him no good in New Guinea; someone might get wear out of them back home. He had brought the shirts across the Pacific because the Army had ordered him to; mailing them home was a silent, resentful, practical complaint.

The next day, Rocky received two letters from his family and three from Margaret Anne. By the end of November, V-Mail service would improve; mail from home arrived in twelve days. At least one of Rocky's letters home arrived, before the end of the fall semester. Margaret Anne wore the orchid for sociology class.

۞

November 19 was a red-letter day. The run-around pattern continued, but the 71st Group was getting its first warplanes and men to fly them.

Our Group was assigned 14 P-39Qs this morning. The colonel sent an order to the 82nd Squadron at Milne Bay to send over 14 pilots to fly locally for two days before taking the planes over the hump to Dobodura. Wilkey, Gilbert, Dixon, Wilkinson and myself hurried around getting operational information so the pilots could fly immediately upon arrival. We needed call words for the planes—the Fifth Bomber Command referred me to Fourth Fighter Sector, who referred me to Fifth Air Force HQ, who referred me to Fifth Bomber Command, who then gave me the call words. Late this evening Lieutenant Dixon stated the colonel was griped because higher HQ had changed their mind about the planes.[19]

The P-39 Airacobra was a single-engine fighter. Built by Bell Aircraft in Buffalo, it was perhaps the oddest fighter airplane used by the United States during the war. The P-39 carried .50-caliber machine guns, but its signature feature was the armament in its nose, a 37-mm Oldsmobile cannon firing through the propeller hub. To fit the cannon into the nose, the engine was moved to the center of the aircraft, behind the pilot; the engine pulled in air through a scoop intake behind the canopy and drove the propeller by a long crankshaft under the pilot's feet. Pilots liked the P-39 because they stepped into the cockpit through a door, rather than climbing in through a canopy, and because they sat high over the wings, with a bubble canopy, giving an exceptional field of vision to both front and back. Without an engine in the nose, the P-39 was phenomenally streamlined. It was slightly faster than the P-40 (though neither was as fast as a Zero) and it was beautiful in flight. The drawbacks of the P-39 were its limited range—there was no space in the fuselage for a fuel tank—and that it was under-powered. Its Allison engine had only one single-speed supercharger; there was no further space in the fuselage for a turbo-supercharger. This meant that the P-39 performed well only up to 12,000 feet, far below the height at which warplanes fought in the Pacific. (Chuck Yeager liked the plane, which he flew in training; and on the Russian front, where the Luftwaffe and Soviet Air Force fought at lower altitudes, Russian aces flying P-39s shot down scores of German aircraft.) By 1943 the P-39 was a work-horse fighter, a solid and effective aircraft, but one that lacked the range and performance that would make the P-51 Mustang a star.

The P-39 was the warplane flown by the 82nd and 110th Squadrons.[20] The 17th Squadron was equipped with B-25 Mitchells. The B-25 was a two-engine medium bomber, built by North American Aviation. In the Pacific, where most B-25s flew, the plane generally had a six-man crew. Three officers sat in front—the pilot and copilot, with the bombardier/observer looking out through the plexiglass panes of the nose, while three enlisted men manned the top turret and waist guns. The Fifth Air Force added .50-caliber machine guns to the airframe, to create the Fifth Air Force's strafer gunships—also known as "commerce destroyers," for the hundreds of Japanese ships that they sank.

The P-39s arrived, and the pilots transferred in; they flew the planes two days at Moresby, to familiarize themselves with the aircraft, and then they went over the Owen Stanleys to Dobodura. The Group HQ unit remained at Moresby and struggled on.

> Today we were inspected by some Signal Corps colonel. He wanted to see our traffic diagrams, our installations etc, our personnel, and was surprised to find we had no equipment, and that our personnel were working for the bomber command. He questioned us if we could direct artillery and naval fire, strafe, bomb, photograph, and the colonel assured him we could. Then the Signal Corps colonel went into one of those communications net mazes describing how we would operate. After a while Colonel Sams asked him where he would set all the equipment, personnel, etc. He slowed quite a bit and said he would return later. I said "I'm tired of asking vague questions about a vague unit which is over here for a vague purpose and in the end we receive

vague answers." Colonel Sams said, "Who isn't!" Later the colonel called someone and during the course of conversation asked "When will they know what unit we'll be assigned and our purpose, who we'll work with?" After hanging up, the colonel said we would probably know Monday.[21]

They did not learn this on Monday; they learned it on Thursday, November 25—Thanksgiving Day. The holiday was marked by traditional services and headquarters politics.

Chaplain Smith held services in the enlisted men's recreation hut. Several of the 82nd Squadron officers who are here attended. Turkey was served for dinner for both officers and enlisted men.

At approximately 1300 today a teletype came to our headquarters announcing the formation of a Reconnaissance Wing. The Wing headquarters will be created from the personnel of the 71st Reconnaissance HQ and the 6th Photo and Mapping Group. Tonight there is much discussion as to whom the command will be given. Besides our Colonel Sams, there is a Colonel Hutchison of the Photo Group who is qualified for CO. Yesterday we received a new T/O (Table of Organization) for Reconnaissance Group HQ. Under it we are authorized a colonel, three lieutenant colonels, eight majors and others. It cuts the enlisted communications section down to 16 men.[22]

To Rocky, the organization chart looked top-heavy. It showed plenty of concern for colonels and majors—no interest in first lieutenants. Whittling down the number of communications men would mean problems when radio traffic was heavy. There had already been trouble with the enlisted men; Rocky was having trouble with Master Sergeant Fribourg, his right-hand man. Fribourg was cracking up. "Sergeant Fribourg called on me late at night to say I was not handling the section right and he wanted to know of everything going on—he pointed out that Lieutenant Ball was taking the men off without his knowledge, and he did not know what to do."[23] That week, problems had come to a head.

> For the last several days Master Sergeant Fribourg, my communications chief, and I have been "on the outs." Lieutenant Ball says it all started when he and Fribourg went to the 90th Bomb Group, where he (Master Sergeant Fribourg) got a little too much under the belt. He then called Lieutenant Ball, and asked him for more liquor and Lieutenant Ball refused. Fribourg became angry especially when he learned Lieutenant Zock was carrying a few quarts of beer for his friends. (Lieutenant Zock was accompanying Lieutenant Ball and Fribourg.) The next morning I observed the Master Sergeant was very ill for obvious reasons, so I took it on myself to relieve him of any work that morning. Instead of ordering Fribourg to leave the men to do certain things which is the normal channel of command, I did it directly, and he took offense because it hinted he wasn't capable of work in that capacity. As a result, he is on the "outs" with both Lieutenant Ball and myself.[24]

Tension was accumulating in the men, who did not know where they were headed. That tension might make an aging master sergeant drink too much; it might make a lieutenant prone to boss around a sergeant.

That night, in the officers' club, the mood was downbeat—subdued even for a holiday evening far from home. Chaplain Smith had organized a fishing trip off Port Moresby harbor and a trip to Rouna Falls. That had not helped enough. Rocky wrote:

> Tonight I am recording today's events in the Fifth
> Bomber Command officers' club. There's one nurse here,
> one dog, one blackjack game (Lieutenant Zock and Lieu-
> tenant Scott were rumored to have won over £1,000
> three nights ago) one craps game, and four lieutenants
> are about to play doubles in ping pong.[25]

Rocky and his section had their doubts about the new wing. Colonel Sams would have felt the uncertainty, too. The 71st Group officers were waiting on events: they wanted Sams to get command. (He had more service, they pointed out, more hours in the air, and he had graduated from West Point three years earlier than Colonel Hutchison.) Some officers vented gripes about the service. Lieutenant Beck, the Montana rancher, complained about nurses and WACs (Women's Army Corps) being coarsened by Army life. Captain Seitz the dentist complained that the Medical Corps was run by doctors. Flight Surgeon Knauf talked about fungus on men's knees and hands. Only in talk of Australian girls was there a spark of high spirits.

> It is reported frequently that leaves and furloughs are
> given after one has been in New Guinea four months.
> There are also reports of those returning from Australia
> from leaves that the Aussie girls want to marry Ameri-
> can soldiers in order to be US citizens after the war, and
> they (the girls) are quite eager to satisfy the US soldiers
> regardless of their rank. One hears frequent stories of
> officers going to Sydney, meeting a girl and living with
> her for the duration of his leave. One soldier said he
> never saw so many pregnant women as in Sydney.[26]

On the Saturday after Thanksgiving, Rocky flew to Dobodura with Colonel Sams and an entourage of other lieutenants, to confer with a battalion of the Seventh Marines. The Marines were scheduled to land in New Britain; 71st Group aircraft were to provide air support. Rocky noted that the radios used by the Marines for artillery spotting were adequate for liaising with the Group's P-39s. Then Sams and his entourage returned to the 82nd Squadron camp area and held a quick inspection.

> Returned to camp. Inspected communications. Listened to the enlisted men gripe about the officers. They stated the men were detailed for officers' mess without additional pay, the officers had showers but they didn't, etc. Captain Schafer told about the water which was taken from the river this morning but had not been decontaminated.
>
> The campsite of the 82nd Squadron is near the Victory Chapel and shaded by tropical trees. The only permanent building is the mess hall, with a concrete floor. The camp area had not been policed. The officers' latrine was a disgrace to the organization, however they had soft toilet paper and that particular item cannot be overlooked. If a urinal could be built and the latrine flyproofed no doubt it would help the morale of the organization. The site being adjacent to the jungle naturally had more animals and insects to contend with, consequently elevated tent floors would be desirable.[27]

Having tent floors was wishful thinking, at least for airmen recently arrived on the east side of the Owen Stanleys. At Lae, just up the coast, the only airmen with wooden floors for their tents, beside a general and two colonels, were five GI prisoners in the stockade.[28]

Sunday morning, Colonel Sams, Captain Meyerhein, and Rocky hitchhiked back to Moresby, catching a lift on a B-24. They arrived at 0920, Rocky wrote, in time for church. "Slept most of the afternoon, ate, attended evening services, read manuals on the radio equipment in the B-25 until 0100 in the morning."[29]

As the week began, there was little to talk about. Maj. Ralph Baker was in Brisbane and could not get the Group's equipment shipped to the Group's airmen. Maj. Archie League had flown to Brisbane to help, but had returned with nothing. Their prized radio truck had taken $1,500 damage on its way from Laurel to California; supposedly it had been repaired. No one could say when their gear would reach them.[30] "All I can say is damn," Colonel Sams was writing, in his own journal. "Equipment located and in Baker's hands in Brisbane and ADVON cannot give sufficient priority to get it up prior to January 1st. Why does every army have to operate in any such fashion."[31]

There was news coming. Rocky caught a hint: "The colonel, with a great deal under the belt, announced at the officers' club last night that he was leaving the Group."[32] Within two days it was clear what Sams had meant. On December 1, 1943, the 5212th Photographic Reconnaissance Wing (Provisional) began operations, and Photo Hutch became Wing commander.

6

HEADQUARTERS

In Rocky's long relationship with the military, there was one case of love at first sight. When he encountered *Catch-22*, he fell madly in love with what Joseph Heller said about the wartime Army Air Forces. Rocky thought that the only fictional thing about the novel was that Heller had put together on one air base all of the odd and neurotic characters who had played their part in the war. And the experience had been like that, he thought, the way in which things seemed to happen again and again: there were times when you had trouble figuring out what day it was, because every day you did the same things.

Rocky was not Yossarian, of course. And Colonel Hutchison was by no means Milo Minderbinder.

。

His name was David William Hutchison. He was thirty-five years old.

In his photos, Colonel Hutchison looks Midwestern, moderate and bland and business-like. Something in his gaze and the set of his jaw says that he believed in working hard to get ahead, and not cutting other people slack. He was a favorite of George Kenney. There was one night at Nadzab, Kenney wrote, when an air-raid alert sounded.

In this public relations photo, Col. David W. "Photo Hutch" Hutchison blinks in the glare of the photographer's flash. Posing with Colonel Hutchison is his right-hand man, Maj. Lester Tockstein.
Photo courtesy of the Edward J. Peterson Air and Space Museum, Peterson Air Force Base, Colorado

Photo Hutchison and three members of his staff were playing bridge by lantern light in a tent near the Nadzab strip. Hutch had just bid a grand slam, which had been doubled. The opening lead had been made and the dummy hand laid down just as the siren blew. Someone moved to turn off the lights. Hutchison would have none of it. He was going to play that hand, war or no war. Pulling his pistol from his shoulder holster, he laid it on the table and announced that the siren meant he had five minutes before the bombs began to drop, that he could play the hand in less time than that, and he intended to play it. The hand was played. Hutch made his bid. The lights were extinguished and everyone ran for a slit trench. A few minutes later the all-clear signal was sounded and his opponents tried to explain to Hutch that the hand should not count as they had not had their minds on the game. It was no use.[1]

Kenney liked commanders who could build him forward airfields. He liked even better commanders who built forward airfields and gave him stories to tell.

Mineral Point is a small town in southwest Wisconsin. In its hey-day, before the Civil War, the town was known for its lead and zinc mines—like Galena, Illinois, a short drive south, the county seat where Ulysses Grant once clerked in a harness store.

David Hutchison's father, who farmed outside town, was a Republican assemblyman and state senator. Two of his sons won appointments to the United States Military Academy. Each retired as a major general. David Hutchison's career was at first undis-tinguished. Finishing low in his West Point class, he entered the Air Corps, where he flew biplane bombers in the Canal Zone and pursuit planes in Michigan. Ten years out of West Point, still a lieu-tenant, Hutchison transferred to photo reconnaissance. He may have thought of Grant, marking time in Galena, offered his chance when a great war demanded his service—and in 1941, as America armed for a second world war, Hutchison's opportunity came.

In August 1941, as a member of an Army Air Force studying damage wrought by the Luftwaffe, Capt. Elliott Roosevelt arrived in London. As FDR's son, his presence underlined the United States' commitment to the Allied cause. American newspapers from Maryland to Alaska ran a wire-service photo of Captain Roosevelt on a hotel rooftop, looking out on the battered city. Beside him stands a stocky man, also in Air Corps uniform, squinting slightly, raising his arm to point out something that the president's son should notice. Of the newspapers that ran that photo, most mis-spelled this officer's name as Maj. D. W. Hutchinson.[2]

In the first months of war, Elliott Roosevelt and David Hutchison served together at Bolling Field, in the southwest corner of the District of Columbia, and at Colorado Springs. Roosevelt was by then the colonel commanding the Third Reconnaissance Group, and Hutchison was the first CO of a new air base built to train photo reconnaissance groups.[3] Being a reconnaissance officer, and knowing a president's son who was also a reconnaissance officer, must have helped Hutchison's career. Thanks to Elliott's service, the president had a family interest in reconnaissance flying—he would have been the readier to strengthen the Fifth Air Force by sending it a reconnaissance group. As Elliott Roosevelt's personal friend, David Hutchison would have been well placed to wangle a transfer overseas, with his forces to follow him.

There had been only one reconnaissance unit in the Southwest Pacific, the overworked, heroic Eighth Photo Squadron.[4] Hutchison arrived to establish a full reconnaissance group. He flew missions himself at first, learning the terrain. He brought in refrigerated film, which gave better definition and stronger contrasts. He worked out that his tired recon pilots had an average of forty-six combat missions each, grounded the squadron, and wired Hap Arnold to send replacements. When recon planes began vanishing, Hutchison pressed for fighter escorts, and got them.

Well before he called for Australians to land at Kaiapit, Hutchison had built up credit with their commanders. He had flown above the Markham Valley with Major General Alan Vasey, commander of the Australian Seventh Division, pointing out the landing zones at Nadzab. Hutchison knew to protect and impress his guest: the number of fighter planes covering the flight were matched only by the number of cars that met the plane when they landed—a "young convoy," complete with Red Cross canteen truck, photographer, and MP escort.

Hutchison also worked the press. He let war correspondents hitchhike by air to the front line: when American paratroops and Australian artillerymen parachuted over Nadzab, a B-17 from the

Sixth Photo Group flew over the drop zone with Hearst newsman Lee Van Atta and Vern Haugland of the Associated Press. Back in Wisconsin, the *State Journal* and *Racine Journal-Times* noted his every promotion and decoration. Prominent among these, in July 1943, was the Distinguished Flying Cross, which Hutchison received alongside another Wisconsin airman, also little known at the time, 1st Lt. Richard Bong.[5]

Colonel Hutchison was not a man to waste time. On becoming Wing commander, he immediately called in the officer who would be in charge of Wing communications. Rocky wrote:

> Colonel Hutchison the new CO of the new wing called for me to call at his office in the afternoon. Before going, I put on a clean uniform, polished my brass and shoes, and gathered fragments of communications data available. The colonel asked me several questions and upon discovering I could not answer them, requested I contact the Fifth Bomb Group and secure all available data. That I did by contacting Captain Elvin and Captain Morrison.[6]

That evening, as assiduously as he had polished his shoes and his insignia, Rocky worked past midnight preparing a report for Hutchison. The next day he got an early start. There was a meeting that afternoon, where the commanders were choosing who would move over to Wing HQ: "Several officers and I for one are sweating out the news."

> Woke early. Went to Sixth Photo Group area to contact the communications officers, who were still on their way here from Brisbane. However, the enlisted personnel gave me the necessary info and data on signal equipment and communications personnel in the Photo Group and in the three squadrons. The 25th and 26th Squadrons have

> P-38s and the 20th Squadron has B-24s. Gave report to
> Colonel Hutchison and was told to contact the Fifth Air
> Force signal officer for additional info. Returned to camp
> area. Slept three hours due to working on the colonel's
> report until almost 1 a.m. last night.[7]

On December 6, Rocky scored a victory: he saw his name on
the list for Wing HQ. He was glad for that, even if there were two
asterisks. He was going as acting signal officer, not as communications officer, and he was holding a post for which the Wing
T/O required a major. This meant he stood to lose his post if any
actual Signal Corps officer could be obtained or a plausible major
appeared.

Hutchison demanded a broader, ambitious radio grid than the
one that Rocky had worked on for the 71st Group. The colonel
listed nine radio nets that the Wing would require, with further
links leaping across the ether to three air task forces and a teletype line to Fifth Air Force command. Wing HQ would have fourteen transmitters, all the way up to a thousand watts; each air task
force would have four SCR-299s, the radio-truck transceiver that
the Group had been so anxious to recover.

Rocky had been gathering information on radio nets, and now
he redoubled his efforts. A SCR-299 transmitter broadcast on only
350 watts; he quickly looked for information on the thousand-watt
transmitters at Fifth Bomber Command, RAAF Reconnaissance,
and Navy Air Operations. He talked to the communications officer at the Eighth Photo Squadron, which had a similar situation
with its B-17s and P-38s, and with Major Tockstein of Sixth Photo
Group (already marked as one of Colonel Hutchison's men). Lieutenant Long, Fifth Air Force's assistant radio officer, another officer low on the totem pole, called Rocky with questions about the
new wing.

At the 25th Photo Reconnaisssance Squadron, Rocky drew
Lieutenant Hartbard into cooperation: "He's a second lieutenant

and a little down in the dumps because his job calls only for a first lieutenant. He asked when I got my promotions and after learning I was a second lieutenant for nine months he rested a little more at ease." From Hartbard, Rocky heard a rumor that was almost true: that Hutchison was in charge of the Wing because he was a friend of the president's son, Jimmy Roosevelt.[8] Other officers seemed less energetic.

> Most every time I walk into any of the Fifth Bomber Command's offices, there's usually a chess game in progress and especially is this true in the Signal Office.[9]
>
> The other day at Fifth Air Force headquarters, I saw several second lieutenant navigators and bombardiers. Upon asking why flying officers should be kept at a large headquarters, I was told many were the ones who volunteered to come over here before finishing school and the ones around are the worthless ones. Also, the disciplinary problems are collected at HQ to burn documents, carry messages and be present when the circumstances require an officer.[10]

Staff officers seemed to offer little actual help. At Fifth Air Force HQ, Rocky caught Colonel Croxton in his office. Croxton was a West Point man, a lieutenant colonel at the age of twenty-six. Rocky wrote: "We talked over the air-ground communications of the new wing and he asked: 'Know what you're doing? Do you know you have one helluva job ahead.'" Someone told Rocky that Croxton knew nothing about signals but had "a helluva lot of bull"; he was a pilot put in as acting signal officer, a figurehead who interviewed communications men by asking questions his sergeant had written out for him.[11] At Fifth Bomber Command, Rocky found Captain Morrison. Morrison told him only that the plans for the Wing communications had been changed. Then he seems to have talked about himself: about arriving in Australia in

December 1941, and not having been home since, and consoling himself with a girlfriend, "some woman corporal in the Australian auxiliary who has a husband somewhere."[12]

〄

That December 7, nothing happened, Rocky wrote. The next day, he received his orders placing him on detached service with the Wing.

The Wing existed, but it was slow to take shape. Officers moving there had parted on bad terms with the enlisted men in their sections.

> Called the communications section together and told them goodbye. Since each officers' club member could buy a quart of gin for a half pound, most of them gave it to the HQ enlisted men as a gift. Several enlisted men became drunk and upon doing so broke all rules of military conduct, called on the officers who gave them the gin and asked why they couldn't have more, and became angry when turned away.[13]

Moreover, it was uncertain why transfers were being made—no one could be sure whether officers selected for the Wing were being signally favored or silently ostracized. "I have met several of the officers of this particular newly activated unit, and their first impression is very favorable, in fact too favorable. Also, several of the officers and enlisted men look and their names indicated they are Jewish."[14]

The problem was not that Rocky did not want to serve with Jews. Rather, when he saw his name on the transfer list, he worried that he was being sent off into the unknown. For all he could tell of command decisions, the 71st Group seemed to be casting off its Jewish personnel, and him along with them.

It was well known that commanders transferred men into new units as a way of getting rid of them—"shunting the crud," as James Jones put it.[15] No serviceman wanted to be transferred out

of a unit where he had friends and where he occupied an authorized position in which he was doing well. Rocky spoke with a
friend from the Group who was also bound for the Wing.

> In evening had long talk with Captain Seitz. I told him of
> the Jewish situation in the Wing HQ, also that they were
> only authorized a Signal Corps officer and not a com-
> munications officer such as I am. He advised me to see
> Colonel Sams (who is now with the 82nd Squadron fly-
> ing missions at Dobo). It is believed that the colonel dis-
> likes Jews for there are only two Jewish officers in his
> Group—all others have been transferred. Seitz said he
> had heard that Major Gordon of the 82nd Squadron
> would be relieved of his command. (This would be a
> good move.) His father had given him this advice when
> he entered the Army: Get your reports in on time and
> keep away from Jews. Seitz stated the American base
> hospitals are overrun with Semitics.[16]

If the command were finally going to get rid of Gordon, a
squadron commander, the command was ready to get rid of anyone. That was why Rocky was concerned about the Wing being
authorized a signal officer but not a communications officer, and
why he was discussing anti-Semitism with a dentist named Seitz.

Perhaps there was bias, perhaps not. When Wing HQ was
scratched together, of those transferred there, men named Tock-
stein, Niederhofer, Hoverman, Hollywood, Sheffel, and Titefsky
were outnumbered by men with names like Dixon, Boyer, Foliart,
Wagoner, Godfrey, Burke, and O'Steen. Chaplain Smith thought
Colonel Sams did not like Jews, but Rocky knew that Smith and
Sams did not get along. If Sams had wanted to transfer out Jewish
officers, he could hardly have missed Lt. Ray Weinstein in the 82nd
Squadron (unless Sams considered Weinstein a fellow Southerner;
Sams was from Meridian and Weinstein was from Shreveport).[17]

"In Fifth Air Force HQ everyone was afraid of someone else." Major League had said that, after what he had seen of ADVON in Port Moresby and General Kenney's staff in Brisbane.[18] Rocky remembered that comment, and his diary reflected how contagious that anxiety had become. It was why Hartbard was ill at ease about promotions, and Croxton dodged meetings, and lieutenants shined their shoes and buffed their collar bars, and everyone studied the transfer orders. It might be why older airmen drank, sergeants and colonels alike. It deepened suspicions about Jews, no matter how competent those Jewish airmen seemed. It helped men condemn, in comrades and allies, flaws that they themselves conspicuously shared. Rocky found one complaint so unexpected that he noted it in detail.

> Heard from Captain Morrison of the Fifth Bomber Command that several Dutch military officers who had left their families in the hands of the Japs are now in Australia living with Aussie girls and charging the US and RAAF ungodly prices for their services, such as $6 per hour to fly and many pilots log passenger time.[19]

Whatever the Dutch pilots might be earning, their war had been cheerless. For some it had been painful. For a year and a half before Pearl Harbor, after the Germans overran their homeland, the Military Aviation units of the Royal Netherlands East Indies Army had waited for the Japanese to overrun their airstrips. Their air force, based on a tropical archipelago, had been peculiarly strong in flying boats—Catalinas, Fokkers, and aging Dorniers with fore-and-aft propellers. When the Japanese finally came, the Dutch were quickly beaten out of the sky. Fleeing south, they stumbled and were massacred. At Broome, on the coast of northwestern Australia, a squadron of Zeros swooped down on a flotilla of Dutch flying boats that had moored there after escaping the

East Indies. In half an hour the Zeros strafed and sank fifteen flying boats, many of them still packed with refugee women and children.

In New Guinea, until the planes wore out, Dutch pilots flew German Dorniers for the Allies. Other Dutch airmen shouldered part of the Allied war effort: commercial pilots on routes across Australia. War correspondent John Lardner noted that they flew their DC-5s tirelessly, almost ceaselessly, sleeping in the shade beneath their airplanes—and without smiling. Flying Dutchmen, Lardner called them, with a pun that hinted at exile and restlessness and loss. Families and property were dear to the Dutch, Lardner wrote; the pilots who had escaped from Java would do what they could to avenge the one and regain the other.[20]

How pharisaical was it for Captain Morrison, who sat safely on Fifth Air Force staff, with an Australian girlfriend who already had an Australian husband, to speak ill of flyers who chased Australian girls and were doing well out of the war? But it was safe to speak ill of the Dutch, with their silver guilders and ungainly flying boats, exiles who fought on only at the sufferance of larger Allied nations.

Rocky continued work. Acting signal officer was a post worth having. He turned from radio nets to telephone systems. Things seemed to have turned a corner.

> Was called by Colonel Hutchison to make it possible for the Wing to construct a telephone system. Figured it would take 60 telephones for Wing HQ; Signal Company; HQ Squadron; and the 6th and 71st Groups. Went to the Fifth Air Force to see Captain Alexander about switchboards; he referred me to a lieutenant in Signal Supply who said if we failed to get switchboards by requisition to that he would give us two on memorandum receipt.[21]

Rocky was no longer on the outs with Sergeant Fribourg. Fribourg was recovering from other problems now, and working with him brought coincidental benefits.

> In afternoon collected my communications data and went via jeep to the 171st Army Hospital to contact Master Sergeant Fribourg, who was there for what the men call the GI's, which in the medical lingo is dysentery. The nurses were a bit coarse-looking and their faces showed more age than their legs. Surprisingly they were wearing skirts, I forget the color, and blue blouses. I commented about the sea breeze to one of the nurses and incidentally she was the first woman I had spoken to since October 2nd.[22]

Although he worked for Hutchison in the Wing, Rocky still reported to Sams in the Group. On December 12, at the end of the day, Colonel Sams addressed his officers. There was news, or what might pass for it.

> Colonel Sams called a meeting of all Group officers at 1745 in front of his tent and passed on to us the following information which is not to be discussed. First, we are now the tactical unit of the 5212th Photo Wing. Our mission is three-fold: short-range reconnaissance, long-range reconnaissance, and ground support. Second, we are receiving B-25Ds for the 17th Squadron and it is rumored they (the 17th) will in time be converted into a B-24 unit. Third, the planes of the 82nd and 110th Squadrons may be changed to P-47s. Fourth, the 82nd Squadron pilots are having a great time flying up and down the coast even though they shot up one of our own barges but fortunately no one was killed. Fifth, the flight echelon of the 17th Squadron are on their way across.

Sixth, the 110th and 25th Squadrons have been ordered up to New Guinea. Seventh, the Group HQ will probably move over the hump in two months. Eighth, we will move to the new Wing area in two weeks. He asked if there were any questions and then dismissed the officers.[23]

As he had done after the 71st Group reached Port Moresby, Colonel Sams did his best to shut down griping. But while Sams could forbid debate, he could not speak with finality. He could not say where three of his four squadrons were—only that they would be ordered up. He was forced to warn that happenstance might change his airmen's role—that they would fly whatever warplanes reached their theater. He acknowledged, with mirthless irony, the war's mistakes and casual risks—the 82nd Squadron's attack on friendly barges. He could say that his men and his headquarters would move, but not where. Ironically, no matter how clear and emphatic his language, Sams could speak only of vague units and vague purposes.

7

PALACE COUP

Late on Monday night, November 29, at the Fifth Bomber Command, a party ran on from the afternoon into the evening, and beyond. Rocky wrote about it the next day.

> Had another big time in the club last night—someone was firing a .45 caliber arm, about 2 a.m., another got the bright idea of igniting ½ lb charges of TNT at 10 minute intervals and also around 2 a.m. I heard a woman's scream.... Chaplain went to squadrons over at Dobodura.[1]

What happened at the officers' club that night was never laid out for public view. It was investigated, but it was a matter whose corners no one may have seen fully: not the officer who was firing off .45 rounds, not the colonel who was savaged by the dynamite, not the woman who screamed (whoever she was), not by the two generals who learned enough of the truth, buried the story, and flexed the matter to serve their advantage, and not by the chaplain who complained. That was Chaplain Smith of the 71st Group, Rocky's pastor, his roommate on the *General John S. Pope.*

෨

For Rocky and the rest of the 71st Group, the scandal slowly broke. On Wednesday evening, December 1, two nights after the shenanigans at the officers' club, Rocky stopped in at the Fifth Bomber Command camp theater. That night, an audience of enlisted men was staging its own satirical revue.

> At the show the enlisted men passed a collection box for the officers' ammunition fund for the benefit of those officers of very high rank who have the habit of firing several rounds around 2 a.m. and igniting ½ lb charges of TNT which threw dirt on the enlisted men's tents. Heard one rumor that one of the chaplains wrote the chaplain of Fifth Air Force and reported the misconduct. Yes, there's always an eager one in every crowd.[2]

There was war news that day, too—it was a date trimmed in black for the 90th Bombardment Group, the Jolly Rogers. For that bomb group, the December 1 raid on Wewak was one of the most slapdash and bloodiest missions of the war. Rocky wrote on:

> During the morning several squadrons of B-24s and B-25s passed over. At three when the B-24s were over Wewak they were jumped by six Jap Zeros who shot down four B-24s (one crew had to bail out over the target, and one bomber made it back to Dobodura on two motors) though the P-47s who were flying escort and cover were hot in pursuit.[3]

The Wewak raid had a complicated operations plan. The lead squadron was to bank north around Wewak, then circle round to attack from seaward. The main force, two squadrons, was to fly straight to Wewak, directly up the Markham Valley. Because the main force had a shorter route to the target, it was to delay its bomb run until the lead squadron was coming in from the sea, so that both attacks would be made simultaneously. The group would then reassemble and fly back to Moresby.

By the time the 90th Group reached Wewak, however, their formation had been disorganized by the weather. Rather than reforming, the bombers flew on, strung out in a long line along the flight path. This gave the Japanese antiaircraft gunners time to be ready for the squadrons arriving later and time for the Japanese fighters to scramble. At the last minute, the mission fell apart. The main group of B-24s did not delay its bomb run. "The group leader called up and said to go in one way and then went in a different way himself," the lead squadron's lead pilot recalled. "That sort of left me out by my lonesome with the squadron, and before I made my run we were hopped by Zeros. . . . They were on us for about thirty minutes."[4]

When the Jolly Rogers returned to Moresby, the men on the runways could see how bad things had been even before the bombers landed: they were flashing red passing lights to warn that they had wounded men on board. "The planes were cut to ribbons, and the meat wagons were scurrying from one to another to gather the wounded and the dead."[5]

By evening, the Fifth Bomber Command had treated its wounded and prepared to bury its dead. The bloody snafu above Wewak seemed distant from the enlisted men's satiric, sarcastic charity drive for the officers' ammunition fund. However, there was a connection to be drawn there—one that would trouble Mac-Arthur's two most senior air commanders.

⟡

Chaplain Smith had brought to light a scandal. He had complained about a night of drinking, gunfire, and dynamite—drunken, reckless, dangerous misconduct.

Within three days, Chaplain Smith's letter reached Douglas MacArthur himself. The gunfire and the dynamite had kept the camp from sleeping until late on Monday night. On Friday morning, with his own hand, MacArthur passed the chaplain's letter to George Kenney. That same afternoon, Kenney sent the letter to Ennis Whitehead, head of ADVON. The chaplain's complaint was now in the hands of the two generals who commanded the Fifth Air Force.

George Kenney was never more flattered than when Douglas MacArthur called him a buccaneer.[6] Kenney was never happier than when raiding enemy ports and sinking enemy men-o'-war and telling stories of his airmen's derring-do. (Not for nothing did Kenney allow the 90th Bomb Group to call themselves the Jolly Rogers and paint their aircraft with a modern version of the pirate sign, a skull and crossed bombs.) No one would have mistaken Ennis C. Whitehead for a buccaneer. They might have mistaken him for a prosperous businessman or (he had a cheerful grin, beneath a monumental nose) a genial small-town mayor. Like Eisenhower, Whitehead came from Kansas, and also like Eisenhower, Whitehead was shrewder than he looked. He was square and stolid and used those qualities to mask a formidable intelligence and a biting wit. Those who knew his ability called him Ennis the Menace. Nor was Whitehead's record as a buccaneer any less colorful than Kenney's. In his day, Whitehead had been a test pilot and flown across continents and parachuted away from stricken aircraft.[7] He had flown combat missions in New Guinea until Kenney ordered him to stop.[8]

When Kenney arrived in the Southwest Pacific, Whitehead was the first officer whom he asked to see. They worked together for the rest of the war, in a close command partnership. They did more than collaborate; they colluded.[9] Kenney, in Brisbane, planned strategy and tactics with MacArthur and lobbied the War Department for men and planes. Whitehead, in New Guinea, actually planned the air strikes and ran the day-to-day air war. Many tactical plans are scrawled in his handwriting.[10]

Gen. George C. Kenney and his second-in-command, Gen. Ennis Whitehead, confer. Kenney shuttled between Brisbane and New Guinea, commanding the Fifth Air Force and dealing with Gen. Douglas MacArthur, while Whitehead ran the Advanced Echelon forward headquarters at Port Moresby (and later from Nadzab). USAAF

Chaplain Smith's letter may no longer exist. It is not in certain files where it ought to be. Kenney and Whitehead are the last men into whose hands it can be traced. They read it with care and comprehension: given the details in Chaplain Smith's letter, Kenney and Whitehead grasped what and whom he was talking about. Wittingly or unwittingly, Chaplain Smith had lodged serious accusations against the colonels who ran the bombing campaign in New Guinea. Moreover, by happenstance, Chaplain Smith had leveled these charges precisely when a scandal might do most damage—during an episode of stealthy political maneuvering within Fifth Air Force headquarters.

Kenney and Whitehead acted quickly to investigate Chaplain Smith's complaint—and they were just as careful to hush the case up. They were careful, competent, thorough men, and what they buried seventy years ago may never be completely recovered.

🔊

To Kenney and Whitehead, the repercussions of Chaplain Smith's letter were immediately clear. The complaint was an explosive charge that had to be immediately defused. Kenney wrote, on December 3, Friday afternoon:

> General MacArthur handed me the enclosed letter this morning and asked for a report on it. His attitude at present is that it is probably nothing more than a howl from a screwball chaplain but I know that he expects a thorough investigation on it, nevertheless. . . . I feel that it can result only in one of two things. If the accusation by Chaplain Smith is correct, some drastic action will have to be taken regardless of the rank and position of the parties involved. If, on the other hand the accusations are false, I intend to try Chaplain Smith for false and malicious statements to the prejudice of good discipline.
>
> The last paragraph on page 1 of Chaplain Smith's letter contains some smoke that may have come from a fire. Pappy Gunn is the officer referred to. The incident, which was probably a foolish prank, is relatively unimportant. The business covered in paragraph 3, however, is something to be investigated. [11]

Kenney and Whitehead knew the party that Chaplain Smith had described. They had been there when it began. They knew that the chaplain's complaint implicated Col. John "Big Jim" Davies and his staff at Fifth Bomber Command, who had hosted the party. It implicated the party guests, too, the colonels who were running the air war in New Guinea—the CO of each and every bomb group: Art Rogers of the Jolly Rogers; Harry Hawthorn of the 43rd Bombardment Group, the group that called itself Ken's Men; Clint True of the 345th Bomb Group, the Air Apaches; Larry Tanberg of the 38th Bomb Group, the Sunsetters; and Jock Henebry, who led the Grim Reapers of the Third Attack Group.

Once assembled in Moresby, the bomb-group officers discussed with Davies the plans for continuing the air war. After that meeting, the colonels moved out to Fifth Bomber Command for a party—for both beer and booze, Jock Henebry recalled.

With them went another colonel, a man to whom the bomb-group colonels owed much: Paul Irwin Gunn, usually called the legendary "Pappy" Gunn. Gunn was known for working hard and living hard. He was a born pilot and brilliant autodidact engineer, the man who had built the Fifth Air Force's strafer gunships. Gunn came from Arkansas and often played the role of the hard-drinking hillbilly, but he was more; as well as packing machine guns onto Kenney's bombers, he had organized workshops to build the packages that held the .50-calibers and riveted them to the bombers, and he worked as an equal alongside gifted civilian aeronautical engineers. If Gunn drank (which he did), this may have been because his wife and children had been captured by the Japanese in the Philippines, and he was haunted by the peril that they faced.[12]

The celebration was a victory party. The bomber groups had demolished Wewak at the end of the summer. They had spent October and early November attacking Rabaul and now had handed off that Japanese stronghold to the Navy. The bomber squadrons were being rebuilt, and the colonels believed that they could, for a moment, relax. Most of them were still in their twenties. They liked swooping and soaring and strafing with .50-calibers, and they had blown the Japanese off the map. The celebration was a promotion party, too, to celebrate Davies' taking over Fifth Bomber Command and Jock Henebry being raised to the rank of lieutenant colonel.

Big Jim had barely begun the party when authority appeared—Kenney and Whitehead walking uphill to the officers' club. Kenney announced that Henebry was being promoted, Pappy Gunn unpinned the silver oak-leaf badge from his own collar so that Kenney could pin it on Henebry, and Kenney said that they would cut the orders in the morning. And then Kenney was finished, Henebry wrote, and they all went back to the beer and booze.[13]

Kenney and Whitehead left early. Later on, Pappy Gunn was one of the first officers to call it a night. He made his way to a shelter near the officers' club and fell asleep. Meantime, the party continued and took a reckless turn. Kenney wrote: "Someone, I didn't think it was necessary to investigate too far, got a half stick of dynamite, set the fuse to delay about five minutes, and placed it outside the hut opposite where Pappy was sleeping. The gang lit the fuse, hurried into their beds, pretending to be asleep, and waited for the explosion. It came on time. . . . Pappy, tangled in his blankets and mixed up with the cot on top of him, crashed up against the thin cardboard wall of the room."[14]

Without a word, Pappy Gunn dressed, staggered away, drove to the airstrip and flew to Australia. His chest hurt, at least one rib was broken, and he stayed in Australia nearly a month. For once, Gunn was silent. He said nothing about the party or the dynamite to Kenney.

This is the story as Kenney gave it. It is not untrue, in that it accounts for what happened. But Kenney was writing from memory, at best; and even sixteen years later, the story had parts that he would have wanted to leave obscure. Kenney had learned more than he put into print.

Pappy Gunn's son, Nathaniel, told a story whose details fit what Rocky heard that night. Nathaniel Gunn wrote that Big Jim Davies, "slightly tipsy," had dreamed up a practical joke to play on Pappy Gunn. With three other officers, Davies slipped out to the ordnance tent and found a canister, "a 'small' explosive device used for loading the parafrag bombs." Big Jim and the other officers went to a hilltop above the camp area and rolled the canister downhill towards the tents. "There's his tent. Gimme the bomb," Davies reportedly ordered. "You guys better stay low 'cause he's gonna come out shooting!" The canister bounced downhill, bounced again, and rolled against the wall of Pappy Gunn's tent. The charge exploded and blew Pappy Gunn out into the campsite; his lungs were collapsed, and he survived only because a foot-locker had shielded him from the full force of the blast.[15]

If Davies and his sidekicks were setting off TNT at intervals, as Rocky heard, the interval might have been the time needed to arm each charge and set it rolling. If the pistol firing came after the last explosion, that might have been Pappy Gunn staggering to his feet and returning fire.[16]

When Kenney first read Chaplain Smith's letter—as Kenney's overall story goes—the Fifth Air Force commander knew only that there had been a party at Fifth Bomber Command, and that his nonpareil aeronautical armorer had left the officers' club and flown off to Australia without explanation. Chaplain Smith apparently did not know the identity of the officer in the last paragraph on the first page of his letter. But Kenney could tell that it was Pappy Gunn, and he knew what sort of warning to give Whitehead. Drinking and firearms and dynamite meant scandal.

Kenney could be a convivial man, but he ran his senior officers tightly. The Fifth Bomber Command party had been a chance for men who had fought hard to blow off steam, and then it had all gone wrong. Drinking by aviators was hijinks and might be overlooked. Drunken officers firing pistols in the dark was different; drunken colonels rolling dynamite into a bivouac of sleeping airmen was categorically different.

A credible report of hard drinking by group commanders leading to drunken horseplay with dynamite and firearms was something Kenney could not tolerate. At Wewak, Kenney's strafing planes had caught the Japanese bomber squadrons as they were taxiing out for takeoff; bare minutes had given the Fifth Air Force its victory. Kenney lived in apprehension of hundreds of Japanese warplanes massed above the equator, waiting to fall upon his bases in New Guinea as his warplanes had surprised the Japanese at Wewak. ("Around the arc from Soerabaja, Java to Rabaul, the Nip had three times as many airplanes as we had," Kenney wrote. "Why he didn't take us out I don't know.")[17] Attack aviation demanded a careful balancing of risks and precise timing, and Kenney could not afford commanders whose drinking might throw off the calculations. It was more than scandal and embarrassment that he feared. A drunken commander might cost him the squadrons for which he had argued and pleaded—might lose him air supremacy, set back the air war, cost him his own command. Kenney had before his eyes the example of a general whose drinking had been blamed for such a disaster. On the morning when the war began in Manila, Maj. Gen. Lewis H. Brereton, MacArthur's air commander, had let his warplanes be caught on the ground by the Japanese. Brereton was a long-serving commander, but he could never shake off the aspersions that this debacle had happened because he had not yet sobered up from a party on the night before.[18]

Whitehead knew to take Kenney's hint about smoke and fire. Two days later, on Sunday, December 5—before the end of the weekend—Whitehead wrote back. Clumsily, making his first error in the first line, he pecked out his own warning: "Am tying this myself so be tolerant." This hand had to be played very close to the chest, Whitehead understood—so close that a two-star general should type his own report.

First, Whitehead knew, he had to deal with the charges brought by Chaplain Smith. He knew already that he would have to discipline senior officers. Beyond that, Whitehead had another problem to deal with in his bomber force—failures of leadership. The colonels' drunken gunplay on Monday night had been followed on Wednesday by the Jolly Rogers' botched raid on Wewak:

butchery in the air, ambulance sirens wailing on the runways at Moresby. Finally, in handling these problems, Whitehead had to play a long game. Fifth Bomber Command was a crucially important position—and a plum position, which officers would vie for. Stateside, there were many senior officers whom he and Kenney considered unfit for command. Keeping them out of the Fifth Air Force was a constant and difficult task; in wartime, officers were eager for combat commands, and other air forces were ready to shunt their second-raters to the Southwest Pacific. If Whitehead demoted Davies, if he shipped senior officers home, he would have to ensure that their places were taken by men whom he and Kenney trusted. That made the matter even more complex and confidential. Not only should Whitehead do his own typing, he would have to write elliptically.

Whitehead began by saying that he wanted none of the three generals who had been suggested for transfer to the South West Pacific Area (SWPA). One drank too much, one had begun to grow old, the last was a "never-was," worse than a has-been. Nor did Whitehead favor retaining an officer already in New Guinea, Big Jim Davies.

> I do not believe that Davies has what it takes. He has been a very great disappointment to me. . . . He has that quirk which makes him want to dissipate his forces. From the administrative angle, the investigation which Gephardt is now conducting may or may not eliminate Davies regardless of his capabilities as a tactical commander. Until such time as the I.G. (Gephardt) completes his investigation, Davies should remain on the job here. The investigation should be completed tomorrow or the day following and will be forwarded promptly. When I go over the testimony, the I.G. may have some added questioning to do.[19]

In this photograph of Fifth Air Force officers (veterans from the 27th Bomb Group), Col. John "Big Jim" Davies stands at the top of the steps, looking away from the camera, while Paul Irwin "Pappy" Gunn grins among the junior officers at the base of the stair.
Fifth Army Air Force; from Gen. Robert G. Ruegg's family's copy of "The 27th Reports," courtesy of Douglas Ruegg and Gerry Kersey of the 3rdattackgroup.org website

How closely did Whitehead watch his men? In the above group photo of Fifth Air Force officers, taken on the steps of an officers' club in Australia, a score of officers are packed into the stairs. At the top of the steps, Davies stands, a tall, handsome, dark-haired man, quietly looking away from the camera. Alone among the officers, he has not troubled to take a beer stein out of his hand.[20]

Rogers of the 90th is burned out and I feel should go home not on leave but for keeps. Bomber Command changes can of course wait until we complete the investigation of

Chaplain Smith's allegations. Gephardt did tell me tonight that it appeared there would be no cause to try Smith for false and malicious statements. I fear that there will be some officers en route to the 11th Replacement Depot for disposition. We can settle bomber command personnel problems at that time. I have not been satisfied with the leadership of the 90th Group since early November. It put on a very poor show at Wewak on December 1st.[21]

There were simply too few competent officers, Whitehead concluded. "I could also send Photo Hutch to Second Air Task Force but that would eliminate our handling recco from Advon."[22]

Whitehead had given Kenney warning. He confirmed that the drunkenness and shooting involved Big Jim Davies. He had told Kenney that nothing supported putting Smith on trial, which meant that he felt the chaplain's complaint was valid. He wrote that he expected to replace junior officers and settle Bomber Command personnel problems—which meant that the charges were serious, requiring action both high and low. Under the smoke, Whitehead confirmed, there was considerable fire.

౿

By the weekend, there were hints—had anyone known to read them—of a scandal brewing. On Sunday, December 5, Rocky went to church services in the morning, and then again in the evening, one of a dozen 71st Group men who turned out to hear a second sermon. "Chaplain Smith told us that movies would be shown at the theatre on Sunday night hereafter. He is rather disgusted."[23]

Movies were already being shown most evenings. The Special Services officers who ran the outdoor cinemas had no particular reason to start Sunday-night features. Smith did not break confidence, but likely he was disgusted because he thought Sunday night movies had been started in reprisal, as an attack on the Sabbath. He must have known already what he would face the next day.

On Monday, December 6, the investigation became public. Inspector General Gephart showed his hand. Interestingly, it was not only Chaplain Smith's complaint that Inspector General Gephart pursued; he also examined the enlisted men's objections.

> Today Chaplain Smith was called upon by a major from the Inspector General's Department who came to investigate the shooting and other unbecoming conduct of the high ranking officers in the Fifth Bomber Command. It seems that Chaplain Smith wrote a letter directly to General MacArthur who endorsed it on to General Whitehead. The major took testimony from the unit censor if the men had written of the matter (that they had done) and several of the enlisted men. The general has rescinded permission to carry liquor in Army aircraft.
>
> There is much commotion over the Inspector General's investigation. Major "Know It All" Knauf just learned that Chaplain Smith was the one who wrote MacArthur. It is also rumored that no liquor will be brought to New Guinea by any means. The officers are blaming a certain General Dewitt's wife for such action.[24]

The commotion must have been spectacular, if it reminded someone of General Dewitt—even if this was an old-time Air Corps insider's joke that Rocky missed. In the weeks after Pearl Harbor, Lt. Gen. John Lesesne Dewitt, a bespectacled elderly general, had been head of the Western Defense Command. From the Presidio in San Francisco, DeWitt had warned of Japanese air raids, closed down travel to Alaska, and banned night-time sports, hunting, and prostitution in military zones. At his urging, the 1942 Rose Bowl was played not in Pasadena but in Durham, North Carolina. To joke about Dewitt, or his wife, was to joke that the furor over Fifth Bomber Command had already gone too far.[25]

By the next day, resentment and alarm had found their focus.

> The Inspector General called for Chaplain Smith to come to Fifth Air Force. It is reported that all officers' clubs in New Guinea now close at nine o'clock. Many of the units have heard that Chaplain Smith was the one who wrote MacArthur. Many of the officers in the Group, though agreeing the shooting was uncalled for, criticize the chaplain because we are here as guests of the Bomber Command and consequently should be more hesitant before writing the generals about our hosts' conduct.[26]

Whether the early-closing order was formal, or because closing early would make their stocks of liquor last longer, servicemen's club bars were closing at 2100 hours.[27] At the Fifth Bomber Command, Rocky wrote, "the bar closes at nine now because of the

Chaplain Smith stands by the chapel at Dobodura in early 1944. After a drunken party at Fifth Bomber Command, where senior officers set off dynamite and fired pistol shots in the middle of a sleeping camp, Smith wrote to Douglas MacArthur. Colonels were busted, but Smith was transferred away from Port Moresby. 82nd TRS, in AFHRA archive

chaplain's letter to MacArthur. Also the officers will not associate with the men of the Group on this account. Night before last, the officer in charge of the club came at ten o'clock, turned out the lights and replied to the blackjackers' protests, 'The chaplain's orders are to turn out the lights at ten.'"[28]

Whitehead had given Inspector General Gephardt the two days he thought the investigation would need. On December 10, Kenney wrote back.

> In regard to the Bomber Command, I have delayed answering your letter until I hear from you about results of the investigation of Chaplain Smith's story. If Davies is capable of handling Fifth Bomber Command or a task force, the situation can be taken care of by reprimand, and perhaps some house cleaning around Fifth Bomber Command Headquarters. If, on the other hand, Jim has decided to substitute drinking for attention to duty, I will see what I can do toward transferring him to some other theatre or back to the United States. I will talk with you further on the matter when I see you in Moresby. In the meantime, unless conditions are too bad I would prefer to have him act as temporary bomber commander.[29]

Whitehead already thought conditions at Fifth Bomber Command were too bad. Two colonels would have to go, Colonel Davies and Colonel Rogers at the 90th Bomb Group. Whitehead also knew that he would have to discipline an officer who outranked even a colonel: Brig. Gen. Frederic H. Smith, his own chief of staff. That would have to be handled very diplomatically; General Smith was the son-in-law of Adm. Ernest King, Chief of Naval Operations. Nor could Whitehead send General Smith home while Smith was running the air campaign over New Britain.

Rogers went first. He left the Jolly Rogers on December 17, only two weeks after Kenney first read Chaplain Smith's letter. Kenney told Rogers that he looked awful, and sent him home with a Silver Star, a Distinguished Service Cross, and vague words about coming back when he was rested. Rogers never returned to the Pacific.

Shortly before Christmas, Whitehead moved against General Smith. He cited medical reasons for Smith going home. In wartime New Guinea, flight surgeons were flyers' physicians, but they were also commanders' chamberlains, servants who quietly did their masters' bidding.[30] Whitehead obtained a letter from a senior flight surgeon concerning the medical condition of his chief of staff. The letter spoke of General Smith's "definite climatic and operational fatigue," a "gradual decline in health."

> The undersigned feels it his duty to recommend that at the completion of the present offensive plans, and at the completion of General Smith's task at the advanced goal, he be returned to the Continental limits of the United States for a period of rehabilitation. It will mean that the future services of this valuable man will be saved. I feel it my duty to recommend these measures. General Smith's rehabilitation could only be completed in the United States. . . . General Smith is not aware of this letter and the undersigned hopes it will be honored just that way.[31]

At Whitehead's direction, this medical evaluation was utterly confidential. A lieutenant colonel took it from the flight surgeon and delivered it to Whitehead himself.

Davies and Smith were shipped home together. In Brisbane, outside Lennon's Hotel, they ran into a familiar face from ADVON, Bill Hipps, Whitehead's operations chief. Davies and Smith said that they had been ordered home for what had happened with Pappy Gunn and the dynamite. Smith was traveling with a British medal, a recommendation to Eisenhower, and the story that he had been worn down by the tropics. Davies may have been handled less gingerly; he had already been shipped home once before.[32]

There remained one last loose end: Chaplain Smith. It had been proven that the chaplain was not a screwball, and that his charges had not been either false or malicious. That did not mean that the Fifth Air Force command would forget Smith's letter.

8

FIRST BATTLES

In the Southwest Pacific, men and material were in short supply. "It was a poor man's war," General Eichelberger remembered. "The miracles of production managed by American factories and American labor were slow to manifest themselves Down Under. We were at the end of the supply line." It was a poor man's war because the Allies spared few troops for it. Lean, sick divisions and battered air groups struggled to save Australia and defeat Japan—without rest, because there were no replacements. "This may answer the question," Eichelberger concluded, "'Why didn't you relieve those tired men in New Guinea?'"[1]

In the last weeks of 1943, Rocky and the 71st Group knew that they were moving toward the front. They had met the Japanese in combat; they had shot down an aging dive-bomber and traded fire with antiaircraft gunners. They knew that their jeeps were already wearing out and that they were losing aircraft—not to Japanese fire, but in crack-ups on the runway. They learned how shortages shaped the war in New Guinea—kept men on the front lines too long, shaped attitudes that airmen held toward the materials with which they fought. They learned as well to listen to enemy broadcasts and follow camp talk, for news was equally in short supply.

In mid-December, two rarae aves were sighted in Port Moresby, a chatty young woman and a four-star general. They were seen as signs of change—that Douglas MacArthur's army and George Kenney's Fifth Air Force would go into action soon.

> Major George Knauf stated: "When I was at the base hospital this afternoon General George Marshall entered the ward and asked where the combat patients were. Upon learning none were in the hospital he cursed and went down the ward asking, 'What are you here for?' 'Malaria, sir; Malaria, sir; Malaria, sir.' Marshall: 'For Christ's sake, isn't anyone fighting here except the air force. Hasn't anyone been shot at? Where are your officers?'" It is interesting to note General MacArthur was not present, however there were several major-generals along. Heard one rumor that the Sixth Army would go into operation soon.
>
> This afternoon while Foliart and I were walking to the mess hall in the new area, we noticed a crowd of soldiers around a jeep, and we found a plump Red Cross girl serving cold orangeade to the men. She had a five-gallon can in the rear of the jeep and was pouring it into paper cups. Because the girl was returning and because we, Foliart and I hadn't been close to a girl, let alone ride and talk with one, we rode to the Fifth Air Force. She said 24 Red Cross girls were in the area (Port Moresby) and several on their way. She could not nor did not give any reason for being in the Red Cross except she just got tired staying at home. She has been on the island (New Guinea) almost two months and was bragging to the nth degree about how much she knew about strike missions, time, number of planes, et cetera.[2]

Gen. George Marshall had flown eastward from the Mediterranean theater, after the Cairo Conference had concluded. The last leg of Marshall's trip, across the Indian Ocean from Ceylon to the northwest corner of Australia, was a flight of more than three thousand miles. Marshall crossed the ocean with no fighter escort, no islands underneath, and no Allied forces or territory between his transport plane and the Japanese airfields on Sumatra and Java. His landfall in Australia was on the same stretch of coast where the Zeros had caught the Dutch refugee flying boats and where Japanese warplanes still ventured.[3] Eight months before, similar risks had been weighed by another commander: Isoroku Yamamoto had flown to Japanese bases in the Solomon Islands. Yamamoto had died because American codebreakers learned his schedule and American P-38s intercepted his plane. Knowing himself how Yamamoto had died, Marshall had planned his journey and flown in secret.

In New Guinea, Marshall and his aides flew over Lae. They counted the wrecked Japanese warplanes piled up at the airdrome there, 150 aluminum carcasses, ten squadrons' worth. (When Washington generals saw the aircraft boneyard at Lae, George Kenney wrote, they "admitted that for the first time they realized we had a real war on our hands.") They circled Nadzab and admired the immense airfields being carved into the kunai grass, bulldozers and trucks crawling along the roadways, transports landing constantly. Kenney boasted that there were no roads to Nadzab— that his men had sawed truck chassis in half, stuffed the steel pieces into C-47s, flown them in, and welded them back together. "General Marshall got a great kick out of the story, especially when he discovered that it was true," Kenney wrote.[4]

🙢

At Dobodura, the 82nd Squadron prepared for combat. Its P-39s were ranged along the tarmac—every warplane in squadron colors, olive drab with a white tail and yellow propeller spinner.

*The 82nd Squadron went into combat flying Bell P-39 Airacobra
fighters. The warplanes often bore the names of pilots' wives and
girlfriends. "Little Sir Echo" was flown by Texas pilot Lyndall W.
Tate. The name alludes both to the Bing Crosby tune and to the
classics—Tate's wife was named Echo, after the nymph.*
National Archives via the collection of Robert Rocker

Eileen, Julia, Reba, Ruthie, Maxine, Snooks—there were no
pin-up girls painted on the noses of the squadron's P-39s, but the
warplanes bore the names of wives and girlfriends. There were
other names: "Calamity Ann," "Brooklyn Bum," and "Sack Rat."
The P-39 of Lyndall Tate, Rocky's compartment-mate, was "Little
Sir Echo." This sounds odd for a fighter plane, but then Tate's wife
was named Echo. The "Rockford Rocket" was flown by Lt. Verne
Murphy, from the prairie country of Illinois. In the air Murphy
was a daredevil. In peacetime he had been a violinist. With a limp
and bad kidneys, Murphy was hardly the picture of a fighter pilot.
Murphy was generally silent and "looked to be a 4-Fer," Rocky
wrote; when Murphy talked, he was interesting, and many thought
him the best pilot in the Group. Lt. Charles Wesley Borders, who
would fly in three wars, thought that Murphy looked like Charlie
Chaplin and yet was the only pilot who ever outflew him. Borders'
own P-39 was the "San Antonio Rose."

In *Guinea Gold*, the military newspaper of the Southwest
Pacific, the work done by the 71st Group was being noted, albeit
briefly. "Arawe Area: Our attack planes bombed and strafed the

village and jetty in the Adi River"—that might have described the squadron's role in supporting the landings on New Britain. Or perhaps it was "Madang: Our escorted medium units bombed the airdrome and supply installations at Erima Plantation, causing explosions and fires. One parked enemy plane was burnt."[5]

The squadron had been heartened by its first public recognition, a mocking threat from the other side. During *The Zero Hour*, the Japanese propaganda radio broadcast, the disc jockey promised death and destruction to the "yellow-nosed devils" who had arrived in the Pacific. "Instead of lowering our morale, our gang cheered mightily," Major Gordon wrote. "We had been NOTICED!" The jibe might have been meant for American troops in general. Westerners stereotype Japanese by their slanted eyes, Japanese stereotype Westerners by their immense noses—"yellow-nosed devils" might have been a slur flung out by a Japanese DJ at any American troops, but the 82nd Squadron was glad to take the insult personally.[6]

The 82nd Squadron (as Colonel Hutchison told Major Gordon) was a reconnaissance unit. Its planes were not to operate as fighters unless directed. If they flew as fighters the Army might count them as fighters and that would undermine the Fifth Air Force when it asked for new fighter-plane groups.[7] Escorting bombers and dogfighting with Zeros was work best left to squadrons that flew P-38s. There were other necessary missions that the P-39s of the group could fly. Combat reconnaissance, short range or long range, meant patrolling the coastline, sinking Japanese barges, strafing Japanese bases.

To hunt Japanese barges was to strike against the enemy's supply lines—part of the attack aviation that General Kenney endorsed. Given heavy losses among Japanese cargo ships, MacArthur wrote, the enemy began using barges to supply their troops in New Guinea. To protect these boats, the Japanese emplaced antiaircraft guns, "scores of heavy caliber shore batteries to cover their lugger and barge movements." Nonetheless, by pressing home attacks, Allied warplanes and PT boats forced luggers to travel by night, and eventually squeezed off Japanese supply altogether. "The wholesale destruction by our planes, submarines and PT boats of enemy coastal vessels, transports, barges, schooners and sailing craft in the Southwest Pacific Area gradually paralyzed enemy efforts to supply, reinforce or evacuate the remnants of his armies. More than 5,000 of these craft were destroyed."[8]

"Colonel Sams has been over the hump for several days," Rocky wrote on December 16. "He told Colonel League last night that the present staff for Wing HQ were only interested in photo reconnaissance and combat recco was secondary."[9] The story was not that simple: Colonel Sams knew photo reconnaissance, but combat recco was his new love. Tired of waiting for the 17th Squadron to arrive with their B-25s, he moved to Dobodura and checked out as a pilot, to fly the P-39. In California, the 82nd had flown lumbering observation planes. The P-39 flew twice as fast and climbed twice as fast, and the engine roared from behind the cockpit. Sams stepped out of his Airacobra, grinned, and called out, "It's just like strapping a bumblebee to your ass and taking off!"[10]

Sams was known as an aggressive pilot, and the reputation was fairly earned. On one mission, he wrote, they had received both heavy and light ack-ack fire. "It causes a peculiar feeling to sit up above and see the fire coming from the guns and realize that they are shooting at you. One more of mild surprise than anything else and a tremendous desire to go down and knock them off."[11]

At Dobodura, before Sams came down from Moresby, Gordon had enjoyed a free hand with the 82nd Squadron. He had stopped playing the martinet; he flattered himself that his squadron ran itself. (This meant doing nothing: as Sams' flying inspection had shown, the officers' latrine was disgraceful, Gordon's men were not policing the area, the water was not being purified, and the

enlisted men felt sufficiently oppressed that they dared to complain to the colonel.) Gordon winked at his pilots brewing hooch,
and he did nothing to intervene at the camp of the 17th Squadron's
ground echelon, where every tent seemed to have both a bunker
and a still.[12]

Gordon had heard that Sams had heart problems and should
not be flying single-engine aircraft. He tried to wear out his superior with long or difficult flights—which did not work. On one
mission, Gordon saw the smoke of a Japanese antiaircraft gun
underneath Sams' P-39. Gordon said nothing. He turned the flight
homeward, mentioning bad weather and watching his gas gauge.
Then Gordon noticed that Sams was ignoring his radio calls.

> When I attempted to lead him through a rainstorm, he
> turned back for some reason. I had no choice but to pick
> him up and try to climb over the weather. . . . We barely
> made it and, as I sat in the cockpit filling out the flight log,
> my scare at our close call turned into a fast burn at him
> for getting us into that situation. As I stalked over to his
> airplane to figure out how I was going to chew him out,
> I noticed a crowd of Marines gathered about. He proudly
> showed me a hole in his wing where a 20-mm shell had
> gone through. When I told him I had seen them firing at
> him, the roles were reversed and he chewed me out for
> not telling him so he could go back and attack![13]

Whatever Gordon was, Sams was the fighter pilot, and Gordon
wasn't. Sams was the pilot who flew low enough to be shot at,
who led the flight out of the rainstorm, and the one who did the
chewing-out. Not for nothing was he a colonel and a group commander.

Something else had happened, an utterly negligent accident or
a wanton crime. Rocky reported that Lieutenant Moody had fired
into a native village.

> The 82nd Squadron sent eight planes on their first mission which was to familiarize the pilots with the surrounding country. The planes escorted a bomber which was dropping leaflets above and northwest of Lae. Captain Moody fired into a native hut with a 37-mm and the roof was blown off.[14]

The Group "frowned on Moody" for firing on the village, Rocky wrote, and Sams may have dealt with this, quietly.[15] One pilot from the 82nd Squadron would spend months grounded, pending the outcome of the investigation.

At Dobodura, a Japanese midnight raid caused the 71st Group's first casualty in the combat zone. Enlisted man Charles Morris was in the hospital with a fractured skull, hip, and three lumbar vertebrae—knocked down by a truck in the darkness, as some men ran for cover and other men tried to drive without headlights.[16] Other airmen banged themselves up in crack-ups, wrecking their planes. Lyndall Tate stalled in mid-air when coming in for a landing; the P-39 fell the last ten feet to earth. Pete McDermott cartwheeled and wrecked; when the stitches came out of his forehead, he would be flying the "Brooklyn Bum 2d." When Ray Weinstein was landing, his motor cut out—he tore up the landing gear, bent the prop, and tore out two wing guns. Doc Schafer stood line duty on the airstrip all day one day. They had sweated out thirty-two takeoffs, he summed up at dusk.[17]

Like Tate, Weinstein and McDermott had traveled out from Laurel on the *John S. Pope*. There were a few other new pilots, like Lt. Mike Moffitt, who had flown out from California in a four-engine C-54.[18] The squadron roster had been filled out with men who had been in New Guinea longer—sometimes much longer. Schafer noted: "One little fellow has been here for a year and flown 75 missions. He's only about 5 feet 6 inches and weighs 115 pounds." This was Lieutenant Zaleski, of Wayne County, Michigan.

This group photo, taken in early 1944, shows 82nd Squadron pilots lined up in front of a P-39, while mechanics pose on the wings of the airplane. The pilot at the left end of the line is Lt. Bill Shomo (always the skinniest, youngest-looking pilot). Next is Flight Officer Gerald Phillips; then Lt. Robert McCalpin, without a helmet; then Lt. Plez Moody, with a cigarette in his right hand, and Lt. Charles Wesley Borders, with a cigarette in his left hand. Next comes a flyer named Temple, whose name appears rarely if at all in squadron records. Next is Lt. Richard Plahn, with the shoulder holster, and Lt. Charles Weber, closest to the camera. Sitting among the mechanics, behind Lieutenant Borders, can be recognized burly, fair-haired SSgt. Ralph Winkle, and at left, against the fuselage, distinguished by his brilliant grin, Sgt. Bill Ursprung. Collection of Michael Moffitt Jr.

Two years earlier, two days after Pearl Harbor, when the Army announced that it was creating the Colin P. Kelly Jr. Aviation Cadet Unit, Zaleski had been first in line at the Air Corps recruiting station in Detroit. His eagerness appealed to Army recruiters and his height appealed to Army photographers, who liked taking pictures of a pint-size fighting man.[19] The P-39 had a small cockpit, which fit Zaleski well. He had been flying with a squadron that had converted from P-39s to P-47 Thunderbolts; the talk in camp was that he might have transferred to the 82nd Squadron because he was too short and light to fly a P-47, a warplane that weighed five tons. He liked to fly low. On one mission, Wesley Borders saw Zaleski's propeller splash through a wave-top (when they checked, the blade-tips were bent).[20] Zaleski went by Zeke, or "Zero Zeke." His Christian name was Maryan, as can be seen on his headstone at Arlington.

Rocky continued to pull together information on communications and navigation systems. The paper war had begun, Rocky commented—a war within the Army. Sometimes, quartermasters would not issue material to squadrons; that had delayed construction in the Group's camp at Moresby. Other times, quartermasters would not issue material to a Wing. There were further rules on priority, and beyond that the problem of finding material and catching in his office the man who could issue it.

> With Lieutenant Kepler, the radar officer over here on detached service because he simply didn't want to sit around Bomber Command HQ and read and work crossword puzzles, I started out to secure the signal equipment authorized for our new headquarters. First: called on our next higher signal officer, which secured how to requisition the equipment. Second: filled out registration and took it to the 912th Signal Company who told us they could not issue any equipment to newly activated units. Third: we returned to find our unit was never activated. Fourth: finally got hold of a memo stating all new units could draw equipment at the United States Army Service of Supplies (USA SOS). Fifth: We prepared requisition to USA SOS—took it to them and were told that the 912th Signal Company would issue the equipment.[21]

Paul Kepler was a friend; Rocky often drove around Moresby with him. They would fill out many requisition forms and hand them in to Service of Supplies staff. They complained about late mail from home. They dropped in at the Australian radio direction-finding station at Moresby and heard how the RDF (radio direction finding) station at Salamaua had buried its radio tubes when the Japanese landed and then dug them up and gone back into business when the Allies recaptured the town.[22]

Rocky had another friend on the Wing HQ staff: Lieutenant Dixon, with whom he had traveled out on the *John S. Pope*. Butch Dixon, like Rocky, had grown up on the Midwestern prairie—west of Indiana, in South Dakota. While Rocky had been raising show calves, Dixon had been gentling horses. They both had a background in the Group and came to question how it had been taken over by the Wing.

> Lieutenant Dixon and I went to Port Moresby to the PX this afternoon for no good reason. While we journeyed back we discussed the officers at Wing HQ. Most of the personnel there are either assigned for political reasons, that is to secure a higher grade, or because they happen to know Colonel Hutchison or "so and so's" father who knew someone else. On paper we have been in operation more than one month and all we have done has been to keep four typewriters going continuously. Do not know what would happen if our clerks failed to show up some morning.
>
> Most of us thought there would be no "red tape" over here but—it's worse than in the States, especially in the Signal Corps. It's common knowledge that the 912th Signal Company, which supplies most of the Port Moresby area, has at its head a captain who has not kept up with the supplies on hand and is now afraid to issue equipment though he has tons and tons of it; why, he doesn't know where it is located.[23]

Dixon would have known about Army routine and red tape; he had spent three years in the cavalry after high school. He would also have understood Army politicking: he had started toward West Point as his senator's second choice. His brother later spoke of his hardheadedness and perseverance. He had studied hard at West Point, done well, must have trusted his own abilities. In summing up Butch, his brother spoke twice of *determination*.

Finally, after weeks when Major Baker had said "not yet" and trucks had been sent to the Moresby docks and called back again, the Group's equipment was arriving.

> Camera arrived. Boats unloaded. The weapons carriers (1¼ ton trucks) for the Group had to be assembled here. The axles; chassis with motor installed; fenders; wheels with tires; batteries, came in one box and the bed cab came in another. Time for assembling each truck—two days.[24]

The Group would need the weapons carriers: the jeeps were failing. Driving back from Moresby, "something happened to our jeep which caused the lights to dim and the cylinders failed to fire. Sergeant Sims stated that the jeeps had been driven over 17,000 miles since our arrival."[25] The teletype printers had been damaged on the trip across the Pacific. The radios arrived in good condition, and as soon as possible the communications section had them working.

> Now that our radios are set up we tune to our favorite station, Radio Tokyo—such songs as "Smoke Gets into Your Eyes," "Little Brown Jug," "Home on the Range," "Old Black Joe," are a few of the songs that are played. To be truthful, they offer the best music in the Southwest Pacific.[26]

⟲

New Guinea was a wilderness of coconut plantations bustling with jeeps and planes. The mixture of the modern and the primitive was not unfamiliar to servicemen who had grown up in the early decades of their century. Indianapolis was a cornfield with street lights, H. L. Mencken had said. Washington, D.C., counted fifteen thousand open privies.[27] The Southwest Pacific was a frontier; servicemen faced the problems and discontents of their civilization as well as the challenges of the jungle.

In New Guinea, airmen built their own camps. GI pyramid tents were hot: airmen learned to find a spare parachute and hang it inside the tent, under the tent peak and stretched out to the walls: this could lower the inside temperature by 15 degrees or more. Tents were built on wooden frames, which stretched them so that men could stand up inside. Lumber for frames and floors came from crates at first, later from felled timber or (best of all) Navy stockpiles. The sides of the tent were rolled up for ventilation; the openings were screened with wire mesh or burlap. A weighted strip of burlap hung down to cover the doorway.[28]

In an air unit, the Utilities Section had the task of making bivouac sites livable—setting up buildings, power, running water, showers, laundries, "and in general adding a bit of city life." The 17th Squadron cheerfully noted that "lacking certain essentials such as tools and lumber, it became quite fashionable to beg, borrow, or steal from all and sundry. At first borrowing caused the most trouble. . . . Begging had its day, too, but stealing produced the best results—for a while!" They praised their own Utilities Section: "Most significant of Sergeant Kelly's work is the efficiency of the Sarge and his crew in 'Moonlight Requisition.' If the article desired is to be had in New Guinea, Kelly can and will get it—and the amazing part is that it's all legal."[29]

The 17th Squadron had abandoned discretion, joking about theft. The Air Force surgeon general described the same situation with staid understatement.

A system of barter was developed throughout the Pacific theaters, with the most valuable trading material being any type of alcoholic beverage. This bartering system continued through the war despite directives from higher headquarters which prohibited it. The units having the best barterers had the best camps, and in this respect flying units were fortunate in being able to obtain supplies of liquor in Australia by means of leave and "fat cat" planes. In many units it became the custom to pool all resources and use the results of barter for the common good of the entire unit, although not infrequently such material was used for personal advantage.[30]

The 71st Group took less than a month to venture into this new market. It was a Special Services officer who led the way.

> Yesterday Lieutenant Zock departed on the unit's first beer run. To give examples of the orders, Mr. Jackson ordered a case of bourbon. Liquor furnishes recreation and a means of exchange with line units who cannot secure liquor as easily as the Air Corps and with the natives and for incidentals such as lumber, scrub brushes, etc.[31]

Fat cats and midnight requisitions, booze to be traded for scrub brushes—Port Moresby could be a free-wheeling, wide-open place; but a unit could congratulate itself too easily. The Group quickly learned that other servicemen did not scruple to take advantage.

> Last night several of the officers at Dobo went into Moresby to the officers' club and someone stole their jeep. One sergeant told me a switch should be placed in the circuit so therefore no one could steal the jeep easily.[32]

Note the disappointment; note also the sergeant's lack of outrage. Stealing a jeep was not the same thing as stealing a car. Stealing a car was a crime between individuals. Stealing a jeep was an improper transfer of equipment. All jeeps belonged to the military, and someone who drove off with a jeep could enjoy its use only if his unit added the vehicle to its own motor pool. Gen. George Marshall hailed the jeep as America's greatest contribution to modern warfare; lower commanders overlooked how such invaluable material might have been acquired. "Institutional theft," one veteran called it, a Marine from whom New Zealanders had rustled jeeps and who had stolen them back—part of servicemen's inclination to pick up anything of value that was free.[33]

Stealing a jeep was dubious, but it was part of a practical, commendable unit policy: to garner for a group or squadron as much useful equipment as possible. The serviceman who stole a jeep lived out part of the self-image of the traditional fighting man. "A fiction beloved in all armies," James Jones wrote, is "the tough, scrounging, cynical soldier who collects whatever he can get his hands on."[34] Stealing a jeep was easy: jeeps started with switches, not keys, precisely so that any serviceman could use them. It was virtually risk-free: jeeps were indistinguishable, and no MP could tell a stolen jeep from one whose use was duly authorized. Ernie Pyle had recently written: "Jeep thievery has been practiced on such a scale over here that it's practically legitimate."[35] Stealing a jeep was scoring a goal. It was getting away with something. It was what any fool who did not trouble to lock up his jeep should obviously have seen coming.

In Port Moresby, officers were beginning to feel that rank had its privileges. Chaplain Smith had heard of cases in which those privileges went too far.

> Chaplain Smith pointed out that a large refrigerator had been issued to a certain special officer for keeping various food stuffs and other things which are better when

cool for the enlisted men, but instead, the officer has it in his own tent for his own private stock of liquor. He also told about a certain colonel in the quartermasters who did not issue a refrigerator to a medical section because he needed it for his stock, but some inspector found him out and now the machine is being issued to keep serums.[36]

One of the war's best generals would define bluntly the duty of an officer: not to eat, drink, smoke, sleep, or rest until his men have had the chance to do the same.[37] Those officers who lived better or rested sooner were the ones whom the enlisted men resented most, and whose self-aggrandizement chaplains and inspectors noted. For servicemen had not stopped drawing lines between conduct and misconduct, and sometimes those lines were enforced.

Looming up over everything else was the impending move over the mountains. On December 15, Rocky mentioned the American landings at Arawe, on New Britain, but noted one other piece of news first: the Air Transport Command had moved an entire bomb group's personnel and equipment from Port Moresby to Dobodura in two days. More news came later:

> Major Tockstein and Colonel Hutchison returned from Nadzab where they selected a site for our future camp. The enlisted men had somewhat of a party tonight. According to one rumor alcohol was flowing quite freely. Staff Sergeant DeYoung said that he would never tell anyone of the conditions the men live under on the ships coming over. He said several of the men never washed. Good blackjack games at the club.[38]

It was still unsure when the Wing would move. In the meantime, preparing for the move made worthless work that had been done at Port Moresby.

> Major Tockstein told me that all Wing construction here
> would stop immediately, that means the large head-
> quarters building for which the concrete has already
> been poured will never be completed. Also the exten-
> sive telephone plans I have drawn up cannot be used.
> Attended communications officers meeting at ADVON
> Five at 1300. Plans and communications problems for
> the future invasion were discussed.[39]

Rumors were that the 71st Group HQ would move to Nadzab in
two weeks, the Wing HQ would move to Nadzab in four weeks,
and that the entire Fifth Air Force would move to Nadzab by the
first of February.[40] Even with the move drawing near, commanders seemed disinclined to offer specific details.

> Went to Wing HQ in afternoon. Had a conference with
> Captain Stump at 1930. He said the Fifth Air Force opera-
> tions officer must decide exactly what we (the Photo
> Wing) were going to do before a communications plan
> can operate.
>   I asked Lieutenant Dixon, now in the Wing's A-3
> operations section, how the Wing would operate tacti-
> cally. He said he did not know nor did Colonel Hutchison.
> Lieutenant Colonel League said he wasn't sure.[41]

ⓢ

He told me, it is rumored, rumor had it, a new rumor, lots of rumors—
Rocky wrote often about talk in camp. The *Officers' Guide* counseled that "the conveying of gossip, slander, hard criticism and
fault-finding are unofficerlike practices," and that servicemen in
wartime should not speak about matters on which they were not
completely informed. "In casual conversation it is wiser to follow
this guide: 'All the brothers are valiant, and all the sisters virtu-
ous.'"[42] Rocky and his fellow officers scarcely followed those pre-
cepts—but camp talk was not all slander and scuttlebutt.

Theodore Caplow, a sociologist-turned-soldier who won a Purple Heart in the Philippines, spent part of his time in the Pacific studying how reports traveled by word of mouth among American servicemen. He found that, contrary to expectations, many reports became more accurate as they traveled. When soldiers shared rumors, they were testing what they had heard against what other men had heard, and trading news with comrades whom they trusted. Building on this, Tamotsu Shibutani, a Nisei sociologist who had known both wartime internment and infantry service, defined rumor as improvised news: news generated informally, news that is assessed and revised as it travels.[43]

In New Guinea, official plans were guarded and definitive pronouncements were rare. Lieutenant Dixon didn't know and neither did Colonel Hutchison. A cartoon in *Yank Down Under* snooped on two generals in a washroom—"Heard any good rumors lately?" one asks the other.[44] Common soldiers manned teletypes and listened to radios (even to the enemy, when they chose). In this environment, servicemen talked about what mattered to them. As improvised, camp talk might be reliable or unreliable—but camp talk took the place of official news.

Finally, war news came, from close at hand. "Reports come that one of the P-39s in the 82nd Squadron shot down a dive bomber (very old—fixed landing gear type)."[45]

Delta Graham, a first lieutenant from Kansas City, shot down the Japanese plane, a Val Aichi D3A dive-bomber. On Saturday afternoon, December 18, Graham had flown out to the Huon Peninsula as wingman to Lt. Bill Pictor. Pictor flew low, searching for Japanese, Graham flew behind Pictor, keeping a lookout; a second flight flew high cover at 10,000 feet. It was the end of the day. Radio contact was poor. Pictor missed Graham, went back to look, joined up with him, and saw his wingman grinning through his canopy.[46] "On 18 December 1943 over Lepsuis Point, Huon Peninsula, New Guinea, at 1735 hours, Lt Graham was flying as end man on a sweep when he saw a Val in back and slightly above him. The plane banked to the left and he cut in behind it, firing a short bust into the root of the right wing from fifty (50) yards. The fuel tank exploded and the Val crashed to the ground."[47]

On Wednesday Graham celebrated. He flew into the airstrip with a slow victory roll, Doc Schafer wrote, "coming over camp he fairly clipped the tops of the trees."[48] Later, when the victory was confirmed, Graham posed for a photo beside his warplane "Maxine," a handsome, cheerful young man, beaming, proud of the Japanese rising-sun flag neatly painted underneath his cockpit. The All-American Boy, Pictor would remember him.

᷂

Christmas week arrived. The 110th Squadron arrived and moved into tents in the Wing area. "Colonel Sams jokingly put out the rumor that half of the men will receive Sydney furloughs at Christmas and the remaining half at New Years."[49] Routine did not change much, Rocky wrote.

> In the evening we attended the movies and saw newsreels, a comedy cartoon, and *Five Graves to Cairo*. Colonel League's tent was invaded by thousands of red ants at dusk and several of us were entertained by sprinkling insect powder around the ants on the tent and watching them die by curling up. It's being rumored the invasion of New Britain will be Christmas Day. Called on Lieutenant Burt, Fifth Air Force cryptographic officer, and secured info for codes and cipher.[50]

Rocky and Bob Foliart climbed a hill in the evening. "While on the hill we watched a very beautiful girl and Colonel Davies come out of his house on the hill. All the high rank have their respective tents or houses on top of the hills. This location presents the problem of piping water to the higher places and many must install pumps."[51] That link might have been a non sequitur—or perhaps not. Other servicemen implicitly believed that any senior officer enjoyed sex and modern plumbing as privileges of rank. A jeep driver who shared the attitude told Rocky "about the immoral conditions at Sydney. He said all stories are true. When his outfit was stationed there twelve percent of the men contracted common venereal disease."[52]

Life in the military, generally, was structured around duty and release from duty. In the Southwest Pacific, this meant time in New Guinea and leave in Australia—which could be conflated with hardship duty and sexual release. That might be overlaid with another set of opposites: resentment of overseas service and desire to find a way back home.

> Stories of Australian women taking in American soldiers when the latter are on leave reach almost the unbelievable. Many officers expect to "shack up" with some Australian girl during their seven days of leave. Almost everyone in the Air Corps flies south on their leaves which are supposed to be granted every four months. 10% of a unit's personnel may be on leave. Major Knauf stated the Inspector General said this theatre had been removed from the replacement list.[53]

In one paragraph, Rocky's thoughts ran through all these levels—sex, service, leave, the probability of getting to Australia, the unlikelihood of getting home.

On Christmas Eve, Rocky waxed sarcastic: "Nothing of importance happened and no one is expecting a visit from Santa Claus tonight." Rank, protocol, and the chances of war had damped down holiday spirits.

> Many of the men in the squadron headquarters are griping because all the officers had left at Christmas leaving no transportation for the enlisted men. Because

the officers had gone no mail could be sent because no censors were available. The rumor which has been circulating lately was confirmed by a form letter from MacArthur stating he regretted to announce a ship carrying Christmas packages had been sunk.[54]

Christmas Day was better, a Saturday of rest and sightseeing. With eleven other officers, Rocky traveled west of Moresby, along a black-dirt road, until they reached a Motuan village, built out on stilts above a beach. Their guide was a laundry sergeant for whom people from the village worked. They watched children run races and older villagers dance and Australian soldiers present Christmas presents of black trading tobacco.

Later in the day we were entertained and startled when a choir sang "Silent Night" and "I Ain't Goin' Grieve My Lord No More." Several of the men purchased walking canes, carved animals and shell beads. On our pass, which was secured from the local provost marshal, it gave the maximum prices to pay, however no one paid any attention to this because we lost it (the pass). Many of the officers had cameras and in order to get pictures of the stripped to the waist young girls, the girls would not pose for less than one shilling. There seems to be a regulation that in order to send pictures to the US, soldiers must be a certain distance from the girls.[55]

They drove back to Moresby for a chicken dinner. At Dobodura, the 82nd Squadron had turkey, and Doc Schafer drew on his medical stores for a few gallons of 180-proof grain alcohol, cut it to 90 proof, and then mixed in warm grapefruit juice.[56]

At Dobodura, there were no native dances, but there was horse-racing. Many of the packhorses brought over the previous year by the Japanese landing force could still be found around the airfields there. The 82nd Squadron had found a few cropping grass by the side of the road, and one airman, Robert Mooney, a jockey in peacetime, essayed to break them. The horses were stubborn beasts, but they could be ridden (some claimed they were British cavalry mounts, captured at Singapore). The Australians had laid out a racecourse in the open country at Soputa. Doc Schafer watched the ponies gallop there on New Year's Day, with an aircraft wing for a starting post, a bamboo platform for the stewards, a handful of touts accepting bets, and a mass of bush-hatted soldiers lining the rails as the field galloped past.[57]

Not everyone was at the races. Among the mechanics of the 82nd Squadron was a careful crew chief from Houston, Sgt. Bill Ursprung. For the month of December 1943, Sergeant Ursprung

At Dobodura in early 1944, Lt. Bill Shomo posed with his P-39 "Snooks," between the two airmen who kept that warplane armed and flying: armorer Pfc. T. O. Davis (at left) and SSgt. Ralph Winkle (right). 82nd TRS, in AFHRA archive

saw fit to set down only this memory, for Christmas Day: "We worked all day and up into the night changing engines on our P-39s." A week later, he reflected: "New Year's Day. Worked all day changing engine on Staff Sergeant Winkle's plane 'Snooks.' Lieutenant Shomo was his pilot."[58]

In squadron photographs, Ursprung is the man you recognize by his brilliant, blinding grin. As a diarist, he was laconic. During two years overseas, he reported a string of airfield catastrophes. "Staff Sergeant Edwards' plane 'Calamity Ann' caught fire and burned up," he would write. "17th Squadron had tough luck today. One of their top gunners got his head blown off and one of their B-25s came in on her belly." "Lieutenant Lipscomb received second degree burns when he crashed Staff Sergeant Winkle's ship on the runway."[59]

In one photograph, overhauling a P-39, Ursprung seems to be physically wrestling with the airframe. He labored, and the ordnance and armaments and communications sections labored, in conditions that were appalling.

They did not settle down to work on motors and planes in great hangars or on broad concrete aprons, or in spacious repair shops adjoining 300-foot warehouses stocked with parts. Instead, they labored in improvised coral bunkers amid debilitating heat and humidity, in tents, or in huts floored with coco logs and covered with leaky canvas tarpaulins; and they labored without much recognition. In almost every instance, the service unit lived and worked side by side with the tactical unit; its functions were as essential as those of the air echelon, yet it received little credit and no public recognition when squadron or group fought its way through to a critical target against heavy opposition. It was easy to forget that bombs and guns functioned because ordnance personnel had labored to maintain them or that the planes' radar and radio equipment permitted a safe return from a hazardous mission because radio technicians had spent many hot extra hours in perfecting operation of the equipment.[60]

And yet Bill Ursprung never faced the lens of history except with a grin, and his mechanic's-eye view of the air war was never one of mere complaint. His sentences might imply that the 82nd Squadron's pilots were damn fools who inconsiderately crashed the planes on which he and his fellow crew chiefs had expended such efforts—except that his attitude was neither cynical nor sarcastic, never anything but stoic. Once this is understood, his short sentences reflect a terse eloquence.

The day after Christmas, the chances of war and the risks of ambition showed themselves. The Wing woke up on a fogged-in day to the sound of a bomber crashing and its .50-caliber ammunition exploding.

> Early this morning Colonel Hutchison and 16 others crashed in a B-17 on take-off. Two enlisted photographers from the Eighth Photo were killed and the colonel was unconscious for two hours. Many said they could not visualize how anyone got out of the plane alive. . . . Rumored that Colonel Hutchison's back was broken. Chaplain Smith held services and I missed for the first time.[61]

Colonel Hutchison was flying the B-17 that crashed, "R. F. D. Tojo." The next invasion of New Britain was more than a rumor now: troops had gone ashore at Cape Gloucester, and a plane packed with war correspondents was scheduled to fly over the beachheads. Hutchison was piloting their plane in person, as he previously had piloted other Allied notables on other flights above combat zones.

R. F. D. Tojo was a war-weary plane; it had flown with two bomber groups before being handed off to Hutchison's recon photographers. Hutchison took off from the runway at Fourteen Mile Strip at 0549 hours. The base was fogged in, with a zero ceiling, and the airstrip was so dark that two jeeps used their headlights to light the way. The jeep drivers noticed that the B-17 took longer than usual to leave the runway. At 0550 hours R. F. D. Tojo crashed into the trees by the Laloki River. The wreck chewed a gap into the tree line, heaped up twisted wreckage and chopped-up branches, and then the clearing filled with flames. "Rescue squads ploughed a path through the swamp and jungle, evacuating the broken and blood-soaked bodies, under a hail of exploding ammunition," a squadron historian wrote. If anyone got out, it was because the plane broke apart: wings splitting off, propeller blades bending, the fuselage tearing open where the plane crashed down on its belly. Two enlisted men died, and two war correspondents.[62]

Colonel Hutchison did not die, but no one knew if he would recover. Sams took over as Wing CO, and Rocky continued work—pulling radio information together, trying to draw equipment from the quartermasters.

A new piece of information had been added to airmen's stories about the air base for which they were headed.

> Heard about capturing two Jap soldiers at Nadzab who were found eating garbage and wearing US uniforms. Several US shoes, food, etc. were found in the Japs' cave where they had been living for months.[63]

Here, for the first time, Rocky came across the most ubiquitous, humorous, sad-sack figure of the Pacific War: the Japanese soldier in the chow line.

By the end of the war, the Japanese soldier in the American chow line seems to have been reported on every island captured by the Allies. The two Japanese soldiers at Nadzab had comrades who had already been seen from Attu in the Aleutians to Mono in the Treasury Islands. Other Japanese soldiers would edge into other American chow lines on Peleliu and Saipan. They would be detected, amid shouting and panicky shooting, farther west on the New Guinea coast, outside the mess hall tent at Hollandia. On Guam, Marine guards would chase them out of Admiral Nimitz's yard. In the Philippines, they would hide among the families of local girls they had married, only to be dragged off by MPs when their in-laws begged rations and tried to pass them off as Filipinos. They would appear in war stories told by black soldiers of the 93rd Infantry Division, interviews conducted by the Wisconsin Veterans Museum and the Texas Voices of Veterans project, and National Park Service oral history studies of the Aleutian campaign. Decades later, the Japanese soldier would continue to figure in online collections of humorous wartime anecdotes—forever sneaking into the chow line, forever cadging enough to survive, and yet, in the end, forever being clobbered and collared. For it is at the end of the chow line, in these stories, that the Japanese soldier always meets his nemesis, that other figure of military comedy, the grizzled mess sergeant.

At Lae, earlier that fall, General Kenney had seen three Japanese captured at the airfield, where they had been hiding out among the wrecked aircraft. Kenney had seen the Japanese with his own eyes, but the story that reached Rocky from Nadzab was already blurring into the apocryphal.[64] The reports were true to life—and some were truer than life.

◌

"Payday, and games of chance were in order," Rocky wrote as the year ended. "New Year's Eve was celebrated by the officers at a dance at the local Fifth Bomber Command officers' club. Most everyone became drunk including the few nurses."

> The enlisted men had a mild party which was a climax to all the celebration of the 200 men in the command who are being sent home. From reports these men have been in this theatre some twenty-four months and are

of the first three grades of sergeants and [are] being sent home as instructors. Colonel Sams said "they" may adopt a policy of sending men home after being in this theatre for two years. Many of the men express the desire to return but not to New Guinea.[65]

Members of air crews might hope to be rotated home from the Southwest Pacific. Others could not expect that—as the farewell party for the sergeants underlined. In July 1943, General Mac-Arthur had issued a blunt and discouraging directive: "The necessity for an indefinite period for using all available shipping for the transportation to this theater of additional units and of replacements to maintain the strength of the command will operate to prevent the return of individuals or units to the United States under any rotation policy or at the end of any specified period of duty. Except for the physically unfit, for air crew personnel returned under a special policy, and for personnel definitely unqualified for duty in the command, personnel can be returned only under the most exceptional circumstances."[66]

Rocky and other airmen had been disabused, almost completely, of their hopes for leaves and furloughs. They had met airmen at Moresby who had been at Clark Field. "The men here who have been here two years or more (those who were in the Philippines) have become robots. A few believe they'll never be sent back to the States because the replacements aren't coming this way."[67] When a reconnaissance B-24 crashed, killing thirteen crewmen, men talked about the radioman, who had been overseas for twenty-five months.[68] The "replacement pilots" supplied to the 82nd Squadron included men who had been in New Guinea for months already, like Zeke Zaleski.

At Fifth Bomber Command, an intelligence lieutenant had summed up all the official reasons that no one was going home: "General MacArthur has not returned troops to the States at the end of twenty months service, however this may be due to insufficient number of replacements being sent over, and insufficient number of combat teams, and means of transportation."[69] *Insufficient, insufficient, insufficient*—Fifth Air Force men had heard the explanations before, so often that they could recite them as a dispirited litany.

The Army already knew well that MacArthur's servicemen thought they had done their share. Army poll-takers had surveyed soldiers' opinion in the Southwest Pacific, and found that "When do we go home?" was overwhelmingly the question that men wanted to ask their commander. "Single and married men, volunteers and draftees, noncommissioned officers and privates, all believed that they and their comrades had already 'done our share.'"[70] A psychiatrist from the Air Surgeon's Office warned:

> From the day of arrival in the theater one encounters a depressed and hopeless atmosphere which comes from the many who have been here so long and have been disappointed so often by premature promises of an early return home. It is feared that the future mental health of these men and the welfare of their families will be adversely influenced by these situations.[71]

Protest could be read on soldiers' uniforms. Men were stitching Overseas Stripes on their shirtsleeves, arguably more than regulations allowed, to call attention to how long they had been away from home.[72] In *Yank Down Under* magazine, a columnist suggested slogans: *End the war in '44. Back to the sticks in '46. Seven-eleven in '47. Carolina in forty-nina. Dixie in Sixty.*[73]

"Skeptics spoke of the 'Golden Gate in '48,' while cynics contributed 'Join Mac and never come back.'" So the Air Force official history would record. As the year ended, the ground echelon of the 71st Group was slowly sensing what veteran formations had learned: that they might watch flying personnel arrive, serve, and rotate out, while they continued to serve without relief.[74]

9

THE NEW YEAR

"Most everyone woke with a headache," Rocky wrote on the first day of the new year. Then he turned to the Wing announcements, which were important.

> Major Tockstein said we should plan to move twice during 1944. The night before last Major McDaniel called a meeting of all supply sections to determine equipment requirements for 1944. Listed were concrete mixers, water coolers, more jeeps, rubber mattresses, ice-making machines, Coke machines, 2½ ton trucks, larger latrine seats (ready-made), more GI cans—and most anything else which was not directed toward personal comfort instead of winning the war.
>
> It is interesting to note that now definite plans have been made for the movements of units to Nadzab, many organizations are for the first time constructing adequate recreational rooms for the enlisted men. Permanent buildings too. Lieutenant Wilkinson said the Army could leave enough permanent buildings in New Guinea to give each native and his children one.[1]

Colonel Hutchison was not dead—nor was he crippled—but for the moment he was out of action. Colonel Sams was running the Wing, and the 71st Group men were glad to have Sams back. Nonetheless, moving to the Wing meant exile from the creature comforts of Fifth Bomber Command.

Colonel Sams ordered that all officers on detached service with the Wing move immediately to the Wing area and thus we left the Fifth Bomber Command area—with its good food, officers' club, theater, showers.

Our new area is among several scattered trees, and on several slopes. Showers are turned on four hours in the evening and drinking water is always available in the water trailers. The mess is poor. The breakfast consists of pancakes, jelly, butter, coffee, some kind of cereal, powdered milk, bread and sugar.

All the high ranking officers do not eat at the consolidated units, but at the Fifth Air Force. There is no doubt if a few majors and colonels ate with us low ranks, meals would improve.

Talked to the mess officer tonight. He states we are on "X" priority while other units here are up to "C" and "B." Only the hospitals are on the "A" list which means they can draw 90% over and have first selection of all foodstuffs. This low priority explains our being without eggs. The mess officer stated whenever he mentions the Wing, the source of supply will not issue him anything.

Also reported there would not be any more equipment issued to the Wing. Our unit (the Wing) will draw its necessary equipment from the groups and squadrons.

Yesterday Captain White, assistant A-1 personnel officer, went to use the engineering company latrine (the engineering company is attached to the Wing) but the guard wouldn't permit him to enter, for he was not

a member of the engineers. The captain was quite disgusted and made arrangements with the Wing motor
pool (on which the engineers are dependent for transportation) not to dispatch any vehicles to the company.
And so our war continues.[2]

Bombing missions went out in early morning, the bombers flying across the Owen Stanleys to strike Japanese bases on the other
coast. The planes would be home by mid-afternoon, skirting the
thunderheads that boiled up over the Owen Stanleys. Afterwards—
or on the many days when there was no flying—the squadrons
relaxed. "Usually there's a softball game between two of the units
and when darkness comes everybody goes to the mess hall to
write letters, read, play checkers, chess, games."[3] One night Rocky
read short stories in *The American*, a love story and a war story
about Sicily.[4] At the Fifth Bomber Command movie theater, the
evening could be hit or miss.

> Went to the theater this evening. A thousand (estimate)
> sat for one hour waiting for the show to begin. The men
> spent the time visiting, cursing, and fighting mosqui-
> toes, and a few sang familiar songs. Finally some cap-
> tain made the announcement: "Due to the inefficiency
> of the Special Service Officer, there will be no picture
> tonight." A second lieutenant entertained all in the club
> by playing the piano.[5]

Camp life was often slow. "Many of the officers have taken
up woodcraft in order to have something to do. Captain Williams
and Mr. Jackson are making rubber band shooters. Major League
is shaping a miniature dugout out of mahogany."[6] (The woodcraft was not entirely adolescent; men fired rubber bands at the
monster tropical bats that flitted around the camp.) Other airmen

made rings out of Australian florins—Captain Seitz the dentist punched and ground out a ring for his daughter Susan.[7] A Post Exchange sold necessities and trinkets: "candy, soap, razor blades, cookies, occasionally watches, lighters and fountain pens. A frequent statement: What I wouldn't give for a Coke."[8] Rarely, there were other opportunities to spend their pay.

> After dinner two Aussie soldiers came to the officers' camp area selling gold rings and crosses. For no good reason they carried a bottle of gold dust. Captain Seitz pronounced the articles gold but did not estimate the percentage content nor did he purchase any. The soldiers said they had panned the gold while fighting on the northern part of the island. Captain Meyerhein, Major Knauf and I bought a cross and a ring respectively at £10.[9]

The rings were heavy enough, the officers figured, that if they weren't solid gold, the rest of the metal had to be silver, and so the crosses and rings were worth it. Next day, however, doubt crept in. "Captain Meyerhein spent the day wondering if the cross contained any gold. Whittling continued."[10]

Chaplain Smith had started a discussion group and Captain Meyerhein gave lectures on the progress of the war. The men of the 17th Squadron had classical music.

> Private Wilk, a teletype mechanic with the 17th Reconnaissance Squadron, was an A-1 violinist in civilian life. When he was drafted into the Army he wrote to the War Department asking to be removed from all KP duty because the soap was ruining his hands—so—he was sent to a teletype school. Now that he is in New Guinea a certain major it is rumored has "found" Wilk and is requesting he be put into Special Service sections.[11]

Casmere Wilk was from Brooklyn. His aficionados wanted to keep him with the camp—he played real music, a comrade wrote.[12] He would go on serving with the 17th Squadron.

There were rumors about women in the war zone. Inevitably, the women belonged to someone else.

> It is being rumored tonight that General MacArthur and Mrs. MacArthur and her staff of women are moving to Port Moresby. The men are wondering if they'll have to wear ties to Moresby now.
>
> It is reported the movie actor John Wayne and two girls are here. No one is excited about it though.
>
> There are several reports of Jap women fighting in the north. One report states that a soldier after bayoneting a "Jap" and cutting the clothing discovered it was a female. Evidently as the Japs withdraw their troops they are taking their women along too.
>
> Captain White showed me a bit of Jap propaganda dropped along the front lines. The propaganda was a photo print divided into two sections. The top showed a "YANK" having sexual intercourse with a naked "Australian Girl," the lower portion showed an "Aussie soldier" chasing a native woman in the jungle. There was a little note along the margin calling attention to that the Yanks were with the Aussie girls while the latter fought the Japs.[13]

Rocky was fortunate in getting letters from the girl who wore his fraternity pin. "Margaret Anne writes that the latest fad at home is young girls wearing a chain holding a wooden pistol—yes, 'Pistol Packin' Mamma!'" In mid-January, well ahead of Valentine's Day, he mailed her two rings. "One I made from a florin and the other was a gold one secured for £10 from an Aussie. They were censored and sent air mail."[14]

Moresby was no longer a besieged fortress. It was safe, almost civilized. Men said that civilians would be allowed back, or that high-ranking officers would rotate through to get combat status and be eligible for transfers home.

> Lieutenant Kepler states that most of the high rank in the bomber command secure their flying time in non-combat planes. There is a sweater hanging in the Fifth Bomber Command officers' club which is worn only by officers on the night before they go home or when they receive their promotions and all drinks are on them.[15]

There were men who weren't going home yet, and hadn't been promoted, and who didn't drink. Rocky and other airmen lounged or wrote letters in the communications tent or the dispensary, anywhere with screen windows and electric lights. (In the mess hall, due to a shortage of window screen, burlap was tacked up over the windows.) There they read *Guinea Gold* and *Yank Down Under* and pulled in news on the radio. Rocky remembered the ringing bells of the BBC Overseas Service.

On Sunday, January 9, the servicemen's radios pulled in a news report from the world after the war. Rocky recorded:

> Talked to several enlisted men at the dispensary tonight. The men were young and two were drafted directly from college. They were looking forward to returning to school following the war and were in hopes the government training program would include college courses.[16]

Rocky would live to recognize the difference that the Internet made to the world—but this anecdote shows how quickly news has always flown among people to whom that news matters. "The government training program" being discussed in Port Moresby that night was the Serviceman's Readjustment Act of 1944—the GI

Bill. On the night that Rocky talked with the college-boy draftees, American newspapers were reporting on the plans that the American Legion had announced for demobilization benefits, "a bill of rights for GI Joe and GI Jane." Via radio, the day's most important news had traveled halfway around the world. Ten o'clock at night in Port Moresby was seven o'clock in the morning in Indiana. The servicemen in New Guinea that evening were discussing a story that their families at home were only then reading in their Sunday newspapers.[17]

There were reminders that news and the mail came under scrutiny in wartime. There was the Group's first public security breach:

> Lieutenant Zock, the 71st Group Special Services Officer and Physical Training Officer, former Louisiana high school football coach, has been griping for quite a few weeks because he was not receiving any mail. Yesterday one of the clerks, a private by the way, in the Wing message center, who records and reads off the record, all the incoming mail, told me the following. "Today we received a letter concerning Lieutenant Zock. He had been using a code, the first letter of the first word in each paragraph and the censor at Brisbane (where the officers' mail is censored) caught it. The Fifth Air Force sent to the CO of the 71st a few of Zock's letters and suggested he be court-martialed under the 104th Article of War." Zock had sent home that he was in Port Moresby, et cetera.[18]

James Zock was from Acadia Parish, in the Cajun rice country. He was a personable man, a good choice for Special Services; Rocky had noted him playing blackjack and carrying home beer and taking charge of the Group's first beer run. In this case he had stretched bonhomie too far.

The code that Zock used was one that many servicemen had heard about. It was so familiar to Army counterintelligence that censors were trained to look for it. The offense was equally familiar: in Pacific theater censor logs, "intentional revealing of geographic location" was the most common violation of censorship regulations.[19] Censors looked for such letters and intercepted the ones they found but the offense was generally considered a minor infraction. That Zock faced punishment under the 104th Article of War sounded dread and ominous. In fact, it meant that Zock faced "company punishment," the lightest level of Army sanction: no stockade time, no fine, nothing more than extra duty or a restriction to camp.[20] The punishment could be as light as an order to rewrite the letter properly.

Spreading the word about Zock being caught may have been the point of the postal clerk's gossip. The clerk may have meant to warn other officers not to write letters that included code—and the clerk may have known to whom to give that warning. Before shipping out, Rocky had arranged both with his mother and with Margaret Anne that he would use the same first-letter-of-the-paragraph code in his letter to them. Margaret Anne recalled that he sent a few letters using the code and then stopped it—because it was too complicated, she thought. Or perhaps Rocky took the point of the warning.[21]

Rocky was getting up to speed in the communications section. Early in the month, as Colonel Hutchison assembled staff for the Wing, he had been concerned about his posting.

> Captain Heuer of the Signal Corps joined the Reconnaissance Wing HQ as signal officer, now where I'll go is another question. I am not authorized in Wing HQ but Major Tockstein said they would keep me—why? That's a good question.[22]

Now Rocky had part of an answer, a reassurance. Colonel Sams asked him to draw up a communications plan to be used at Nadzab.

With Lieutenant Kepler, Rocky continued to press for radios and electrical supplies. Their struggles with the Army Service of Supplies had become intense and epic. The most complex struggle began with a simple requisition for electrical supplies.

> We first took the requisition to a USA SOS officer (United States Army Service of Supplies) who politely said the requisition would have to come through channels—so off to the Air Service Command—there we were told to rewrite it—having done so we returned to the Service Command only to be told no action could be taken because the person who had ordered the requisition rewritten had gone to Australia—thus two days delay. Upon Major Steward's return (he ordered the rewrite) we were told none of the equipment existed so we stopped and Lieutenant Kepler went to Nadzab. There he contacted Major Althause who said the Air Service Command had hundreds of transformers.
>
> Kepler returned—we made another requisition—went to Air Service Command and Major Steward mumbled around and finally said he would take the requisition but first we would have to get the approval of USA SOS—so again we went to SOS. Here Captain Brennan, the Engineering Officer, was very polite and said the Air Service Command and not he was responsible for our supplies. He called Major Steward and asked "What the god damn it to hell are you giving these boys the run-around for." Back we went to the Air Service Command where the major literally grabbed the requisition and said we would get immediate action and he would have the equipment in two days.

Two days later we saw the major and he said the requisition was at USA SOS in Lieutenant Colonel Ross' office—we went to see Colonel Ross who in turn had never heard of the requisition. The colonel called the major—ate his ass out—and then with the lieutenant-colonel's aid we found the requisition and took it to the colonel. He approved the articles.[23]

That would not be the final skirmish. Any victory might be undone, or arrive trailing further obligations.

Today we got a teletype writer from the 912th Signal Company. The set was in banded boxes so I didn't open them at the warehouse. The boxes were taken to Wing HQ, opened, and we found the teletype itself broken and several fragments loose in the box. I immediately took the set back to the warehouse and secured another, but the captain wanted me to send him a complete report and write out a salvage report on the equipment. And so our paper war continues.[24]

The Fifth Air Force had its own form of reveille. Rocky woke up most mornings to the sound of C-47 cargo planes heading east, revving their engines for the climb across the Owen Stanleys.

One by one the units in the Port Moresby area are being flown over the mountains. Usually the units are alerted two days before they are scheduled to leave by air freight. All equipment is packed, stacked in individual areas determined by cubic feet and weight. The night before leaving, the equipment is loaded into trucks in readiness to be moved to the planes around midnight. Generally, not all the planes scheduled are available, for example, nine planes were to take part of the 960th Engineers

> to Nadzab this morning, but only three were present. Everything possible is sent by air—radio sets are removed from trucks, so are generators, etc. And all larger items are sent by boat. Yes, buildings too are airborne. Our headquarters building is 117' x 50' and is put together with bolts. Takes three days to dismount and crate away in airborne dimensions.[25]

The cargo planes were bound for Nadzab, and everyone was talking about the move. People said Nadzab was cooler at night than Port Moresby and that the malaria rate was low. The Wing had heard that their first assigned camp area lay underneath two feet of water. They had also heard that Fifth Bomber Command was building a headquarters with screen windows and a concrete floor, and that the 960th Engineers had indulged Bomber Command's pampered staff officers with a swimming pool.[26] There was envy in that—distrust, too. Rumor said the engineers should have been building revetments instead of swimming pools.

> The Japs bombed Nadzab today. According to the reports the regular fighter cover was out when the Japs came in. They made six runs on the airdrome and no planes offered opposition. Several P-40s and a C-47 were shot down and a B-25 strafed on the ground. Several stated the US planes were not dispersed as they should have been.[27]

There were risks to a move, in New Guinea weather: "One officer of our Group said you couldn't help but find your air route from Buna because the course is marked with wrecked C-47 planes."[28]

Nadzab was northeast of Moresby. Other airplanes were heading south. Some were official flights carrying servicemen to Australia on leave; others were fat-cat runs to bring back food and liquor.

Several of the larger units here have officers stationed down in Australia bringing liquor, Cokes, and other luxuries. Two weeks ago the Fifth Bomber Command sent a plane down to Townsville to bring back ice cream for the men and officers.

Here in New Guinea the personnel in the bomb units fly to Australia on what is called the "beer run." Since liquor can only be secured in Australia, these missions are frequent. One sergeant suggested a small brown jug be painted on the plane to show the number of beer runs.[29]

It was going to be a long time before Rocky could count on getting leave in Sydney. In the meantime, New Guinea had attractions. One Monday, after Rocky had pulled Sunday night watch as Wing duty officer, he and Foliart and Kepler had the afternoon off and drove to Rouna Falls in a borrowed jeep. "We went swimming naked in one of the cool whirlpools below the falls although we were told not to by the MP because nurses frequent the falls."[30]

John Wayne's USO tour was still in town, offering one of the most curious stage shows of the war.

Tonight John Wayne appeared at the Fifth Bomber Command Starlite Theater. The show smelled, however, one fellow who sang two classic songs was superior.[31]

John Wayne had come to the Southwest Pacific, far from newspapers and photographers, while his lawyers were settling the terms of a divorce. Onstage, Wayne was the master of ceremonies—but he was not the strongest presence. That would have been the fellow who sang classic songs, Benjamin DeLoache.

DeLoache stood six feet four inches, as tall as Wayne. He had debuted with the Philadelphia Symphony and would teach voice at Yale. "Ben, I'd look like a fool if I put on that cowboy thing of

Lt. Delta C. Graham of Kansas City, here with his P-39 "Maxine," was the first flyer in the 71st Group to shoot down a Japanese warplane, on December 18, 1943. On March 1, 1944, Graham crashed during a strafing run, possibly hit by enemy fire, and became the first 82nd Squadron flyer to die in combat. San Diego Air & Space Museum

mine," Wayne had told DeLoache, "but I can introduce you, and you'll get the biggest audiences that you ever sang for in your life." In the concert-hall world, DeLoache was renowned for having sung in the American premier of *Wozzeck*. During the troupe's three-month tour of the SWPA, he switched to standards and show tunes (many from the new musical *Oklahoma!*), and Wayne finished the show with "Minnie the Moocher."

The audiences in the jungle had been the best in the world, Wayne told people back in Hollywood. The servicemen were starved for news from home, happy to yell and relax at a show. What the GIs needed was letters, cigars, phonograph needles, and radios. And there was something else, the craggy Western hero added, in his slow homespun drawl. The GI bands needed America's help, too. People should send them reeds, strings, and orchestrations.[32]

§

There was other news, which Rocky heard at Wing headquarters. In the 110th Squadron, two more pilots had been killed.

> Lieutenant McAlarney of the 110th Squadron was killed yesterday due to hitting a tree in Uligan Harbor when he was on a strafing mission. The rescue officer at ADVON Five said if he was not killed, he was a Jap prisoner.
>
> Lieutenant Anderson failed to return on January 20th. He was also in the 110th Squadron. The squadron sent over searches on the 20th and the next two days but were unable to locate him though they did sight something. Last night when I was duty officer down at Wing HQ the message came via Aussie Radio that Lieutenant Anderson, Plane No. 26, crashed at Kasipi Swamp, near 146° 54' 8° 28' on 20 January and he was buried near the Rest House there. The Australian lieutenant who telephoned the call said it may have taken the runner three days to reach the radio station. Also it is worth noting, only two numbers of the plane's six numbers were reported, evidently there was a great impact.[33]

Gerald McAlarney was a New Yorker, from Astoria in the borough of Queens. Eugene L. Anderson was from Minnesota. For McAlarney, it was eminently clear what had happened. He had gone in too close on a strafing run. His wingman saw it all:

Approached the target on the right side of Uligan Bay directly in front of me. He made a steep dive into the target firing a long burst. His shots were to the left of the barge which he was strafing. He made a turn to the right to move his line of fire on the target which was behind a tree jutting out into the bay. As he made this turn he was very close to the ground. His right wing struck the tree well below the top. The plane cartwheeled to the right and went over into the water nose first. I estimate his speed at about two hundred and sixty (260) miles per hour when he struck the tree.[34]

As for Anderson, no one knew what had happened; he had vanished into the overcast. The morning Anderson died, his flight was climbing through a maze of clouds—80 percent cloud coverage up to 13,000 feet (the height of the mountains). Above that, the sky was still more than half clouds, and thunderheads were looming up. Anderson was wingman to Dick Minton. Minton headed into the overcast and Anderson followed, while the rest of the flight steered around to the northwest, following clearer weather. No one who knew him ever saw Anderson again. The overcast still hung over the mountains, and the flyers who went out to search for the wreck knew better than to fly into those same clouds again.[35]

At Dobodura, Doc Schafer saw more carelessness and recklessness. Lieutenant Tate of the 82nd Squadron had buzzed the camp of the 17th Squadron—"dove down on their outside latrine and scared a couple of fellows off the throne besides blowing laundry off the line." Lt. Needham Graves had been strafing a Japanese motor convoy and dived in so low that he clipped a palm when he pulled out. A P-38 pilot had killed himself while showing off: "He was stunting over the field, pulled up to about 700–800 feet and did a wing-over and didn't pull out soon enough. Trees were knocked down for what seemed like a half mile."[36]

Schafer had begun to see the strains of combat fatigue. Some officers had no eagerness to fly. They were nervous and irritated, smoked too much, had poor appetites, and were losing weight; "sleep not good, and one has nightmares." Two had wives back in the States who were expecting children. They had sallow complexions—that was the Atabrine that they took to prevent malaria.[37]

Schafer knew exactly what to look for. Army psychiatrists had studied combat fatigue in exactly the same context, another fighter squadron flying P-39s in New Guinea, only a few months before. The same symptoms stood out:

> A continuous sensation of mental and physical tiredness (especially severe in the late afternoon), tiredness at the completion of one mission, the early onset of fatigue while flying, irritability, lassitude, boredom, loss of aggressiveness, and loss of appetite.
>
> Listlessness and lethargy were evident. No one seemed to have the energy to do anything. The usual horseplay was lacking, bickering replaced kidding and joking, the regular afternoon volleyball and horseshoe games practically ceased. Boredom was widespread—no one had a sustained interest in anything. Most ominous of the changes was the gradual decrease in griping about anything, particularly the mess. . . . Finally, a number of the pilots simply quit eating. Weight losses varying from 5 to 30 pounds per man prevailed. An eager, alert, aggressive squadron became a tired, indifferent and listless one.[38]

Actual combat might invigorate a squadron, temporarily; combat as a routine wore a squadron down. Carbon monoxide leaks often weakened flyers. A pilot who belched up Australian bully beef into his radio mike might feel sickened and distracted for the rest of the mission. A flight of listless fighter pilots—what an oxymoron—would be easy prey for an enemy who stayed alert. Diet was important; pilots had energy only if they kept eating. That was one of the reasons that the military allowed air units to fly fat-cat runs to Australia: steaks and fresh vegetables were food that men could be counted on to eat. Atabrine held off malaria, but it had vicious side effects. It made soldiers' skin turn yellow, upset digestion, and sometimes, as it built up in the blood, became toxic and caused psychotic incidents.[39]

Colonel Sams could see more of the psychological terrain. In the 110th Squadron, Sams had just lost McAlarney and Anderson—two crashes due to errors, accidents that well-rested pilots might have avoided. He had had to ship a third man to Australia, a probable mental case. Yet another man had quit flying strafing missions (he was scared, Sams thought). Two other officers were bickering and Sams wanted to transfer them too.[40] Sams held a conference, and Rocky heard details. "Captain Moody who was a hot-shot pilot back in the States is reported to have become careless and doesn't care to fly missions," he wrote.[41]

Sams whirled into the 82nd Squadron's camp and demanded that leave rotations begin immediately. He arrived on Thursday; he wanted the first batch of pilots to start for Sydney on Saturday. Sams gave the order to Gordon, the squadron commander. Gordon sidestepped the responsibility for making a choice—he handed off the duty to Schafer. Schafer was surprised to be entrusted with this command decision, but he chose quickly—leave went to the ten pilots with the highest number of missions and hours of flying time. In not much more than a month, the highest man in this group had flown sixty-three missions and ninety-eight hours, while the lowest man had flown forty-nine missions and seventy-five hours. Luckily, all the pilots showing strain were included.[42]

Amid the tension and the fatigue, there was one piece of good news. The 82nd Squadron got back a pilot who they thought had been lost.

> Lieutenant Bailey was forced down at sea in his P-39 and he was able to bail out. According to the reports he was but a mile offshore of another island when the accident occurred but due to the current, he was carried away to

sea. For twelve days he floated and some lucky sea gull spotted Bailey and resulted in the pilot's only meal. Most fortunate too—the gull had just swallowed two fish.[43]

Bailey was the first man from the 71st Group to go missing and be rescued. He was sent to Australia to recuperate. He would treat it as a one-man fat-cat mission of his own. Meantime, the war went on, with its dangers and complaints.

> Today came the news that a lone Jap plane raided Nadzab at dusk yesterday, striking one lone Negro in the shoulder.
>
> Night before last we had a blackout and rumor reported three enemy ships overhead. I was in the mess hall as usual writing letters when the blackout began. We officers went outside and talked until the lights came on again. Lieutenant Dixon returned from Nadzab and reported that a whole hilltop had been cleared off for General Whitehead.
>
> Talked to the Wing Sergeant Major yesterday who was quite disgusted with everything: "If I was offered $100,000 or a discharge—I'd take the discharge."[44]

Colonel Sams was also hearing his men's gripes. An enlisted man had told him, "From the personal standpoint I'm ready to go home but from the professional viewpoint, I will never go home."[45] The comments seemed different, but they rhymed.

There had been friction between the enlisted men and the officers. Rocky had seen this in the movie-theater protest of the promotion party dynamite shenanigans. He had sensed more, as shown in his comments that enlisted men's recreation rooms had begun to be built only when the Fifth Air Force was moving on.

The officers, the older ones, are saying it was never like this before the war. Now the enlisted men feel as though they are as important as the officers. It is reported several men resent waiting on the officers at mess. (The officers eat on plates and with regular fork and knives whereas the enlisted men eat from their GI mess kits and wash their eating ware in a large can of hot water.)[46]

One of Rocky's tent-mates, Captain Williams, was said to sleep with a .45 under his pillow, for fear of the enlisted men. (The enlisted men told Rocky that.) Rocky's other tent-mate, Mr. Jackson the warrant officer, pressed Rocky the new lieutenant to shovel gravel

On the east coast of New Guinea, the 17th Squadron lived and worked in a sea of mud. United States Air Force Academy, McDermott Library, Small MS Collection No. 1479: photograph taken and donated by Fred Hill.

for the floor of the tent, an idea that Rocky did not welcome. "Told Mr. Jackson to blow it out his barracks bag," he wrote.[47] Colonel Sams was washing his uniforms side-by-side with his lieutenants. Neither he nor Rocky wanted to pay what enlisted men were asking to do laundry (32¢ a shirt, which worked out to twelve dollars a month). He'd be damned if he'd wash dirty clothes, Sams announced, it would only cost him twenty dollars a month—but for Sams, parsimony outweighed disgruntlement. While he griped that he would pay to have his khakis laundered, the colonel was scrubbing his clothes himself.[48]

More mail arrived. Rocky received a letter from Professor Kirklin at Franklin College. Kirklin's son was serving on the Italian front. There were rumors from Italy that units there would be returned to the States after six months in combat. "From my own viewpoint, such a move isn't good because once the men are returned home, they'll lose their combat fitness," Rocky considered.[49] One hears sour grapes in that. MacArthur's headquarters had announced a plan to give furloughs, stateside, to soldiers who had served in the Southwest Pacific for eighteen months and spent six months north of Australia. There was a catch: no units would be furloughed, only individuals. (The 32nd Division would not return en masse as in 1919, parading through its men's Wisconsin hometowns.) More particularly, individuals could return only as transportation allowed.[50] Servicemen in the SWPA had learned already how few men could qualify for travel homeward across the Pacific.

In Indiana, it had been a hard winter. The newspapers carried stories about disastrous fires and men who died drinking methyl alcohol. Hunters waited in long lines at Vonnegut's Hardware for shotgun shells—strictly rationed, one box to each customer. Along Sugar Creek, gray foxes were seen, beasts long vanished from Indiana; the Mechanicsburg Christian Church ladies' guild organized a fox hunt, killing enough to earn sixty-five dollars in state bounties. In Sheridan, the hitching posts were taken down on Main Street. An itinerant speaker who called himself a Christian Jew told a congregation about his escape from France. Bill Terhune, a farmer's son whom Rocky would have known, went missing when his B-26 was shot down by the Germans over St. Omer.[51]

At the Boyer farmhouse, they had bought a Philco radio, the family's first. They listened to it during the dinner hour. "The War-opean news," Van called it—they listened in hopes of hearing more about the Pacific. Anndora recalled that dinner was silent; nobody talked, except the announcer on the radio.

At Franklin, Margaret Anne was the editor of *The Franklin*, the college weekly paper. She also belonged to the Franklin College War Council. On the campus, men were few and far between. Any young man who had a uniform to wear did so, even those who belonged only to the Civil Air Patrol. Her mother warned her against having her head turned, since they all looked alike in uniform. It was front-page news, underneath the photo of Monte Cassino, when the story of Norman Vandivier's last flight was read on-air during a national radio hookup; the Vandivier family were listening to the broadcast, but had not been told about it in advance. Over Christmas, Margaret Anne and some college friends went to a dinner at Camp Atterbury, hosted by a unit training there, the 106th "Golden Lions" Division. The next Christmas, she would remember, that same division was the one overrun by the Germans in the Battle of the Bulge.[52]

∾

On February 8, after six weeks' recuperation, Colonel Hutchison was back at the Wing, and Colonel Sams returned to the 71st Group. "Colonel Sams is the best CO I've ever known," Rocky wrote.[53] With Hutchison's return, the officers' gossip began again.

> We have quite a lot of stories from the rumor department today. First, Major Minnock of the A-1 personnel section said Colonel Hutchison ordered him not to secure

any more officers for Wing HQ because it was being rumored "down South a Recco Wing HQ cadre was being organized and would move up to take over our present set-up." The major and a few other high-rankers are quite disgusted because it would beat them out of their chances of promotions. It is whispered in every tent the only reason the Wing was organized in the first place was to create possibilities for promotions. It has been said [that] to become a member of Wing HQ, it wasn't what you knew, but who you knew. Another description is, never were so few controlled by so many. "Brown nosers" is a term or rather a sort of adjective used to stereotype those individuals who were called ass kissers in civilian life. Anyone who puts in a long hard day, always working, is called an "eager beaver."

Was duty officer last night. The duties of such a capacity are to take action on any situation which may arise, receive all teletypes, safe hand documents, and fight mosquitoes throughout the night. Before coming from beneath my mosquito bar this morning, I placed my head as near as possible to the bar without touching it. Only a few seconds later the insects located me and within a minute or two I counted ten mosquitoes sitting on the net near my head.[54]

The oddest story came from the Weather Central section, where Rocky's friend Lieutenant Foster worked. It was an example of meteorological accuracy combined with wishful thinking. The Reconnaissance Wing was going back stateside, someone had said, or moving on to India; it was leaving New Guinea because New Guinea had too many days when clouds and rain made photography impossible.[55]

Two pilots died that week, on combat missions, but in accidents. Rocky knew one of them well and penned a short, moving elegy.

> Captain A. Q. Smith, 110th Squadron, is reported as miss-
> ing in action. He was one of the finest fellows I have ever
> known, as a pilot, a Sigma Alpha Epsilon brother, and as
> a gentleman.[56]

Alfred Q. Smith flew out of Gusap at noon on February 12. The planes headed toward Saidor, over the Finisterre Mountains, where some peaks rise higher than 13,000 feet. There were broken cumulus clouds at 10,000 feet. There were eight planes in the mission, two flights of four P-39s.

> The first flight climbed above cumulus clouds, but three
> ships of the last flight entered the clouds at approximately
> 1,000 feet below top of cumulus. Pilots entering cloud in
> their order [were] as follows: Capt. A. Q. Smith, Lt. D. N.
> Nordeck, Lt. H. W. Babinsky. Lt. D. N. Nordeck and Lt.
> H. W. Babinsky broke through shortly afterward, but no
> more was seen of Capt. A. Q. Smith.[57]

This time it was the leading pilot who never came out of the cloudbank. The two planes in the rear of the flight, in the scant seconds of flight time by which they were following Smith, gained just enough height to scrape clear of the mountaintop into which Smith crashed.

Smith's family was from Atlanta. He would have been an SAE at Georgia Tech, the Georgia Phi chapter.[58] It was years now that Captain Smith and Lieutenant Boyer had been out of college, but it mattered to them that they were fraternity brothers—and perhaps that Foliart was a Sigma Chi alum, and that Major Tennille had belonged to Beta Theta Pi during his years at Chapel Hill. Junior officers were young men who received many more orders than they gave and were glad for any friends they might find: from flight school classes, or in college days—or even from adolescence. *Yank Down Under* ran regular columns in which servicemen offered to trade unit patches, as if the Army were an extension of the Boy Scouts.

One more pilot died that week, another flyer from the 110th Squadron. The way that he died was one of the few war stories that my father told.

> It was reported late this afternoon one of the 110th Squadron pilots was killed today when the pamphlets which he was dropping over Madang, were carried into his air scoop causing motor failure. The two wingmen on the mission also found pamphlets in their scoops.[59]

1st Lt. Paul P. Swanson was the pilot who died. At 10:35 in the morning, four planes from the 110th Squadron came down to a hundred feet over Ulugan Plantation, dropping leaflets. Two planes banked right, while Swanson and 2nd Lt. Jesse McNeill turned around and headed back over the plantation. McNeill saw Swanson head toward the coast and go lower and thought that his leader had picked out another target; then he saw Swanson's P-39 stall above the treetops, crash, and start a furious fire.[60]

The P-39 Airacobra had windows that could be cranked down like car windows and through which propaganda leaflets could be thrown. Swanson died that day because no one had thought what would happen if leaflets were thrown from the cockpit of a plane in which the air intake was behind the cockpit.

Finally, the waiting and the rumors were over. Wing HQ issued its orders: the 20th Mapping Squadron would move on February 14, the 26th Squadron and Sixth Group HQ the day after that, and finally Wing HQ on February 17.

> Usually every afternoon the Owen Stanley Mountains are covered with thunderheads which rise to several thousand feet, thus prohibiting the C-47 transport

planes from flying. Usually the clouds break up in early morning and thus traffic starts and often the planes will make two trips on a mission. At an early hour, usually six, a weather plane takes off towards the mountains and sends back weather reports at ten-minute intervals and when the pass is reported "clear," the transports take off and return at ten to carry across another load. The equipment and personnel to be transported eat breakfast at midnight and have everything loaded in the planes by 5 a.m. The second mission personnel eat breakfast at 3 a.m. and are ready to load at 8 a.m.[61]

That left a handful of working days—everything to be done at the last minute, plenty of delays and waiting times. Rocky and Kepler checked again on the transformers for which they had fought so long with Service of Supplies—the gear over which Captain Brennan and Colonel Ross had cursed out Major Steward. The transformers were in Milne Bay, they learned; all they had to do was get them.

A volcano erupted on the east coast that week, spewing ash as far west as Moresby.[62] It set a tone of violent energy. Flights were being scheduled; duffel bags were being packed. Pilots rushed through on their way back from leave: "I have heard that the women in Sydney were willing, and I expected to find them willing, but not that willing!" one marveled as he caught his flight.[63] The B-17 that the Wing used as a unit cargo plane was booked. Rocky and Kepler grabbed a night out on the town, or at least at the Australian officers' club, a four-course dinner with a five-piece band. Old paperwork was being burned, and haste made waste— double-checks, second-guessing, and quick judgment calls.

Two days ago I lost a secret letter attached to an outline project. The letter I believe was burned with other documents but not being sure of this, I submitted a certificate stating the letter was lost. Captain Williams said I had better submit a statement to the effect it was burned because if it was lost, the inspector general department would investigate our headquarters and cause trouble.[64]

The pace did not relent; nor did the pattern of hurry-up-and-wait. On February 17, the day Wing HQ was scheduled to move, Rocky found a last-minute chance to get to Milne Bay and pick up the transformers.

> This morning the B-17 was available so Major Davis took off for Milne Bay where I expected to pick up electrical supplies, then on to Nadzab, but ten minutes from Milne the weather closed in, so we returned. We flew over one large plantation (640 acres) located ten miles from the coast on a lazy river and the landscaped lawn reminded me of a fashionable hotel. Beautiful.[65]

New Guinea might be beautiful, but the lesson was not to fly into the overcast. It was a farewell that fitted Port Moresby. They packed up the camp and waited for the C-47s.

> This is being written with the aid of a campfire for tonight our tents have been struck and all our equipment is loaded in large 2 ½ ton trucks which are parked single file leading up the hill toward the mess hall. Originally we were allotted twenty planes for movement in the morning but at 8:30 tonight, higher headquarters called saying only three planes would be available for the first mission (6 a.m.) but the original number could be had for the second (9 a.m.) mission. Major Warner had planned to move from the area at midnight to the planes, have them loaded by three and then permit the men to sleep in the planes.[66]

This was the last entry that Rocky made in Port Moresby. He wrote his next entry from east of the mountains. He summed up twenty-four hours of hustle and delay, a few bright hours on a beach, a long night's labor, and a sunrise takeoff.

> We were supposed to be flown to Nadzab this morning. We had only three planes left and since all our equipment was packed there wasn't too much one could do so—Foster, Foliart and I took off in the jeep assigned to me. We had dinner at the Australian Officers' Club at Moresby primarily because we didn't care to eat the canned rations being served at the unit mess. Foliart and I had our hair cut, by an enlisted Aussie who hadn't been home in 18 months, in one of the three barber chairs on the island.
>
> Following lunch we drove eastward searching for a road to Bootless Bay which I had spotted the day before. On one occasion we reached the beach of the bay only to find remains of barbed wire entanglements in the water and agreed it was no place to swim.[67]

They drove on, through miles of Australian camps, and finally revved the jeep over a ridge that looked down on the bay. A boatload of Motuan families splashed ashore, and a lieutenant and a nurse drove up. Foliart bought four shillings' worth of bananas and they combed the beach for stones.

> Returned to camp, went to the Fifth Bomber Command for dinner, attended the theater, returned at 10 p.m. only to find Major Warner waiting at the orderly room to tell us the trucks would leave the area for loading the planes at midnight.
>
> That we did. Most of the planes were loaded by 4 a.m. Jeeps gave us the most trouble as it takes five men and a

damn good driver and I didn't prove to be a damn good driver. After the planes were loaded the men went to sleep. At 6 a.m. the crew chiefs arrived and engines were warmed up and checked. Several of the men visited a Red Cross shack nearby which served coffee and sandwiches *free*. At 7:10 our pilot arrived and so immediately we were off along with several other C-47s.

Our route took us up the coast several minutes, turned, and went over the hump. The terrain was as expected. The view of the Markham Valley is one of the most beautiful spots I have ever seen—open at both ends with mountains reaching to the clouds on either side. Locating an airstrip was easy. Immediately upon our stopping in one of the areas cleared for such from the grass a Negro on a motorcycle opened the door and asked who we were. Off he went. Soon a truck arrived with five Negroes who immediately unloaded our plane and took the equipment to the camp area.[68]

They were in Nadzab now—on the east side of the mountains, where the fighting was. At Wewak, they heard, the Japanese had received reinforcements—bombers and paratroopers. (And this was true: the Japanese Fourth Air Army had moved to Wewak, with its twelve flying regiments, as many as 754 warplanes.) Against this threat, airmen were carrying pistols and gas masks and digging foxholes. Captain Williams said they would win the New Guinea campaign in four months. No one else agreed. They thought they would fight in New Guinea for another year, and that they would not win the war until 1947.[69]

10

NADZAB

In the spring of 1944, the Fifth Air Force base at Nadzab, which six months earlier had been a plain of kunai grass beside the Markham River, boasted of being the largest air base in the world. Men who flew in were amazed.

> I couldn't believe my eyes. I saw taxiways with hardstands to park airplanes curving every which way and half a dozen long runways abuilding. There were hundreds of heavy bombers, medium bombers, light bombers, transports, spotters, and fighters—P-38s, P-39s, P-40s, and P-47s—as far as I could see. Three of the heavy bomb groups were there or were in the process of moving in—the 380th was still down near Darwin—and it seemed to me that most of the rest of Fifth Air Force was at Nadzab. . . . The housing areas stretched from the hills that rimmed the northern side of the valley all the way south to the banks of the Markham River, which was where the 22nd Bombardment Group was. The entire complex was twenty miles square.[1]

Fighter Command was at Nadzab, Bomber Command was at Nadzab—ADVON had moved across the mountains from Port

154

Moresby. Colonel Hutchison's Reconnaissance Wing was at Nadzab, too. There were four all-weather airfields. Airfield Number
Two was a short no-nonsense fighter strip; the other three airfields each had two runways, each runway stretching out to six
thousand or seven thousand feet, lengths that could handle any
bomber yet built. Some runways were paved with steel Marsden
matting; others, luxuriously, were paved with asphalt. There were
fifty miles of all-weather taxiways. They ran by straight lines and
angles away from the airstrips, among countless loops and whorls
of dispersal areas, the tank laager of George Kenney's aerial army.

In the deadliest days of the Battle of Britain, the Luftwaffe had
struck each target with more than a hundred bombers. At Pearl
Harbor, Admiral Yamamoto had sent in two waves of aircraft, each
of 180 bombers and fighters. At Nadzab, there would be revetments and hardstands for more than five hundred warplanes.

At Nadzab, Fifth Air Force warplanes were shedding their camouflage.[2] There was a flying circus on the tarmac, the gleaming
new P-38s flown by Dick Bong and Tommy Lynch, General Kenney's favorite aces.

Bong's and Lynch's P-38Js were fresh from the Lockheed works
in Burbank. Bong trimmed his plane in red—wingtips, stabilizers,
nose, and propeller spinners. Lynch put black-and-white stripes on
his tail, wings and spinners, and painted snarling tigers' mouths
around his air intakes. Yet the paint was not what airmen remarked—
"it was the uncustomary brightness of natural metal," Bill Yenne
has written.

> In World War I, when the pilots of Baron von Richthofen's
> Jagdgeschwader I had started painting their aircraft in
> garish colors, they earned the appellation "Flying Circus."
> Those who saw Lynch and Bong, with their brighter-than-
> normal Lightnings, revived the term, and the pair of aces
> became the V Fighter Command's two-man "Flying Circus."[3]

Surrounding the airfields were broad cities of tents, laid out in quadrangles, each square-cornered tent rising to a central peak. There was a bustling PX. There was a full hospital, the Army's 117th Station Hospital, run by a scion of the Mayo family, and an outdoor theater that could seat thousands of servicemen (John Wayne's troupe had been the first show on that stage). Airfield construction battalions had pushed a road through to Lae on the coast, twenty miles away, to a huge new pier and new warehouses and massive fuel tanks, and then built a pipeline beside the road.[4]

The setting was spectacular. The notes of a correspondent in George Kenney's entourage reveal all the color that black-and-white photos of the war drain out.

> The very peaks are draped with white clouds, and this was on the best day, General Kenney remarked, on which he has ever come over "The Hump." Mr. Rawlings, Saturday Evening Post correspondent, pointed out "the rumpled faded green carpet hills" which are the foothills to the high ranges flanking the Markham Valley. The combination of these folded hills covered with knee deep green grass from some angles and waist deep green from others and barely covered with green from yet other angles, with the towering black monsters behind them, is most effective.
>
> The wide stretch of the Markham Valley is spread over by Nadzab strips, Nadzab airplanes. . . . The great air set-up is neatly arranged, and no attempt has been made at camouflage. It is far better fixed than Moresby and is a giant mushroom city of cardboard and copper wire and canvas.
>
> Hot, very, around midday; cool enough at night for a blanket. The clouds pile in at dusk, and are usually oozing about underneath the mountain peaks for hours after daybreak. The river itself is a sprawling wide thing, yellow colored and with patches of brown bed showing every few yards.[5]

Another airman was more rhapsodic. He felt that the Markham Valley was more beautiful than the Shenandoah:

The planes flew virtually at tree top level, skimming across knolls and statuesque solitary coconut palms, surrounded by kunai grass as tall and taller than a man. On the mountain sides we spotted a few native villages of three or four council houses of the Iroquois American Indian type. No natives were visible at any time. From the air the panorama unfurled like a travelogue. . . . The only thing missing was the giraffes.[6]

With rough cabins and tents pitched among trees, parts of Nadzab looked like a Boy Scout camp. The operations shack was an old Lutheran mission schoolroom, with a grass-thatched roof. At the airfields, men lashed together logs to build control towers and flight controllers clambered up on rickety rung ladders.

Other parts of Nadzab looked like a frontier boomtown, a place knocked together from cheap lumber and 55-gallon drums. The officers and enlisted men scrounged plywood and pool tables and bars for their clubs and tacked up girlie pictures and mirrors. The barbershop offered screen windows and a homemade barber chair. At the open-air theater, the audience sat on crates and bombcasings and the stage's backdrop and hangings were made from parachute silk. There were softball fields, and a newspaper, and service bands, and visiting celebrities. If there were Japanese soldiers sneaking into the chow lines at Nadzab, they must have figured they would pass unnoticed in the crowd.

As at summer camp, new arrivals were happy to settle down in comfort. Veterans of the early days at Moresby recalled their sleepless nights there, the long-running show of Japanese bombers and spotlights and antiaircraft fire, and mused that the war had lost its punch. Men also sensed that the respite of life at Nadzab was temporary. Officers thought that they would move on in four months. The Navy had demolished the Japanese citadel at Truk, so the war in the islands above Australia was probably over. Likely the next move would be to the Philippines.[7]

Rocky heard no more of the rumor that the Fifth Air Force brass had a swimming pool—there may have been only a swimming hole created by a dam in the river. He did not complain again about mess hall food. He had learned that some airmen ate much worse than he did: there were radar station outposts where rations were pitched heavily out of a C-47 and the food was so bad that men came down with jaundice.[8] He found life at Nadzab could be comfortable. At the same time, he noted, with the rest of the headquarters staff, that some of the officers at Nadzab lived more comfortably than others.

> Went to ADVON headquarters and found all buildings with screen wire and concrete floors. It is rumored that the general's house, which has a large screened porch around it, also has chrome plumbing. How those higher headquarters do suffer. And as yet our mess hall has no concrete floor. Today I heard a major in our unit griping over the fact he wasn't to have a concrete floor in his tent whereas all the majors in other units had them. Lieutenant Colonels Darnell and Smith are having a 30' x 15' building constructed for their quarters whereas everyone else sleeps in tents. None of the headquarters buildings have been completed even though an advanced echelon has been in the area for three weeks. The Wing HQ building was once almost constructed when it fell over as dominos will.[9]

Rocky had heard of scorn directed at Fifth Air Force staff. "It is being said that when the enlisted men of a certain engineer company completed the officers' club at ADVON Headquarters, they all canceled their war bond allotments."[10]

Some officers thought precautions were being neglected. Others thought that the privileges of rank had been pushed too far. "One fellow stated that if the Japs only knew it, they could send a plane down the Markham Valley and down several transports any day in the week. Another added he wished to hell a Jap did come down the valley and blow up the goddam general's house."[11]

Like other boomtowns, Nadzab had labor problems. The protests were louder than at Moresby. In a night-fighter squadron, a typed manifesto of enlisted men's demands was posted. After calling for "fair play," the proclamation fired off a list of grievances:

> Officers must have their latrine first. Officer tents are erected in advantageous positions. Officers have special washstands constructed by the enlisted men at the expense of work hours required more urgently elsewhere. Officers grab the showers first. Officers use squadron tools and equipment for personal use. Officers take a jeep to themselves. Officers' attempts to have enlisted men, gunners, and cook's helpers wait on them in tent and at table. Officers have uttered threats to shoot enlisted men found within the area of the officers' tent.[12]

The airmen of Nadzab were particularly disgruntled about their latrines. East of the Owen Stanleys, where troops and planes were assembling to fight the Japanese, latrines and sanitation were caught in a garish new light. Nadzab was notorious for both mud and dust. Slogging through mud and coughing out dust, men had been forced to dig cesspools for their squadrons—enough cesspools for an entire aerial army.

Even more than waiting at table—even more than lieutenants resenting higher officers' cement floors and wooden cabins—enlisted men resented digging latrines and building showers for officers. Men quarreled over latrines because latrines were of prime importance in the tropics. The historians of the Air Force

Medical Service later wrote: "Without doubt, the screening of latrines, plus the proper construction of latrine boxes, was the most important sanitary measure that could be carried out."[13] As the war moved northward, onto coral islands where troops were crowded into beachheads, it would be over latrines and plumbing that tempers would increasingly flare.

There was another level of enlisted labor about which less was said. At Nadzab, the black service troops of the Southwest Pacific, engineers and quartermasters, the black troops on motorcycles who had met Rocky's outfit on the airstrip, had built on a heroic scale. They had laid down the Marston matting of the airstrips and the gravel highway to Lae. They unloaded the C-47s into which Kenney's airmen stuffed their jeeps. When a crash-landing plane chewed up the Marston matting, they dashed in and cut out the jagged strips of metal and patched in new matting so that the next flight could land. The black engineers lacked heavy equipment and had to beg it from white engineer units. They had bolt-action Springfield rifles; white soldiers had new Garand semi-automatics. They worked under white officers who had been exiled from Brisbane—officers who didn't bust sergeants who ruined equipment, or who cursed at them on parade, or shot themselves.

The black engineers were not being granted leave in Australia, not since they had brawled with white infantrymen. The airstrips were the only place where they could drive trucks or motorcycles freely; on military roads, MPs pulled them over, often, for speeding. But nonetheless, where the black engineers and quartermasters went, planes were unloaded on the double, and warehouses went up, and roads and runways stretched out until they could handle the traffic of the war. And if the Japanese had attacked in force—sent in a raid that was more than a lone airplane dropping a bomb that wounded a lone black man—the black air base security battalion would have been among the servicemen running to the antiaircraft guns.[14]

Colonel Sams was back at the 71st Group. He flew back and forth along the eastern slopes of the mountains, whirling from squadron to squadron, storming into operations tents. At Gusap, he thought young Captain Lonigan lacked the experience to command. "I arrived to live with the 1101th," he wrote, "and have hopes of straightening out the squadron. Secured water pump, cement, two portable buildings and generally put my nose into everything." At Nadzab, he transferred a master sergeant, a tech sergeant, a lieutenant, "and raised sundry other hell."

During Sams' whirlwind five-day inspection tour, he was flying a P-39, not the B-25 that had been issued to him as Group commander. When he returned to Nadzab, he learned that his bomber was missing. Amid the bustle of the move over the hump, with personnel shuttling back and forth between bases, the plane had been missing for three days already. That meant Sams was missing seven airmen who had been on board the bomber—two sergeants, one corporal, one new pilot, one freshly minted West Pointer, his operations officer, and his dentist.

> Dixon, Meyerhein and Seitz are reported as missing on a plane from Dobodura. Seitz once told me he wanted to have another child before coming overseas and maybe it would be a boy because he, Seitz, might not come back.[15]

Three of Rocky's friends were dead: Dixon, Seitz and Meyerhein, people with whom he spent time and talked—and Butch Dixon, with whom Rocky had driven around Port Moresby and slouched through staff meetings, had been the pilot flying. The evening that he learned about the crash, Rocky did not write much. What the day meant to him stands out less in his two sentences on the plane crash than in the fact that he said no more about it. Nor, in fact, could anyone have discussed the crash, except by conjecture. Nothing was known about the crash, nor has anything ever been learned about it.

Colonel Sams opened an investigation, but he blamed Dixon. Sams had issued orders not to fly without a qualified copilot; Dixon had violated them. Sams regretted Meyerhein's death, "for he was afraid of flying and did so only from a sense of duty."[16]

Dixon had scheduled a flight from Dobodura to Gusap. The Missing Air Crew Report mentions one witness: the flight surgeon for the 17th Squadron, standing line duty on the airstrip that day, who saw Dixon take off in Sams' B-25. He saw nothing worth reporting. The weather conditions say more: "low ceiling, and rain along the route."[17]

By February, it was the middle of the rainy season. The Army had cautioned soldiers about rain in the tropics.

> When it rains in the islands it really does rain, even though the downpour doesn't usually last long. You can hear the rain coming from a long way off, heavy and dull just as if someone had turned on a whole lot of shower baths, and when it hits it is like a wall of water.[18]

In the air, the rain fronts were deadly. It was not simply that the weather hid the mountains; the battlements of cloud were as treacherous and lethal as a minefield. Osmar White once got out of a transport plane and counted thirty rivets popped out of the port wing by air currents en route.[19] The route that looked safest might actually pose greater dangers. An experienced pilot explained what it was like inside a squall:

> There would be dark, dark columns and light columns, and we would head for the light columns. It was the natural thing to do. Well, that was the worst thing that you could do, because that's where the shear factor, of the updrafts and downdrafts, was at its maximum. That's why it looked light. Whereas, heading into the darkest part of the cloud was the safest.[20]

Gen. Ennis Whitehead penned a grave, intense narrative of what could happen inside the cloud banks of New Guinea. Whitehead had determined to test the flying skills of Lt. Col. Arthur Rogers (the 90th Bomb Group commander whom he would later ship home). Whitehead checked out a bomber, had Rogers take the controls, and ordered him into the weather.

> There was a layer of middle cloud and Rogers walked into it. He hit turbulent air and turned back and pulled out of it. Our gross weight at take-off was approximately 64,000 pounds. Despite his first experience in [the] turbulence, he pushed in on instruments again and hit extremely turbulent air. As soon as the turbulence began, he started a 180 degree turn. . . . In a few seconds we had a rate of descent of 3,000 feet per minute and an indicated airspeed of 230 miles per hour. The copilot was obviously quite frightened but did cut the throttles to [idle]. I talked to Rogers, giving him his indicated air speed, his rate of descent, and kept repeating the old formula, "Center the needle and then center the ball." He did this just before we hit an [updraft] that gave us a rate of ascent of a little over 3,000 feet per minute.[21]

Centering the needle (on the turn-and-bank indicator) was to ensure that the aircraft was flying straight. Centering the ball ensured that the plane was flying level, that neither the right nor the left wing was lower. Watching the airspeed was the best way to ensure that the plane was not diving or climbing. Unless the plane were flying straight and level, the gyrocompass and artificial horizon would be worthless—and the plane would even more readily be knocked or spun around by currents of air.[22] It would be hard for any pilot to maintain this balance, to respond to the updrafts and downdrafts about his plane, while at the same time flying a safe course through clouds and over mountains.

Whitehead's account of flying through a cloud bank is remarkable for its sangfroid. In the tight, precise tone of his sentences, the flat understatement of an experienced pilot describing a deadly hazard, one can detect the alarm that has been carefully pressed out of the words.

Even Colonel Rogers of the Jolly Rogers could be battered by the turbulent weather of New Guinea—even when he had Ennis Whitehead for a flight coach and a copilot who knew when to cut the engines. Whitehead's narrative is a cautionary tale. It warns of what likely happened that rainy February day, inside Colonel Sams' B-25: of an instant when the bomber became unstable, when instruments became worthless, when air currents shifted violently, where a copilot did not know enough to help. Whatever Lieutenant Dixon encountered in the wet, gray weather above the low ceiling, it overmastered him.

§

Colonel Hutchison was putting together Wing command, preparing to hand off Wing command, and preparing to take over an air task force (which he knew would be folded into the 308th Bombardment Wing). It was a task he knew well. He had first mastered it in Colorado, when he went as CO to an airfield outside Colorado Springs. In the first months of the war, commanding an air base had usually meant building the air base.

> Personnel often moved into an air base long before completion of even the most essential facilities. In such a case, training might be conducted under canvas with construction proceeding on all sides, the instructor in his lecture competing with the noise of hammers and concrete mixers as well as of the ubiquitous trainer "buzzing" the field. Flying would begin with the completion of a single runway. Thereafter heavy construction equipment became an impediment to flying, the movement of aircraft and fuel trucks an impediment to the contractor's job. . . . A

field became alternatively a dust bowl or a morass with each change in weather. Primitive living conditions, make-shift classrooms, and overcrowded shops remained characteristic.[23]

Carpenters were working on Hutchison's quarters. At the Wing command site, HQ offices were being hammered together, plywood sheets over frames of two-by-fours, screen wire and burlap in the windows. There were plenty of bulletin boards and folding chairs; men were nailing together bomb crate lids and two-by-fours to make tables. Rocky commented:

> Routine—dull—boring—and damn the typewriters. Captain Cummins has worked two whole weeks on a saw-mill which is no doubt a great weapon to be used against the Japs.[24]

But Cummins' sawmill had its uses—not as a weapon of war, but as an engine of commerce. At Nadzab, to control a sawmill was to hold a stake in the growth of the vast tent city. As airmen felled timber to improve their camps, any sawmill proprietor could keep, as a fee for milling the timber into lumber, fifty percent of all the cuttings.[25] Cummins' sawmill brought in lumber for the Wing, which could be used for senior officers' quarters or could be traded for liquor, which in turn could be traded for generators or refrigerators or comestibles or the use of a bulldozer.

Squadrons arrived from the Sixth Photo Group, Hutchison's old command. In the Sixth Photo Group, there were bona fide heroes: reconnaissance flyers Arthur Post and Alex Guerry, from the Eighth Photo Reconnaissance Squadron. Post and Guerry were skilled pilots with hard-earned medals on their chests and dozens of missions under their belts; six weeks before, on a stateside war bond tour, they had strolled with starlets on their arms. Post had been shot down over Rabaul, escaped into the jungle, and been rescued by a Navy submarine; Guerry had power-dived through a flock of Japanese fighters, scattered them, made it home, and been written up in *Reader's Digest*.[26] Rocky listened to them when they talked—did it help that Major Guerry was also an SAE brother?—and heard Guerry laugh off the articles. "The story goes, he acted as if he had guns in the plane and chased a Jap plane into the sea. But according to the Major's personal story—when he was jumped by the Japs, 'I dove fast—and really got my ass home—and to hell with those Japs.'"[27]

For his adjutant, Hutchison had picked a 71st Group man, Rocky's former tent-mate Captain Williams. Williams did not inspire confidence, however, and Hutchison doubted him.

> During December it was reported a native was killed up along Salamaua and Lieutenant G___ of the 82nd Squadron was held responsible and was confined to quarters, where he has been sitting ever since. Evidently another letter came today asking why a court-martial hadn't met. Colonel Hutchison called Captain Williams who evidently had lost the original letter, and asked "Why in the hell haven't you done something? You've let a good pilot sit around for two months."[28]

Within Wing HQ, the pressure did not slacken, and tension went beyond commanders' rivalries. Hutchison used his authority when he could. He also exercised the privileges of rank.

> Everyone is griping because last night when 10 p.m. came at which time to shut off the generator which furnishes lights to the camp area and is located in same, Colonel Hutchison yelled from his tent where he was playing poker, "Turn on that fucking generator," and until 2 a.m. the colonel continued to play while the men couldn't sleep—but that's a colonel's privilege.[29]

Colonel Hutchison found fault with Wing communications. Since he returned, no more had been heard of the communications plans that Rocky had drawn up for Colonel Sams. Hutchison had been a base signal officer himself once, and he had his own ideas about what he wanted. In the Wing, the phone system and radio nets were not yet operational—bad news for the communications officer, but Rocky had been hamstrung by a lack of resources. He had no men to do the work and had to beg telephone wire from units that had telephone wire.

> Colonel Hutchison wrote a letter to the ADVON Chief of Staff stating that in all his Army career he had never seen such a deplorable communications system. Result: the ADVON sent a captain over to see me to see what the trouble was, and learned I had no one in my section, nor was authorized a section, had to bum my line, etc. Yesterday I asked for six linemen, Major Tockstein wrote the order and I received five draftsmen and one clerk.[30]

It was hard for Rocky to read his new CO, and the experience was not pleasant. In the meantime, Rocky's own men were causing further problems.

> Sergeant Palermo is being sent on a ten-day rest furlough. Reason: last night he was on the teletype machine and wouldn't permit traffic to move, he merely chattered on the machine. This is the first time he has ever been out of the way as an operator, and it came on quite suddenly.[31]

The furlough did not start soon enough. The next day, Rocky's teletype man had a complete breakdown.

> Sergeant Palermo has been placed in a psychological ward. Captain Doyle (A-2 intelligence section) states that

most of the mental cases start by the victims believing they are overworked.[32]

Sergeant Palermo's collapse raised unhappy questions about the pressures of the war and the limits of therapy. Nobody wanted communications tied up; nobody wanted a trained teletype operator sent to a psych ward; everybody could complain of being overworked; and nobody was going home.

Giving Rocky five draftsmen and a clerk had not been enough to get the phone lines strung. Colonel Hutchison called again, and again a staff officer came running.

> Colonel Hutchison wrote the chief of staff at ADVON and stated that in all his years in the Army, he had never seen communications in such a deplorable condition. As a result, Lieutenant Colonel Bestic of ADVON sent Captain Daroff over to straighten things out. He came—period.
>
> Word of General Patton striking a soldier in Italy has come in and the men have received it with mixed feelings.[33]

When Colonel Hutchison said that Wing communications were deplorable, Rocky took that personally. He knew that a first lieutenant would not likely win any argument with a colonel. He resented that Hutchison could get him in trouble, and that Hutchison's lackey Major Tockstein would not get him the linemen he needed. He resented that his teletype operator had picked this particular minute to go crazy. He resented staff officers looking over his shoulder for failures, and meantime doing nothing to straighten out his problems.

Rocky's resentment was masked thoroughly, but not completely. In the dialect of the American Midwest, hard feelings are expressed in oblique comments, and he had been reared by parents who preferred silence and sarcasm to complaint and discussion. Nonetheless, the bitterness is there. Rocky's feelings about the situation in Nadzab come through in his comment about the overseas news. There was plenty of good news from the war fronts as winter ended: Russian advances, European bombing offensives, the Navy's raids on the Marianas, a successful strike against Rabaul.[34] Rocky mentioned none of this. Instead, he mentioned George Patton slapping a soldier in Italy. What was on his mind that day was a soldier being mistreated by a commander.

At the end of February, as the Allies prepared to move northward, there came reminders that the war remained to be won. The 25th Photo Squadron returned from a successful mission to the Japanese base at Hollandia. "The pictures showed nearly two hundred bombers and sixty fighters on an airstrip without a single bomb crater, within 530 miles of our camp. The rumor quickly got around and some of the men it is reported started digging foxholes."[35] Allied momentum built; the start of the campaign was measured by circling warplanes and empty runways. "Planes have been overhead off and on all day," Rocky noted. And then, as if thinking that so many flights might spot something in the mountains, he added, "No report from Dixon, Meyerhein, or Seitz."[36]

> Major Crouch flew over the Admiralty Islands to take pictures in spite of the weather. He returned two hours overdue. It became known late this afternoon the landing on the Admiralty Islands will take place tomorrow which is a month or two ahead of schedule. At first some thought we would attack Hollandia first and then go on to Manus Island. If the Japs knew of our attacks and counterattack with strikes we would be in simple words, in one hell of a mess. It is rumored that every plane in New Guinea will be off the ground tomorrow.[37]

Sixty miles north, at Gusap, the Japanese raided in daylight. A flight of Japanese fighters flashed across Strip Number Five at lunchtime—four fighters, two passes, and then they roared out of sight. The 110th Squadron climbed out of their slit trenches and hunted down the damage: one bullet-hole in a P-39, a handful of bullets dug up in the engineering tent, a ragged row of holes in the operations shack.[38]

Over Nadzab, during the daylight, Allied planes were the only planes in the sky. Men began to discount the risk of attack by the enemy. There was a three-shot alert in the middle of the night, warning of an air raid; no one got out of bed. A bulletin board warned that the Japanese were expected to attack within two days: "Only the eager ones carried their helmets," Rocky wrote.[39]

> Had another Red Alert last night—rather early this morning. We were awakened by the thud of guns and the noise of the flares. On paper everyone is supposed to dress, take their gas mask and gun to their respective foxholes and remain there until the alert is over. When the alert occurred, the sky was clear and the moon was out. Everything was quiet. A few of the more eager ones went to their foxholes, while several, including myself, cursed the noise and went back to sleep.[40]

Rumor had it that there were still 220 Japanese warplanes at Hollandia and another 200 on Wakde Island, also within easy range of Nadzab. A counter-rumor, which justified men who rolled over and went back to sleep instead of diving for shelter, was that the Japanese lacked aviation gas.[41]

Junior officers continued to gripe, among themselves, about their commander. Lieutenant Kepler told Lieutenant Boyer that Colonel Hutchison had given an aerial tour of the war zone to a personal friend, "a maritime inspector" from Milne Bay.[42]

(Hutchison might have pointed out how useful it would be, given the supplies now being brought to Nadzab from the port at Lae, to befriend Navy men at the huge Milne Bay entrepot.) Enlisted men and captains chimed in.

> Colonel Hutchison's house is almost completed with its three rooms, built-in showers and water flushed toilet. All outside walls of the house are screen wire. Corporal Jenkins who was installing the lights said: "Why does he have such a fine place when we enlisted men have no light nor even floors in our tents? But then too, if I were a colonel, I would have the same thing." Captain Jack Chapin said he saw a teletype message from one brigadier general to another general which said: "Brad, I have a nice long drive up to my house and I do not have a car to get up and down the hill. What can you do about it?"
>
> No one seems to respect Colonel Hutchison. Many report he will not back up his own men and is merely a politician. Today the electrician came and said the colonel wanted 220 volts to his tent in order to operate his refrigerator—so now we must get a transformer from somewhere to get 220 volts. The colonel will also have an electric stove in his four-room house and will not eat at the officers' mess.
>
> Because the officers' mess is not completed, the officers are eating with the men. The officers' hours are 0730–0815 at breakfast. Often Colonel Hutchison comes at 0900 and jumps on the mess sergeant for not having hot food.[43]

At the officers' club, the mess officer had not met the operating schedule and was not staying within budget. On March 28, Rocky wrote:

> Last month our officers' mess officer said the club would open on March 15th and then he took off for Brisbane with £2 from each officer to buy liquor—he returned last week with more promises about wine, ice cream, the type of service etc. and asked for an additional £5.[44]

There was more troubling news. Australia was going to be put out of reach, people said. "It is rumored that Port Moresby will soon be made a rest center and troops will not be sent to Australia on leave. It is a known fact the leave ship has stopped running."[45]

Chaplain Smith was at Nadzab. He had been spending his time at Dobodura with the 82nd Squadron. He helped with the baseball and swimming programs, and the squadron photographer caught him standing in the door of the Victory Chapel. Smith was thinner than he had been before shipping out, looking less hearty perhaps, but younger—still one of the tallest officers.[46]

> Chaplain Smith is transferring out of the 71st Group to an Air Engineering Outfit. The chaplain at first welcomed the change because he and Colonel Sams never got along. But two days ago he learned that Fifth Air Force knew nothing of the move; evidently ADVON is arranging the transfer. Now the chaplain believes he is being moved to a front-line outfit as a result of his reporting the colonel's action at Fifth Bomber Command. If true, this backs up the reports that the CO of the 90th Bomb Group said that the chaplain would be reassigned.[47]

Rocky was also switching units; the Wing Table of Organization had caught up with him. A genuine Signal Corps lieutenant had been found to serve as signal officer for the Wing, and an Air Corps major had been found to fill the major's slot that Wing communications officer called for.[48]

Rocky never spoke of being demoted. Nor did he ever discuss how, within weeks, he was made a Wing communications officer once more—so either he was quickly restored to favor or he was deftly shuffled sideways. He did comment obliquely, by quoting a live-wire clown: "Corporal Dare, motor pool noncom, said he overheard a second lieutenant say that his job called for a major and he hopes the war will last enough until he gets it."[49]

"Lots and lots of new rumors," Rocky observed. There were so many that he began to categorize them. "From the military standpoint, Wewak is out of commission but everyone expects our next move to be against Tadji"—then again, the bombers seemed ready to hit Hollandia, or maybe Wakde Island.[50] Meantime, news from the war meant accounts of "friendly fire."

> Reported that the 82nd Squadron shot up two Navy PT Boats, one Navy barge and one Marine barge today. Kepler said the 90th Bomb Squadron sank an American sub some time ago and that's why the order has been not to make passes at subs. It is reported a B-24 of the Bomber Command made a recco flight up to the Philippines for the first time. Their plane was out for twenty-two hours. The other night the 90th Bomb Group made a strike on the Hollandia air strip with several other squadrons and they missed their whole target area and only two bomb craters could be spotted on the five fields.[51]

From the nonmilitary standpoint, the most interesting scuttlebutt was neurosis in the headquarters staff.

> Several of the high-ranking young officers in ADVON were pilots in the Philippines and though many were once perfect, they are now what we called a little bit off!

One who is A-4 logistics officer of Fifth Air Force stands up on his desk several minutes of the day because it helps him think better.

Major Crouch, West Point, has been a major since '42 and his name should be spelled with a "G." He went to the latrine yesterday and found an enlisted man over one of the four holes, and the major waited outside the latrine until the enlisted man came out.[52]

Women had arrived at Nadzab, Army nurses for the hospital. They arrived bearing a heavy burden of malicious gossip.

Lieutenant Powell told a story tonight, when we were talking, about the nurses' quarters over at ADVON which were miles from the nearest hospital (evidently for airborne nurses). Out at Moresby, only two elements had a sewage system, the General and the Red Cross girls. The system once became inoperative and upon cleaning it, the workers found the equivalent of three bushel baskets full of used condoms.[53]

Envy of commanders was common, in the sense of universal. Slanders on the virtue of WACs, Army nurses, and Red Cross girls were common, in every sense. Far from home, their plans and careers disrupted, their lives put at risk by the chances of war, servicemen "clung more tightly to the women they loved and remembered," Ann Elizabeth Pfau has perceptively written. Equally—and unfortunately—servicemen also turned against women in uniform a long-nurtured resentment of their own hardships: WACs and nurses "represented the possibility of female independence at a time when men were particularly dependent on women's affection."[54]

Red Cross girls had not reached the Markham Valley front. For Nadzab, the Red Cross wanted to set up a "post club" the size of a mess hall, located near the landing strip. General Whitehead frowned at this and emphatically scrawled: "We will have day rooms at Nadzab *but no clubs.*" To the Red Cross, he snapped back:

> We have our camp areas separated from the airdromes as much as transportation permits because airdromes are normally the principal targets of enemy bombing attacks. Furthermore, when our men are at the airdromes they are on duty. There are always some who take undue advantage of any "loafing" facilities afforded them. We cannot, therefore, mix recreational facilities and duty in the airdrome area.
>
> I hope you will realize that we are engaged in a war of movement. I expect this movement forward to be accelerated. The faster we move forward, the sooner this war will be won.[55]

Airmen would have to make do with the tea brewed on primus stoves by Australian YMCA teams, volunteers who had been at Nadzab since the earliest weeks.[56]

The United States Navy had arrived at Nadzab, too: a squadron of long-range patrol bombers from the Solomons. The Navy pilots were soon telling the same stories as Fifth Air Corps pilots—about flying eight hundred miles to bomb airdromes in China, and trips home when they threw out guns and cameras and oxygen bottles and reached the field with twenty scant gallons of gas in the tanks. Then there were stories about earlier battles.

> The Navy's communications officer who was in the battle of Midway said they torpedoed the Japs at masthead height at 150 yards in PBYs. When they were ordered on the mission they received the following introduction, "We are very sorry that we have to order you to do this but we've got to hit them with everything we've got"— and they did.[57]

Particulars of the fighting at Midway had been slow to reach the public. In New Guinea, in 1944, the best way to learn what had happened at Midway would still have been to ask an aviator who had flown there. Perhaps in conversation one might learn how a doomed attack had been made at masthead height, or other details of how a friend had died.

The officers' club opened a month late. The first night the cooks offered real potatoes and ice cream.[58] The club opened in time to welcome the officers of the 91st Reconnaissance Group, stepping out of a B-17 from Australia—six full colonels among them, Lieutenant Foliart told Lieutenant Boyer.[59] It was not only junior officers who saw how top-heavy this made things. Rocky reported: "The high rank is arriving with a full colonel in its A-3 operations area and to quote Major Guerry (the major has been acting A-3 operations officer and his father's president of Sewanee College), 'Damn it. I could have controlled a lieutenant colonel but not a full colonel.'"[60]

There were hopes for consolation. They had been in New Guinea for five months now, they could think about leave, and Foliart had been putting together plans.

> Foliart said today everything is going to be all right at Sydney. He reports that Lieutenant Hilgerson says that when you get to Sydney, contact the Red Cross girls, who, realizing what the Americans from New Guinea want, "fix" the fellows up with dates who are willing to give the Americans what they want. Foliart also said that around Macquarie, the rest area, there were lots of married women who were also willing.[61]

Previous rumors had been false; airmen were still traveling to Australia—and even for Rocky and Foliart and other non-flying officers, the idea of leave in Sydney was becoming more than a daydream. Hilgerson was a gaunt, bespectacled old man of twenty-five. If he spoke from experience, and spoke well of his experience, it boded well for anyone else. In Nadzab, meantime, there were signs that a new campaign in the air war was building. Rocky's friends the Wing meteorologists had finally been overwhelmed: "The weather section, which has been working twenty hours per day, broke last night when Jensen became ill and Foster said what the hell." And yet their work had been successful: the Fifth Air Force had raided the Japanese airstrips at Hollandia. "Reported 1/3 of the planes there we destroyed whereas we lost none. This raid's success was far different from the first."[62]

11

FROM MINIMUM ALTITUDE

After the war, when Rocky and Margaret Anne were graduate students in Bloomington, Rocky's sister Anndora visited their apartment. While she was there, by happenstance, there was a sudden roar, a light airplane zooming low above campus. In the same second she heard the plane buzz, she saw her brother dive for the floor, hands caging his head. This was two years, at least, after Rocky came back from the Pacific.

Rocky was working on a doctorate in psychology, in a department that B. F. Skinner had run. He himself would have explained his dive for the floor as respondent behavior, an action triggered by a stimulus. That much anyone might understand. What others would not have understood so well was the conditioning behind the response. It was not only Japanese aircraft that Rocky had learned to fear—he had learned to fear American aircraft as well—and there was more than one way in which the recklessness of American pilots would follow him home.

When Rocky talked about the war, he never spoke in terms of glamour. The 110th Squadron called itself the Flying Musketeers, and the 71st Group called itself the Strafin' Saints, but those were nicknames that Rocky never used. Nor did he speak of airmen's conduct in terms of bravery. He spoke well of pilots who watched out for their wingmen, and was glad to remember enlisted men he knew who held a position until morning when no one would have blamed them for clearing out during the night.

There was one squadron in the Group that flew as if there were something glamorous in combat. The 17th Tactical Reconnaissance Squadron, under Maj. William Tennille, bore the official sobriquet of the Wreckoneers. More often, they employed another nickname: they called themselves the Fighting Seventeenth.

The 17th Tactical Reconnaissance Squadron, with its B-25s, had arrived in New Guinea during January. On January 28, 1944, a Friday, the squadron flew its first mission, a reconnaissance over the Bismarck Sea. Nothing was sighted, but the squadron was unfazed. At month's end, the squadron history reported: "All missions have been successfully accomplished but to date no exceptionally

"Little Joe," a B-25 from the 17th Squadron, stenciled with a war's worth of bombs for missions flown, profiles of ships sunk, and a Japanese plane to mark a combat victory
Courtesy of Eastern Oregon University, Pierce Library, Fred Hill World War II Photograph Collection. Taken and donated by Fred Hill.

*On an antiaircraft gun captured by Australian forces
near Hansa Bay, Japanese gunners painted stencils of
Allied warplanes to mark aircraft that they had shot
down. Some may represent planes from the 71st Group.*
Australian War Memorial, Photo 075932

important sightings have been made. Particularly since we commenced active operations the morale of the Squadron personnel
has been particularly high."[1]

On their seventh day of combat flying, February 3, the 17th
Squadron sighted and bombed two destroyers and a freighter.
They reported one direct hit and claimed that another bomb had
skipped completely over the target.[2]

Two days later, Capt. Bert Smiley's flight raided Muschu and
Kairiru Islands, far northwest, above Wewak. They bombed a
freighter and a gunboat, strafed barges and the shoreline, and
barely made it home. Lieutenant Pruitt's B-25 came back to Finschhafen with its top turret shot away, the gunner dead, its hydraulics full of holes, and the tail mangled. Lieutenant Young's plane

was hit eight times, once in a box of .50-caliber ammunition that caught fire and began to explode; the navigator grabbed a fire extinguisher and put out the flames before the plane shot itself down. Young's bomber limped home to Dobodura and crash-landed, a total loss. Captain Smiley's own plane was not hit but nearly crashed anyway: "[H]e spotted a barge which was strafed with such viciousness," his copilot wrote, cheerfully, "that we nearly piled into the side of the mountain."[3]

"Smiley somewhat put his neck out on this mission," Colonel Sams wrote. "Results good, price high."[4]

Two days later, the 17th Squadron paid a higher price. This time it was Major Tennille leading C Flight. At 2:15 in the afternoon, at Bunabun Harbor, thirty miles north of Madang, Tennille spotted five barges, "partially camouflaged," riding in the harbor. That the barges were in open water in broad daylight, and only partially camouflaged, suggests that they were bait. The flight roared down to masthead height.

Still in echelon formation the flight leveled off to an altitude of 100 feet from 1,500 feet and swept on the target. Approximately 80 to 100 yards from the shore where the partially camouflaged barges were located, bursts of A/A broke out from the center and both sides of the harbor. The fire from the side appeared to be heavy of 75 mm caliber, that from the center, medium of 40 mm caliber. The A/A came as a complete surprise and caught the flight completely off guard. The bursts were about 10 to 15 seconds duration. They were intense, medium and heavy and accurate. The lead plane was not hit, the center plane was first hit in the left and then also in the right engine. Both immediately burst into flames. The left wing was also hit as well as the fuselage which broke off at the tail assembly. The nose of the damaged ship fell into the water and began burning.[5]

The second plane was flown by Lieutenant Brown. With him died his copilot, navigator, and three gunners. Rocky wrote:

> During the last two days the 17th Bomber Squadron lost three planes. One exploded in air when hit by ground anti-aircraft or "ack-ack." Lieutenant Brown was the pilot and known and respected, by all, from the lowly to the righteous. The other two planes were shot up but made the return to the strip where they made an emergency landing.[6]

Colonel Sams heard the news, and listed the names of the officers he had lost. There was talk of converting the entire 71st Group to medium bombers; that would mean higher casualties. He looked

This reconnaissance photo, recording a glimpse of a hut and a bridge, shows how difficult it could be for American reconnaissance patrols to spot targets in enemy territory. Courtesy of Eastern Oregon University, Pierce Library, Fred Hill World War II Photograph Collection. Donated by Fred Hill.

in on the 17th Squadron during his flying tour, and his report was mixed. The squadron was having a streak of good luck—so far. Two flight leaders had each sunk a freighter, but he doubted one officer; the man had "no more sense than a jackrabbit."[7]

🌀

Major Tennille was the only officer in the 71st Group about whom there has hung any sort of legend, or reputation, or notoriety. Tennille was known as a hot pilot, a leader who dived into the attack, and a squadron commander who feuded with his group commander—qualities that made him popular with most of his men.

> "I would like to meet that pilot," commented Lt. Col. C. Darnell, who is known as one of the greatest P-38 Lightning pilots in the Southwest Pacific. He was speaking of the pilot of a fast-moving B-25 Mitchell medium bomber that went flashing past the Headquarters building, then pointing almost straight up, it streaked into the blue New Guinea sky.
>
> "He's the first pilot I've seen that can fly a B-25 like a P-38," said the Colonel, and that was no exaggeration, for every time a B-25 came roaring in low over our headquarters building, it was known to be Maj. William G. Tennille, Jr.
>
> Major Tennille was intent upon giving the Nips all they had coming to them, regardless of the danger involved. Many times he landed on jungle-cut strips to remain overnight, refuel, and then take off the next morning to give the Japs another dose of explosives. Under his leadership his squadron was fast building a reputation, with enemy barges sunk, ammunition dumps hit, and supply dumps left blazing.[8]

The low, roaring passes were not simply daredevil flying. They were contumacious retorts to authority. When Tennille's bomber was roaring overhead, it was because Colonel Sams had just chewed out Major Tennille. Whenever Sams chewed out Tennille, Tennille would buzz Sams' office tent. Each buzz shook up the tent and knocked down Sams' gear, people in the 17th Squadron said; it was good for a laugh on the old man.[9] To adorn its squadron history, the Fighting Seventeenth commissioned a portrait of its late commander. The portrait shows Tennille looming above a foreground scene, in which a B-25 is climbing steeply after buzzing a camp.

In February 1944, friction was building up, within the Group and within the Wing. Rocky heard of a command conference in which Sams seems to have been bushwhacked.

> Colonel Sams returned a few days ago only to find Colonel Hutchison and Major Tockstein in his tent. Two hours later Colonel Sams was gone.[10]

When a man is waylaid by his boss and his boss's minion, nothing congenial is afoot. No wonder Sams flew out as soon as he could reach the airstrip. Sams the group commander did not get along with his superior at the Wing. Neither did Major Tennille the squadron commander get along with his superior—Sams. Tennille is likely the unnamed 17th Squadron officer who Sams thought had no more sense than a jackrabbit.[11]

As much as Tennille, Sams was an aggressive leader. But unlike Tennille, Sams knew that as a commander he had to count losses and prevent them where he could. Sams could see that in two weeks of combat, Tennille had lost two bombers and nearly lost two more—and that the man seemed to be proud of that. Tennille had gone for the decoy barges at Bunabun Harbor and the hailstorm of Japanese flak had caught him by surprise. He turned in reports that called his B-25s "Rogers" ("five Rogers went on the mission"). This seemed to be aping the veteran 90th Bomb Group, with their Jolly Roger skull-and-crossed-bombs insignia and their sickening roster of casualties. Worse, Tennille was letting pilots take out bombers on solo visual reconnaissance missions, which was like letting men swim out alone to look for sharks.

Tennille's own officers were complaining about his recklessness. After the major swooped into the Japanese ambush that killed Brown, Tennille's copilot and navigator had asked to fly with a different pilot.[12] With that record, and that loss rate, someone had to knock some sense into the commander of the Fighting Seventeenth.

Tennille's men knew him as determined and insistent, "a 'Colonel-talking' CO if there ever was one."[13] On the squadron's way overseas, he had argued with base commanders until his men got passes and hotel rooms. He let any member of the squadron, not only officers, order viands and liquor for fat-cat flights. Most recently, to celebrate the second anniversary of the squadron's formation (and likely to take his airmen's minds off their casualties and wrecked bombers) he had thrown a party for the enlisted men, "complete from soup to nuts," with liquor and a band.[14] Carroll Anderson, a P-38 pilot and air historian, found that airmen from the 17th Squadron felt that their commander had spoken up even when it counted against him:

> Some knew he had been a major for a long time. . . . He had a knack for speaking up to the brass when it might have been expedient to remain quiet. Some of his men thought this was the reason he had been so long in grade.[15]

The men of the Fighting Seventeenth could think well of a commander who, like them, seemed at odds with authority. Moreover, behind the desire to take the war to the Japanese, Tennille and his men had something else in common: the hope of getting home soon. The air crews of the 17th Squadron believed that after two hundred hours of combat flying, the war in the Pacific would be

*Taken during an Allied air strike against the Japanese base at Madang, this reconnaissance photo was worked up by intelligence officers to highlight the features of that anchorage and its defenses. "W. R. C."
stands for W. R. Carpenter & Co., the Australian enterprise known for its copra plantations, company stores, and steamship lines.* Directorate of Intelligence, Allied Air Forces SWPA, in AFHRA archive

over for them. They would look back on this as naiveté, but it explains why they flew so many missions so soon. Their mission was "armed reconnaissance," as their squadron historian put it: "Name the mission and we will do it."[16]

෯

During the last week of February 1944, the 17th Squadron took on a curious, important mission. The Admiralty Islands, north of New Guinea and west of New Britain, offered the Allies great opportunities as the next objective on MacArthur's northward campaign. The Admiralties would be a gift to the Navy: sheltered between Manus Island and Los Negros Island was deepwater Seeadler Harbor, six miles wide and twenty miles long. The Japanese had used the Admiralties to ferry planes to their airfields on New Britain and the Solomons; capturing the islands would cut this route and isolate Rabaul. Taking the Admiralties would also allow the Allies to leapfrog past the Japanese army at Wewak and move forward along the New Guinea coast.[17]

The Army official history notes: "Kenney, who had experience in New Guinea with quick seizure of airfields by light forces, had a scheme in mind for another such operation"—a "reconnaissance in force" to seize Los Negros, with its airfield at Momote Point. With the Admiralties secured, Kenney wrote, "we could jump the next show up the New Guinea coast to Tadji or maybe even to Hollandia." MacArthur endorsed the suggestion; it put the cork in the bottle, he said.[18]

Kenney believed that the Japanese held the islands with a small garrison, or perhaps had secretly evacuated all of their troops. On February 23, seeking evidence to support this theory, Kenney sent reconnaissance planes over the Admiralties. The planes he chose were from the 17th Squadron.

For ninety minutes, three B-25s from the 17th Squadron circled over the Japanese airdromes on the Admiralties. They drew no flak and they saw no Japanese soldiers. Gradually, the bombers circled lower and lower, until they made a final pass at treetop level. "Nil signs of enemy activity," they reported. "No barges, no washing on the lines, no attempt to clear the doorway in front of the hospital at Lorengau wrecked by bombs, no detours around bomb craters on roads; grass was growing in the craters on both Lorengau and Momote strips."[19]

For the pilots and gunners in the B-25s, this was a tense, repetitive, endless exercise. They were daring the Japanese to shoot at them—and each time that the Japanese did not shoot, the bombers came back to taunt the enemy again. The air crews had no illusions about Japanese antiaircraft fire, not anymore; it was less than two weeks since they had seen the Japanese shoot Brown's plane in half. They knew that each time they flew lower, they became more vulnerable—targets for machine gunners, even for infantrymen with rifles. On their final pass, the bombers buzzed the Momote airstrip, roaring over enemy territory at the lunatic height of twenty feet. At this point, it was not only enemy gunfire that the airmen needed to fear: any bobble of wind or unseen radio aerial or twitch of a pilot's carpal tendon would have brought them down.[20]

The 17th Squadron's mission to the Admiralties on February 23 played an ironic role in the Pacific War. Because the flyers saw no Japanese activity, MacArthur brushed aside contrary reports from combat scouts and was persuaded to land troops on Los Negros. A thousand soldiers from the First Cavalry Division went ashore on February 29. They found at once that the Japanese were still there—enough of them to require a month of hard fighting. The conclusion that the Japanese had abandoned Los Negros was

Maj. William Grant Tennille, commander of the 17th Squadron. Tennille was said to fly his B-25 like a P-38, and the foreground shows him buzzing Fifth Air Force HQ at Nadzab—which he did frequently, particularly after quarreling with superiors.
From Strike! The Story of the Fighting 17th

a humiliating but ultimately fruitful error. Seeadler Harbor gave the Navy a splendid advanced base, a better anchorage than Simpson Harbor at Rabaul, and the capture of the Admiralties invigorated the Allied drive westward along the coast of New Guinea.

Six days after the mission, the Fighting Seventeenth prepared its report for the month of February. In discussing the Momote mission, the squadron historian was uncharacteristically sober. By the time this report was typed, the men of the 17th Squadron knew that they had been fooled twice over—by the Japanese and by themselves. The Japanese had been at Momote all the time: crews of antiaircraft gunners, maintaining absolute silence, discipline, and fire control. The flyers now knew that they had steeled themselves for combat and if they had met combat they would have died. They had come back alive from Momote only because their enemy saw advantage in letting them live.

The squadron historian concluded, defensively:

Our record for the month of February has been outstanding considering our planes for the most part go out on long over-water reconnaissance alone. . . . In fact other groups in this area refer to us as the "eager beavers." Perhaps we have been foolhardy at times, but we have had a fine record while learning a great deal. Some of the jobs we have tackled have been too big. But we know better now.[21]

⑤

Delta Graham, who had shot down the 71st Group's first Japanese plane, died on March 1, 1944, killed over the coast north of Madang. "Heavy anti-aircraft fire was observed in the vicinity of Nagada, which was accurate, intense, and heavy," Captain Elvin wrote. "An airplane flown by Lt. D. C. Graham was seen to snap-roll, recover, nose pulled up to avoid crashing, and a high-speed stall resulted, followed by a snap-roll and a crash into trees on the river bank south of Prinz Heinrich Harbor. His plane was observed by Lt Weinstein to explode and burn seconds after crashing."[22]

Lt. Maryan Zaleski, the five-foot-six pilot who had joined the 82nd Squadron, died on March 6, 1944. In February, after more than a year of combat flying, Zaleski had received the Distinguished Flying Cross, for "continuous operational flights."[23] On Monday, February 28, Zaleski buzzed the squadron at lunchtime. Doc Schafer wrote:

> Today, [while I was] sitting there with a mouth full of hash, a yellow-nosed P-39 suddenly roared down, came across the field almost touching the ground directly toward the mess hall. At the last moment he pulled up into a vertical climb, nipped the leaves and sent the tree tops thrashing. Many of us facing the outside almost fell off our benches and choked on the hash. Zeke (Zaleski) surely gave us a buzz job.[24]

The next Monday, Zaleski buzzed the squadron again. The moment was just as sudden and scary, and sadder. Succinctly and diplomatically, the squadron historian wrote: "1st Lt Maryan J. Zaleski crashed from minimum altitude near Horanda Airstrip shortly after take-off."[25]

Sergeant Ursprung laconically wrote: "Lt. Zaleski (Zero Zeke) crashed into the jungle while buzzing our engineering section."[26] There is a sardonic undertone here; Ursprung may have been one of the mechanics whom Zaleski was buzzing.

Colonel Sams added a postscript: "Zaleski crashed and burned just behind the strip. Poor chap had his 300 combat hours and would have gone home shortly."[27]

Usually, a pilot's death left no body to bury. For Zaleski a funeral was held. A truck carried the casket, covered with a flag, at the head of a string of jeeps. Six pilots were pallbearers. Chaplain Smith read the service, a squad of airmen fired three volleys, and a bugler played "Taps."[28]

Lieutenant Graham and Lieutenant Zaleski each received the Air Medal, posthumously. Zaleski's decoration came as an Oak Leaf Cluster, for he held the Air Medal already, as well as the Distinguished Flying Cross.[29] George Kenney had a policy of awarding medals whenever he could, because he could not give more tangible rewards: "I knew that little bits of pretty ribbon had helped in World War I," he wrote, "maybe they would help in this one, too."[30]

Lieutenant Colonel Croxton was dead now, too, killed in a plane crash. General Whitehead wrote the letter of condolence.[31]

Close calls continued. Lt. Warren Sparks of the 82nd Squadron nearly died during one strafing mission at Madang, chasing a convoy of Japanese trucks. The trucks spotted the P-39s and turned off the road into a coconut plantation. At low level, the palm fronds could not be seen through; only by climbing to three thousand feet and looking down from directly overhead could the pilots locate the parked trucks. Sparks recounted:

To attack, we had to come in at a very steep angle in order to keep the target in sight. . . . I started firing and only the left-hand .30s fired, throwing me off the target. I reached up and turned the wing guns off, got back on target and started firing. By that time, I should have already started to pull out of the dive. Realizing this, I pulled back sharply and the old 39 went into a high-speed stall and continued dropping, palm trees getting bigger and bigger. I eased back on the stick, got out of that stall, and then gently started to pull out knowing I was going to take the top off that palm tree and hoping I didn't get down far enough to hit the trunk of the tree. After I bounded off the trees, everything was still operating but I was getting a lot of vibration. After landing, damage was noted as large gashes in leading edge of wing and a slightly bent prop. There were at least three other instances during this period when other pilots topped a palm tree.[32]

Lieutenant Shomo also had two close calls. He toggled the landing gear switch instead of his flap switch—the same fool mistake that Gordon had made. Shomo scraped to a belly-landing on a drop tank of gasoline, on a steel Marston matting runway, but somehow his plane did not catch fire. The next day, over Madang, Shomo strafed a parked Zero; the plane blew up, and the explosion knocked his P-39 into the tree line. Yet again, thanks to luck or fate, Shomo made it safely back to base.[33]

The 82nd Squadron lost another pilot in these weeks, but the squadron did not know it yet. Lt. Harvey Landrum, with fifty-one missions under his belt, had gone on leave to Sydney. On March 22, on his way back, Landrum reached Port Moresby. With twenty-one other servicemen, he crowded on board a B-24 that was taking off for Nadzab. From Moresby to Nadzab was a forty-five-minute hop, so brief that men hitchhiking back to their outfits were willing to stand on the catwalk over the bomb-bay. The plane flew into the overcast and never emerged. Nothing more was certainly known for almost forty years, until the crash site was found and American forensic specialists identified the dead, listing Landrum among them.[34]

Lt. Mike Moffitt and another pilot were hunting barges off New Britain and decided to refuel at Cape Gloucester. They would give the ground crews an air show, they decided, and buzzed the runway for its full length—gave everyone a haircut, they called it. The Gloucester controller ordered them to land. When they stepped out of their cockpits, they found themselves facing Col. Robert Morrissey. As a young lieutenant, two years before, Morrissey had shot down the first Japanese fighter claimed by the 49th Fighter Group. He presently ranked high in Fifth Air Force fighter command and he was not amused. Morrissey ate around their asses, Moffitt said afterwards, and after that ass-chewing he never gave any more haircuts to colonels.[35]

At the end of March, the 110th Squadron lost a plane and a pilot. Richard Floyd Minton, from Orange County, Indiana, crashed his P-39 near the strip at Gusap. Minton was the youngest pilot in the outfit. Back in January, when Anderson vanished, Minton had been the pilot whom Anderson followed into the overcast while the rest of the flight circled around the cloud.

The squadron history said little. It reported that on March 29, 1944, Minton was "on a test hop," five miles south of Gusap, at 3:35 in the afternoon. "Cause unknown. Plane was last seen in vertical dive by unknown transport pilot. Plane was totally destroyed." Doc Schafer heard a different story—that Minton had done nine slow rolls over the runway, losing altitude, disappeared, and crashed a few miles away.[36]

Rocky heard more. Minton had been doing the "test hop" required after a plane had been serviced. In doing the slow rolls over the airdrome, Minton had been dipping his plane's wingtips in the kunai grass. The kunai grass stood six or seven feet tall, and it took no particular skill to dip one wingtip; any pilot could swoop down, level out, dip one wingtip, and then soar up again. Dipping one wingtip and then righting the plane and dipping the other wingtip took notably greater skill, because the pilot had to maintain speed throughout, while watching the terrain. A thoroughly reckless pilot might even attempt to dip one wingtip after another by doing a low-level barrel roll above the kunai—an airshow trick that could be completed only by an exceptionally skillful flyer. Minton had tried to dip both wingtips; he may even have tried to do the barrel-roll stunt. He was not an exceptionally skillful flyer, and it was even more reckless to do show-off maneuvers when testing a plane that had just been serviced. Whatever Minton was doing, he never got his second wingtip out of the kunai grass. He snagged the wingtip, crashed the plane, and died.

To this crash, there was a sequel. There were two links between Rocky and Dick Minton. Rocky knew Minton from the service;

Margaret Anne knew him from high school—she and Minton were both from Paoli. After the war, Minton's family had his body brought home and reinterred in Bloomington. Rocky and Margaret Anne were married by then and attending Indiana University, both in graduate school. They attended the ceremony. When Minton died, his family had received an Air Medal and a letter from his commanding officer. The family sensed, from some phrase in the letter, that something had been glossed over. Minton's mother was particularly troubled. She buttonholed Rocky at the memorial service and pressed him to tell what he knew—sixty years later, Margaret Anne recalled how fiercely determined she had been.

"That was the only time I lied," my father observed. I do not know what he said or did not say.

12

QUAKES AND TREMORS

In late April, late at night, an earthquake shook Nadzab. The quake came amid weeks of portents and turnabouts. There were new Allied landings in New Guinea—new victories for MacArthur. The Fifth Air Force had hammered the Japanese, and the weather had sprung a deadly trap. Torrents of rain cut off water supplies. The 91st Photo Reconnaissance Wing drew alongside the 5212th Photo Reconnaissance Wing: men who were discouraged at one wing found themselves welcomed by the other. Air task forces were becoming bomb wings. Colonel Hutchison had left, and Colonel Brownfield had arrived.

᭛

The Wing had its own newspaper now. It began as the *Wallaby.* After higher-ups noted that its masthead misspelled "reconnaissance" and that a column rendered the Wing commander's name as "Huchinson," the paper changed its masthead, shuffled staff, and became the *Wing-ding.* The *Wing-ding* featured European war news, comics, pin-up shots, and sports stories on the Nadzab softball leagues. The first issue appeared on April 1, and the columns were packed with inside jokes. The Special Services projectionists would be screening *The Sheikh, Birth of a Nation,* and a

Pathé newsreel, *Dewey Captures Manila*. Colonel Hutchison was warned that Major Tockstein had invented a crooked cribbage board and wanted to raise the ante to two pounds. The paper joked twice about Captain Cummins and his sawmill, in the same way that other newspapers would joke about real-estate developers. The *Wing-ding* also ran a famous-last-words column, which made hackneyed jokes about first sergeants and jungle juice. One famous-last-words quote was ascribed to a pilot: "Now watch *me* buzz the area."

On the march toward the Philippines, the next stop was Hollandia. MacArthur planned to land at that Dutch outpost, far up the New Guinea coast, bypassing Wewak. To support the landings, the Navy's Task Force 58 had raided Palau.[1] The Japanese Fourth Air Army had its headquarters and warplanes at Hollandia, and the Navy promised to give air cover for the beachheads only if the Fifth Air Force had destroyed the enemy warplanes beforehand. George Kenney promised to do that by April 5. "Everyone except MacArthur looked skeptical," Kenney wrote, but Kenney was as good as his word.[2] Against Hollandia, the Fifth Air Force threw every bomber and long-range fighter that Kenney could muster: 65 B-24s on March 30, 68 B-24s on March 21, and 63 B-24s on April 3—this time with 171 strafing planes, A-20s and B-25s.[3]

For those not flying, the air war showed itself in runway accidents. Men could become inured to the mirthless irony of a war passing without notice or other men dying because equipment failed.

> You would think we would have a great deal of excitement on a day like today because we were throwing every plane available into the raids on Wewak, Nubia, and Hollandia, but instead, I don't remember a plane flying over all day long. Of course the planes going over never attract our attention.

Rumor out that the Wing will go to Burma. Another B-24 blew up this morning. The one yesterday was taking off, a tire blew out, all men except two escaped before the "instantaneous" bombs exploded.

Also secured a hot-plate from the mainland. Kepler said that Lieutenant Colonel Smith and Lieutenant Colonel Darnell have two iceboxes full of gin, wine, and one case of beer and whiskey.[4]

Lieutenant Boyer was between assignments, a supernumerary officer at the Wing. For once, he wrote not in straightforward sentences but by accumulating vignettes.

An occasional bomb exploding due to grass fires, the movies every Wednesday, Friday, and Sunday nights, continuation of the rumor that a photo wing is going to Burma, our planes flying over the extreme western part of New Guinea, the successful raids on Wakde and Hollandia, the expectations of our next move, filling out section supply lists for the forthcoming movement, listening to the Navy men tell about their past experiences because the present ones are too dull. The Navy came here expecting lots and lots of excitement on their 2,000 mile patrols but so far only three have seen any Jap aircraft. And rumors as to what will happen to the 91st Recco Wing which was the unit which was scheduled to take over the 5212th.[5]

Very shortly, Rocky would learn that the 91st Photo Reconnaissance Wing was more than an idle unit top-heavy with colonels. He sensed something of this already; the comment about the Navy flyers showed a streak of humor. Along the road from Lae, there arrived the forces that Rocky had hoped to see, the 347th

Signal Company Wing—linemen, clerks, repairmen, and cryptographers. They answered to the new 91st Wing signal officer, Maj. Hubert Chenery.[6]

As a field-grade officer, Major Chenery commanded resources of which First Lieutenant Boyer could only dream. The entire Signal Company was thrown into construction work, cutting and hauling timber and setting up 75-foot antennae. Chenery asked to be loaned the communications section of the Fifth Photo Technical Squadron, and he got it. He requisitioned materials. He complained about the generator and got more power. He got the radio net up and working. He loaned three men of his own to Fifth Air Force to set up a radio-teletype system, to help build a transmitter out of abandoned radio parts. This may have been Rocky's doing—he knew his circuitry, and he never lacked a box of old radio gear.

Major Chenery was a trim, dark-haired man of forty. He had worked for two decades with telephones and phone lines—with the New England Telephone & Telegraph Company, where he had kept the lines humming during winters in Vermont. In his manner there was something voluble, even avuncular.

> Major Chenery, signal officer of 91st Recco Wing, and I went to ADVON this morning. As we passed the Red Cross quarters at the bottom of the hill, he saw two girls who had come over on the boat with him. We stopped, we talked, he drove the girls up to their quarters which were 100 yards from the highest-ranking officers. Upon the invitation, we visited their quarters only to find them quite dark and the concrete floor dirty from mud. The major said three of the Red Cross Girls on the boat were "little lambs." He continued by saying he took it on to himself to explain the facts of life to one of the girls. From discussions among the men, prostitution among the nurses and Red Cross girls is common, and their prices start around three pounds ($6.436).[7]

Rocky was a healthy young man far from home, unexpectedly brought into proximity to young women. He was also a churchgoing math major. Sex and Red Cross girls had gotten under his skin. That shows, in the way he figured the costs of prostitution out to three decimal places.

April 9 was Easter Sunday. Chaplain Smith flew up to Saidor and preached in mid-afternoon; Sergeant Ursprung attended. At Nadzab, the same weekend, a thousand servicemen crowded into the mess hall to celebrate Passover. Afterward it was reckoned that only half of the celebrants were Jewish.[8]

North of Nadzab, that same Easter afternoon, four P-39s from the 82nd Squadron were flying coastal reconnaissance, looking for Japanese barges. Capt. Dick Karr and Lt. Mike Moffitt were flying high cover, with Claude Augustus Diffenderffer and Lt. Tommy Sellers flying low as strafers. Diffenderffer was twenty-two. He had just made first lieutenant and he had done well flying low element. In January he had machine-gunned thirty Japanese soldiers, infantrymen surprised by one of his strafing passes, and in March he had shot down a Japanese bomber, which he spotted sneaking across the treetops.

As the flight neared Uligan Harbor, Karr reminded them to skirt the place. As reconnaissance pilots, they knew that Uligan was well defended—heavy antiaircraft guns, lots of them, well sited and well protected, firing shells that exploded in black bursts of shrapnel. The gunners were good shots and usually opened fire when a plane came within four hundred yards.

The flight banked out and away from shore. They were two miles out, only twenty feet above the water, when the Japanese opened fire. At the first shot, Diffenderffer's plane exploded. The last that Sellers saw of Diff's P-39 was the yellow propeller spinner.

A radio call came in, asking the flight to come back. The voice on the radio claimed to be Poker One, as if it were Diffenderffer calling for rescue. The pilots knew better; they knew that the

Japanese listened in on American radio frequencies. They stayed off shore, far enough to be safe. There was no trace of the plane, they found, only an oil slick burning briefly on the water.[9]

🌀

A week later, Rocky wrote a long, broadly ranging diary entry. He would have spent the day indoors, under canvas or the tin roof of a mess hall, for the rain that day was ceaseless and the news was bad. In the Fifth Air Force, April 16, 1944, was remembered as Black Sunday.[10]

> Weather played strange tricks today. Usually all weather conditions follow the New Guinea coast and as they near New Britain go out to sea. Yesterday there was a front over the northwest part of New Guinea and the weather officers believed it would move at the normal rate and thus Hollandia would be open today. Instead of moving at its usual speed, according to Lieutenant Jensen, the front reached 50 miles per hour. The planes going north found closed weather conditions, had to fly instruments all the way back and even Saidor was closed. It is reported that 26 planes did not reach their home bases tonight. Several report those that did were carrying only 10–15–20 to 35 gallons of gas in their tanks.[11]

To hit the Japanese base at Humboldt Bay, near Hollandia, Kenney and Whitehead had sent a huge air armada across the mountains: 58 B-24s, 46 B-25s, and 118 A-20s, covered by 40 P-38s. The strike was successful. However, except for the heavy bombers, Humboldt Bay was at the limits of every plane's range. When the weather front closed in behind them, shutting off the way home to Nadzab, the P-38s, B-25s, and A-20s were trapped. The 431st Fighter Squadron tried to fly over the storm; they climbed to 25,000 feet, saw that the thunderheads still towered a further

25,000 feet above them, and thought better of the idea. The command pilot found the coast at Madang, slid down to the lowest of altitudes, and flew sixty miles above the breaking surf to Saidor. There the squadron waited it out—"parked our planes and sat on the wings and witnessed the panic."[12]

Saidor was a forward air base, little more than an emergency landing strip. The airstrip was sound and surfaced but the rest of the place was a churned-up sea of mud. Doc Schafer was at Saidor. "Rained like hell all day," he wrote. "Torrential rains," wrote Sergeant Ursprung, who was also stationed at Saidor.[13] There were dozens of desperate pilots lost in the overcast above the landing strip—and on the ground beneath the clouds, there was worse, a series of crashes and collisions in the pouring rain.

The steel airstrip matting was slick with water. The first plane to land skidded off the airstrip. The control tower told pilots to land "toward the water," meaning Dekay's Bay, but confusion arose immediately—the rain had flooded low-lying ground, and there seemed to be water at both ends of the airstrip. A reconnaissance P-38 and a B-25 landed from opposite ends of the runway, simultaneously. "Everyone was shouting, the ambulances were screaming, but they came together in the center of the runway with a terrific explosion and both planes burst into flames." For fifteen minutes no plane could land, while airmen ran to put out the fire and bulldoze off the wreckage.[14]

Doc Schafer followed the confusion in the air and the carnage on the runway.

> The ceiling was down to a couple of hundred feet. One B-25 hit the runway so hard, he bent his landing gear out sideways so that the tips of his props just cleared the ground. Just heard that 11 planes cracked up this afternoon trying to get in, all low on gas and instrument weather. . . . Besides the 11 ships cracked up on the strip, six P-38s ran out of gas and crashed into the bay, pilots bailing out. Three

B-24 photo ships are missing. Other 38s and A-20s, low on gas, were directed to head for Nadzab. How many got there is questionable. Tonight the field is packed with planes. Thirty heavies of the Fifth Air Force's 93 are here. Every taxiway, road, and open space around the strip is jam packed.[15]

Three A-20s, light speedy attack planes, put themselves out of action, one after the other: one banged into a B-25, one wrecked itself at the end of the runway, one slid into a parked P-47. Two B-25s collided on a taxiway. Another B-25 skidded sideways and its wheels collapsed. A P-38 dodged a B-24 but turned so sharply that it bent its nose wheel; its propellers shrieked as they hit the matting. Another P-38 pilot dropped out of the overcast and found himself flying scant feet directly above a B-25, which was also coming in for landing. He gunned his engines and raced ahead of the bomber, then dropped down wheels-up on the last yards of the runway (a neat piece of flying; no aircraft brake could have slowed the plane). The plane slid through wreckage and buried its nose in a mud embankment. The pilot lived.[16]

There were engineers still clearing and grading at Saidor, the 860th Engineering Aviation battalion—Chaplain Smith's new outfit. They revved their cranes and bulldozers across the landing strip, pushing off airplanes or towing away chunks of wreckage, as the field beside the airstrip filled up with parked aircraft, and the gray clouds pressed down overhead, and the rain kept coming down hard.

Across the Fifth Air Force, everyone realized that the day was a disaster: the airmen and engineers at Saidor, Rocky at Nadzab, and higher commanders in bases farther south. Back in Port Moresby, perhaps to keep the press from asking questions about why so many warplanes had not returned, Capt. Richard Bong (normally quiet and reticent) spent the afternoon talking to war correspondents. Bong kept the newsmen talking that afternoon, on into the hours when men play poker, while teletypes buzzed elsewhere in Moresby and Nadzab and Saidor, trading messages about which warplanes had landed where.[17]

At one time, Rocky heard, there had been six warplanes burning simultaneously on the airstrip at Saidor. The toll of aircraft lost to the weather finally ran to twenty-six, almost two full squadrons.[18]

Closer at hand, there was news from the Wing and the Group—personal frictions, transfers, gripes, and continuing discontent.

> Kepler received four Christmas packages sent during October. Men are less optimistic as to the length of the war—most of them say at least two more years.
>
> The report is out that Private DuBois threatened to shoot Corporal McMannus, and the result is that DuBois is being sent on rest leave tomorrow morning.
>
> Some time ago the line chiefs etc. of the 17th Squadron went practically on strike. Major Tennille called everyone together, had a gripe session, and Captain Wallace, squadron engineering officer, was relieved and Lieutenant Wilkey from the 71st Group replaced him.
>
> From most everywhere comes the report that the Japanese prisoners who are fortunate enough to reach the American interrogators believe they are actually fighting "somewhere" in the United States or in Australia.[19]

The Japanese who thought they were fighting in the United States were not the only servicemen whose commanders fed them convenient illusions. "About a week ago Major Gordon, CO of the 82nd Squadron was returned to the States," Rocky added. "It is believed such action was the only sure-fire method of relieving him of his squadron."[20] It had taken the Fifth Air Force five months, but they had finally shipped home Major Gordon. Gordon went cheerfully. His orders said he was returning on a classified mission; it was a lecture tour, he discovered, which shortly thereafter, for whatever reason, was canceled.[21] Gordon would see service later in China, but he had ducked his last decision and cracked up his last airplane with the 71st Group.

There was another major piece of news, worth recording on Black Sunday. Rocky wrote further:

> Late last evening we heard the rumor that Colonel Hutchison would be sent to a task force and some colonel in the Service Command would become CO. Yesterday the 5212th Recco Wing became non-existent and we were assigned to the 91st Photographic Reconnaissance Wing Headquarters. No one can understand why Fifth Air Force put in a commanding officer who does not know and admits it, anything about photography, when last week they assigned a colonel who has 14 years' photo experience to the Air Service Command.[22]

ᔕ

At Nadzab, as well, the storm front had caused problems. The runoff had been too much: "The dam which holds the water for our photo labs and showers was broken and it is rumored one week's labor will be required to repair it." The dam was out for four days; men could stand outside and wash off when it rained, but no one could do laundry. The problem was fixed, in the end: "The most indispensable piece of equipment in New Guinea is the bulldozer," Rocky opined.[23]

Liquor had ceased to be a private commodity, something hoarded by fat-cat flyers or sold by the drink in officers' clubs. Liquor was reaching the marketplace; it had acquired quantity and price. On April 20, the Wing officers' mess was selling from its stock: "bottles of whiskey (approximately one quart) for 16 shillings per bottle, wine for 4 shillings, gin for 8, and a bottle of rum 8 shillings."[24] Two weeks later, prices were higher: the officers' club offered "three quarts of beer, and any quart bottle of wine, bourbon, or gin, for one pound."[25] (Units may have been trying to stockpile liquor or buy it for resale. The Eighth Fighter Squadron, its communications officer said, was going to be issued a B-25 to make beer runs.) A hitchhiking soldier told Rocky that he had bought two quart bottles of whiskey in Lae for £7 per bottle, and that an infantryman at Saidor paid £20 ($64) for a bottle of American Scotch.[26] There was some failure in the market. "The HQ Squadron supply sold four bottles of beer to each officer tonight for one half pound. The enlisted men are quite griped because they were not sold any."[27]

Fat-cat and beer-run planes were flying. All of this set the stage for Lieutenant Bailey's ice cream swindle.

> During the afternoon of two days past, Lieutenant Jensen came up to me and whispered "Can you keep a secret?" (a nod was sufficient assurance). "Tonight at 7 o'clock if you will meet Foster and me here in the Wing headquarters we will get you a pint or so of ice cream." I immediately contacted Kepler and told him about the date and to be present. 7:15 found us at the door of the PX awaiting Lieutenant Bailey to open it. He led us into the room—started to open what looked to be an ice cream container packed with dry ice. After that he took a container, reached into the depths, staring, as we likewise were staring but ours was anxiety and do you know what the damn fool brought out of the package— *dehydrated* ice cream. He already had our money and thus charged us $160 for two pounds of ice cream which when mixed with water will make something like 15 gallons of ice cream. Thus we too have a black market in New Guinea.

But last night we had a big rain and caused a tree to fall which fell in Lieutenant Bailey's tent. Oh what sweet revenge—so says Jensen.[28]

For one evening, at least, for anyone who had no duty and could obtain a pair of field glasses, there was a glimpse of a genuine girl from back home.

Had a stage show last night which consisted of one girl and a master of ceremonies and a military band and an audience of three thousand soldiers. Nothing out of the ordinary happened and consequently it just goes to show you we American soldiers do have chivalry.[29]

Jeanne Darrell was the songstress—slim, dark-haired, twenty-one, and "lovely (with an accent)," the *Wing-ding* announced. Miss Darrell began with "My Heart Tells Me" and the audience stopped the show with demands for an encore. The *Wing-ding* critic mused, "she was the first American girl in many a day for most of us; we didn't blame the men for howling." Instead, "we quit counting the songs after 'Mairzy Doates' and just sat and envied the guys with binoculars."[30]

It was on a stage, singing, that American women proved least disappointing. On a Wednesday-night date, three Army nurses proved that the gossip about them could not be entirely credited.

Three officers, Lieutenant Foliart, Lieutenant Leon, and another one, just returned from a date with three nurses. Foliart was quite disgusted because all that his would let him do was to rub her belly—and really to quote him, "All I got was my blanket dirty, someone stole my quart of whiskey and a few god damn kisses. We went out and sat on a hard rock half the night."[31]

The leave planes were still flying between New Guinea and Australia. Now motor pool NCOs, as well as combat flyers, were reporting that Australia's young women did not disappoint.

> All the enlisted men who are returning from Macquarie, the Fifth Air Force rest camp, say it is a good place to go. Plenty of food, things to do, and lots of women. Corporal Dare just returned and reports if a fellow stays sober, he will be socially accepted. He said the Red Cross girls conducted dances and trips. He said the women are okay too. On his last day he went out on the beach and had intercourse with a girl during the period of four hours, reached four climaxes, so he says.[32]

Recon photographer Sergeant Cahill had a more trenchant comment. "Staff Sergeant Cahill said the only venereal cases reported in the Wing were the ones the combat crew members contracted in Townsville."[33]

At Nadzab, the airmen were waiting for what would follow their strikes on Hollandia—the infantry's next move up the coast. "Everything, as far as we know, is ready for the big invasion," Rocky wrote.

> One item which we never expected overseas is the common conversation among all ranks about our future movements. Everyone knows the invasion of Tadji was delayed one week and we are expected to move into there on the 23rd of April and into Hollandia the first week of May. Plans have already been drawn up in the Sixth Group HQ about their installations at Hollandia. In fact, there isn't any security. Three weeks before units moved into Cape Gloucester everyone knew it, the same way. Saidor, same way.[34]

All of this would very nearly come to pass—but improvised news was not the truth. As the airmen of Nadzab waited for the landings, they might have recalled other rumors that had not been borne out.

On April 14, as rumor had had it, the invasion was taking place that day.[35] There had been a rumor that the Allies had a secret airdrome in the Philippines.[36]

There had also been a rumor that the troops had landed already, by night. That made sense, Rocky had thought, because at night the infantry going ashore could spot Japanese snipers and machine-gun nests by their muzzle flashes.[37]

There had been a rumor that Army and Navy personnel would be rotated home after fourteen months overseas, and Foliart began talking about what he might be doing in fourteen months. Then Jensen, whose wife was eight months pregnant, met another weather officer who had been overseas for twenty-six months.[38] There had been a rumor that personnel would be rotated home after thirty months.[39]

On April 21, an hour before midnight, an earthquake shook Nadzab. It was a strong quake, a shock that awed seismologists in Bombay. "At 2300 we had two very distinct earthquakes some two seconds apart and the second was very strong and some later estimated it would have cracked concrete floors. Everyone hopes it tore up the whole Japanese Empire."[40]

The next morning, instead of rumors, there was banner-headline news. The boldest landing of the New Guinea war had taken place, five hundred miles up the coast.

> Today is the day. All our planes were scheduled to take off at dawn but for some reason, none did—today was the day. At 8:30 this morning we got our first reports of the invasion and the following notes appeared in our war room.

TANAHMERAH. Attacked by the 24th Division at 0700. Two Regts, the 19th Regt and the 21st Regt, were in the initial assault. This action is the strategic ace in the hole since it is thought most of Hollandia's area defenses are around Humboldt Bay. By dusk tonight it is hoped that the 24th Division will have advanced to the western edge of the Hollandia airdrome with 11,000 in action. Naval Bombardment for 30 minutes and 15 minutes before the assault.

HUMBOLDT BAY. Landing made at 0700 by the 162nd and 186th Regts after 30 minutes of Naval Bombardment and 15 minutes of Naval A/C strafing. 4 Beaches were hit simultaneously by the two Regts. By dusk tonight there will be 11,325 troops in Hollandia. By D+4 there will be 17,325. These will be part of the 41st Division.[41]

The two beachheads were twenty-five miles apart, at either end of the headland of the Cyclops Mountains. From them, American regiments moved inland, to seize the Japanese airstrips and supply depot at Hollandia. The landing went well, the Japanese fled, and Allied troops captured countless Japanese supply dumps, the richest prize of the war: "pyramids of canned goods," Allied commander Robert Eichelberger wrote, "tarpaulin-covered hills of rice which looked like Ohio haystacks."[42]

Dazzling in its conception and magnificent in its execution [wrote William Manchester] the Hollandia lunge would have been beyond the talents of all but a few of history's great captains. In retrospect, it looms as a military classic, comparable to Hannibal's maneuvering at Cannae and Napoleon's at Austerlitz. It is, of course, less famous. That may be attributed to a curious principle which seems to guide those who write of titanic battles. The higher the casualty lists, it appears—the vaster the investment in blood—the greater the need to justify them. . . . The total cost at Hollandia, including the mopping up, was just 150 GI lives.[43]

"Tonight we listened to the U.S. and Britain as well as Tokyo to find what would be said about the Hollandia invasion," Rocky recorded. "Some of the fellows are expressing the opinion that we'll be in the Philippines by Christmas."[44]

ຈ

As of April 22, a new officer commanded the Wing: Ralph Orville Brownfield. Brownfield had fifteen years' service as an officer. He claimed to have been a barnstormer; he had joined the Air Corps early, cracked up three airplanes, and become a service officer. The record of his career, it has been said, "describes unpleasant things like lawsuits and accidents."[45] The Air Force moved him from Wright Field in Ohio to Australia in May 1943. There Brownfield ranked as theater service commander. He seems quickly to have decided to do what commanding officers do. He had subordinates whom he could transfer between facilities, he had facilities between which he could transfer subordinates—and he floated an idea that George Kenney immediately shot down. Kenney wrote bluntly:

I understand that you have been toying with the idea of rotating personnel between the service squadrons and the depot organizations of New Guinea and the mainland. I do not think the idea has much merit. The only thing that would make sense would be exchanging personnel who are doing exactly the same type of job. . . . Outside of occasional freak cases of this nature, I would like to have you drop the whole idea.[46]

The airmen of Nadzab had their own opinions of the Service Command staff; they thought they were incompetent pencil-pushers who lost equipment and rejected their requisition forms. Brownfield took over the Wing beneath a cloud of prejudice. His priorities as commander did nothing to disperse it. Four days after he arrived, he embarked on a dubious mission:

> Early this morning Colonel Brownfield, the new Wing CO, took off in a B-25 to fly to Hollandia for the mere purpose of being the first pilot to land a bomber on the newly captured Hollandia strip. It was rumored two other planes were racing with him—but—one hour after his takeoff, ADVON got the word the Japs were shelling the strip and the communications section was asked to inform him not to land and that we did via radio naturally. The colonel was disgusted. Colonel Brownfield is one of these officers who believe neat charts win battles. He is strictly a paper man.[47]

Three days later, Brownfield held a meeting that made things no better. What his men remembered was that he admitted a lack of experience, criticized Wing staff, threatened transfers, and showed a robust concern for his own comfort.

> Colonel Brownfield held a staff meeting this morning and was quite griped because the A-1 personnel section did not secure medals for a few of the boys just after they had accomplished their feats. The colonel said that he would have to transfer many of the officers from the Wing because of being over strength and over in rank. And that he knew little of the type of work that we are supposed to do therefore it would be up to us to inform him what each section was supposed to do.
>
> The colonel closed his meeting by asking how to chlorinate his water. A new wing is being built into the colonel's house.[48]

The colonel's house might be under construction—but the Wing faced more pressing needs. The mess hall was in poor shape: "Staff Sergeant Cahill stated that Major Pratt, Wing flight surgeon, made his sanitary report that the officers' mess wasn't fit to feed hogs in."[49]

Rocky held a new position; he was now communications officer for the 91st Wing. Colonel Brownfield sent in a staff photographer to document his unit's operations. The photographer posed Rocky with his clerk, Pfc. Spragg. They look cheerful and serious and are studying a document. Another photo, less artful and more revealing, shows Foster and Jensen looking haggard as they work amid their charts in the weather office. The Chemical Warfare section, under Captain Ogden and Lieutenant Beyer, busies itself

Col. Ralph Orville Brownfield took over the 91st Photo Reconnaissance Wing in April 1944. He made himself known for trying to garner medals and planning a dream house in a war zone. 91st Photo Reconnaissance Wing, in AFHRA archive

with phone calls and files. Major Chenery and Lieutenant Hilgerson consult while Lieutenant Phillipo makes notes. On the opening page, Colonel Brownfield stares out at the reader, behind his blotter, desk set, and memo boxes.[50]

As the month of May opened, the communications officer network had pulled in a report on the war in Europe. Lieutenant Kepler had heard it directly from Lieutenant Cook, communications officer at the Eighth Fighter Squadron. "Lieutenant Cook, a friend of Lieutenant Kepler, who knows some officers that just returned from the mainland, says while down there, one dated an Australian auxiliary who worked for a colonel and she said the second front would open on the morning of May 10."[51]

Rocky thought that Allied intelligence had, "in GI language, screwed up by the numbers"—American planes flew without opposition over Wewak and Sawar, the last Japanese strongpoints.[52]

> Lieutenant Powell said in reference to the Japs' side of strategy for the Hollandia area, "Let's just put in a few anti-aircraft guns and go home, too." According to our war room bulletin board, only 2000 soldiers were at Hollandia whereas a month ago the figure of 20,000 was for the same area. Also it stated 24 American pilots are prisoner at Wewak and the reason that the Japs didn't remove their planes from Hollandia was because of the scarcity of pilots.[53]

Rocky was glad to share Powell's joke about the Japanese choosing to leave. He was glad to hope that they might reach the Philippines by Christmas and that the fight had gone out of the Japanese. American prisoners had been reported at Wewak by Radio Tokyo broadcasts—also by Indian Army prisoners of war who had served the Japanese as coolies and been liberated when the Americans took Hollandia. Any hopes regarding American pilots held at Wewak were futile. No prisoner of war held at Wewak survived the war, and only four airmen survived out of the dozens of Allied POWs taken to Rabaul.[54]

Officers were saying that they were glad that that son-of-a-bitch Hutchison was gone, now that he was not there to hear them. They were learning, however, that the problems of the Wing had not been solved by a change in command. Foliart reported that promotions had been frozen for all ground officers in the Fifth Air Force, and Sergeant O'Steen reported that all leaves and furloughs would be frozen for a month.[55]

> The officers of the 91st Wing have arrived and according to Staff Sergeant Hiester, all officers received a promotion before being sent overseas. Lieutenant Colonel Ilgenfritz called a meeting of all officers saying that we were 100% over in strength. He said that the new men arriving, with higher ranks than the heads of departments here, naturally created a problem.
>
> Lieutenant Ball said that the men of the 110th Squadron were all applying to be returned to the States upon reaching their 37th birthdays. It is rumored by Lieutenant Jensen that a certain captain who arrived with the 91st Recco Wing Advanced Echelon saw the conditions here so he immediately asked to be returned to the States and day before yesterday—he went.
>
> It's Lieutenant Colonel Guerry now. He is 25 years old and has gone from a second lieutenant to a lieutenant colonel in ten months, says Major Chenery, his bosom friend.
>
> Lieutenant Jensen said that everyone was so up in the air about the invasion of Hollandia whereas here in the theater it was just another day and just that.[56]

Guerry had been promoted again, Jensen was feeling dour, the Wing was grumbling—but against this background, the 71st Group was keeping up the air war. The 82nd Squadron claimed to have hit five more camouflaged barges, and the 110th Squadron reported that it had hit four: the barges refused to burn until one pilot bombed them with his drop tank and the gasoline caught fire. The 17th Squadron raided Hansa Bay with fifteen planes, and Colonel Sams led another mission along the coast above Madang; they saw no shipping, and shot up a plantation reported to house a Japanese supply depot. Only at Uligan, where Diffenderffer had been killed, did the Japanese fire on them. "I've got to figure some way to knock out that outfit without getting hurt," Sams wrote. "They have already nailed me for two fighters and a bomber crew."[57]

Skip-bombing ships and strafing land targets formed the essence of "attack aviation," the doctrine that George Kenney had so forcefully preached. Kenney had won many converts—but there were officers who knew the risks of low-level attacks and remained unconvinced. When Kenney praised attack aviation to Hap Arnold, Arnold took him to task. As Thomas Griffith has written: "Based on his experiences in the Southwest Pacific, as well as his previous leanings, Kenney believed that the low-altitude, high-speed tactics of attack aviation were sound and 'in evidence every day all over the world.' Arnold informed Kenney that his instincts were flat wrong: 'Attack tactics have *definitely not* as you state proven sound "every day all over the world." When these tactics were attempted in Europe, the results were disastrous; on one mission, eleven out of eleven airplanes were lost.'"

The italics are Arnold's own—a forceful attempt by America's top air commander to hammer this point home to Kenney. Arnold knew what heavy flak could do; Kenney had not seen it. As Griffith continues: "In reality Arnold's analysis of the situation was more correct than Kenney's. Because of the weakness of Japanese antiaircraft fire, especially on merchant ships and around the Japanese airfields, Kenney was unaware of the losses capable of being inflicted on large, low-flying aircraft by such weapons."[58]

The experience of the Group in May 1944 would back up what Hap Arnold said. Someone else whom Rocky knew died on a low-level mission—Hugh Mosher from the *General John S. Pope*.

Mosher was in the 17th Squadron; he had made captain. He would have been a bombardier if they had used bombardiers in skip-bombing. Instead, on low-level missions, the pilot dropped the bombs while the bombardier, now called the observer, looked out through the plexiglass panels in the nose of the plane. To ride in the nose of a B-25, said Joseph Heller, who rode there himself, was like being "a goddam cantilevered goldfish in a goddam cantilevered goldfish bowl."[59]

Mosher's bomber was the second plane in the flight on a day when the 17th Squadron raided Japen Island, at low level. When the lead plane opened its bomb-bay doors, the payload of four 500-pound bombs fell immediately, unexpectedly. Mosher's plane was caught in the explosion; the blast smashed in its cantilevered nose and a bomb fragment hit Mosher in the forehead.[60]

Also dead on a low-level mission was Lt. Harry F. Harrison of the 82nd Squadron. He had been the last plane in a four-man flight attacking Awar Plantation at Nubia, up at the north end of Hansa Bay, strafing the airstrip and the plantation buildings. It was eight in the morning and they were lingering over the area— which may have been unwise. Flight leader Captain Moody called for everyone to head home. Moody's wingman answered, and Lieutenant Borders answered, but not Harrison. His P-39 had vanished. They flew back to the shoreline, checked out to sea, circled the plantation, searched for an hour, until their fuel ran low—but saw no oil slicks on the bay or ocean, no scorched crash site in the palm trees.[61]

ᛦ

Colonel Hutchison had not been "sent" to an air task force. He had been promoted to head his own air task force and was on the way to commanding his own bombardment wing.

The air task force was an innovation in command structure made by the Fifth Air Force. Like its model, the naval task force, it was an independent frontline air command. As Thomas Griffith has written, "since the distance, environment and equipment of the Southwest Pacific made it impossible for commanders to dependably communicate with the units at the forward airfield, the commander of an air task force . . . had 'complete authority to handle any situation.'" The air task force was the command that took over at each forward jump of the air blitz, "an advanced headquarters that was flexible in size and assigned aircraft for a specific task."[62] To maintain consistency with larger Army Air Force command structures, each of Kenney's air task forces was characterized as a bombardment wing. "Although the names of the organizations changed, [the bomb wings] continued to function as the old air task forces and controlled many different types of aircraft for various periods of time, depending on the operation. In this regard these three bomber wings were unlike similarly named wings in any other theater, which only contained bomber aircraft. Every operation in the Southwest Pacific would have an air task force, only with a different name."[63]

Hutchison was at Hollandia with the Second Air Task Force. The Allied ground commander at Hollandia was Robert Eichelberger, who had beaten the Japanese at Buna. Eichelberger threw himself into the engineering work. "To me the stench of hot asphalt became a fragrance," he wrote. He posted a letter to Ennis Whitehead: "We are working night and day to make those strips and the road leading thereto worthy of the name. Our problems are many and varied. . . . Hutchison has been fine. He is easy to get along with, appreciates his own problems, and knows exactly what we are up against. If the planes don't fly it will not be his fault."[64]

From their new vantage point, on the actual terrain of Hollandia, both Hutchison and Eichelberger would begin looking for new airfields. The airfields at Hollandia were overshadowed by the Cyclops Mountains, a ridge that topped 6,500 feet, forcing bombers to climb too quickly. The Japanese airstrips were inadequate for American warplanes: "A Jap Zero weighed about six thousand pounds. An American bomber weighed about sixty thousand pounds, and needed good ground and good underpinnings, and a long stretch of hard-surface runway for a take-off."[65]

At a higher level of command, Douglas MacArthur and George Kenney were also looking for the next airdrome to seize. MacArthur began spinning out plans to his staff. William Manchester memorably captured the scene. "The General was off on one of his soaring flights of rhetoric, telling his staff that Hollandia was only the first of several bounds he meant to make. Now that the Japanese were in disarray, he wondered aloud, why not leapfrog another 120 miles west to the enemy airdrome in the Wakde Islands, and then leap 180 miles more to the island of Biak, guarding the mouth of Geelvink Bay, New Guinea's largest inlet? Kenney was elated—'the Philippines,' he wrote, 'didn't look anywhere near as far as they did a few months before.'"[66]

Of all MacArthur's generals, Kenney was the only commander who favored pressing on up the New Guinea coast—but he was equally enthusiastic. The war for airfields was continuing, Kenney reflected. To keep the war front moving, he figured, he needed four or five more airfields. There were places farther along the New Guinea coast where he could count on good ground and good underpinnings. "I was abandoning the Dobodura area and Port Moresby. . . . I wanted to keep on going and take over Biak where the Nips already had three coral runways. Coral was good stuff. Where there was plenty of coral, the engineers could give us a field in a matter of a few days."[67]

In May 1944, I think, Rocky went to Sydney. He had been planning to go there with Foliart, and there is a gap in his diary that
a trip southward would explain. A few artifacts from that trip,
whenever it was, survived to tell the tale. Rocky had money
to spend; he bought several huge, heavy sterling silver serving
spoons and shipped them across the Pacific to Margaret Anne.
He bought a book at a library sale. It was still in his papers, sixty-
five summers later, wedged in among old issues of psychology
journals and briefcase kits for the Wechsler and Stanford-Binet
intelligence tests.

And there is one story that Rocky told that might still be traced
in yellowing blotters in the archives of the New South Wales police
force. They were walking back to their rooms, one night, when
the streetcar caught up with them and the bell clanged like crazy
and a familiar American voice shouted at them to hustle and get
on, they had thrown off the conductor and were driving the thing
home themselves. (My father told this story once, thirty years later,
forty years ago now. Was it Foliart who shouted, or was it Foliart
who was walking beside him?)

It was almost three years now since Rocky took the bus for
Camp Atterbury. It was six months now that he had been in New
Guinea. He had been shuffled between an air group and two
reconnaissance wings; half a dozen of his friends were dead, and
some of his other friends had been promoted. It was a year since
he had typed a letter to Margaret Anne from his radio truck.

Colonel Sams determined to check out as a pilot in the P-38.
He took up one Lightning, warily noted how the flaps worked,
otherwise found it as easy-flying a plane as he had ever flown. He
felt like mastering the plane completely. The next day was Sams'
birthday, his thirty-eighth. He took up a different P-38 for fifty-
five minutes. The seat had been moved forward five inches and it
told. "Almost impossible to handle on ground due to close coupling
and cramping legs," he considered. "One year older. So what," he
wrote.[68]

13

CAPE WAIOS

"The officer leading those bombers was too aggressive," my father once said. "He and all of his crew were killed. But he wanted to be sure he hit that cruiser, and if he hadn't been that aggressive, they wouldn't have hit those destroyers like they did."

Thinking aloud, Rocky left the comment hanging. In Rocky's diary, however, there is only one officer who fits that description. That is Maj. William Grant Tennille Jr., commanding officer of the 17th Squadron. On June 8, 1944, off Cape Waios, New Guinea, Major Tennille attacked what he thought was a Japanese cruiser, carrying the 17th Squadron into the battle after him. In the fight off Cape Waios, which lasted ninety seconds, the 17th Squadron earned sixty Distinguished Flying Crosses. Nineteen of these honors were posthumous.

🌀

American troops landed on Biak on May 27, 1944. The landing was bungled and left the invasion force out of place on a hostile coast. The terrain was difficult and the Japanese fought well, and it was months, not weeks, until their resistance was broken.

The Japanese planned to ship reinforcements from the Philippines, from Davao on the island of Mindanao. They loaded soldiers on destroyers, to make a quick run south past the Moluccas, escorted by cruisers and a battleship.[1]

After dark on June 3, at 9:30 in the evening, the reconnaissance paladins of the Sixth Photo Group phoned Wing headquarters. Lieutenant Colonel Guerry and Lieutenant Colonel Darnell asked for the photo codes so they could fly in the morning.

> There has been great excitement today. By noon everyone knew of the convoy and the rumored number varied from 57 to 76. Lieutenant Sill of the Bomber Command said that the Fifth Bomber Command had sent a strike out to hit it and the planes returned all shot up. A destroyer was sunk. He further added the navy had only a small squadron of Catalinas in the vicinity but two battleships were heading down this way but would take two days to get here. At eleven it was rumored the first echelon of the Japs were 70 miles off Biak which we had just invaded.
>
> At eleven the weather reports from Biak stopped coming in. At ten our radar stations at Wakde went off air and did not call until 7:30 in the evening. A few believe all outgoing messages are being censored. Due to radio failure Major Chenery sent Lieutenant Boone and two enlisted men to Wakde to see what was wrong. Several believe the Japs will reinforce Biak, others believe they will retake Wakde.
>
> Late this evening the Bomber Command was to send out another strike and our four strips here were practically barren. During the evening we heard no news because ADVON was withholding everything. However it was rumored that contact with the convoy had been lost due to a weather front which the Japs had been following down from the Philippines.[2]

There were barely a dozen ships in the convoy; rumor and speculation magnified this into the huge fleet of which Rocky heard. After seeing American patrol planes, the ships put in to the Japanese anchorage at Sorong, around the northwestern tip of New Guinea, to wait there until the ships could more safely finish the run.

On June 4, the Japanese launched an air strike on the Allied cruiser force patrolling the waters off Biak, and damaged the USS *Nashville*. This cheered the Japanese, and more comfort came the next day. After dark on June 5, a handful of Japanese flyers took off, tasked with bombing the American air base at Wakde. They would achieve a devastating success.

The Japanese had been driven out of the skies during daylight, but they steadily continued to fly missions by night. Japanese night bombers were often mocked as "Washing-Machine Charlie" (or "Piss-Call Charlie"), and it is often thought that such missions were flown only to disrupt the sleep of Allied servicemen. This is not so. The Japanese had shifted to a strategy of asymmetrical warfare—aerial guerilla warfare, which was surprisingly successful. Plane per plane, the Japanese may have destroyed more enemy aircraft by small night-bombing raids than the Americans destroyed on Japanese airstrips during massed-plane daylight raids.

Wakde lies just off the coast of New Guinea. For night bombers, it offered a perfect target: it was an island made of white coral, easy to find because it literally glowed against the dark ocean. A night fighter pilot recalled that "the coral island in equatorial moonlight made a target that was all bull's eye. . . . Coral strips in the moonlight shine like a shavetail [lieutenant's] first gold bar, and you would swear that the Nip can't miss you, even from 20,000 feet."[3]

Wakde is also a small island, barely long enough to hold a mile-long airfield, and only half a mile wide. Every acre had been crowded with parked aircraft, drums and tanks of high-octane aviation gas, ammunition dumps, and bomb dumps. Not only were there newly landed American bombs on Wakde, there were stacks of captured Japanese munitions that American ordnance teams had not yet defused.[4]

Late on June 5, the Japanese night bombers homed in on Wakde. The night was overcast, but the moon was nearly full, and they spotted the island through a break in the clouds. Rocky heard from Staff Sergeant Wawrzynkiewicz what happened next.

> "It was dark and Hollandia was closed. A plane called the tower and asked to enter the traffic pattern. The men in the tower believed it to be a plane which couldn't make Hollandia, gave the plane the necessary instructions. The plane came over the runway and at the far end he dropped several bombs right on top of several planes." One of the pilots who had sunk a destroyer went down the following morning to paint in the ship on the nose of his plane only to find just two motors lying on the ground.[5]

Colonel Sams was on Wakde, visiting the 17th Squadron, and waited out one air-raid alert. After an hour, when nothing had happened, Sams climbed back into his cot—too soon.

> I was just dozing off when the first bomb whistled in. I hit the back edge of the tent as the bomb hit directly one of our large bomb dumps. . . . We sat out that attack watching the glare of fires and listening to the ack-ack, the detonation of our own and Nip bombs, and the 75-mm dumps going up and gas tanks and drums going up. The 90mms flashed and whooshed, the 40s and 20s cracked and the PT boats made so much noise with their engines we thought the whole Nip air force was in the area. The fireworks finally slowed down and we heard the second

run approaching from the west. This Nip laid his string down the same side of the runway as the first. He hit direct three P-38s, one B-24, and a bomb fuse dump. Believe you me we had some tall fires.[6]

The antiaircraft guns fell silent, and the men of the 17th Squadron climbed out of their foxholes. Wakde would have been fire and darkness: pillars of flame, billowing smoke, twisted wrecked aircraft, bombs exploding. Slender palm trees, bright in the glare against the black ocean night, strangely tall above the fire and wreckage. And the tableau would have been peopled just as strangely, by hundreds of half-naked GIs in underwear and steel helmets. It would have been half a scene of apocalypse and half a study in hell-lit humoresque.

The raid on Wakde that night was the worst blow ever suffered by the Fifth Air Force—"probably [the] most successful strike against an Allied field in this theater," MacArthur's intelligence chief immediately fumed.[7] Samuel Eliot Morison estimated the loss at about two-thirds of about a hundred planes; Sixth Army sources reported nine planes destroyed and ninety-three damaged.

George Kenney and Ennis Whitehead had taken a calculated risk in pushing their forces forward. "We were crowding Wakde to the limit," Kenney later admitted.

I knew we were inviting trouble by parking aircraft almost wingtip to wingtip on Wakde, but we had to have our fighters forward to maintain cover over the shipping constantly unloading at Biak. . . . So we stacked them in and relied on attacking the Nip airdromes to keep the Nips from attacking us.

The Nip, however, refused to play the way I wanted him to, and for a week, beginning the 5th of June, until I got some night fighters operating at Wakde, he put over some mean night attacks. On the night of the 5th a Jap

In early June 1944, the Japanese staged night air raids on the Fifth Air Force base on Wakde, a small island crowded with Allied warplanes and packed with munitions and aviation gasoline. By June 8, so many American planes had been destroyed or damaged that only ten bombers were in shape to fly a mission against a Japanese destroyer convoy: the B-25s of the 17th Tactical Reconnaissance Squadron, "the Fighting Seventeenth." Those B-25s are seen here on the far side of the burned-out P-38. National Archives Photo SC 258444 (Signal Corps Photo # SWPA-SigC-44-13084)

bomber blew up a bomb dump and had everyone on the island believing that an earthquake had hit the place. Between the Jap's bombs and our own we lost several hundred drums of gasoline and three P-47s. Two nights later I lost ten more airplanes on the ground, and, the night of the eleventh, the devils dug holes in the runway that took us all the next day to fill in and burned up another four airplanes.[8]

Kenney was using both his voices here—the voice of the aggressive general and the voice of the public relations man. Never was any spokesman bolder and more disingenuous than he was in this explanation. It might be true, technically and literally, that the night bombing had destroyed gasoline stores and three P-47s.

But the greater truth was that, as an air base, Wakde had been put out of action. Scores of American warplanes were damaged and unflyable—many would have to be junked. Sergeant Ursprung put it tersely: "Japs raided Wakde and damaged all but five ships."[9]

On the morning of June 8, 1944, after several nights of Japanese air raids, there were only a handful of flyable American bombers on Wakde Island: the B-25 gunships of the 17th Squadron. That morning they would have to fly. During the night, reports had come in that the Japanese convoy had reappeared, once more steaming south toward Biak.

The flyers of the 17th Squadron were still calling themselves the Fighting Seventeenth, but they had been chastened. They knew now that, on Momote, they had been the victims of a bleak practical Japanese joke. They had come back alive from their reconnaissance only because the enemy had let them live, and the information they gave had been dead wrong. The First Cavalry had landed, relying on their information, and the troops had nearly been overrun by hundreds of Japanese infantry. The credit of the 17th Squadron was shaken and their reckless confidence had been exposed.

In March the squadron members showed caution. They saw dozens of barges, but struck at few. They reported their coups conservatively now: they were damaging more barges than they destroyed. The single-plane "long over-water reconnaissance" missions came to an end. They started flying organized bombing missions instead. Some senior officer, probably, had taken firmer control. (This was the period when Sams was chewing out Tennille and Tennille was buzzing Sams' tent.) Significantly, Ennis Whitehead sent the squadron a letter, calculated to soothe anxiety and envy.

Only a comparatively short time has passed since your organization joined us in this theater. You may therefore think that we "old-timers" will be reluctant to share with you credit for what has been accomplished here. But do not underestimate yourselves. Do not think that your work of the past six months has gone unobserved or unappreciated. Your great versatility and combat efficiency merit the highest praise. Your part in our combat operations has been an essential one, and you have performed it consistently well. In operations yet to unfold, I know that your part will be no less essential, and I am sure that your performance will be no less commendable. May all your common memories be proud ones.[10]

In April the 17th Squadron flew assigned photo reconnaissance and bombing missions. In May it flew bombing missions, almost daily. It moved north to Wakde on May 25. American troops had gone ashore nearby, at Sarmi, and the squadron found itself shuttle-bombing the mainland on short-range ground support missions. The squadron history reported: "Because the airstrip on Wakde Island was only a few minutes flight from the target two or three of these missions were frequently performed in a day. It is of interest to note that due to the proximity of these targets to our camp the ground personnel took great delight in observing an entire mission from the beach on Wakde Island. From this point of vantage they could see flames and the high columns of smoke which arose from damaged oil stores and supplies."[11]

These were short missions, but they counted as missions and they racked up hours of combat flying—the sort of statistics that could win men Air Medals and get flyers rotations stateside. Even Major Tennille was rumored to be looking for a way home. Tennille had been in the Army since 1940. He had a wife named Sarah and now a three-month-old baby, William Grant Tennille III, a boy he had never seen. He had joked to his operations officer that he wanted to get home so that he could stop his wife feeding the baby orange juice and get him started on whiskey.[12]

During the Japanese night raids on Wakde, the 17th Squadron lost six planes damaged on the night of June 5–6. They had another bomber shot up on a mission on June 6. At dawn on June 8, the squadron counted its losses yet again. They were heavy: the previous night's bombing had destroyed two B-25s and damaged three more.[13] The strength of the squadron had been reduced to ten bombers. And yet those ten B-25 gunships were the only bombers available on the Fifth Air Force's front line.[14]

On June 8, 1944, Maj. Bill Tennille was thirty years old. He was from North Carolina. The family was well known in Greensboro and in Winston-Salem, where his father ran the Hotel Robert E. Lee. Rocky knew Tennille as the officer who had gotten sore feet during training hikes at Laurel.[15]

Tennille was "a smallish man," "almost frail," according to the Air Force publicists who first told his story. "He had dark curly hair and a fine smile, and he had a vast contempt for the war." In combat, they claimed, he lacked fear, "because he used to say that the war could not touch him that way. He laughed a great deal and he joked with his men, and the war could not touch that."[16]

The *Wing-ding* spoke of Major Tennille in a similar vein. "Characterized by a pleasing Southern accent, and with a mischievous twinkle in his brown eyes, the young major, only 29 years of age, was admired by everyone who knew him. . . . He was a friend to enlisted men and officers alike."[17]

All this is easily said. Nonetheless, there seem to be firm corners of substance to this eulogy. It is of one piece with Rocky's remark about how Tennille had settled complaints about his squadron's engineering section—that he heard the mechanics out, and then replaced the engineering officer. Perhaps Tennille's background in the hotel industry had trained him to handle complaints rather than fighting them, or taught him the value of skilled labor, or given him practice in the art of managing and pleasing large parties.

Some of his men doubted Tennille, because he readily put them in harm's way. Other men liked Tennille, perhaps because he shared the limelight and whatever glory the squadron earned. Most squadron histories are by-the-books typescript formularies. They use columns of figures to set forth dry reports of missions flown, munitions expended, damage done, and damage taken. The reports of the 17th Squadron go far beyond that. Their pages assiduously narrate each and every encounter with the enemy, no matter how minor. They energetically press for recognition of each and every airman involved—calling for Air Medals, Bronze Stars, Soldier's Medals, any decoration for which a man might qualify. Ground crewmen, whom flying officers often forgot, are profiled at length—"Old Bo" the ace mechanic, for example, who had joined the Third Cavalry in 1916 and whose expertise deserved recognition with the Legion of Merit.

Major Tennille had trouble with Colonel Sams—everyone saw that, and they chuckled when Tennille got his own back by buzzing the colonel's tent. Bert Smiley liked Tennille. (After the war, Smiley married Tennille's sister.) At the same time, Smiley clearly saw in Tennille the same qualities that Sams did: that Tennille was an enigmatic leader, restless, overbold—a skilled pilot, but a maverick. "Bill was his own man and nobody could tell him what to do," Smiley recalled. "He had a lot of confidence in me as his operations officer, but I'll admit, I didn't know what to think of him sometimes. He was a wild man, but absolutely fearless."[18]

On June 8, breakfast was flapjacks and coffee. Then the pilots were called to the operations tent. As the only bombers available, they had been ordered to attack the convoy.

The original plan was to pattern-bomb the convoy—to hit from high altitude. Because of the overcast, plans changed. Smiley was at the front of the tent, by the chalkboard. He was outlining the mission as operations officer; he was also scheduled to fly the lead plane. Smiley laid out a skip-bombing attack. He and his wingman would attack the two cruisers, while the remaining eight planes hit the four destroyers that were towing barges. If the squadron attacked all six vessels simultaneously, he considered, this would scatter the antiaircraft fire.

Others remembered a difference on one very critical point. The original convoy had included cruisers, heavier ships than a threadbare squadron of medium bombers could be expected to handle. "If the cruisers were still in the convoy, or if the ships in the convoy were so deployed that the firepower from the cruisers could be brought to bear on planes attacking the destroyers, the planes were to return without attempting the attack."[19] In short, the squadron was not to attack cruisers—either to preserve the few frontline bombers that the Fifth Air Force had, or to encourage the cruisers to steam on into waters where Allied cruisers could deal with them.

The mood in the operations tent was not good. For two weeks now, the Fighting Seventeenth had been on the receiving end of the war—taking its own share of bombs and machine-gun fire. Wakde was the first time that the squadron had been bombed and strafed, and the airmen had learned to fear and hate it. They spent their nights in foxholes and began each morning counting the damage that the Japanese had wrought. The night just passed had been the squadron's worst. Once in the air, the pilots knew, things would be no better.

They would have twenty P-38s flying high cover, which should keep off any Zeros, but Japanese fighters were no longer a serious problem. The serious problem would be Japanese antiaircraft fire. They had seen Japanese antiaircraft fire now, and they knew that the numbers were wrong. Ten bombers were too few to send out after a convoy of warships. Lieutenant Sciortino kept thinking that they had been trained to bomb and strafe, not attack naval vessels. Lieutenant Strawn thought that they would get the hell kicked out of them.

Smiley finished the briefing. At the front of the room, on a chalkboard, he had matched up the crews who would fly with the ten B-25s that were fit to be flown. Smiley asked for questions; and when he did, Major Tennille walked up to the chalkboard, rubbed out Smiley's name as mission leader, and replaced it with his own.[20]

The most dangerous course of action that a leader can adopt, John Keegan has eloquently written, is to advance on his own, in the hope that his example will draw his men in his wake.[21] Tennille had chosen to take that course of action. He wrote in his own name and dared everyone to follow him. The Old Man was sitting in on this hand himself.

Fifty missions might send him home, Tennille may have figured. Fifty missions and a valorous raid on a convoy would be better.

The air crews began climbing into the truck to head off for the runway. "Bring us a couple of Sugar Two Stacks," someone shouted after them. (A Sugar Two Stack was shorthand for the largest class of Japanese freighter.) "Sugar Two Stacks, hell," someone called back, "we'll bring you a couple of destroyers and a cruiser or two." That was bravado; not everyone assumed it. As the men were climbing into their B-25s, Captain Lind made a different remark: "If we find those damned ships, I'll be cashing in my chips today."[22]

The bombers began taking off at 0930. Tennille's B-25, another pilot remembered, lifted its nose wheel, bounced down on its main wheels, bounced up again and stayed in the air—lifted off nose-high, which was risky, but then climbed fast.[23]

Tennille's bomber had no nickname that men recalled (unless it was "Twenty-Five"). Howard Wood was his wingman in "Thumper." Sumner Lind was next in "The Straggler," with his wingman Fred Rimmer flying "Little Stinker." Glenn Pruitt in "Dragon Myasz II" ("Dragon Myasz I" had been one of the B-25s shot to pieces in February) had for his wingman Albert Wolfram in "Eager Wolves." Wesley Strawn flew "Miss Cue"; Don Machnikowski flew his wing in "Mitch the Witch." Archie Trantham of Cape Girardeau flew "The Mad Mizurian" with Robert Beck, a Hoosier, in "Sacramento Belle."[24] Each plane carried two 500-pound bombs and one 1,000-pound bomb. One 500-pounder was to be dropped first, then the thousand-pounder, then the last 500-pounder. All bombs were set with instantaneous nose fuses and four- to five-second delay tail fuses, ready either for high-altitude bombing or masthead-height attack.[25]

For three hours the squadron flew northwest. Their escort planes overtook them, P-38s from the 432nd and 433rd Fighter Squadrons, Clover and Possum Squadrons of the 475th Fighter Group, Satan's Angels. The mission flew northwest along a weather front. There were two layers of overcast, at five thousand and ten thousand feet—rain all along and dark blocks of cloud below. When the formation flew into the weather front, four fighter planes strayed away.

At 1250 the 17th Squadron had reached Amsterdam Island, off the northern tip of New Guinea, four hundred miles from Wakde. They had seen no ships. The weather was still patchy. Then a call came in from the four strayed airplanes: Possum Blue Leader, a hundred miles behind them, circling near Manokwari. He had spotted the convoy: "They appear to be freighters," he said.[26]

The convoy was off Cape Waios, labeled False Cape on the maps—not a cape at all, but a promontory on the long, curving coast. The bombers swung to the north, banked eastward, flew south-southeast. At 1315 they spotted the convoy. Some flyers must have taken comfort in Possum Blue Leader's report—hoped that the ships were merchantmen. They could no longer hope that. The ships had heeled sharply to port and cracked on speed in a way that no freighter could. They were warships: destroyers at least. The ships were formed in a rough pyramid. One was leading, another steaming 1,200 yards behind it, then came two

Off Cape Waios, in a short, savage melee, the 17th Squadron attacked a group of Japanese destroyers conveying enemy reinforcements to Biak. In ninety seconds, the squadron earned sixty Distinguished Flying Crosses, nineteen of them posthumous. Courtesy of Eastern Oregon University, Pierce Library, Fred Hill World War II Photograph Collection. Donated by Fred Hill.

larger ships, 400 yards apart—each large ship trailed by a smaller vessel, 660 yards apart. "Jesus Christ, they're cruisers," somebody said. There still was reason to call off the strike.

At that moment Tennille came on the radio, and simultaneously his plane began to dive. "My wingman and I will hit the destroyer and cruiser on the left flank and divert their fire," the pilots heard him say. "Pick your targets."[27]

There were, in fact, no cruisers in the convoy. The Japanese warships were six destroyers, two of them longer than the others.

They were the *Late Rains, Early Summer Rains, White Dew, Spring Rains, Spreading Waves,* and *Shore Wave:* the *Shigure, Samidare, Shiratsuyu, Harusame, Shikinami,* and *Uranami.*[28]

The destroyers bristled with antiaircraft guns. The *Uranami* and *Shikinami,* the largest ships, each carried as many as twenty-two 25-mm fast-firing cannon and ten heavy 13-mm machine guns. The *Shiratsuyu* may have carried almost as many antiaircraft guns: at least one of her turrets had been replaced with double- and triple-mounted 25-mms. The remaining destroyers—*Shigure, Samidare,* and *Harusame*—each carried two triple-mounted and one double-mounted 25-mm cannon, as well as 13-mm machine guns. Beyond this, the *Samidare* had ten additional 25-mms in single mounts, and the *Shigure* had fifteen.[29] The Japanese 25-mm antiaircraft gun was fed with 15-shell ammo boxes, which meant that it fired in short bursts. (Japanese antiaircraft crews learned to fire first and then dive for cover from any strafing plane that made it through their barrage.) The gun was heavy-handling, shook hard, and blinded its crew with its muzzle flash, but it would hit at one thousand meters and within eight hundred meters a triple-mount could be uncommonly lethal. At masthead height, where skip-bombers flew, even the ships' machine guns were formidable.

The destroyers at Cape Waios had gone through more than two years of hard fighting. They had seen the Solomons and Rabaul and New Guinea; they had landed reinforcements and drawn off regiments in retreat; they had torpedoed their weight in American warships; they had taken blows and returned to fight again—all the ships were veteran destroyers. If a tiny ship like a destroyer can be famous, some were even famous destroyers. The *Shikinami* and *Uranami* had led the Japanese convoy at the Battle of the Bismarck Sea.[30] The *Shigure, Samidare,* and *Shiratsuyu* had sailed in the celebrated 27th Destroyer Squadron of Captain Tameichi Hara, and the *Shigure* had been Hara's flagship. During the biggest American air raid at Rabaul, Hara's destroyers had been the first ships to get under way. They had drawn up outside the harbor, firing flak that broke up the American formations, and that morning *Shigure* had claimed five bombers.[31]

The destroyermen had seen hard service. They were disgruntled and angry. For months they had been sent out to fight their navy's battles, while the battleships and carriers sheltered in harbor. Now they had been sent out again. They had steamed out of Sorong just after midnight. Since dawn, under the rain and the black overcast, they had been watching for the American bombers. Now the bombers were here. They had their own fighters above them, six Zeros and four Oscars; they saw the big American P-38s roar into the attack and the Japanese fighters break away into a cloudbank. So the destroyermen could count on no one else; they would have to fight the bombers on their own—but they had handled bombers before. A turret gun fired and a waterspout rose astern, between the ships and the bombers. A radioman began yammering in English: *"Turn right, turn right, what altitude are you?"* Make an airplane dodge or a single pilot doubt and that split second of confusion might be enough.[32]

Tennille and his squadron bore down on the convoy, roaring in from astern, low above the dark water, closing fast. The loaders clipped on the ammo boxes. The gunners drew breath. They trained their cannon and caught the planes in their gun-sights, and they shot the first three bombers out of the sky.

Tennille's plane was the first to make a bombing run. Wood was his wingman and followed him into the dive.

Wood was hit first, a thousand yards short of the convoy. His plane's wing was shot off and the bomber crashed and sank. There were black clouds of flak exploding now in the air between the planes and the ships, and more waterspouts. Tennille was firing, shooting at the gunners who were shooting at him—the pilots could see the bullets churning up water. Tennille reached the left-flank rear destroyer and dropped a bomb and lifted over the ship, heading on to sink what he thought was a cruiser. Lieutenant Pruitt saw the bomb miss and then he saw Tennille's wheels drop down from the bomber's wings and fire flare up along the fuselage. "Tennille, you're on fire!" pilots were shouting.

"So long boys, I'm taking the big one," they heard Tennille say. They kept shouting to him on the radio, but heard no reply. They saw Tennille's bomber soar over the ship. They could not see if he had dropped his last two bombs. The whole B-25 was on fire now. For a second they thought Tennille was trying to ditch, and then the plane stalled and flipped over and hit the water cockpit-down.

In "Dragon Myasz II," Lieutenant Pruitt could not dodge and flew through a waterspout. He went for the lead destroyer, fired at soldiers he saw on its deck, dropped his bombs, and pulled out on the far side of the flak. He and Lieutenant Lundberg, his copilot, both thought that they had put all three of their bombs on the ship. The plane flying their wing caught up with them, Lieutenant Wolfram. Wolfram had gone for the same destroyer and thought he had hit it, too.

Lieutenant Trantham and Lieutenant Beck pulled up from their bomb runs. They had hit the second destroyer; they thought they had hit it twice.

Lieutenant Machnikowski pulled out of his bomb run swearing. He had strafed the destroyer that Tennille had gone for but flak had banged up his plane and jammed shut his bomb-bay doors. Captain Lind, the third pilot to go in, had cashed in his chips. Machnikowski had been behind Lind and saw what happened. Lind had gone for the same destroyer and dropped two bombs that hit and then as Lind cleared the ship the Japanese ack-ack had hit him and blown off his right wing and his plane exploded and went in. The ship had gone down by the stern and Machnikowski thought he had killed some of the sailors as they ran up the slanting deck.

While Lind was going left, Lieutenant Strawn had gone for the right-flank rear destroyer. The destroyer turned across Strawn's path, putting a long broadside of guns against him. This was when they would kick the hell out of him, Strawn thought, and then suddenly the flak stopped. The decks in front of him looked empty. (Were the gunners ducking down behind their empty guns?) Strawn pressed the bomb release switch but it wouldn't work. Strawn's smart-aleck observer from New York City asked Strawn sharply if he saw anything he liked and Strawn said he had been shopping around, and this time the switch worked. Captain Lind's wingman, Lieutenant Rimmer, came in with Strawn. Rimmer's left engine was hit and flak had punched through the nose of his plane and his observer was bleeding to death out front with his leg blown off. Rimmer thought either he or Strawn had hit the destroyer once. Strawn thought he had put a 500-pounder through its side.[33]

The bombers gathered where Pruitt's plane was circling, out of range of the Japanese cannon.

Pruitt set a course for Wakde and took the lead. One B-25 made it home, then crash-landed. Another bomber, when they checked it on the ground, had its escape hatch battered shut by flak and a hole shot through one blade of its propeller. The squadron had dropped nine 500-pound bombs and five 1,000-pound bombs, and fired 14,500 rounds of .50-caliber ammunition. Lt. Morris Oberhand, Rimmer's observer, died in the Wakde hospital the next day.[34]

Against these costs and losses, Rocky heard the claims that were being made:

> Ten B-25's of the 17th Squadron attacked four destroyers and two cruisers yesterday. Three destroyers sank immediately and the other was left burning. Three planes were shot down by the anti-aircraft fire from the cruisers, among whom were Major Tennille, Captain Lind et cetera. Lieutenant Lundberg said he dropped two 500-pound bombs and one 1000-pound bomb on his destroyer. The battle lasted approximately one and one-half minutes.[35]

The Japanese reckoned a different toll. The *Harusame* had been sunk, but the *Shigure* had rescued more than a hundred of her crew. On the *Shiratsuyu*, four crewmen had been killed. On the *Shikinami*, two sailors had died and the depth charges had been set afire. Officers ran aft and jettisoned the depth charges before they could explode. The convoy steamed on to the northwest coast of Biak, which they reached around dusk. Just short of midnight the destroyers cast off the landing barges (which carried some troops ashore) and then, outrunning a larger force of Allied cruisers and destroyers, dodged away and raced home. Most of the soldiers taken on board for Biak were landed back in Sorong the next day.[36]

The pilots thought they had set the ships afire. Probably, they mistook minor superficial blazes for conflagrations: bombs striking a warship's deck set small fires and may give the impression that the vessel has been generally set ablaze. Larger and more spectacular flames—equally illusory—can result when a warship shifts quickly from cruising speed to flank speed, as excess oil burns in the engine exhausts, causing flames to shoot out of the smokestacks. (The *Shigure*, once, racing to flank speed after a surprise night-time air strike, was spared a second attack because the American pilots saw flames shooting from her funnels and concluded—the *Shigure*'s radiomen heard this on the air, in English— that they had set the destroyer afire.)[37]

"The 17th Squadron made history in this theater today but at heavy cost," Colonel Sams wrote. Sams flew to Wakde and drew the unit out of combat.[38] It would be weeks before the 17th Squadron flew another mission.

At Nadzab, the airmen had heard how badly the Fighting Seventeenth had been shot up—heard also that General Kenney was pulling the bombers back from Wakde because the Japanese night raiders were knocking out too many of them. The offensive seemed to have stalled. There was hopeful news from a different theater—so important that commanders at Nadzab made a late-afternoon announcement and the *Wing-ding* rushed out an extra edition. On June 6, Rocky heard of the Normandy landings, "that the second front had been opened along the northern coast of France. . . . Fellows are now optimistic and hope the war will be over this year," he wrote. "The men are betting that we will be in Paris by the Fourth of July."[39]

14

SUMMER

By July, the war had moved beyond Nadzab.[1] To the northwest, the fighting continued. On Biak, American soldiers were making slow headway and American airmen were hunkered down behind whatever shelter they could find, waiting for the enemy snipers and mortars to be cleared out. Not since Buna, nearly two years before, had infantry combat been so bloody. The Japanese fought doggedly; they stalled the invasion, dominated the airfields, and threw off MacArthur's timetable. Ironically, the savage fighting at Biak was the other side of the relaxation that men found, briefly, in the tents and thatched huts of Nadzab. Until the Japanese could be driven out of their caves and bunkers, until American warplanes could fly from Biak's airstrips, the American air wings could not move forward.

> Lieutenant Foliart said that Lieutenant Cole heard that the Fifth Air Force is one whole month behind schedule. It has been a consistent rumor for three months that our Wing was to be established in Biak by June 1st but it is believed by all that we will not arrive there until the latter part of August.[2]

So for these few weeks, in every sense, for Rocky and the rest of the airmen at Nadzab, the war was almost a thousand miles away. There were stage shows, softball leagues, Red Cross girls, and food worth eating. Celebrities visited. Latrines became grandiose.

> Yesterday we had fresh pork for both lunch and dinner. Upon asking the mess officer if it was quartermaster's issue I received the reply, "Yes, but it is hospital rations. We had to give the quartermaster's personnel a little gin for it." Major Chenery said the lumber (American pine) used in the construction of the new officer's latrine cost approximately $300. It is beyond question the best in New Guinea.[3]

Creature comforts had caught up with the 71st Group and the 91st Wing, but so had envies and contempts that were familiar parts of American life: rivalries, racism, and office politics. Rumors abounded—men began thinking that the war might end, and about what might come after.

On the hills above Hollandia, on a picturesque mountainside, a headquarters building had been built for Douglas MacArthur. It was not elaborate, only three prefabricated buildings bolted together, but it would contain a palace's worth of arrogance, adultery, scandal, and disgust.

MacArthur's aides had the building painted white, and here perhaps his problems began; only lately, and belatedly, had the general announced that he would not run for president. The HQ seemed to look down on the grit and smoke of the beachhead. As William Manchester put it: "Stories about [the house] circulated throughout the Southwest Pacific, gaining in the telling until troops spoke of 'Dugout Doug's White House' and 'his fabulous villa overlooking dreamy Sentani,' and indignantly canceled their war bond purchases."[4] They were not the only ones who resented what they saw or heard.

Kepler returned from Hollandia and said the following orders had been issued: One, all showers will be completely enclosed. Two, no swimming in the nude by anyone. Three, men cannot walk in the nude within their area. And all this is because General MacArthur has a home on a hill which overlooks the Hollandia strips and the general's wife and the Chinese maid for his boy will live at Hollandia and they, the females, would be embarrassed, if they saw a nude human figure (male).[5]

Until this time, MacArthur had been running the war in the Southwest Pacific from Lennon's Hotel in Brisbane. MacArthur's troops were ready to believe the worst of a commander who lived in an Australian hotel while they sweltered under canvas in the heat and rain of New Guinea, and who now—they believed—looked down on them from luxury and a mountaintop. At the 91st Reconnaissance Wing, Rocky wrote:

The subject of discussion at the breakfast table was General MacArthur's home at Hollandia. One officer said he had heard a battalion of engineers were required for its construction and the roadway leading to it. A rumor has it that immediately upon the WACs' arrival in Australia, Fifth Air Force issued the order that officers may date enlisted personnel.[6]

The airmen were wrong to hold MacArthur's white house against him. They were absolutely right to connect it with WACs and sex.[7]

Lt. Gen. Richard K. Sutherland, MacArthur's chief of staff, had a wife and daughter in Washington. In Brisbane, he had begun an affair with a much younger woman, Elaine Bessemer-Clarke, an Australian socialite. Even in wartime Australia this was reckless: Elaine Clarke herself was married already, and her husband was a prisoner of war, captured by the Japanese at Singapore. To keep Elaine Clarke nearby, Sutherland had her commissioned into the WACs, as a headquarters receptionist.

In the bustle of Brisbane, many Australian women worked around Allied headquarters, and Elaine Clarke was not conspicuous. That changed in April 1944, when Sutherland brought her north to Port Moresby, to Government House, the forward headquarters for the Southwest Pacific. Not even Eleanor Roosevelt had visited Government House. MacArthur encountered Elaine Clarke there, unexpectedly, when he walked half-dressed and bare-legged into the living room. Embarrassed but composed, Mac-Arthur told Sutherland to send her home to Australia. Within weeks, Sutherland had disobeyed that order. He brought Elaine Clarke to the villa at Sentani.

To vaunt his power as chief of staff, Sutherland brought Elaine Clarke with him to the officers' mess of General Krueger. (This was a calculated insult: Krueger held toward stray women at his dinner table the attitude to be expected from a stern soldier born in Bismarck's Prussia and reared in the Midwest that inspired Grant Wood's painting *American Gothic*.) Elaine Clarke commandeered for herself a jeep used by a lieutenant colonel, coveting its padded seats. Sutherland was the son of a United States senator; he had grown accustomed to arrogating authority to himself. Now he began to muse aloud that MacArthur had become an old man, and that he himself was running the show.

From the beachhead, the soldiers could sense hauteur and privilege in the headquarters, and they held it against MacArthur. The general had earned this, perhaps, with the failings that counterpointed his intelligence and self-reliance—his vanity, pride, and Olympian remoteness. In the end, which was still months ahead, MacArthur would not be mocked, he would not see his own authority flouted, and he would take risks in the field, perhaps enough to balance his fondness for the comforts of headquarters. For now, Sutherland was to enjoy his idyll, and the servicemen's envy continued to simmer.

In Wing headquarters, the gossip was also about sex and archi-
tecture. Colonel Brownfield was determined to build for himself
what amounted to a mansion in a combat zone. Pointed comments
were made about this, sotto voce.

> The subject now under discussion is Colonel Brown-
> field and his staff's house which is to be constructed at
> Biak. The rumor goes it will be a six bedroom, one recre-
> ation room, one dining room, one kitchen and two bath-
> rooms complete with lavatories.
>
> Major Chenery, our signal officer, has expressed many
> sarcastic remarks about the house. In all confidence,
> he told me that all Colonel Brownfield talked about at
> the dinner table was how many girls he had had inter-
> course with during the last week. It is hell being here in
> New Guinea and being awakened by feminine laughter
> from the colonel's house some fifty yards away. Chaplain
> Perkins reproved Lieutenant Colonel Sellards, the Wing
> flight surgeon, quite severely, because frequently a Red
> Cross girl was seen leaving the lieutenant colonel's tent
> early in the mornings.[8]

In 91st Wing HQ, without missing a beat, as if encoding communications, officers switched from questioning their CO's com-
petence to questioning the value of their new outhouse.

> The subject which is receiving the greatest attention is
> the new officers' latrine. The hole is, according to one of
> the fellows who dug it through the hardpan, approxi-
> mately twenty feet deep. The top on the framework
> for the seats, containing two rows of four holes each,
> back to back, is made from the best of American pine,

imported pine, the mahogany that lies around isn't good enough. I am wondering what Chic Sale would say to this situation.[9]

Chic Sale was part vaudevillian and part homespun Midwestern humorist. His masterwork was *The Specialist*, a novella-length monologue by a carpenter about the finer points of building outhouses. His name became a nickname for outhouse, and Rocky was not the only serviceman to speak of Chic Sale when discussing latrines in New Guinea.[10] This was to be expected in a war where flush toilets were rare—but to speak of Chic Sale, or of a Chic Sale, also carried overtones of sarcasm and satire.

Chic Sale began *The Specialist* as a vaudeville routine. It reached print in 1929, became a bestseller, and remains in print today. Its humor is subversive—earthy but never actually scatological, dancing around forbidden subjects by dwelling on outhouse construction and furnishings. (For example, when called in by a farmer because his hired hands are spending too long in the privy, the carpenter observes: "I looks at the seats proper, and I see what the trouble was. I had made them holes too durn comfortable. So I gets out a scroll saw and cuts 'em square with hard edges.")

Latrines demanded so much hard labor and so much attention that they held an outsized place in memories of the war. With a preternatural irony, and a peculiar note of nostalgic cheeriness, Chic Sale's straight-faced discussion of outhouse construction was echoed by Army Air Force medical historians.

While one common type [of latrine] was made from oil drums, the only really satisfactory one was the deep pit latrine which was in turn surrounded by a screened insect-proofed structure with automatically closing doors. Properly constructed, these structures could be removed from latrines and placed over new ones, thus conserving time, energy and materials. . . . It should be noted that the

246 Chapter 14

Quartermaster latrine boxes described in Army training manuals were never seen among Air Force units! But it was found by experience that boxes should be made from seasoned mill lumber and furnished with close fitting covers that could not be propped open. Unseasoned or rough lumber developed too many holes to be successful.[11]

When servicemen marveled at the concern and jealousy being lavished on latrines in New Guinea, they spoke of Chic Sale. Their talk about latrines and bathrooms was as satirical as *The Specialist*— just as Sale was poking fun at Midwestern middle-class prudery, they were obliquely mocking the commanders who used those facilities. One of Rocky's comments underlined how self-conscious and theatrical this mockery could be. "Everyone is looking forward to see Bob Hope and all the others. Saw some soldier with a movie camera taking pictures (making the gestures anyway) of the officers' new latrine."[12]

In the Pacific, there was plain evidence of how commanders' demand for comfort and convenience could sap the strength of an offense. On Guadalcanal, two summers before, the Japanese had landed to build an air base. They landed without opposition, brought in thousands of laborers, enjoyed almost two months in which to complete their work—and yet, no Zeros ever flew from the island. When the United States Marines landed and captured the base, they were amazed to find the airstrip empty but the camps complete. "Our enemy were sybarites!" wrote Marine lieutenant William Whyte. "The officers, we discovered, lived in a tent city at Kukum with concrete floors, and they had brought with them a perfectly astounding collection of pornography. They had electric lights, steel-covered air-raid shelters, and elaborate concrete privies."[13]

What Whyte saw on Guadalcanal was not lost on him. He would go on to write *The Organization Man*, about the Japanese officers' American counterparts, small-minded corporate men who preferred to be conventional and comfortable rather than original or daring. Nor was General Krueger blind to what would happen if American senior officers arrogated to themselves the construction materials that his offensive would need. Krueger could be particularly alert to officers' asserting dubious privileges. He may have heard what the Marines had captured—or he may have remembered his own youth. Krueger had been an enlisted man in the Pacific himself once, during the Philippine Insurrection forty years before. Krueger became the airmen's man of the hour.

> The mess officer said, when I made a comment about the colonel and his staff's home to be constructed in Biak, "General Krueger, commanding general of Sixth Army, said we would live under field conditions on Biak and there would be no palaces." [14]
>
> Captain Chapin said last night that General Krueger was the person who issued the order that no more individual units would erect buildings. His policy is that the only constructions will be mess halls and warehouses and headquarters and all will be prefabricated and he is issuing material according to the number of men. [15]

The *Wing-ding* had found its footing. No longer did it reprint the canned service biographies that Fifth Air Force publicists handed out when a new CO was named; now reporters turned out feature articles on high-ranking personalities like Colonel Darnell and Colonel Guerry. There were outhouse jokes, about an outfit's "super deluxe sixteen-holer . . . the most pretentious 'Chic Sale' in New Guinea." There was a gossip column on the 71st Group. There was continuing coverage of camp softball, in which Lieutenant Zock led the 71st Group Strafers against the Dumbos, Eight-Ballers, and Photolites. The *Wing-ding* also featured the cartoon temptress "Willful Winnie of New Guinea," a lissome young woman whose flowing hair and hourglass figure recalled the

Gibson Girl and whose misadventures with propeller wash anticipated the problem that Marilyn Monroe would have with sub-
way vents.[16]

As well as printing news, the *Wing-ding* dealt in code and camouflage. The paper answered to an "Advisory Committee" of officers whom Rocky would have recognized as lackeys of Colonel
Brownfield (Lieutenant Colonel Ilgenfritz, Captain Williams, and
Major Tockstein). When the paper made subversive suggestions,
it did so subtly. The *Wing-ding* did not speak of tension between
enlisted men and officers—rather, a question-and-answer column
advised enlisted men that they would be required to salute captured enemy officers, as per Provost-Marshal regulations. The
Wing-ding did not gripe about rotation policy. Instead, it printed
as front-page news the names of the handful of men who actually
left for home on rotation—a lieutenant and thirteen NCOs under
the April quota, eleven sergeants and a private first class for May,
a bare dozen a month out of the thousands of men at Nadzab.[17]

No one else was going stateside, for their replacements were
still hard to find. Hap Arnold had delivered to George Kenney one
group of fighter planes and pilots, leaving it to Kenney to find
ground crews from men already in the Southwest Pacific. The
Fifth Air Force hunted for men, wherever they might be found.

> Over at the Fifth Air Force officers' mess, several Chi-
> nese young men wait tables—so the story goes, coming
> from a sergeant in Ordnance at Wing HQ. These Chinese
> were shipwrecked along the coast of Australia, made pri-
> vates in the Fifth Air Force, and became waiters in the
> Fifth Air Force officers' mess. They cannot speak English
> and at the present time a Chinese second lieutenant is
> teaching them to speak English.[18]

In Australia's prisons, Kenney had found an unexpected resource:
"over a hundred Chinese cooks, stewards, and mess-boys, refugees

from British ships that had been sunk in the Far East." Denied entrance to Australia, they had been quartered in Australian jails. Kenney enlisted twenty likely men: "It not only released twenty men for my new fighter group but provided me with some excellently trained mess personnel."[19]

Steadfastly, inexorably, Kenney and MacArthur held back from rotating servicemen home. To this discouraging record there was another side. MacArthur's war in the Southwest Pacific was a war of maneuver rather than a war of blood. Kenney's war stories were of pilots who fought against long odds and armorers who did much with little. When Kenney heard how lightly the Allied air commanders in Europe spoke of their casualty rates, he was outraged. He fumed:

Jack Murtha on his return with Sutherland [from a military conference] told me of a statement made by Colonel Loutzenheizer in Washington to the effect that any air forces commander who was taking less than fifteen percent casualties was obviously inefficient and should be relieved of his command. If this is the attitude Washington has become accustomed to, and they are all talking blood thirsty figures over there, it is a poor lookout for the morale of the lads actually doing the fighting. Washington has become calloused to the terrific losses the air forces are taking in German occupied Europe; they boast about figures which make one's hair stand on end.[20]

Because Kenney and MacArthur could not count on replacements, they proved respectful of their men's lives.

War news came in two kinds. The news from overseas was cheerful. On July 20, Rocky wrote: "The most frequent comment today is, 'The news today from all the fronts is the best we've heard.'"[21]

Hours later, the news seemed even better. "Heard late last evening there was a revolt in Germany, and Major Clark the chaplain could be heard from his tent making very optimistic prophecies."[22] Reports from the Southwest Pacific itself were grimmer. For the flyers of the 71st Group, these were troubled weeks. An officer from the 17th Squadron told Rocky that the squadron had taken 30 percent losses since coming overseas.[23] Another flyer gave a report on what to expect, farther north:

> Lieutenant Rogers of the 17th Recco Squadron said that in Biak the Japs were living in the so-called caves which were air conditioned and many caches had been found. He added that at night you could hear the Japs' motor, for their air conditioning plants, running. There is an order out now that Air Corps personnel cannot go Jap-hunting with the infantry because too many pilots have been killed.[24]

It was more than Japanese resistance that had delayed the Fifth Air Force's drive northward—geology and sickness also posed obstacles. At first, Rocky heard that the Wing had not moved to Biak because there was not enough water for the photo labs.[25] There was also a deadly epidemic of scrub typhus:

> It is a consistent rumor that many men are dying of typhus up north. Kepler told me eighty men had contracted it on Owi Island, and today at noon Lieutenant Scott, A-2 intelligence officer, said 800 cases have been reported on Biak. We have heard for a long time that only forty percent of the cases survive. Spragg reports that they (the Engineers) will burn off the whole area before we will move. No doubt this explains our delay in moving and being a month behind schedule.[26]

Colonel Sams had played nursemaid to the shot-up 17th Squadron and brought its bombers back into action. The Fighting Seventeenth began to talk of new exploits as well as of its casualty rate. Captain Wise and his crew were shot down near Halmahera and rescued the next day by seaplane. The Japanese intervened and were driven away. Lt. Bertram Sill, of Brooklyn and Long Island, fought off the attack. "Lieutenant Sill, who was flying escort to the PBY or Catalina of the Navy who picked them up, shot down his second plane, a medium bomber. When the plane shot at them, Sill maneuvered into such positions that all gunners could get a shot at the plane."[27] Sill flew a B-25 gunship, but he did not roar into dogfights; he fought by judging spatial relationships and setting up shots for his gunners. Perhaps unsurprisingly, he had been a skilled machinist before the war and was renowned within his squadron as an ace when bridge was being played.[28]

Elsewhere in Colonel Sams' domain, there were troubles. He flew to Tadji: "Worried about the condition of P-39s of 82nd and 110th and the resultant attitude of the pilots. My boys are too damn good to worry about their planes unless there is something wrong, and I very well know that these planes are worn out and will cost lives unless replaced."[29]

There had been a complicated session of aeronautical horse-trading. Hap Arnold had agreed to ship enough P-38s to the Southwest Pacific to equip the Seventh and Eighth Fighter Squadrons, which had been flying all-but-obsolete P-40 fighters. Sams agreed to take these P-40s for the 82nd and 110th Squadrons. In exchange for taking P-40s now, the 71st Group would be the first group in the SWPA to receive P-51 Mustangs. At the same time, the Group was promised new P-39s. The P-40s, when they arrived, looked old. They were clearly hand-me-downs, bearing nicknames and girlie pictures painted on by former pilots. When the P-39s arrived, Sams inspected them and found that the planes were not new: they were practically worn out, each with two hundred to four hundred hours' time on them. They were no better than the battered warplanes that the 71st had been flying since it reached New Guinea.[30]

I very well know that these planes are worn out and will cost lives unless replaced. Sams had done some canny work, but he knew that the deal was, in the short run, a devil's bargain.

And Sams knew that the problem was not only the aircraft; it was combat fatigue, showing itself in negligence and bad judgment. In the 82nd Squadron, somebody else's P-47 ran into and chopped up a P-40, Lieutenant Weber touched down short of the runway and knocked off a wheel, and Lieutenant Murphy cracked up on landing—"the Sunday jinx hit us again," Sergeant Ursprung wrote, matter-of-factly. Lieutenant Lipscomb landed wheels-up on a belly tank of hundred-octane gas. The plane cracked up and the gasoline burned; Lipscomb was blistered on his hands and arms and only his goggles saved his eyes.[31]

Errors were creeping into flyers' routines. Lieutenant Pictor recorded how it could happen.

After peeling off for our usual tight landing pattern, I got the red light—someone taxiing across the strip. Almost immediately, I was given the green light and decided we could still make it. The wheels must have still been coming up because I got no warning signal. A great landing—no wheels! Sergeant Deets was racing along the strip in his jeep. He told me the belly tank scraped off and burned beautifully, but I was okay—only a little unhappy. Fortunately, the report blamed it on battle fatigue. That night Captain Parks and I tried to wash down the event.[32]

Pictor was a veteran pilot, but he was making bad snap decisions, feeling unhappy, drinking to forget problems. He saw "battle fatigue" as something different from his own performance, even when the accident report named the problem.

Colonel Sams himself was feeling the pressure. "Still hanging around Group, inertia's got me," he wrote in mid-July. The next day was worse: "Don't know why I continue to have headaches. Sufficiently frequent nowadays to have me worried."[33] He himself had been shaken up by bomb blasts, but he would not acknowledge—not any more than Pictor—that the steady tension of combat had impaired him.

At the 110th Squadron, Lt. Gabriel Eggud dropped a bomb from too low an altitude. The blast ripped off both wings of Eggud's plane and must have shredded the fuselage too; what was left of the P-39 exploded before it hit the ground.[34] This was what had killed Mosher—and a very similar error, in June, could have blown the entire 17th Squadron out of the sky. Carelessly, ordnance men had loaded regular fragmentation bombs (which dropped straight and were fused to explode on impact) on a mission when the flyers thought they were dropping parafrags (which floated down on parachutes, giving the planes time to clear the blast zone). Equally carelessly, no flying officer checked what sort of bomb his plane was carrying. Colonel Sams wrote: "Strafed and bombed Japs west of Tor River. All planes received some bullet holes and bomb fragments. Operations said we were carrying parafrags and we (damn fools) didn't realize we were carrying straight frags and came in too low. Least number of hits on any plane five. One plane had his left rudder destroyed and one tire punctured. Anyhow the Nips got part of the bombs and all of the strafing which was plenty and all our crews learned a lesson the hard way."[35]

Even for airmen who did not actually trade shots with the Japanese, the tensions of combat made themselves felt. "A crash, fire, and explosion would clean out about a city block, with debris, including human parts, everywhere," an airman remembered.[36] Sergeant Ursprung noted tersely that a staff sergeant had committed suicide and another soldier had gone insane.[37]

Army psychiatrists had already warned that the combat zone of the air war extended wherever an air strip operated. "Aeroanxiety," the psychiatrists called what resulted.

Most cases of aero-anxiety complain of nervousness and fear. The fear is brought on by repeated exposures which endanger one's life. An engine may fail on take-off, or a tire may blow out as the plane rushes down the runway. With a full load of gasoline and four thousand pounds of bombs such incidents may become tragic affairs. And those who have witnessed such affairs readily know the mask of fear on the men's faces. . . . The amazing fact is that 90% of the injuries received are of a minor nature, *but the degree of mental scarring runs high.* While some show little effect from such handshakes with death, others exhibit marked degrees of anxiety. All show *some* effects.[38]

With aircraft so war-worn, with pilots whose acuity was fraying, losses occurred that were inexplicable—both in the sense that they were mysterious and in the sense that no good explanation, of any sort, could be imagined for them. On July 3, at 8:30 in the morning, two first lieutenants from the 110th Squadron, John T. Evans and William J. Sparks, were raiding Wallis Island. They were flying P-39s. Sparks' plane was a P-39Q/6, a plane that the squadron had been flying for months. As Evans went in for a strafing run, he saw Sparks pull up and fly past him, heading out to sea. When Evans finished strafing, Sparks was nowhere to be seen. Oddly unconcerned, Evans continued strafing for another quarter-hour, "presuming that Lt. Sparks had returned to Tadji Airdrome." Evans then flew into base alone. They sent him straight back to Wallis Island, with an escort, to look harder and without presuming anything. It did no good. Nothing more was ever seen of Sparks.[39]

There had been two PT boats nearby. Evans considered: "Sparks could have glided near the boats if he was forced to make a landing in the sea at that time." Then he added a final clause: "provided he had control of the ship." Those who flew or serviced war-worn aircraft would see in that phrase the suggestion that the engines or controls had failed.

The 82nd Squadron lost another pilot, 2nd Lt. Joseph Grenda. "Took off and had engine trouble, he failed to get back to runway, went into ocean and drowned," Sams summed up.[40] The crash may have been more abrupt. Sergeant Ursprung suggested that Grenda arced straight from the airstrip to the ocean: "Lt. Grenda, test hopping Corporal Calderon's ship, crashed into sea—one mile from the end of the runway." The squadron history offers a different explanation: "While on a routine test hop this pilot was engaged in acrobatics." Sadly, all of these explanations seem consistent and plausible.[41]

Grenda's death may have put to an end a scandal that had quietly hung over the 82nd Squadron for months. This was the court-martial that Captain Williams had ignored and Colonel Hutchison had brushed aside—the case in which "a native was killed up along Salamaua and Lieutenant G____ of the 82nd Squadron was held responsible" and confined to quarters.

While P-39s from the 82nd Squadron were firing over the bay near Dobodura, ricochet rounds struck and killed several villagers in a canoe. Rocky had heard the pilot's explanation: "The rumor said G___ had his guns stick the day before so he went out over the water to test them on an old barge." The case had been taken seriously. Investigators questioned Papuans who had been on the water that day, as well as Australian antiaircraft gunners on a nearby beach. Inquiry focused on the 82nd Squadron because it had the most planes flying nearby; it seems to have ended without formal charges, because no witness could tell which sort of airplane had done the firing.[42]

In the flight echelon of the 82nd Squadron, there were three Lieutenant Gs: Delta Graham, Needham Graves, and Joseph Grenda. Graham and Graves may be ruled out. Both of them were flying in January, when Lieutenant G___ was grounded. Grenda does not seem to have been flying then. Nor had he (unlike Graves and Graham) been named for an Air Medal by the time of his death. Had Grenda been flying regularly, he would almost certainly have flown the missions and hours needed to earn that decoration.

⑤

Sutherland was not the only general with a personal WAC. General Kenney had a WAC in his entourage, Lt. Beryl Stephenson, another Australian woman with a U.S. Army commission. Unlike Elaine Clarke in her tailored white uniform, Lieutenant Stephenson wore regulation olive drab: polished brown lace-ups, buttoned-up tunic, flat-topped kepi. Even so, she was conspicuous on the womanless airfields of New Guinea, a pretty woman in her twenties keeping company with a general in his fifties.[43]

Men talked about General Kenney's WAC, as they talked about captains rating nurses, or the costs of prostitution, or Chaplain Perkins taking Doc Sellards to task for keeping a Red Cross girl in his tent overnight. More stories spread among the junior officers.

> Kepler told me about his boat trip over. "We had several Red Cross girls and nurses aboard and after dinner there was a scramble to get blankets, rush up on deck to some secluded corner, spread the blanket and lay with one of the Red Cross girls. I had never seen so many acts of sexual intercourse in one place in all my life. Everyone was off to war."[44]

The rumors had it that women in uniform were promiscuous. The rumors also had it that women in uniform were inaccessible— at least to enlisted men and junior officers. Servicemen were willing to repeat these stories because they jibed well with the grievances that they harbored (just as they were willing to rumor that Japanese soldiers sneaked into their chow lines because this jibed with their belief that the war was going well).

Rocky listened, one July evening, to a group of sergeants discussing "the post-war woman situation."

> First sergeant: "I certainly wouldn't marry a girl who was in a uniform during the war. It makes them coarse." Second sergeant: "I'm wondering often about the nurses. The officers certainly won't marry the nurses, especially those who came overseas, and the enlisted men won't marry them because they wouldn't associate with them during the war."[45]

The second sergeant expressed a crucial point. No airman complained about the boldness of Australian girls, or about officers chasing skirts in Australia—that competition was open to all. When servicemen griped about the promiscuity of WACs and nurses, they were also griping about sexual privileges unfairly claimed by officers. About this same time, in Europe, *Stars and Stripes* cartoonist Bill Mauldin made the same point—he drew a cartoon that showed enlisted men lining up at the front door of a USO show, while officers waited at the stage door with bouquets.[46]

The servicemen's mean gossip about nurses and WACs was sharpened by envy of higher-ups' quarters and comforts. Enlisted men and junior officers resented higher officers' luxury—lechery, carnality, excess, extravagance. They envied a man who had his own bedroom and bathroom, a place to take a girl that did not involve getting a clean blanket dirty and sitting on a hard rock half the night.

At a USO show, a soldier might grab at one of the women dancing on stage.[47] Much more often, airmen carped about superiors' privileges. Rarely did any resentment go further. At a Nadzab squadron, where a petition had been circulated and a squadron meeting broke up in angry shouting, a corporal relieved himself on the CO's desk blotter (and got himself sent home with a Section 8 psychiatric discharge).[48] Down on the coast at Milne Bay, racial tensions were stronger, and it ended in violence.

> Tonight at the dinner table Lieutenant Bristowe, who is
> serving as Assistant Judge Advocate of Fifth Air Force,
> told of the cases he was trying. He said all the charges
> involved intoxication. He told about seven soldiers
> being hanged at Milne Bay on charges of murder and
> rape. Someone spoke up and gave these details of two
> rapes at Milne Bay. An officer and a sergeant had taken
> two nurses out to the beach one night and while lying on
> the sand, three Negroes came and while one threatened
> with a knife the officer and sergeant, the two others
> raped the nurses. Also, there have been reports of Red
> Cross girls being raped but no confirmation.[49]

What Bristowe spoke of had begun four months before, on
March 15, in the evening, with two Army nurses riding in a jeep
to the beach at Milne Bay. They were white; there were no black
nurses or Red Cross girls in New Guinea. Their dates were a lieutenant and a sergeant, both also white. Just short of the nurses'
curfew, the nurses and their dates were surrounded by a group
of black enlisted men. The black soldiers mobbed the jeep, bran-
dished a knife and a club, said that they wanted the girls themselves, and pulled the nurses out of the jeep. Two assailants were
half-hearted; one nurse said she was having her period, and fought
them off. The other nurse was held down and raped, five times.

The defendants were tried by general court-martial at Milne
Bay, before a panel heavy in officers from the Quartermaster Corps
and headed by a Dental Corps lieutenant colonel. A seventh black
soldier who had been present gave a statement to investigators,
after which he apparently was tried separately by a special court-
martial (which could not have imposed the death penalty). Some
effort—not extensive—was made to clarify which defendants had
gone beyond threats and assault to commit the physical act of rape.
The trial lasted two days. All six defendants were found guilty.

They were sentenced to hang and, after their sentences were reviewed and confirmed, were hanged on October 2.

The first American serviceman to hang in the Southwest Pacific, in November 1942, had been Edward Leonski, a Signal Battalion private convicted of strangling three women in Melbourne. In Leonski's case, the crime seemed peculiar to the individual: Leonski, who had been called a mama's boy when growing up in New York City, preyed on older women. However, for the officer who commanded the Oro Bay prison, the black soldiers' deaths raised broader issues. The warden was troubled by the fact that although the wartime Army was predominantly white, more than half of his prisoners were black, most of them jailed for assaulting superiors or disobeying orders. He did not excuse the crime, but he linked its punishment to the color bar that his country still tolerated, and to a climate that allowed sexual license to white soldiers but denied it to black troops. The hangings, he wrote, had been a wartime tragedy.[50]

The thatched roofs of Nadzab had begun to show wear; men lashed tarpaulins across them to keep out the rain. The base had grown up into itself. When the Allies landed at Sansapor, at the northwestern corner of New Guinea, in Nadzab there was "nil excitement, in fact no one seemed the least bit interested. Spragg said a fight took place at the enlisted men's club the other night when one soldier stuck another in the back with a knife."[51]

The clubs boasted pool tables, refrigerators, and Coke machines. The PX was not as established as the one at Moresby, but it sold Australian candy, watches, and cigarettes. (The candy was popular, watches were welcome, and north of Nadzab men smoked only when the quartermaster had cigarettes to issue.) "Our meals now equal those we had in the States, steaks, eggs, butter, potatoes, apples, oranges," Rocky considered. There was a reason that Rocky had not been talking about washing his clothes: the Wing laundry had three machines and was handling two hundred bags a week.[52]

Lieutenant Beyer, chemical officer, is being transferred from the Wing to join an outfit which will stay at Nadzab to train new arriving personnel. Last night when Beyer told Major Chenery, the signal officer, of his transfer and what the unit's objective was, the Major expressed his wishes by saying he wished he could become the base signal officer for this would have the following advantages: no chance of being killed, the food would be good, one would get his leave every six months, the WACs would be here by then, and this particular area (training) would close immediately with an armistice, and so consequently he would be sent home first.[53]

A foresighted signal officer was selling photos of the pin-ups painted on warplane noses, and art flourished in other ways.[54]

The captain who is Wing Statistical Officer is also a short-story writer. Foliart to me: "The captain has completed a story which takes place in a foxhole and gives the conversation between two Marines during shelling by the enemy." The captain is submitting the story for a contest. He has never seen a Jap, no enemy territory and the nearest to the actual front he has been is six hundred miles.[55]

Colonel Brownfield had shaken up the Wing by shuffling his lieutenant colonels. Lieutenant Colonel Darnell and Lieutenant Colonel Smith, whose iceboxes Kepler and Rocky had envied, left the Sixth Photo Group, and Lieutenant Colonel Post took over. "Because Lieutenant Colonel Darnell was relieved, many of the Sixth Group officers spent last night along the bar at the officers' mess—getting stinking."[56] The officers' mess had evidently replenished its stock of liquor. Only one air base north, drinking problems were different. Rocky heard from Sergeant Niederhofer, an old friend from Group HQ.

Niederhofer, who is with the First Airdrome Squadron
at Gusap, said the men at his base were drinking absolutely everything. He further added they had developed
a craving for the hydraulic fluid used in the airplanes
and consequently it is impossible to have any in reserve
for the planes.[57]

Niederhofer was in town for the Jack Benny show. The USO
show ran two nights in Nadzab, with almost twelve thousand servicemen watching each night, and was broadcast live on Radio
WVTB of the Armed Forces Radio service (1480 kilocycles).

Niederhofer and I went to see the Jack Benny Show with
Carole Landis and Martha Tilton and a few others. The
show was good but the use of profanity by all members
of the cast degraded the production. We saw the show
at an anti-aircraft unit and throughout the performance
all the anti-aircraft beacons were focused at a point
above the stage, with their beams of light forming great
pyramids. We came from the show with one thought: no
matter how much sex is twisted and suggested towards
you from the stage, the boys will always applaud and
bring back the good musicians.[58]

Jack Benny opened at Nadzab with the same joke that he had
told the year before on the coast of Africa: that the place looked
like Waukegan.[59]

"We hear your show on the radio," commented a bystander.
"When we have radios," chimed in another.
  "I don't see why you fellows don't get radios. . . . Why
don't they send radios?" Benny mused, half to himself.
  "Why don't they send relief?" prompted a Signaller . . .
followed by a burst of applause.[60]

With his comment about blue language, Rocky may have been the only critic. Jack Benny had his violin and a flawless self-deprecating cheapskate routine. Carole Landis won every serviceman's heart. In the *Wing-ding*'s photos, she is a revelation: a slim young blonde actress with bright eyes and the sort of smile that is rightly called megawatt. The Photo Reconnaissance Wing was full of photographers and each pressed in to take her picture: Miss Landis at the microphone (she did her own singing), Miss Landis on a different microphone, harmonizing with Martha Tilton, seeming to faint in Jack Benny's arms, wearing a skirt and girl-next-door gingham, glamming in a low-cut gown, posing in a flight jacket—the most tireless of good sports when it came to dining in the mess hall or autographing an airplane nose. "The demand for pictures of the Jack Benny show has far exceeded the supply," the *Wing-ding* observed. "A close-up of Carole Landis has become a commodity worth a pile of 'bobs' and 'quids.' . . . So the Wing-Ding has put on its glad rags, sharpened its one pencil and now presents three full pages of the show."[61]

Col. Alex Guerry handed to the *Wing-ding* editors another photo: Miss Landis dining with two familiar officers in neckties and ribbons and flyers' wings. The officers are Major Guerry and Major Post, as they had been six months before. The scene is a Los Angeles night spot. Miss Landis, as always, is beaming; her smile dazzles the camera. Guerry's smile may be even brighter; he looks as though the evening has just begun. Post has barely tasted his coffee. He looks alert but subdued, as if wishing the spotlight might swing somewhere else.

From Hollywood, Guerry and Post had traveled back to New Guinea—Guerry to fly more missions, Post to have Colonel Brownfield for a boss. For a few weeks, anyhow, they had made it back home. That counted as news. The *Wing-ding* ran the photo on page one.

On the Nadzab control tower, someone posted a sign: "Change here for Tsili Tsili Port Moresby Milne Bay Dobodura Lae Madang Wewak Tokio." No signboards pointed home, but the road ahead was marked. At month-end, Rocky wrote, "Lieutenant Colonel Ilgenfritz departed for Biak to aid or rather direct the construction of our new camp. Major Smith, in our A-4 logistics section, said that Colonel Brownfield told Ilgenfritz that if he didn't get anything else done he was nonetheless to get Brownfield's house completed."[62]

15

MOVING UP

Even as servicemen tacked up photos of Carole Landis, while offi-cers at Wing HQ quietly traded comments about Colonel Brown-field, a typist was pecking out an order.

> The following AC O & EM, Hq & Hq Sq, 91st Photo Wing
> Rcn, APO 713 Unit 1, WP by mil acft to APO 920 o/a 3 Aug
> 44, on TD, for purpose of carrying out instructions of CO.
> Upon completion of TD will return to proper sta. No add
> expense to govt atzd: 1ST LT ROSCOE A BOYER 0856663
> S/Sgt William J Hiester 33168726.[1]

Rocky would spend the next week on Biak, traveling by mili-tary aircraft and without incurring additional expense. Early on, he would see firsthand the battlefield—dry, dusty, bloody—of which Nadzab had heard all summer.[2]

⟲

Biak is a coral island. It is the opposite of an atoll; the reefs from which it is built have been pushed above water into sea cliffs and hilly inland terrain. The coast is lined with reefs and mangrove swamps. In 1944 there was one road, running along the beach. A formidable line of bluffs, covered by jungle, rose above the beach: General Eichelberger, who had been commandant at West Point, was reminded of the Palisades on the Hudson. The center of the island was corrugated with hills and ridgelines. There was dense rain forest, with thick undergrowth, but the terrain itself was chokingly dry. The rain that fell on Biak soaked straight down through the coral and did not run off in streams.

The people of Biak spoke Malay as well as their own tongue. They sailed plank boats, not dugout canoes, and their smiths worked in iron. They were renowned as traders—also as fighting men, warriors who fought with the straight-bladed Malay cutlass. They owed fealty, in theory, to the queen of the Netherlands. In their own islands, they followed *mambri*, "brave men," and they had waged their own bloody war against the Japanese.[3]

On Biak, around the village of Mokmer, there was a coastal plain, eight miles long and more than a mile wide. This plain was one of the two most significant features of Biak, because airfields could be built there. Behind the plain, commanding it, too steep for men to climb without using their hands, rose a jungle-covered ridge that hooked east to reach the coast. Inside this ridge was the other geographic feature for which Biak would be remembered: the caves. These were huge sinkholes from which caverns radiated and between which tunnels had been dug. The Japanese had placed mortars and machine guns in the caves and surrounded them with pillboxes and bunkers, defenses that blended into the undergrowth. To man these, the Japanese had more than 11,000 men. Just over half were construction engineers and laborers from Formosa. The rest were veteran infantrymen and blue-clad Japanese marines. Like the Japanese on the Admiralties, the Japanese troops on Biak concealed themselves with absolute discipline. The American 41st Division, when it went ashore, thought it faced less than a single enemy regiment.[4] Of such expectations the American troops were soon disabused. The Japanese fought from gun emplacements hollowed out in the coral cliffs, ambushed and man-handled American battalions on the coast road, and—rarest of events in the Southwest Pacific—sent tanks into battle to crush American columns.

⟨§⟩

Even for Colonel Hutchison, Biak proved a slow and difficult nut to crack.

Hutchison had landed soon after the infantry came ashore, planning to get American airfields up and running. The Japanese thwarted that. Instead of sending his engineers forward, Hutchison was forced to wait—while the Japanese battered an American battalion and sent it stumbling backward along the beach, while the 41st Division dragged itself through the dry backcountry, while Lieutenant General Eichelberger relieved the division commander, and while American infantry seized the plain and climbed the ridge and pondered how to drive the Japanese out of the caves beneath them.

While the infantry fought in the brush, Hutchison brought American warplanes into action. Two Fifth Air Force publicists wrote his story, presenting him as the hero of the Biak campaign: innovative, brave, and clever, slightly rueful but never daunted. "Alongside the battle fought on Biak by American infantrymen against the Jap defenders—and it was a fight in the worst of Pacific traditions . . . there was a sort of junior tussle conducted by 'Photo' Hutch against the enemy Samurai. Hutch's lower-case war, a private and fairly exclusive little conflict, fell into two parts. Hutch who commanded the air task force on Biak lost out on the first half and came back strong to finish top man in the second try."[5]

Hutchison flew low-level reconnaissance in a light plane, studying enemy positions and calling in air strikes. Above one position, he counted eight Japanese machine guns. "'The Nips looked up at me,' he said. 'They waved at me. They laughed. . . . They kept sticking their fingers to their noses. They didn't even take a pot shot at me with their machine guns, although, God knows, they could have hit me with a pistol bullet,' he continued morosely. 'They wanted me to see how fine they were and they wanted me to go back and tell the boys.'"[6]

He directed fighter sweeps, strafing attacks by P-40s—that did not work. Next he tried bomb runs by B-25s, using delayed fuses, so that the bombs would dig into the coral before they exploded. That did not work either. Hutchison tried a third approach, a strike by heavy bombers, with eight B-24s dropping thousand-pound bombs. He lulled the Japanese into believing that the heavy bombers circling overhead were bound for other targets, until the bombers suddenly struck: "From the low altitude of four thousand feet they dropped sixty-four one-thousand-pound bombs, thirty-two tons of explosives on an area three hundred yards long and seventy-five yards wide. And then the infantry attacked. . . . Hutch felt good. 'I always get curious and look up when I see airplanes,' he said. 'I figured maybe the Nips would get curious and look up too.'"[7]

The story is full of war-movie touches, applied either by Hutchison (who was hardly unassuming) or by two journalists who had learned their craft in the tabloid era of *The Front Page*. But with Eichelberger's infantry working their way overland, and Hutchison's air task force dropping bombs on the hills at the eastern end of the Mokmer airstrip, Biak was deemed safe enough for Air Corps personnel. The Allied drive toward the Philippines could resume.

In Nadzab, the Wing headquarters was coming to appreciate the struggle on Biak. They had lost men there, after the landings: Captain Hancock and his B-25 crew, shot down above the beachhead, by mistake. Men were making dirty jokes about Biak, and the tenor of dirty jokes had deteriorated.

The best joke of the war: Another soldier was inquiring from an old veteran in Biak Island if he had seen or had taken any Jap geisha girls. "Oh, yes, we had one for four days until some second lieutenant came along and made us bury her."[8]

After months in New Guinea, there were no more jocular conjectures about black women looking whiter and whiter; now the joke involved an enemy corpse and necrophilia. If there is irony in Rocky's comment, "the best joke of the war," that only sharpens the sarcasm and resentment.

Biak promised the hardest work yet seen. Lieutenant Colonel Ilgenfritz, the Wing's A-4 logistics officer, had sent back a letter from the beachhead there.

> Supply here is tough. The things we need most to work with aren't here or so we're told. Please send me two cases of drinkables for trading stock from the officers' mess as soon as you can. It will help. We also need more men, some hammers (6–12) which cannot be gotten here, also some 24" or larger pipe wrenches. Two, if possible draw the four 50 KVA generators down there and ship them with the first water shipment. They say we cannot draw them here.
>
> Chenery can send his telephone men any time. Field wire is available. We need more transportation bad. Send some water pipes too if you can. With little suction hose and foot valves. We are badly handicapped because the tractor and rest of shipment isn't in.
>
> Ask Stafford to send my serum syringe and directions and Powell to send me film for my camera. Tell Colonel B. initial progress is slow because of supplies. Getting under way. Will write more fully later.
>
> In haste,
> Ilgenfritz

Major Chenery said that because lumber was so hard to get at Biak, supply might have to fly lumber from here for Colonel Brownfield's house on Biak. The lumber must be tongue-and-grooved.[9]

Chenery was a veteran Bell System manager. He had learned quickly to understand the Fifth Air Force. Being a senior signal officer, with a young communications officer on hand, he did not keep a dog and bark himself. He sent Rocky north. Rocky made no diary entries for a week. When he returned, he sat down and dashed out an entry that stretched across eight notebook pages.

Returned from trip to Biak. Major Chenery sent me up to learn what was wrong with the communications system. Upon arriving, I learned the equipment the 25th Photo Squadron had turned over to the communications team to use was as follows. One SCR-188 (75-watt transmitter) had been saltwater-soaked and was thus inoperative. The large radio set became inoperative when the grid of the PA tube began to go positive and Master Sergeant Morrow couldn't find what was wrong with the bias.

Lieutenant Phillipo who was in charge of the station said that to add to the snafu, Lieutenant Colonel Ilgenfritz first couldn't make up his mind where to locate the transmitters, the power units would not work, the men classified as mechanics were only mechanics on paper, and the men could not draw cigarettes nor receive their allotments which griped them to no end. Lieutenant Hilgerson said first that Lieutenant Colonel Ilgenfritz was going to have the headquarters in a semicircle, then changed his mind a day later and said to leave them constructed as H-type.

Upon my return I talked with Major Williams about the conditions at Biak and when I told him that the Wing buildings were not up, the area had not been cleared of the scrub vegetation, the coral rocks had not been blocked and it was considered quite a laborious operation to hammer them down, no water had been piped to the area, generators had just been installed, and all tents had not been wired, the major asked "What in the hell have they been doing up there for the last three weeks?" Perhaps the major should have been told all the men said they had the GI's (dysentery) the first three days there because of the water. Lieutenant Colonel Ilgenfritz did not escape, although as several of the men pointed out, he did not suffer too much for he had a refrigerator and beer to drink whereas they had neither.

The mess sergeant at Biak said he had lost fifteen pounds in one week but he was not sorry he had come with the party, because "of course it is rough up here, but it makes one think he's doing more for the war effort." The sergeant's mess hall was a small structure, about 15' by 35' in which he had four tables for eating, all his stores, and his two gas stoves. The floor was the unmolested coral ground and one had to watch his step while walking to a table. The food was exceedingly good, fresh meat once a day. However we found several small black insects in our bread. Tropical butter was served all with dehydrated potatoes and cabbage, beets and carrots. Why the Army feeds us so many beets is a mystery. One week at Nadzab we had beets every day. Everyone ate in their mess kits, even the lieutenant colonel, but no one seemed to mind.

Because the B-24s (F-7s) of the mapping squadron will operate from Biak, and thus will need standing weather reports, and because it was practically impossible to call a weather central by phone, I drove to the Sorido airdrome control tower. The strip was being repaired and only an MP was on duty so I proceeded to visit with him. He said his outfit landed six days after the invasion and while unloading, the PT boats shot down four Jap planes in the harbor. In those days everything was blacked out at night "whereas now, no blackout discipline is ever observed except during a raid." He added, "many men had been lost while souvenir hunting, in fact two captains were killed yesterday. The Japs had used rice sacks for protective measures and when these became wet and spoiled, large green flies would breed within them. The flies were everywhere. The spoiling salmon in the wooden kegs added to the stench of the decaying bodies. And another thing, I have been on New Guinea ten months without a furlough. However, I can't gripe. The 41st Division has been here thirty months and none of them know when they are going home. The general of the 41st is a real Joe, he said the other day he was going to teach his men to take prisoners and wear shirts. In fact, this place is already becoming civilized—making us wear shirts. Oh yes, the natives really hate the Japs. You see the Japs took the native women all except two old ones from the large valley down the coast. Saw one native the other day with a sack full of Japs' ears."

Before departing the MP exhibited a sea shell bracelet he was making for his girlfriend.

One night we had an air raid. The three-gun signal was at 4 a.m. We woke, dressed, and sleepily walked outside. For approximately ten minutes everyone stood around saying "Well, let's get it over with so we can go up to bed." Just a few minutes later you could see the shells explode from the ack-ack guns. No one moved and we stood by admiring the display as the motor noise and the firing came nearer. We rushed down to the beach and into the stench of the coral caves (several of these caves have decaying Japs within). We came out when the guns stopped firing and saw the light beams from the beacons in the fleeing Jap plane. In the morning we learned the plane had dropped two bombs and a flare on the dock.

Corporal Dare learned of my presence at Biak and came over to see me. He said he saw the Australian nurse whom the Japs had held on the island. The nurse was flown to the mainland and was reputed to be pregnant.

Lieutenant Phillipo said a boatload of beer came into the harbor but too many boats had higher priority at the dock. Was rumored the men will be rationed to three packages of cigarettes per week.

Late one night I had a long talk with Staff Sergeant Obermann who has been overseas 29 months and doesn't know when he will be sent home. He said, "I always hope I will be home every June, March, and Christmas. The last time I saw my wife was March 1941, I left the States in June—and, Christmas just because it's Christmas. And if you want to know about screwing, you should know about First Lieutenant Southard. He was once one of our best photo pilots. He got his DFC by flying over Wewak, being intercepted, dropping his belly tanks, flying low over the dunes getting the important pictures, then beating it home. He never tried to impress anyone and disliked anyone who did. He didn't go well in the Guerry, Post, and Brownfield clique, who were afraid of him. In order to hold Southard down, he was made mess officer, and after improving the mess, more than ever before, Guerry, Post, and Brownfield were envious, so after being overseas ten months, flying more missions than anyone else, Southard went home with the same rank, probably sent if you ask me."

Staff Sergeant Hiester and I flew back on a C-47. We reached the strip at 0930 and the plane didn't take off until 1300. Aboard were two Allison engines (being sent back for routine maintenance), the pilot, co-pilot, radio operator, crew chief, engine sergeant, two officers from the 41st Division who were going home after being overseas 30 months (the quota for their regiment was 3 officers per month, monthly—they were in the June quota) and three officers from the Engineer Corps. One of the latter was worried if the plane could lift such a load.

Before take-off I had a long talk with the pilot who had been flying in the theater for 13 months and his squadron has never had a casualty. He said when they were flying supplies to the outpost at Tsili Tsili, all the cargo planes were scheduled to arrive and leave at the same time each day. A couple of months later they learned via their intelligence officer that the Air Force was using the cargo ships as bait for the Jap fighters.

He also confirmed the story that at one time one couldn't get lost between Nadzab and Gusap because the route was marked by wrecked C-47s. He said that whenever a C-47 was jumped by a Jap, the pilot would set the plane down in the kunai grass in the floor of the valley.[10]

Heat, stench, buzzing flies, broken equipment. Dysentery. Air raids. Officers muddling things and sergeants doing their jobs. Massacre jokes, sexual frustration, hopes for romance. Young airmen talking about pregnant nurses, middle-aged non-coms thinking about their wives. Envy and rivalry. Soldiers flying south on furlough and aircraft engines flying south to be overhauled, side by side. No beer and too few cigarettes. Rocky's report on Biak is a précis of war in the Southwest Pacific.

The 82nd Squadron was already on Biak. They were used to the Fifth Air Force owning the air above New Guinea but quickly learned that things were different here: as they were docking, they watched four Japanese planes dive-bomb a destroyer.

The 82nd Squadron was used to forward air bases. This was their first time, however, on the actual front line of the war, with infantrymen fighting half a mile away, artillery shells arcing overhead, and dead men being buried by the roadside. Doc Schafer saw the crowded beachhead and the casualties and thought that the place looked like Tarawa.[11] The coral was too hard for foxholes, so they found softer ground around a swamp. Engineers went out to work on the airfield; the Japanese drove them off with grenades. Sentries and antiaircraft gunners sometimes missed and sometimes did their jobs too well, problems that some men blamed on their commander. As Rocky heard it:

> Colonel Hutchison was subject to investigation (he was CO of the forward operations) because one night the Japs infiltrated into our lines and the men were unable to protect themselves because they had no ammunition. It seems the American troops had shot two Americans for no good reason so Colonel Hutchison recalled all ammo from the men. Major Pratt said at first the anti-aircraft guns weren't shooting at the Jap planes. The radar warning was off because one night an air raid sounded and before the men could reach the foxhole, the bombs were already hitting.[12]

After a week, the 82nd Squadron moved to Owi. On Owi there were no snipers—only scrub typhus. Then the Japanese were forced out of the hills and caves, driven back out of mortar range. Hutchison ordered the squadron back to an area littered with the detritus of war. Schafer wrote: "We're moving to Biak. Flew over to see the area. All coral, flat, thick brush, no shade, 4–5 garbage dumps left by the infantry, several decomposing bodies scattered, Jap ammo scattered around in broken boxes, flies so thick you have to keep your mouth shut. . . . What a sanitary headache. Will have to blast holes in the coral for latrines and later a well."[13]

When the pilots caught up with the ground crews, the 82nd Squadron sat out a loud, troubling evening. The camp listened for hours to a painful outburst from Lieutenant Lipscomb, who had been so badly burned but insisted on staying with the squadron. He had been friends with Harry Harrison, the pilot who had vanished in mid-air over Awar Plantation. "Last night Lieutenant Lipscomb got stinko drunk," Doc Schafer wrote. "Before Lippy began drinking, he was sorting out Lieutenant Harrison's things, pictures, etc. They had been very close, classmates in flying school. Several days ago (or a couple weeks) Lippy had to make a wheels up landing, his plane caught fire. At first he could not get his door open. When he did get out, his hands were severely burned. After he got drunk, he talked incessantly of those two things, also wanted to beat up a couple of pilots whom he believed were exaggerating the successful results of their missions."[14]

As flight surgeon, Schafer must have tended Lipscomb's burned hands—handled injuries that should have been treated in a hospital. Another time, Schafer had to make a sudden run-out call, a hundred miles in a liaison plane across the sea to the landing strip at Noemfoor. On a mission over Manokwari, Lt. Bob Wells had been hit in the head. The glass of his canopy was shot out and the cockpit was splattered with blood. Wells had flown back to Noemfoor, sixty hard miles across open water, with the joystick clenched between his knees and holding his head with his hands. Somehow Wells landed, and then he passed out.

Schafer found Wells in the hospital tent. He cleaned the wound as best he could; some bone fragments were too deep in the brain for him to reach. He took out other pieces of skull and shrapnel, sewed shut the dura mater, closed, and started Wells on penicillin.[15] Then Schafer flew back to Biak, where the rest of the squadron demanded his attention. He did not learn, for forty-odd years, that Wells had lived.

The Fighting Seventeenth was on Biak too, what was left of it. The squadron raised a mess hall and nailed on a tin roof, then turned to a tougher project, the officers' latrine. Fred Hill, a gifted photographer who ran the photo lab when there was water to run it, touted up the effort: "288 sticks of dynamite—as many as twenty for one blast—to dig two holes 10′ x 4′ x 8′ and consumed eight days and used ten to twelve men per day." When the latrine was done, he snapped a shot of the work crew, resting—five enlisted men at ease in a row on the seats of the officers' latrine.[16] Officers' tents were the first to get electric lights. Enlisted men had to wait, and some were impatient. One airman swiped a light bulb from the latrine to use in his own tent. The bulb had been marked, the theft was detected, and he was sentenced to move gravel for a week, two hours an evening.[17]

By the pier at Biak there was an Allied cemetery, with six white crosses for Captain Hancock and his crew. The flyers of the 17th Squadron traced out the story. It had been the second day of the invasion, a time when the Japanese were fighting hard. The infantry wanted maps and Hancock was assigned to drop them. When he neared the beachhead, Hancock called the antiaircraft units there, whose controllers used the call sign Ointment. He proceeded with the mission toward the end of the day. "In accordance with instructions from Ointment Captain Hancock followed all identification procedures. After identification procedures Ointment controller cleared him in at approximately 1735, 45 minutes after receiving preliminary instructions for dropping photos. At 1740 Ointment called leader of second flight that Captain Hancock's ship had been 'shot down.' He further added that all clearance procedures had been faithfully carried out by him and that 'it was not his fault.' Instructions were received from Ointment to 'leave the area immediately they are crazy down here.'"[18]

The gunners ashore were tense, and late afternoon was when Japanese air raids were worst. The Japanese bases were west of Biak, while American bases were to the east; "because of the difference in time of sunset at the closest Allied and Japanese bases, Japanese aircraft could remain in the Biak area about half an hour after Allied planes had to leave."[19] Hancock flew toward the beachhead in late afternoon, a time when Japanese bombers were expected, with his bomb-bay doors open—and the antiaircraft gunners shot his plane down. He left a mother in Texas, a wife in California, and a little daughter barely old enough to walk. He died after flying more than fifty missions.

Back in Nadzab, command decisions had grown no wiser. Rocky overheard Captain Cummins tell Colonel Brownfield that the colonel's personal shower would be ready in a couple of days; Cummins had a dam and pump in place to feed the water tank.[20] That was a dubious use of resources. So was the task to which Lieutenant Colonel Guerry had been assigned: to fly to Biak a transport plane carrying the prefabricated sections of Colonel Brownfield's house. With four Distinguished Flying Crosses, Guerry was absurdly overqualified to fly a cargo run. (Perhaps Brownfield called in Guerry because he wanted to keep his building plans quiet; had he asked a transport group to carry this lumber, a transport colonel might have refused to fly lumber into a war zone.)

> The commonest comment of the day: "Will Colonel Brownfield kick Lieutenant Colonel Ilgenfritz when Brownfield gets to Biak and finds out Ilgenfritz doesn't have his eight room house completed." The HQ barber said some of the enlisted men were discussing going over to Colonel Brownfield's chicken lot, catching a couple of hens and having fried chicken.[21]

Another comment was floating in conversation: General Whitehead had said he would rather move one squadron than twenty Red Cross Girls.[22] Rocky himself would have enough trouble getting five enlisted men onto a plane for Biak. August 13 was a Sunday afternoon, and Rocky began loading the biggest airplane the Wing had available—a four-engine F-7, the reconnaissance version of the B-24. Monday morning showed how well that succeeded.

Loaded 5,000 pounds of equipment in an F-7 during the afternoon which will be flown to Biak and the time of take-off is 0600 a.m. tomorrow. Arranged for a truck to pick up myself and five enlisted men to haul us to the plane, and breakfast for the men at 5 a.m.

The switchboard operator called and rang my phone at 5 a.m. and I ate a breakfast of two fried eggs and hot cakes, and found the truck waiting at the designated place at 5:30, but no enlisted personnel could be found. A few minutes later Master Sergeant Johnson appeared and he didn't know where the other men were located. I found two still eating. By 5:45 Sergeant Johnson was loaded and I learned Sergeant Lennox of the Signal Company had already gone. Staff Sergeant Hollinwood wasn't completely packed and Pfc Bloom acted as if he didn't give a damn about moving by waiting until we picked him up and when he did, he decided to go to get a drink and then Sergeant Hollinwood wanted to know if he could go to the latrine. We departed from the area at 0600, arrived at the strip only to find the plane in the process of taking off. Major Warner was quite griped about this situation but nevertheless arranged for us to take a plane tomorrow morning.[23]

On Tuesday, things went better. Rocky gathered a brace of captains for backup, and planned for an earlier start.

The operator woke me at 4:30 and I called Captain Chapin and Captain Sexton, who were going along in the same plane, and called the motor pool to check on the truck which was to take us to the strip. The truck arrived at 5 a.m. as scheduled and because no mess personnel were at the kitchen, we left the area without any breakfast. Arrived at the plane at 5:50, loaded our baggage. Captain Rogers, our pilot, then learned we did not have parachutes, so therefore delayed his take-off until we secured them from 20th Mapping Squadron engineering. The trip up was uneventful and most everyone slept, including the co-pilot. Arrived over Mokmer strip on Biak at 1100 but were not permitted to land until 1130 because of the heavy traffic (Mokmer was the only airstrip in operation). The equipment was unloaded and I went to seek transportation to camp area but found it impossible to get either from the base's air freight or from our own organization. Captain Chapin remained with the equipment at all times while Captain Sexton acted irritated and no one knew why. After all, he wouldn't help anyone load or unload. Reached camp with equipment at 3:30, unloaded, ate, saw Major Chenery who said I would return to Nadzab to find out what was wrong with the radio station.[24]

Major Chenery had made his own way to Biak. He wasted no time in checking up on units based there and taking action on what he heard.

Rumor of the day: When Major Chenery was at the 17th Recco Squadron, an operator told him he intercepted a message from Radio Tokyo that the Japs would use gas and bomb Owi Island off the map tonight. Naturally the Major spread the rumor and late at night Fifth Air Force A-2 intelligence section sent the message to all units stating that the message had been received and we could take it with a grain of salt if we wished. Nevertheless Colonel Brownfield issued the order that all men would have their gas masks nearby during the night.[25]

The radioman was reporting a credible threat, and Chenery was old enough to recall how many soldiers had been scarred and killed by mustard gas in the First World War. On Biak, there was reason to fear gas might be used again: in Japanese arms caches, the 41st Division had captured hundreds of "gas candles," a species of toxic smudge pot.[26] Fifth Air Force was right to take Chenery seriously.

Across the Wing, conversations were laden with irony and ennui. Jack Chapin, the ordnance captain, as he drove Rocky to the airstrip, "discussed without any great interest the enlisted man of the 20th who attempted to swim to the raft along our camp beach and drowned. Jack commented that he was tired of everything. 'I've been overseas so long that whenever I move, I become tired and irritated, but then when the showers are completed and there's shows in the evenings, I become mentally well again.'"[27] Back at Nadzab, men were exasperated but resigned. "Corporal Byrd of the 71st Recco Group asked me if I recalled how carefully we packed our radio truck in the States and then when the unit got overseas, the radio equipment was removed and the truck used to haul garbage from the mess halls."[28]

> Had breakfast with Captain Doyle and Major Baker. Captain Doyle said all air transportation was frozen until Fifth Air Force had moved, which may mean we will go by water. Also, General Whitehead put out the order that no lumber will be flown to the forward bases, and three days later two C-47's flew lumber from Nadzab to Biak for the General's house. Doyle added it was hard to believe what actually goes on over here and the people at home certainly wouldn't believe it under any circumstances.[29]

One man was still cheerful and chatty: Staff Sergeant Cahill the rumormonger—as frank and voluble as he had been about the sad state of the officers' mess.

> Staff Sergeant Cahill, Fifth Combat Camera Unit, gave me the following statistics. One, he had made over $300

selling nude pictures since coming overseas. Two, he would trade nude pictures for choice foods with the quartermasters and Australians. Beer is also secured with such means. Three, the most sought-after picture is one where a woman is sucking a male's penis. Then comes positions taken during sexual intercourse and last, nudes.[30]

At Nadzab, Rocky was staying with Beyer. Beyer was from Beverly Hills. He was the chemical warfare officer, supposed to deal with poison gas or (this was the Fifth Air Force's newest weapon) napalm. Beyer had been married twice already, and he was given to oddball pronouncements. "Last evening Lieutenant Beyer said he missed cold glasses of milk more than he did his wife," Rocky reported. Another time Beyer remarked, "You know what? I have the crabs. I never had them before and always felt I had missed something because everyone else I knew had and talked about their crabs on certain occasions."[31]

Of all Rocky's friends, Beyer was the oddest duck. At the same time, he had a quiet ability to take advantage of situations—he was being sent rearward to Nadzab just when the fighting front was shifting to the Philippines. To get his own teeth cleaned, unflinchingly and without warning, he dragged Rocky into the behind-the-scenes quid-pro-quo market for dental services.

It is known to all that the Medical Corps will not clean a serviceman's teeth because according to their theory, if they began cleaning teeth it would occupy all their time. Lieutenant Beyer had an appointment at the local hospital for some sort of dental appointment. He asked the dentist if his teeth could be cleaned and received no as the answer. Upon completion of the examination, as he was leaving the office, the dentist asked "Oh say, I have a radio receiver from an airplane but need a 24-volt battery to operate it. Could you perchance know someone who could secure me such a battery?" Chuck remembering me said, "Yes, I think I know just the man. I'll check with him and let you know for sure." Dentist: "Thank you very much, and sergeant, put the lieutenant's name down for an appointment to have his teeth cleaned Wednesday afternoon."[32]

Beyer was the one who had heard about Lindbergh—Mr. Charles A. Lindbergh, no longer a colonel, flying with the 475th Fighter Squadron. Beyer had heard about Lindbergh from Major Pratt, the 310th Bomb Wing flight surgeon, who had met him on a trip to the front. Lindbergh was quite pessimistic about the war, Beyer said that Pratt said (and Rocky reported). "And he believes Germany is a long way from being defeated. He didn't know very much about the Japs. . . . Lindbergh further said there would be another World War and this one isn't the last one."[33]

For Charles Lindbergh, the 110th Tactical Reconnaissance Squadron would once have been full of old friends. It was a St. Louis outfit and he had flown in it twenty years before, when it was the 110th Observation Squadron and Lindbergh was a St. Louis airmail pilot.[34] He had come to the Pacific to consult on the aircraft being flown there—in particular, to advise Fifth Air Force fighter pilots how to extend the range of their P-38s. Lindbergh was treated as a celebrity by the fighter-squadron pilots and as an equal by Fifth Air Force brass. There was time for fishing one afternoon, Lindbergh recorded, with General Wurtsmith, Colonel Morrissey, and Colonel Hutchison.[35] Hutchison must have arranged the outing. Hosting and ferrying important guests were duties that he ambitiously assumed—when General Eichelberger needed to fly to the mainland, Hutchison piloted the plane.[36] It was another invitation to be exchanged between commanders; another favor offered to a general who might someday requite it.

‿

Up on the front line, a two-hundred-bed hospital had been author-ized; the doctors were already treating four hundred scrub typhus cases from Owi. "It is interesting to note that natives have never lived on the typhus infested island of Owi," Rocky commented.[37]

> Heard that on Owi all clothing must be impregnated against typhus-carrying insects. All impregnated cloth-ing is marked with a Red "X" on the back. If anyone on Owi is found without the Red X, the soldier, his officer and the unit's medical officer are all fined.[38]

It was at Owi, George Kenney wrote, that he learned some-thing. "When we mentioned the place to the natives around Biak, they told us that no one lived there as the place was 'tabu.' We had heard that word many times ever since coming to New Guinea and had smiled and paid no attention." They had heard *tabu* about Embi Lake, near Dobodura, and later about locations near Nadzab—places where American servicemen moved in and then came down with scrub typhus. Now, at Owi, when scrub typhus struck yet again, Kenney realized what *tabu* meant in the environment of New Guinea. "From then on if the natives said tabu about a place we took the proper precautions."[39]

There was more news from the front line, none of it cheerful.

> Spragg said the mess hall at Biak burned down after an explosion. Several men were burned. This incident came as no surprise because all heating is accomplished by high-octane gasoline. Often when the fire is low, under the water tanks, a bucket of gasoline is thrown on the flame. Most men get burned this way.[40]
>
> Heard today a pilot from the 20th Mapping Squad-ron in Biak was out souvenir hunting and came upon a Jap hand grenade. He picked it up, it exploded, and yes-terday his left arm was removed above the elbow.[41]

At Mokmer Airdrome on Biak, Lt. Douglas Murray of the 82nd Squadron one afternoon clambered a quarter mile uphill from the squadron bivouac to a cave he could see in the cliff face. A sightseeing excursion, he thought. He walked over in shorts and carrying a machete and later acknowledged how foolhardy he had been. Inside the cave was a clutter of gear, helmets and messtins, a pile of newspapers with cartoons and articles—a lot like *Guinea Gold*, Murray thought. Outside the cave was the part that (he wrote) he did not understand then and had never been able to understand later. There was a pole outside the cave, a heavy post, six inches in diameter. "Tied to this pole was the body of a Japanese soldier. His hands were tied behind his back and around the post, and his feet were tied around the post. The following grisly description is the part I do not understand. The top of his head, from just above his ears, was sliced off clean. It was just as if Goliath had swung a mighty axe at a level angle and lopped off the top of his head."[42]

〽

Morale at the Wing continued to plummet. Lieutenants talked about the colonel behind his back, two captains were in quiet revolt—and over dinner on August 19, a field-grade officer entertained dissent.

> At dinner this evening a few remaining high ranks (namely Lieutenant Colonel Ilgenfritz, Major Warner, Major Minnock) discussed the movement of the local color lab to Biak, which is being requested by Colonel Brownfield. At the completion of the discussion Lieutenant Colonel Ilgenfritz said, "I suppose the generals want Captain Powell (Wing color photo officer) to take pictures of their homes. I personally flew Powell to Port Moresby once so he could take color photographs of the generals' homes down there and on the other occasions he flew there for the same purpose."[43]

That was Wednesday night. On Monday, everyone could see how bad things were. A briefing on reconnaissance turned hostile and sarcastic.

> Major Smith returned to Nadzab to get the rest of the units to Biak. He said yesterday the Wing sent six F-5s (P-38 photo planes) over Mindanao and they completed photographing more than half the island. Then someone spoke up and asked: Did the colonel fly one of those planes? Major Smith: No, he wanted to but the general said no, because the colonel knew too much about the next phase against the Philippines. Another question: Didn't one of the squadron's commanding officers tell the colonel, "You know nothing about flying a photo mission. I have a second lieutenant in my squadron who can do a hell of a better job than you, and I'll be damned if I'll let you fly one of my ships on a mission?" Another question: Who flew the missions, won't they all get the DFC? Major Smith: Two men from each squadron. And because they got the pictures before the Navy, they'll sure get DFCs. The pictures really made the general happy and I think he and the colonel got drunk together last night. Oh yes, did I tell you they photographed all the Celebes in one day last week?[44]

The men had gotten wind of Colonel Brownfield being up for a Distinguished Flying Cross, for flying a mission that did not warrant that decoration. Rocky had heard the flippant version of the story: "On Mondays, Wednesdays, and Fridays there will be requests sent out for those to sign up who wish to participate in the war. And on Mondays only, the pilots will be called together, and the following week's missions will be listed, with the medal which will be received by the person who flies it. This policy eliminates debates over decorations. The assignments to the highest-decorated mission are naturally given to the highest rank."[45]

The story was now being repeated with truculence. Major Smith's cheery remark about the colonel getting drunk with the general was hardly news that would placate the pilots.

Two days later, the tension broke. The officers of the Wing learned that an unsustainable trend toward personal aggrandizement had not been sustained.

> Heard in the showers this evening that Colonel Brownfield had been relieved of command of the Wing and was being returned to the States. Major Minnock, who was in the shower, said: "Well, there'll be some changes made now—changes to the good. Conditions certainly couldn't get any worse." Warrant Officer Hene (the source of the rumor) said, "I hope to hell the first thing he'll do is to get a new adjutant."[46]

More of the background soon came to light. The news made sense of Captain Sexton's surliness at Mokmer Airdrome and suggested that there was in fact a God—or, at least, that Fifth Air Force ultimately did know what it was doing.

> Captain Campbell, a personal friend of Captain Sexton, said at the breakfast table, that Colonel Brownfield learned that Captain Sexton had made certain remarks, uncomplimentary of course, about Colonel Brownfield taking his washing machine and other similar items to Biak via C-47. Colonel Brownfield called Captain Sexton into his office and proceeded to eat his ass out (eating one's ass out is the highest degree of reprimand).[47]
>
> It seems that when Colonel Brownfield learned what Captain Sexton was saying about him (Captain Sexton was scheduled to fly to Biak, arrived at the plane, loaded his equipment, only to unload in order that Colonel Brownfield's washing machine could be sent—

result, the captain remained and the washing machine went to Biak), Colonel Brownfield called an officers' meeting and said, "I have never heard of such disrespect as being shown in this headquarters. If any of you have anything to say about me, come and say it to me in my office or I'll have you transferred or court-martialed." No one stepped forward.

It seems as though Fifth Air Force has been hearing of the conditions in the Wing for a long time, in fact they had heard that Colonel Brownfield had gone to the air service command and ordered several flushing toilets for his house at Biak.[48]

About the time that Fifth Air Force decided to relieve Brownfield, *Yank Down Under* newsman Sgt. Ozzie St. George was sketching a cartoon. The cartoon shows an airdrome freight office, where three soldiers with duffel bags are being waved off by a cargomaster with a clipboard. "Sorry, men, but we've got some high priority freight here," he explains, gesturing at a portable latrine, complete with screened windows and an "Officers Only" sign. A shipping tag shows that the latrine is bound for APO 565. This sharpened the satire; it combined mockery of officers' bathroom privileges with soldiers' resentment of the high command, for servicemen knew that APO 565 was Hollandia, the site of Douglas MacArthur's white-painted villa.[49]

When it came to latrines, ill will and envy stretched from the lowest private in New Guinea to the four-star general in overall command. Fifth Air Force command might wink at Colonel Hutchison building a headquarters with indoor plumbing in a rear area, because Photo Hutch had built airfields in forward areas. Colonel Brownfield had made a fool of himself in the air and in the operations tent. There was little to be said in his favor, against the rancor and jealousy that an order for flush toilets provoked in a land of rough-cut board latrines.

⑤

Colonel Sams was in a jovial mood. At Biak, for the first time since Laurel, he had the 17th and 82nd Squadrons together at the same air base. He flew with the 17th Squadron over McCluer Gulf. They saw no Japanese boats, but played a practical joke on two prau schooners by buzzing them and firing the .50-calibers when they were directly overhead.

Sams had been on leave. The night before he came back, George Kenney had pointedly asked Sams if he were flying too much combat—which made Sams think. What he really wanted, he thought, was to carry on until the end of the year, get in four hundred hours, and then quit. In the meantime there was work to be done. He borrowed a bulldozer and considered where to lay out a baseball diamond.[50]

⑤

Captain Campbell was taking bets that the war in Europe would be over by the end of August. An engineer officer predicted that their own war would be over in early 1946. "When up in the forward areas, one never hears how the war is progressing and doesn't have time to think about it," Rocky observed.[51]

Across the Southwest Pacific, dead men unquietly marked the way. On the old Bulldog Track, the trail used by Australian commandos to cross New Guinea, one halt was named "Dead Chinaman" and another "Dead Kukukuku." Each was known by the remains to be seen there—by a moss-covered skull that stared from a hollow tree, by the tribal burial platform that held a warrior's bark-wrapped mummy. From Buna to Nadzab, from Nadzab to Gusap, airmen flew by the trails of wrecked cargo planes. On Biak, there were the graves of men killed by friends in a flash of accident and panic: Captain Hancock and his crew. On the ridge above their cluster of white crosses, lashed to his post outside the cave, the dead Japanese soldier remained a grim, troubling landmark. Murray saw him, so too the infantry, so too American souvenir hunters and the Japanese holdouts who killed some of them, so too Charles Lindbergh. No one recorded who held up that corpse and tied the knots in place, or why, and neither side laid the body to rest.[52]

From down the coast came one more reminder of the war's cost. An Australian brigade near Prinz Heinrich Harbor reported that they had uncovered a body, several months old, legs tied together, in a shallow grave by a bomb crater. There was little to identify it: a pair of flying boots, some scraps of clothing, and a Mae West life jacket on which someone had written in pencil. As they read it, it said D. O. or D. C. Graham.[53]

Colonel Brownfield was out of the war now. The men over whom he had lorded it would head toward a grimmer war under better leaders.

16

BIAK

In January, Major Tockstein had given the Wing fair warning: prepare to move twice in the year ahead. Now it seemed that they would move three times—maybe four. No sooner had Rocky moved to Biak than the island began to seem overcrowded, and talk began of a move to the Philippines.

⟨§⟩

On September 1, the heavy bombers on Owi struck the Philippines: a huge strike, fifty-five B-24s from three different bomb groups, covered by three squadrons of P-38s. Rocky was working the night before in Wing HQ: "Was duty officer and during the evening there were many incoming teletype messages concerning the large strike against Davao in the low part of Mindanao. According to the messages, eleven squadrons will hit the town." The next morning, when he flew out to Owi, he could see how large the raid had been: across the island, the airstrips were barren. An empty airfield meant an air strike in the air. The strike against Davao was against three airfields that commanded the invasion routes that MacArthur's staff was mapping out. The raid was the largest American air strike in months; it was particularly daring since it was staged in daylight.[1]

Col. John T. Murtha was the new Wing commander. Everyone liked him. He had graduated from West Point alongside Sams and gone into the Air Corps as soon as he could earn his wings. Before Pearl Harbor, he had been an air observer for the Army Air Force in England. He liked hunting and bombers were his favorite kind of aircraft. On Biak he had won the Air Medal for strafing a Japanese bunker with the 75-mm gun in his B-25.[2]

Colonel Hutchison had hobnobbed with his commanders, not his officers. Colonel Brownfield had asked his men about chlorinating his water. Colonel Murtha talked strategy with his men. He tied things together: why the invasion planners had overlooked Owi, why Owi had been a tough place to build airfields, why Owi had become essential. Rocky was impressed with what Murtha had to say:

> There has been considerable discussion of the reason the Fifth Air Force ever landed on Owi Island. Before the invasion of Biak, the occupation of the island was never considered, because no Japs or natives were on the island. Also, the terrain of the island was thought not suitable for an airdrome. The island hides a coral plateau which had a perimeter of sand which was suitable for building. However the island was heavily timbered, some of the trees were 150 feet high and four feet or more in diameter.
>
> The conclusion from all rumors points out that the infantry failed to take the Jap-held airdromes on Biak, in fact, for a while, it looked as if they weren't going to, so the Air Force made their own invasion, and told the ground forces to go to hell. Though the dreaded disease of typhus was contracted by a large percent of men, the strip was large enough for many ships and was in operation when Mokmer, the Jap airstrip on Biak, was taken. And now quoting Colonel Murtha, "Had the Air Force

not gone into Owi, it would have delayed several weeks, consequently we could have not sent those one hundred and thirty bombers at Davao so soon. It all merely goes to prove the Air Force is forcing ahead the war in this theater—not the infantry—the good ole Air Force. The same reason goes why you fellows have had to do without showers, or roads, or mess halls, just because the infantry did not get the ground and give the engineers time to move in, therefore that's why we moved in while the infantry front lines were our camp areas."[3]

It is easy to see why his airmen liked Murtha. He acknowledged what they had done without, pointed out how well they had measured up, and gave them credit for helping win the war. Murtha was driving home the point, which Rocky saw, that the war in the Southwest Pacific was an air war. *The Air Force is forcing ahead the war in this theater—not the infantry—the good ole Air Force.*

As air groups moved forward and tents went up, the beachhead at Biak took on the look of a makeshift main street. Note the telephone lines strung by Major Chenery and his linemen. Courtesy of Eastern Oregon University, Pierce Library, Fred Hill World War II Photograph Collection. Taken and donated by Fred Hill.

In the Fifth Air Force camp, organizations were jostling each other, or throwing elbows. When Fifth Air Force ADVON staff arrived, they took over the 91st Wing bivouac, pushing out the Wing staff to new quarters farther down the beach.[4] That led in turn to bad blood between the Wing and the Sixth Photo Group. A deal had been struck, in which only a black engineer unit walked away happy.

> The Sixth Group headquarters officers are highly griped at the Wing Headquarters officers because of the following reason. One of the officers in Wing HQ, who was in charge of clearing the Wing HQ area, went to an engineer outfit and asked for a bulldozer. Being unable to secure one, he offered to give all the fresh meat on a fat cat plane (a "fat cat" is an airplane which flies to Australia twice a week to bring back fresh meats and other food stuffs which cannot be secured in the combat zone), and thus he got a bulldozer to clear the Wing Area—but only the Wing Area. The rub is that the Sixth Group needed an area cleared but were unable to secure one bulldozer yet they had contributed as much per man as the Wing HQ in buying the fresh meat which was given to the Negro engineers. Result: no bulldozer, no fresh meat, low morale.[5]

At Nadzab the Wing had learned to hustle. Lieutenant Boyer and Captain Chapin listened in on a middle-of-the-night construction deal.

> Jack and I were awakened around three this morning by a conversation in an adjoining tent. From the fragments of conversation the following was deduced. Two enlisted men had stolen a truck load of lumber and had brought

it up to trade it for liquor. Evidently the enlisted men knew that the officers needed lumber and had liquor so they came to this area. After considerable bartering Lieutenant Bristowe and Lieutenant Cole secured the load for two quarts of rum. This morning we saw the lumber was planed one-by-eights.[6]

Planed one-by-eight boards were much better than rough construction two-by-fours. Life on Biak, particularly with top-of-the-line lumber like those boards, could almost be comfortable. At the 82nd Squadron camp, in Lieutenant White and Lieutenant Moffitt's tent, screened behind mosquito netting, could be found a washstand, bar, and seltzer siphon. The officers' club had a crushed white coral floor, radio, and icebox. Special Services was screening *Jack London*, which dwelt on London's discovery of a Japanese plan to dominate the world, and *Christmas Holiday*, a film noir that blindsided servicemen who expected musical comedy from Gene Kelly and Deanna Durbin.[7]

On the coral-spattered bluff near Sorido Village, the south coast of Biak Island, sun-tanned, Atabrine-colored men of the 91st Photo Reconnaissance Wing began setting up a pseudo-permanent camp. . . . All through August the advanced echelon had been blasting coral-encrusted stumps with dynamite, erecting mess halls, administration buildings, photo labs, and squadron living quarters. A bulldozer pushed a road through a gliding curve toward Wing Headquarters.

Latrine digging, incidentally, proved to be a task worthy of any demolition engineer's training. Digging details blasted with dynamite, swung picks, and tried to shovel. Finally a semblance of a trench was dug, and coral and dirt levees were piled up around the edges. Neatly-cut seats and screen cages to keep the flies in finished off very-functional latrines.[8]

Latrines were a touchy subject in the Southwest Pacific. After using dynamite, picks, and shovels to dig an officers' latrine, these enlisted men of the 17th Squadron enthroned themselves on the seat box to satirically celebrate their triumph. Courtesy of Eastern Oregon University, Pierce Library, Fred Hill World War II Photograph Collection. Taken and donated by Fred Hill.

"For the first time in many months Wingsters have access to a well-sanded beach and good swimming water," the Wing historian concluded. "Nearly every day men of the advanced echelon took time out for a swim and to hunt for 'cat's eyes' sea shells.[9] It wasn't long until discarded belly tanks became impromptu boats and sailing craft." This tone was cheery—too much so. Men were still drowning off the beaches.[10]

> The Sixth Group officers are constructing a large officers' club on the beach. The club building is a former photo lab and elevated above the water by barrels. While leaving last evening I overheard two enlisted men's conversation. One enlisted man: "What in the hell is that?" Other enlisted man: "The Sixth Group Officers' Club. Suppose now they'll put this whole beach off limits for enlisted men."[11]

Kenney and MacArthur had moved forward by capturing islands for airfields—figurative islands like Nadzab, actual islands like Wakde. On Biak, the air blitz advanced by capturing only a narrow strip of an island. Because the airfields on Biak were located on the coastal plain, the infantry pushed inland only four miles—just enough to ensure that the Japanese could not drop mortar shells on the airstrips. "Infantry patrols still went out on reconnaissance tours of the native villages and jungles, now and then picking up a Nip or shooting down a sniper," the Wing historian wrote.[12]

The antiaircraft officer who shot down Hancock's plane had been busted (so the 17th Squadron heard). There were other stories of the early days on the beachhead, of other times when men had shot too quickly.

> While at Owi this afternoon I met a private who was in the anti-aircraft unit which landed on Biak the first day. When asked of their casualties he related the following: "We have had two casualties, one resulting from an accident and one from enemy fire. The accidental one happened the first night we were here. We landed, set up our guns and when night came, the order was issued that no one would move under any circumstance during the night because it was expected the Japs would infiltrate through the lines. During the night someone must have been dreaming for he yelled 'They've got me' and just a few seconds later the executive officer felt someone touch his legs and lift his feet. The executive officer then shot the person at his feet. Later it was discovered to be our first sergeant. He was a fine fellow, and evidently he was walking in his sleep for he had worked so hard preparing our outfit for the move. He was really a good man."[13]

Men regretted having been trigger-happy, but no one on Biak could yet relax. Michael Moffitt of the 82nd Squadron constantly wore his heavy .45 in a shoulder holster (to keep it handy if Japanese sneaked into camp, and to keep any American from stealing the pistol if he laid it down).

> An engineer major was returning alone in a command car from an outpost construction area, when three Japs came out of the brush in front of his car, holding a white flag. Although much excited, he had them climb on the radiator and fenders, then drove into the main camp area. Might be added that the major was quite unstable due to shock.[14]

In a cave in the cliff above the 82nd Squadron bivouac, two officers from a fighter squadron found a Japanese soldier sleeping. They woke him up, captured him, and brought him (en route to the stockade) to the squadron mess hall. The prisoner ate ravenously. He bowed a great deal, Doc Schafer noted, and "made signs that there was another one up there somewhere."[15]

The 82nd and 110th Squadrons were flying attack missions against Japanese airstrips, working to keep the runways cratered so that no planes could be flown in. They flew missions against the airdromes at Waren, Moemi, and Ransiki, on the coast facing across to Biak, as well as the Japanese base at Manokwari, farther north and west. They hit Morotai, northwest above Halmahera, trying to knock out a Japanese radar station. Some flights went out to Cape Waios, others down the far coast of New Guinea. The bombers of the 17th Squadron went farther out on patrol, crossing New Guinea, heading far out into the empty Ceram Sea.

Colonel Sams led a strike southwest to Wewak, where the Japanese airstrips had been repaired. He was flying a P-40 now. "Those planes have brakes and rudder that are hell on the leg muscles," he wrote. "Make my muscles quiver like they have DTs." Switching from a P-39 to a P-40 meant other adjustments,

*After the 82nd Squadron traded its P-39s for P-40s,
Sergeant Winkle and Corporal Davis posed again—this
time beside a warplane inherited from the 49th Group, a
hand-me-down fighter still bearing earlier pilots' nose art.*
San Diego Air & Space Museum

as Sams found on a mission to Ransiki: "Bombing was okay but
I couldn't find the master gun switch. Did I feel silly. The others
knocked off a boat and fired a fuel dump while I flew around feeling like a chump. I'll know next time."[16]

⟨S⟩

The day after the great bomber mission against Davao, the 82nd
Squadron sent out a much less ambitious sortie. Four pilots flew
out, three in P-39s and one in a P-40. The ones who flew P-39s
never came back.[17]

The pilot of the P-40, who did come back, was 1st Lt. Bill Shomo,
the flight leader. The pilots who vanished were two new second
lieutenants, Gene Ronning and James Rice, and First Lieutenant
Bailey. Bailey was the squadron celebrity who had ditched in

January, gone missing for two weeks, recuperated in Australia, and, on his return, sold Rocky and his friends a packet of freeze-dried ice cream.

The mission was a vague one, "armed recco and bombing mission on targets of opportunity on the south shore of New Guinea, in the Etna Bay region." It was also a long mission—Etna Bay was ninety minutes' flight time out, at the maximum range for a P-39.

Shomo said later that they reached Etna Bay, found a thunderstorm in progress, and decided immediately to return home. He decided to climb to 4,500 feet, through a broken level of cumulus. At 4,000 feet, while he was still in the clouds, his drop tank ran dry and his engine stopped. Shomo dropped to 1,000 feet before he could get his engine restarted. He could not see the other planes; he called to them by radio. The only response was the buzzing noise of someone else pressing down a radio transmitter button. Shomo directed the other planes to rendezvous at Cape Bohia, ten minutes away. He reached Bohia and circled there for half an hour. No one showed up. On the radio he heard no voices, only more buzzing from that unseen transmitter. When his own fuel ran low, Shomo flew home alone.

They searched that day and the next, and found nothing. The only possible piece of intelligence came in early. On the afternoon that the planes vanished, a bomber from the 17th Squadron reported "three P-39s either rat-racing or strafing at Babo, which was many miles north of their target."

There are errors here, more than one, peculiar and fatal. Babo is nowhere near Etna Bay—Babo is on McCluer Gulf, a hundred and fifty miles farther north. If the flight went to Babo, Shomo was completely lost. If the lost P-39s were strafing or rat-racing at Babo, burning precious fuel at the edge of their combat range, that was an error, too.

Shomo thought the buzzing transmitter was another pilot's acknowledgment of his radio calls. Possibly it was a Japanese radio-man holding down his own transmitter button on the American frequency, jamming it. If the three P-39 pilots heard Shomo, they should have taken the warning to head home. Even if they did not hear him, they should have known to head for Biak. Or perhaps the three P-39 pilots were dead already, on a mountainside hidden by the overcast.

Other searches were made; all were fruitless. One pilot recalled: "Bailey was a hard-luck pilot and I believe this was his second time to be missing. He was never found as far as I know."[18]

On this chapter of the air war, Sergeant Ursprung wrote the last line. He noted the loss of the three P-39s and the failure of the searches. Ten days later, he recorded simply, "Completed engine change on Staff Sergeant Winkle's P-40 Snooks." Crew chief Winkle's P-40 was Shomo's trouble-plagued warplane, the one that had stalled and dropped Shomo into the clouds while the other pilots vanished.[19]

✥

The Signal construction crew honored Major Chenery with a souvenir, a Japanese field telephone. Rocky mentioned the field telephone, which means that he coveted it.

There was something larger on which Rocky and Chenery saw eye to eye. There had been some sort of altercation, a quarrel between the staff officers who sent messages and the field officers who actually transmitted the messages and worried about the Japanese intercepting them.

> As the infantry cleared the Jap-constructed airdromes, the tactical air corps units began to locate on Biak and operate from there. This situation developed to be a communications problem—how to relay information from headquarters on Owi to the tactical outfits located at Biak, some miles across the water. This problem was approached as follows—first submarine cable, then later radio teletype, temporary rubber cable, barge transportation and L-5s (liaison-type airplanes) between strips on

Owi and Biak. Naturally the barges and airplane service were put into operation immediately, and also point-to-point coded radio traffic, and a few days later, a five-pair rubber cable for telephone service.

Next came the radio teletype, and because of the great time required to encode and decode messages, the Fifth Air Force ignored all rules of security and sent clear messages by radio between Owi and Biak. They believed however (to quote Lieutenant Colonel Bestic), "We are using FM sets, low power, directional antennae, using several channels, and as far as we know, the Japs do not have any teletype equipment. And if the Japs did pick up our messages they would have to relay them back, then send the orders forward and by that time it would be too late. Look at what has happened, day before yesterday we sent out the frag order by clear radio teletype that eleven squadrons would bomb Davao, Mindanao, and not a single Jap airplane took off to intercept them. Maybe it would be a good thing if the Japs did get a few of our messages because then it would give us a chance to shoot down a few of their planes."

Major Chenery, our signal officer, who knew of the circumstances connected with the radio teletype, made the rule that our Wing would not violate security measures. Therefore we could not send any messages to Owi but would send them by plane.

Next came the submarine cable. For several weeks the fifty-pair cable laid on the Biak beach was something which no one was using. Finally the cable was laid between Owi and Biak and then someone discovered the lack of equipment to complete the installation and the electrical circuits would not operate. Now no one knows when it will be completed.[20]

Chenery and Rocky were the field men. They had found out Bestic, and Bestic knew it: they had caught Fifth Air Force staff transmitting radio messages *en clair* about upcoming daylight air strikes. It is hard to imagine a communication that was more reckless or put warplanes at greater risk. And Bestic knew he was in the wrong; that was why he tried so frenetically to show he was right.

Back in Nadzab, Bestic had been the ADVON staff colonel who did nothing to help Wing communications, except to send over an ADVON staff captain who also did nothing. Rocky had been exasperated then—he remained of the same mind now. He was not ready to let security breaches be explained away, nor was Chenery.

ⓢ

Lieutenant Bristowe, in the tent next to Rocky, was more than a part-time court-martial officer and sight-unseen procurer of lumber. He handled medals.

> Lieutenant Bristowe the Wing decoration and awards officer was scheduled to fly to Hollandia early this morning and will contact Lieutenant General Kenney CG of Far East Air Forces concerning awards for Wing Personnel. Among the award recommendations that he is carrying is reportedly one for the Congressional Medal of Honor (or the highest honor anyway) for Major William Tennille, the Commanding Officer of the 17th Recco Squadron, who led his ten B-25s against four Jap destroyers and one cruiser. It is reported that Tennille flew towards and attacked the cruiser, thus drawing its fire from the other planes. At the end of the battle, only the cruiser remained. Some said the major's plane was going to get away safe but hit the water. One sergeant said no one could have possibly could have gotten out of the plane. Other awards are for the DFC and so on.
>
> Lieutenant Bristowe said that fifty percent of the application for medals are successful for Lieutenant

General Kenney spends his time three ways, (one, tactics; two, awards; and three, with his advisor, Stevie, his WAC captain, who must approve) and because of Kenney's interest in awards, it is quite easy to get one.

Lieutenant Bristowe told me how Colonel Brownfield got his DFC. "Well, you know Colonel Brownfield was a command pilot who had been overseas a good long time. Well, he was due to go home and since his only decoration was an Air Medal and because he was a personal friend of Major General Whitehead, the brass decided it wouldn't be fitting for an old command pilot to return home after several months in this theater with only an Air Medal. So Colonel Brownfield was automatically put down to fly in the next DFC mission scheduled—which proved to be from Darwin to Ambon. Lieutenant Colonel Guerry and Lieutenant Colonel Darnell also flew on the mission, in fact these two went along to navigate the mission for Colonel Brownfield. Perhaps I had better add Colonel Brownfield had but 30 hours in an F-5 (a P-38 reconnaissance plane) when he went on the mission. On the first attempt to photograph Ambon, the area was covered by a heavy overcast, therefore they made a visual reconnaissance. The second flight was more successful but the pictures were inferior, but nevertheless it constituted a DFC flight and the basis of the award read: 'proves that a singly operated unarmed photographic plane is capable of long over water flight.' The feat was not spectacular but navigation was difficult inasmuch as there was but one checkpoint over the entire trip."[21]

Rocky and Bristowe's doubts about Colonel Brownfield's heroism were warranted. The citation for Colonel Brownfield's Distinguished Flying Cross, as recited by Lieutenant Bristowe and recorded by Lieutenant Boyer, closely follows the official wording of the award.[22]

❧

In the 82nd Squadron, Tate the quiet quick-witted Texan and Murphy the daredevil violinist were heading home. Replacement pilots had arrived. "Sure hope they learn fast how to nurse those old P-39s around, otherwise they're dead ducks," Doc Schafer wrote. As the weeks went on, and the Group transitioned to flying the P-40, he added: "Our gang really has a circus up there in their new P-40s. Many of them are wild kids, but okay."[23]

In the P-39, with its tricycle landing gear and nose wheel, pilots had enjoyed a clear, high, all-around view while taxiing; the P-40 landed and taxied on a tail wheel, with its nose high, blocking the pilot's view of what was directly ahead. Pilots landed too hard and broke their landing gear. They hit puddles during takeoff and spun off the airstrip, Lieutenant Braun the new pilot and Lieutenant McDermott the veteran pilot alike.[24]

Lieutenant Sellers tried to take off in a P-40 carrying full tanks of gasoline and 1,500 pounds of bombs—tried and failed and tried again, three times in all. Each time he lifted off, the engine cut out. Finally, in frustration, Sellers gave up and taxied off the runway, without evincing any awareness that he had cheated death three times. Colonel Sams heard what had happened, saw immediately what might have happened, and yelled at his squadron commanders about getting an engineering check immediately when a motor cut out. *Immediately*, he emphasized, "raising the normal amount of hell."[25]

They finally laid a submarine cable between Owi and Biak. The first submarine cable was built to withstand water pressure at depths up to 250 feet. After the cable was laid, it was discovered that the channel between Owi and Biak ran as deep as a thousand feet. Rocky kept flying to Owi and sending messages on paper. Before the Wing left Biak, there was one final mishap. While the second cable was being put in place, a landing craft pushed out of the way the barge from which the cable was being laid, tilting the barge and dumping the spools of cable in 150 feet of water. The base signal area (not Chenery and Rocky) took the blame. The base signal officer, a major, remarked gloomily that when his commander found out about that, he would go back to the States as a Pfc.[26]

Women in uniform were on their way north—so men heard. The *Wing-ding* ran a long profile of an Army nurse. *Yank Down Under* ran a long story about WACs. The magazine also answered, curtly, a letter from three anonymous GIs, clarifying that male and female officers and enlisted personnel had been allowed in May to attend social functions and associate together, but that this authorization had been rescinded by a command circular of July 19. So that meant little visible change, and Lieutenant Beyer made one of his deadpan oddball comments. "Last evening Lieutenant Beyer arrived at Biak and called on Captain Chapin and me. Beyer said he had been reading up on masturbation and learned that it did not result in any physical injury."[27]

> Near our area is a hospital. In the past no nurses have been stationed there but now preparations are being made to receive them. A large steel mesh fence is being built around the nurses' tents and tied to this ten-foot tent on the inside is canvas, prohibiting any one from looking into the area. The barricade has one entrance, and that is guarded 24 hours a day by MPs.[28]

There were signs of other women. A chest of cosmetics had turned up in a Japanese depot. Someone had seen Japanese women, seven of them, in a truckload of prisoners being driven past. They had been wearing bright-colored blouses and slacks, some of them smiling and smoking cigarettes. Doc Schafer considered that the Japanese might have geisha organizations for their soldiers, in the same way that the Allies had the USO.[29]

Met a lieutenant who is now assigned to GHQ as a liaison officer to the 91st Wing but was with the infantry which marched from Moresby to Buna. Upon questioning he said the only Japanese women who have thus far been contacted by American forces were on Los Negros Island in the Admiralties. Here the American soldiers showed their respect but many of the Jap girls walked among the unsuspecting Americans with hand grenades under their arms. The officer said that in the future we would have as much difficulty with the civilians as with the actual Jap soldiers.[30]

On a coral island at the far end of the world, if American women were under lock and key and armed guard, young American men would look for other women. Note that the infantry lieutenant gave this information "under questioning" by airmen. He may have been extemporizing, for his details are closer to fiction than fact. Postwar histories do not confirm that the Admiralties campaign ended in a wave of suicide grenade attacks by comfort women who preferred death to capture and dishonor by enemy soldiers. It had been a U.S. Army nurse who did that—at least on-screen. In *So Proudly We Hail*, a 1943 Paramount Pictures war movie, blonde Lt. Olivia D'Arcy, played by Veronica Lake, slips an unpinned grenade into her blouse as she pretends to surrender to Japanese troops on Bataan—killing them, killing herself, avenging her dead fiancé, and buying time for her comrade nurses to escape.

Perhaps it was coincidental—but it was now, at the same time that Army nurses and WACs could be seen, that there was trouble over Atabrine. The gossip had always been that Atabrine caused impotence or sterility.[31] Now that the Fifth Air Force had moved north from the jungle airfields of Dobodura and Saidor and Finschhafen, malaria no longer seemed such a threat. Nonetheless, the Army kept ensuring that servicemen took Atabrine, and someone stood against it.

> In order that the men and officers take their Atabrine
> pills six days a week, Captain (Doc) Stafford is standing
> in the chow line every day at noon and throwing the pills
> into the mouths of the men. Everyone was willing except
> one, the cigar-smoking Baptist Chaplain Clark. He told
> Stafford he was against the whole affair of throwing the
> pills into the mouths of the men and he would refuse to
> open his mouth. He further added he would go to some-
> one who could do something about stopping it. Doc
> Stafford said the practice of taking pills originated in the
> 41st Division when practically all of its men had malaria.
> Chaplain Clark is becoming most disliked.[32]

Chaplain Clark may have borrowed trouble; he may have
resented being fed Atabrine in the same way that Roman Catholic
priests distributed the consecrated host. Catholic seminarians had
just been given draft exemptions while Protestant religion students
remained liable to be called up, and Protestant chaplains in the
Fifth Air Force complained that Roman Catholic chaplains ran
everything. (Lieutenant Beyer reported that story.) To replace
Father Bradley at the 71st Group, who had gone missing on a
flight to Biak, they were sending in a new man, Father Zielenski.[33]

If Chaplain Clark was disliked, there were reasons that other
men's resentment focused on him. He had held up the chow line
for personal reasons, and in doing so identified himself with Atabrine, sexual frustration, and a situation where authority treated
grown men like children, inmates, and incompetents. He had drawn
upon himself the anger that other airmen felt at these indigni-
ties. Army Air Force psychiatrists understood the process well. In
the Southwest Pacific, they knew, airmen lived under conditions
of stress. "The constant hammering at personnel—'take your Atabrine,' 'use repellent,' 'dress properly,' 'dry out your clothes, blankets, and shoes,' 'drink only chlorinated water,' 'avoid swamp

areas,' 'stay out of the brush,' 'stay out of the native villages,' 'don't walk here'—all had an aggravating influence of negativism on the individual."[34]

No normal human relationships with members of the opposite sex, the psychiatrists had pointed out. *No family life. Close association with a small group of men for long periods of time, with resultant bickering and personality clashes. Four to six men in one pyramidal tent. Unappetizing diet and primitive latrines.* The hardships of the Southwest Pacific wore less harshly on airmen than on infantry, but they nonetheless wore men down.

Yet if the landscape of the theater could not be changed, a responsible commander could make a difference in the character of his command. "Malassignment and malclassification of individuals through promotion and awards" produced low morale, the psychiatrists counseled. Among non-flying officers who had served overseas, only 22 percent of first lieutenants and only 30 percent of captains felt that the promotions always went to the most deserving officers—and flying officers, who had better chances for recognition, felt almost as diffident about their superiors' judgment.[35] This a thoughtful commander could deal with.

New men were arriving on Biak, names and ranks to be typed into unit T/Os. Differences in rank and experience threatened to create friction within the Group and the Wing.

> Spragg told me that the Wing HQ had assigned several enlisted men with high rank to the Sixth Group and 71st Groups and almost immediately, Colonel Sams and Lieutenant Colonel Guerry called on Colonel Murtha and stated they would not accept enlisted men with such high rank, for if they did, they would be unable to promote the men who had been in their organization. The orders were rescinded and the men in question are simply lying around the HQ Squadron.[36]

Late yesterday afternoon a captain from the Ordnance Service arrived to be assigned in the Wing to replace Captain Jack Chapin, my tent-mate. Jack C. said undoubtedly he was going to be sent to the 308th Bomb Wing now located at Hollandia to help make preparations for the invasion of the Philippines. Jack became disgusted when he learned from the captain that he had graduated from OCS in November 1942 and had received his captaincy in January 1944. He was a first lieutenant for seven months and Jack was one for 19 months.[37]

Airmen who had come over on the *General John S. Pope* now counted as veterans. Sams and Guerry deserve high marks for loyalty to men who had served with them.

⚘

There had always been rumors about the war; now there was gossip about peace. The stories began to circulate early in September, when Rocky noted, "There is a daily rumor out that Germany has surrendered or is asking to."[38] The stories culminated in a rumor of the classic sort, the sort that officials wanted to catch and suppress.

Major Crowley returned from Hollandia early this morning with the following information. The officers at Hollandia were all drunk because they had received news that Germany had surrendered. Later at Colonel Murtha's staff meeting they confirmed the rumor. All day long the men were asking if the rumor was so.

Upon asking Major Smith the A-2 intelligence officer about the source of the rumor concerning the surrender of Germany, learned the following: Someone played a practical joke by placing a news notice on the transit officers' bulletin board at Hollandia that Germany had surrendered, therefore all officers passing through saw the item and spread the rumor at their next stop.[39]

The last week in September, Rocky flew down to Nadzab one final time. The trip was different: he left from the air freight office at Borokoe Airdrome, not a shell-pocked tarmac at Mokmer, and the strip was alive with Japanese prisoners and liberated POWs. "Airstrips were never built fast enough for Whitehead's forces," Ennis Whitehead's biographer has written: "Almost as fast as the strips were built, they became obsolete."[40]

> While waiting for the plane, we watched the Negro truck drivers' craps games, and later one truckload of Jap prisoners and two truckloads of freed Javanese and Indians, former Jap prisoners. One of the Indian prisoners said he was a laborer at Manokwari and after the invasion of Biak he was brought to Biak by night and landed on what he called "a very difficult beach." He said letters could be sent to the prisoners but they could not write any.
>
> Later I talked to the MP officer who had charge of the Japanese prisoners. He said there was an estimate of 500 to 1000 Japs on the island. He then related the following: "We picked up a Jap last week who could speak very good English and during the interrogation he told of attending the Bob Hope Show and skipping down into camp areas at night and securing food. Someone told me that a Jap admiral was still at large on the island and it is rumored he has sufficient supplies to hold out for a long time."[41]

Nadzab had changed, too. An air base full of young men now had an educational body on campus, the Far East Air Force's Combat Replacement Training Center. Kenney had asked for years for airmen: now he suddenly had them, because Hap Arnold knew that he would not need them to replace flight crew losses in Europe. Nadzab was crowded with hundreds of new second lieutenants, all fresh from flight training, awed to be overseas. Far behind the

*On Biak, four lieutenants who had been friends since flight
school posed for a snapshot: Jack Prindeville, tall Jim Richards,
Bob Wells (with bandages over a hole in his skull), and Mike
Moffitt with his shoulder holster. Within weeks, two of these
pilots died—Prindeville when his worn-out P-40 caught fire in
flight, and Richards when his new F-6 Mustang was caught
in bad weather.* Collection of Michael Moffitt Jr.

front line, they were wearing pistols on their belts. Nadzab was
becoming the plum posting that Major Chenery had predicted, a
place where officers could expect good food, regular leaves, WACs
for company, and an early flight home.[42]

The young pilots were talking about suicide raids, but they had
never seen one. The only clear sign of combat was overhead, where
C-47s were towing gliders, almost constantly—rehearsing for airborne landings.[43]

🌀

The 82nd Squadron lost one more pilot before they left Biak. On
September 25, the squadron sent eighteen planes on a bombing
mission against Kaimana. Twelve planes completed the mission,
five turned back, and one plane dropped into the sea. Lt. Jack
Prindeville was flying with the formation, at nine hundred feet,

when the belly of his plane caught fire. The other pilots yelled at him to jump. Prindeville dived, got his canopy open, did a barrel roll, and dropped free of the aircraft. He had hundreds of feet of clear air above the water, but either he did not pull the ripcord or his parachute failed to open. The chute opened just before Prindeville hit the ocean; he took half a swing and hit the water flat. Doc Schafer heard that Prindeville made two weak swimming strokes and then went under, Colonel Sams that he sank and dragged the chute under with him. Two pilots circled the area until PT boats and a Catalina arrived, but they saw nothing of Prindeville, and the Navy found nothing.

"He was one of the friendliest of the pilots," wrote Lt. Henry Newton, who had just joined the squadron. "I spoke to him while fixing the bombs just a half hour before. The missions were very successful."[44]

There was another death in the Wing, one that Rocky noted: the commander of the Sixth Photo Reconnaissance Group, reconnaissance pilot Arthur Post.

> Lieutenant Jensen told me that Major Post was killed yesterday. He was flying a piggyback P-38 with one enlisted man in the back (an instrument expert). The major flew low over the camp area and along the water's edge, then he pulled up into a slow roll and then, many believe, his motors cut out and he fell into the ocean. There is no definite proof he was killed, but he was the only person flying locally in a piggyback and was the only one who didn't return.
>
> To us, Major Post was the best of pilots and an individual in whom we had confidence, either on the ground or in the air, but tonight he sleeps eternally in his plane under several feet of water in the bay. We mourn, and will mourn with every remembrance of him who has suffered the fate of many who fly.[45]

Arthur Post was from Milwaukee, where his story can be traced in the *Milwaukee Journal* and the *Wisconsin Jewish Chronicle*. He came to New Guinea when any Allied flight over Lae or Rabaul attracted a flight of angry Zeros. In those early months, Post flew dozens of missions, earning and earning again the bits of ribbon with which General Kenney honored his airmen. Post had earned the Distinguished Flying Cross, Distinguished Service Cross, Air Medal, two Bronze Stars, two Oak Leaf Clusters, and the Purple Heart. In the last months of 1943, Post had zigzagged across two hemispheres. He had gone from jungle fugitive to guest of honor—bounced from the rain forest of New Britain to the ice of Wisconsin, been hailed in Washington, touched down in Hollywood. Post was offered a flight instructor's position, stateside. He asked instead to go back to New Guinea.

Rocky rarely used words like *mourn, eternal, remembrance,* or *fate,* and he wrote without subtlety. But there was reason for Rocky to mourn Post's death. Post was a bona fide hero, the more so because he did not talk about his exploits. He was a skilled pilot who had died in an inexplicable crash. Any airman in New Guinea would have felt that cheerless irony.

At the end of September, the weather turned rough; it was the middle of typhoon season. The 20th Mapping Squadron sent three F-7 reconnaissance planes to the Philippines. One returned without incident, and another scraped into Wakde with its tanks dry and no gasoline left save for the gas in its fuel lines. The third plane was lost. Everyone regretted it, Rocky wrote, because the crew were all experienced men.[46] The same rough weather raised the surf and tide along the beach.

> During the last few days there has been a continuous high wind and the sea has been unusually rough. Many of the officers who built their houses (tents with wooden frames) on gasoline barrels along the water's edge had

to move the constructions or watch them [get] washed away. Among the officers who had to move were the two chaplains, the Sixth Group personnel are teasing the chaplains about building a house upon the sand. No one was sorry the chaplains had to move—in fact most of us found the circumstances highly entertaining.[47]

Colonel Murtha told them that they would move by water, this time and any time to come. "Our unit has been alerted for several days now and all the sections are preparing shipping crates," Rocky recorded on October 2. The officers' club had an open house, using up liquor. Forty gallons of punch were dipped out, ten gallons of which were pure grain alcohol from the flight surgeon's store.[48] They compared depressing notes on earlier trips by Liberty Ship. The 17th Squadron men had spent thirty-two days on board ship, eating dry rations, when the squadron moved up from Finschhafen—longer than it would have taken to cross from San Francisco.

Lieutenant Cook of the Eighth Fighter Squadron said thirty days were required to move the squadron's equipment and ground personnel from Lae to Biak. He said their particular boat was in Humboldt Bay (Hollandia) several days and the enlisted men had dysentery, no toilet paper, no stationery, no reading material, and no mail. He said when they landed, equipment was piled on the beach and almost immediately men from other units began stealing it.[49]

The landing itself, they figured, would go well. The 20th Mapping Squadron had flown missions over the Philippines many times, within 250 miles of Manila, and all of the Japanese airdromes except one were grass strips. There were seven main Japanese airdromes, they had photographed them all, and all the photos showed far fewer enemy planes than expected. Likely the landing would be unopposed—the Japanese had probably withdrawn from the southern Philippines and would withdraw from Luzon if they could.[50]

Before he left Biak, Rocky finally met face-to-face two characters who had dogged his steps since Nadzab.

> Men and officers were along the beach swimming and maneuvering their boats which they had made. Almost unnoticeably, an improvised raft approached the beach and when two officers of one of the squadrons noticed it they believed the occupants aboard the raft were natives. The figures motioned for the officer to come, that they did, to discover two Japanese who wanted to give up. Evidently these would-be prisoners were too exhausted to row any further. When the news was spread of the "capture," everyone swam out to the raft and pushed them ashore. The Japs were so weak that locomotion was practically impossible. When the fellows gave them cigarettes and one man brought a piece of bread from a nearby mess hall and gave it to them, these two men painfully to all of us, rolled over upon their knees and worshipped us.[51]

Rocky could now tell his own version of the story of the two Japanese soldiers in the chow line. It was an anecdote in which, pathetically, life and art were one. The chow line stories mocked the enemy: the soldiers of the Emperor, once so feared and hated, were now glad to pose as nondescript GIs. The stories portrayed a victorious Allied army in which rations were plenteous, if carelessly dished out. Rocky had seen the enemy firsthand now, weak and bedraggled, desperate to surrender, grateful to be given bread and cigarettes.

Any Japanese soldier left on Biak was glad to fall into American hands. Outside the perimeter, the bitter war between the *mambri* and the Japanese continued. It was financed by the Dutch, who offered a bounty of half a guilder for every Japanese holdout killed. Before peace finally came, the people of Biak brought in more than three thousand ears.[52]

Biak was the last time that Rocky saw Chaplain Smith, who had come north with the 860th Engineers. On a visit to Owi, Rocky called on the chaplain. Smith's engineer battalion had been issued new equipment; clearly they were bound for the Philippines. Talking to Rocky, he noted that his new flock kept him as busy as the 71st Group had done.

> He had on his desk a letter written by an enlisted man to his girlfriend in the States. In his letter he told his girl that he had a buddy who had priced sexual intercourse with a Red Cross girl and found it to be up to $100. Chaplain Smith had received the letter from the censor so that the man might be told he should not tell such stories even though they could be true. Smith has told me that the authorities were having a problem in the hospital from the nurses selling lethal methyl alcohol. He further added that he had organized a jazz orchestra and in the first practice night, the members proceeded to become intoxicated.[53]

Chaplain Smith had preached to his men and worked for them and stood up to colonels and handled what generals dished out to him; men from his old unit went out of their way to see him, and one wrote him a fond compliment. "He had the toughest job possible," recalled Warren Sparks of the 82nd Squadron, "trying to save the souls of a bunch of young heathens whose entire attention was devoted to flying, drinking, chasing girls (and catching them), and playing poker. To his credit, he never gave up trying to save us, but he did mellow a lot."[54]

Doc Schafer had started home. He had fungus on four fingers of his hand now; he had soaked his hands in permanganate and mineral oil and boric acid, and had tried copper ionization, still without much success. Of his work he could be quietly proud. He had written two short articles for the *Journal of the American Medical Association*; before he left the Pacific, an offprint of the first piece had made its way to him. The War Department was asking for details on the male hormone kits he had found in Japanese supply dumps.[55] Behind him lay a long year measured in mission whiskey and takeoffs and crack-ups—Morris' fractures, McDermott's stitches, Lipscomb's burns, and the hole in Wells' skull.

Other men from the 17th Squadron were heading stateside, Don Machnikowski and Ray Couk and their crew from Mitch the Witch: Colonel Sams was having their papers typed. "Very few of the old ones left now," he remarked.[56]

Some men were still eager to show that they were playing a part. A private first class whose mail Rocky was censoring "wrote his mother and told her about flying as co-pilot in a B-17. Hope his mother never learns that only commissioned officers fly planes."[57]

At a movie one night, the audience cheered the announcement that Russia would aid the United States in continuing the war after the defeat of Germany. "The first time since coming overseas that the men have shown any enthusiasm over the outcome of the war," Rocky commented. "Maybe we will be home in 18 months after all—maybe."[58]

The Wing was loading a Liberty Ship now. They had heard the Filipinos would welcome them with open arms, and they had high hopes for a return to civilization. There was gossip about where they would land. "Major Chenery said a concrete road, built by an American construction concern, bordered one side of the Wing area. If so, it will be our first sight of a paved road in the war zone. Many men expressing a desire to have their furloughs in Manila."[59]

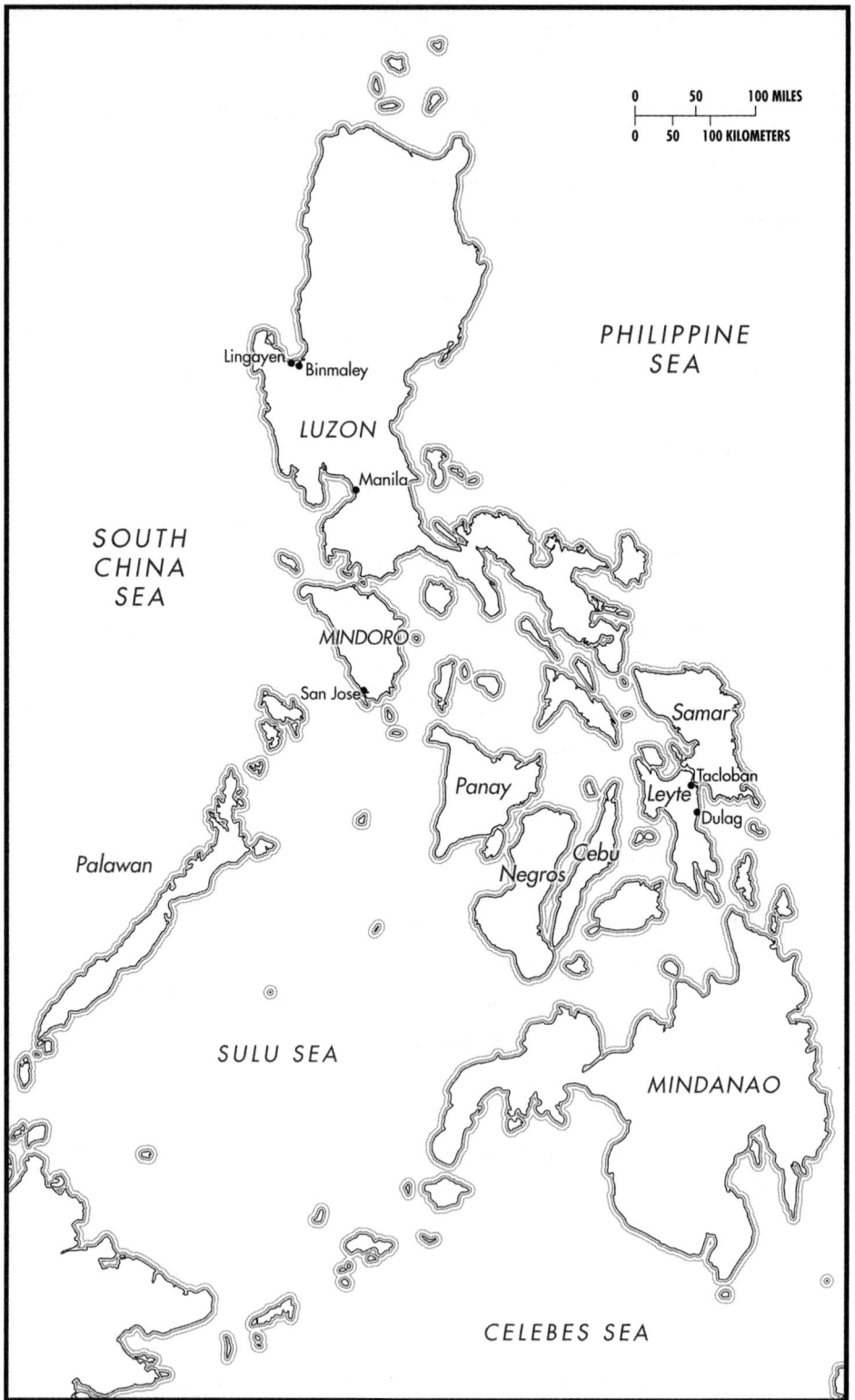

MAP 2. *Philippine Islands*

17

LEYTE

Douglas MacArthur had vowed to return to the Philippines if he had to go by himself in a canoe with George Kenney flying cover in a single-engine Cub liaison plane.[1] On October 20, 1944, Mac-Arthur made good on his promise: he landed on the island of Leyte, on Red Beach outside Tacloban, and announced to the people of the Philippines that he had returned. Kenney splashed ashore beside his commander, soaked to the knees.

The Fifth Air Force had estimated that the Japanese could hit the American beachheads with three or four large air raids a day. Kenney had not counted on small raids, and the Japanese surprised him. As MacArthur's entourage left the beach, three Japanese warplanes strafed the soldiers crowded there. Just after dark, four more Japanese planes strafed. At dawn the next morning, a Japanese dive-bomber came in low across the water, too low to be hit by Allied antiaircraft fire, then pulled up and smashed into the bridge of the HMAS *Australia*—the first kamikaze.[2]

🌀

A familiar officer once more commanded, this time a level higher. Colonel Murtha had moved to the 310th Bombardment Wing and Colonel Sams took over at the 91st Wing—"making the fifth new commander the Wing has had in ten months," Rocky observed."[3]

For Sams, making Wing commander was like breaking out of a weather front. Recent weeks had been hard. He had been shot up on a night mission to Ambon: flak hit his plane and shrapnel bounced off his flak suit, above his heart. "Should call it a good day in that I didn't fight with anyone," he wrote that week. There was a staff meeting with General Whitehead, at which fireworks were anticipated and about which Sams afterwards wrote down nothing. Finally came a last-minute, hand-to-hand, overnight struggle inside HQ: "Was told this afternoon that I would take the Wing. Before dinner, was informed I was to be returned to the States immediately for combat fatigue. To start the fight I got three flight surgeons to conduct a 64. Nothing wrong. . . . Informed by General Whitehead that I would remain and have the Wing."[4]

On October 18, the 91st Wing members sailed, on the *Gilbert Stuart*, a Liberty Ship. They traveled southeast along the coast to Lae, and waited there while a fighter squadron and its gear were loaded—then steamed back north again to Hollandia, where they joined a convoy.

MacArthur had gone ashore; some sort of huge naval battle was raging off Leyte and the American aircraft carrier *Princeton* had been sunk. The officers of the Wing knew no more, not yet. They crowded into the chief mates' room to listen to the *Philippine Hour*, an American broadcast aimed at the Philippines. They scoffed at reports that servicemen had crowded around the beachhead to catch a glimpse of MacArthur, but entertained the idea that Mac might know something about strategy.

> Captain Colle made the following statement: "Although everyone hates MacArthur, he is no doubt our greatest strategist. In this theater there were few or very few men killed. There have been no blunders as the Anzio beachhead etc. Not once have we met any resistance upon our landings: but all other Generals are simply pikers when it comes to publicity."[5]

"Late this evening rumors were as follows," Rocky recorded: "We would not depart from Hollandia until the Jap navy had been driven back; during the last twenty-four hours the Japs have raided the Leyte beachheads fourteen times."[6]

At Tacloban, meanwhile, follow-up waves of landing craft came ashore at the beach beside the airfield and unloaded their cargos on the flat terrain where the First Air Task Force was planning to build a runway. The logjam was cleared by the task force commander David W. Hutchison and his engineers: Kenney had authorized Hutchison to bulldoze into the water any supplies that cluttered the airstrip, and the army quartermasters did not doubt that Hutchison would do it. General Krueger told the engineers that unless the gravel were laid "they would be digging foxholes for their lives within 24 hours." Navy warplanes, orphaned when their carriers were sunk off the island of Samar, landed on the strip at Tacloban. There were more than a hundred of them, they cluttered an airfield that was already overcrowded, and dozens cracked up on the short stretch of steel matting as they landed. Some managed to refuel and rearm and fly out; the rest were among the first obstructions bulldozed. At Tacloban, space was so tight that a war-plane that could not be repaired in twenty-four hours was routinely bulldozed into the sea.[7]

Japanese air strikes continued—and at Tacloban, it was the Japanese who attacked at masthead height. On October 25, at sunset, Kenney and Hutchison were watching Navy torpedo planes land. Suddenly, the last plane in the formation peeled off from its landing approach, roared out over the harbor, and bombed a boat carrying gasoline drums—a Japanese bomber, using the trick that had worked at Wakde. The next day, at the Tacloban airstrip, Kenney spent the day climbing in and out of slit trenches, dodging attacks that came in without warning: "About 500 yards away, just lifting over the palm trees at the south end of the airdrome, were four Nip planes with the lights beginning to twinkle from the machine guns mounted in the wings." Kenney dropped flat behind a jeep and stood up unscathed. Hutchison and Pappy Gunn ducked behind another jeep, but Gunn was not so fortunate; a piece of phosphorus from an incendiary bomb buried itself in his arm.[8]

By noon on October 27, Hutchison and the engineers had laid a strip where P-38s could land: a half mile of steel matting, with another thousand feet of crushed coral. Ennis Whitehead had ordered north as many P-38s as the strip could hold. At the appointed hour, thirty-four P-38s flew in, arrayed in flawless formation, "buzzed the strip and then settled in to stay—the first American Army planes to base in the Philippines since 1942," the official history relates. The Fifth Air Force now had responsibility for the air war in the Philippines.[9]

On October 28, the *Gilbert Stuart* was still anchored off Hollandia. A few officers made their way ashore and reported back that the place was "lousy with WACs." It was Saturday night but no one else made it to dry land. They tuned in to radio reports on the fighting, from American sources, and otherwise.

> This evening as many men and officers who could gathered about the ship's broadcast speakers to listen to Radio Tokyo and the US Philippine Hour. Radio Tokyo reported that the American navy had been defeated in the battle for the Philippines, and that when the American forces attempt to supply those troops already on Leyte, the Imperial Navy of the Japanese would destroy them all. It also reported we had lost over five hundred planes and 128 warships in the conflict.
>
> A Japanese admiral reviewed American operations and said that they exhibited faulty mental capacity of our military leaders or words to that effect. He said it made General MacArthur and Admiral Nimitz look ridiculous. Also, America was throwing everything she had into the battle for the Philippines, because Roosevelt realizes that if he should lose the battle, he will also lose the coming election.[10]

On Sunday morning, October 29, at eight o'clock, the *Gilbert Stuart* got under way. There were nineteen ships in the convoy, guarded by six destroyers. Rocky asked the crew if he could write in their mess room in the evenings. They heard the muffled explosions of depth charges, once, and another time heard that the night before they had passed safely within yards of a floating mine. Some sailors were used to the risks; they had served on the Murmansk run. The airmen sat in the sunlight on the boat deck and discussed Wing photo officers who had never flown a recon mission and whether poison gas would be used when they invaded Japan. They listened faithfully to Japanese radio broadcasts.

> This afternoon we listened to a Tokyo radio program in which a drama was presented. The two characters were Frank (Franklin Roosevelt) and Davey Jones. Jones told Frank that he was receiving so many ships in his locker that it was impossible to take care of them. The drama finally concluded with FDR telling Jones he was too busy with the coming election to bother with reports about the sinking of ships.[11]

On November 4, they made landfall at Leyte. They saw a convoy to port, and two battleships and their escorts, and they prepared to land. They waited all day, and at twilight unpacked their blankets and cots.

> Immediately after darkness the first air raid came, and they continued for the remainder of the night. Our boat was anchored an estimated four miles off Dulag and therefore when the Japs bombed in the Tacloban area, we saw a silent panorama of the raids. Several men cheered the large explosions which took place in the air thinking they were results of direct hits on Jap planes but many officers thought they were phosphorous bombs which

the Japs had dropped. Regardless of what time one would wake throughout the night, one could see explosions of anti-aircraft shells. A few of the more nervous officers did not sleep all night but stayed below decks, thus slept in full uniform, and others undressed and slept on the open deck under blankets on their cots.[12]

They kept on waiting, the next day and the one after that.

Last evening everyone prepared his bed as early as practical and went out on deck to watch the anticipated air raids. Most of the more stable officers believed our ship was at such a distance off shore and since being on the perimeter of the ships that are anchored we would not likely be bombed. However the usual nervous officers were wearing full uniform with helmets, life jackets, canteens. It is interesting to note that all of these latter cited officers are married.[13]

There was a new arrival in the Wing, an ordnance officer named Jensen—a different man from Rocky's friend the weather officer.

A few days ago we had an air raid alert and I took a shower during it. Lieutenant Jensen happened to see me and later told Captain Foster, quote: "He is just a god damn fool."

There was considerable griping last night when the Japs failed to come over. One alert was sounded at 8 p.m. and one at midnight. I slept through both.

Two officers of the 440th Signal Battalion went ashore yesterday to investigate the probable time of unloading and to reconnoiter their camp area, and late yesterday they returned. Their remarks et cetera: It is really rough. You know how dusty the road was at Dobodura, well, it cannot compare at all with the ones on Leyte. Food—there isn't any. When Fifth Air Force has but coffee and prunes for breakfast, and you all know Fifth Air Force would have the best, you know things are really rough. The Bomb Wing would not permit us to eat with them because their rations are short. Tacloban appeared not to have been damaged but all the other towns and villages have been destroyed. Our particular camp area is in a swamp.

This morning our P-38s took off at daylight and climbed to 20,000 feet to wait for the Japs. While we were eating breakfast, five Jap planes came in over the strip, strafed and dropped a few daisy-cutters (bombs whose shells are made from wire) and our P-38s never saw them.[14]

On November 9, after three weeks at sea, they began going ashore. Their new base was Dulag, an airdrome on the coast. The Fifth Air Force had three other airdromes nearby, five miles inland: Buri, Bayug, and San Pablo. None of the airstrips had been surfaced; the runways would need eight inches of gravel laid down before matting could be laid. The airmen were living under canvas, in camps of the unimproved sort. General Krueger had ordered that no lumber—not even shipping pallets or crates—could be used for constructing quarters for officers or enlisted men, until the hospitals were completed.[15]

Meantime, the rain and wind doubled and redoubled: it was their first typhoon. "From the angry immensity of the heavens floods raced in almost horizontal sheets. Palms bent low under the storm, their fronds flattened like streamers of wet silk. Trees crashed to earth."[16]

They got Bayug and Buri into operation, then those fields flooded. The road to San Pablo became impassable. Even at Tacloban, the field was mud—an unadulterated bog, someone called it.[17]

Dulag did not flood. They were laying steel matting, four thousand feet of it. The engineers were working with a foreman from the town. He was personable and got them men who worked hard; he spoke pretty good English. One morning, they found the foreman dead on the road outside the base, shot by American sentries in the night. No one would have been walking down that road unless he were returning from an area that the Japanese still held. The airmen talked about it and concluded that the foreman had probably spoken pretty good Japanese, too.

On November 16, Rocky penned what would be the final entry in his diary.

> Colonel Sams held a meeting of all staff officers in which he related the following: No classified information would be placed on the bulletin board because the natives might remove it. He pointed out that someone had removed two telephone diagrams from the board already. The camp area must be drained immediately. Native labor could be used for this purpose. Latrines must be built for the natives, both for men and women. A barber shop, temporary, will be constructed. In order to speed up work, no shaving around the neck would be done and the clippers would be dipped into a solution before using the instruments on each customer. Each tent would have a native boy who would police the area and build up the floor in order to prevent water from flowing in.
>
> At 6:45 p.m. the rumor spread that the Japanese had broken through our perimeters and were in the vicinity of Fifth Air Force HQ. The MPs along the road were stopping all traffic and permitting only combat personnel to pass. The more nervous men slept with their guns.
>
> While eating supper we watched several P-38s dogfight with Jap planes to the west. Later the rumors reported

the Japs had strafed and dropped anti-personnel bombs on the airstrip, killing two hundred men.

Went to the hospital to visit Captain Foster, who, according to rumors, developed abdominal pains caused from worrying over our frequent raids and from being detailed to help unload the ships.[18]

At this point, Rocky stopped keeping a diary. In the Philippines, things got too busy, he remarked. He had skipped a week already. Now there were rains to deal with, typhoons on the way, air raids, rumors of paratroopers. There were telephone systems to plan and string wire for.

Rocky was at Dulag with the Group and the Wing. At the end of November, Colonel Sams rapidly put down what the rest of the month had been.

This poor neglected record. 23, 24, 25 fair weather otherwise rain daily and nightly. 110th going great guns knocking off destroyers, transports and anything else they can find. Knocked off three Zekes which they contacted over Cebu today. 17th lost one plane and crew to A/A yesterday, Stoegbauer, Thompson and Coey and three gunners. Three planes hit convoy consisting of three destroyers and two transports heading toward Ormoc. They destroyed one of the transports of about 7000 tons. My activity is limited to jeeps and L-5s to Air Force. Air here is ours in daytime but the Nips really come over at night. Two nights ago they dropped one bomb within fifteen feet of Lieutenant Zock's tent and three in 110th area. The same night they landed paratroops between us and the beach.[19]

On Morotai, the 82nd Squadron had received its new F-6s. These were reconnaissance versions of the P-51 Mustang—faster planes than the squadron had ever flown, and the first brand-new planes that the squadron had ever flown. The pilots were as happy as kids with sport cars, someone remembered.[20]

That was the good news, from the daytime. Sergeant Ursprung's journal became a stoic tally of night-time danger: three air raids one night, after another night two raids in early morning, three air raids between 2:30 and 5:30 a.m., two air raids between 2:30 and 4:30, two air raids, two air raids, no alerts, one air raid, two alerts, one raid. Also, he added, "Lieutenant Franklin bailed out of Staff Sergeant Sutton's P-51 when engine quit while changing tanks. He forgot to turn on booster pump."[21]

ℑ

On December 6, before dawn, two hundred Japanese infantrymen slipped silently out of a swamp beside the airfield at Buri. They had a Filipino guide and they had reconnoitered well. Across the muddy airfield, a few Air Corps service units were bivouacked. At the top of the bluff above them, half a mile away, were the tents and plywood buildings of Fifth Air Force Bomber Command.

It was still dark, and the airmen at Buri had sentries out. At sunrise, when the sentries left their posts, the Japanese attacked. They overran a signal company—silently, with their bayonets, spearing radio operators and telephone linemen. The signalers fell back to the road embankment, were hit with a burst of machine-gun fire, and fell back again. The Japanese pressed on and struck a black airfield construction battalion. It is said that a cook left the breakfast chow line, picked up his rifle, and killed five Japanese. Other men joined in. They fired until they ran out of ammunition, then sent a man sprinting to ask Fifth Air Force for more. It was a wild waste of ammo, white officers thought—"promiscuous firing" was the Army term—but the black troops broke the Japanese charge. An ordnance company scrambled out of their blankets, fell back on their workshop, made it a strongpoint, and held the line. Sherman tanks came up, and American airborne troops. By late afternoon the Japanese had been driven back to the far side of the airstrip, and the situation seemed stable.[22]

At this point, about 6:30, when the Americans considered that the day was won, a squadron of Japanese bombers flew overhead, in flawless formation. A minute later, the airmen at Dulag and Burauen heard bombs exploding from San Pablo. Five minutes behind the bombers came a flock of transport planes. They were C-47s, everyone thought, and then someone saw that the planes only looked like C-47s: they were actually Douglas DC-2s—prewar planes, not American planes—Japanese transports. They dropped three hundred Japanese paratroopers.

The Americans on the airstrips were outnumbered and outgunned. They left the airstrips to the Japanese. At San Pablo the paratroopers ran amok.

> They were singing, shouting; three were playing musical instruments—a jew's-harp, a harmonica and a small horn, evidently some kind of identifying and rallying instruments. They shouted, "Hello . . . hello . . . where your machine guns . . ." . . . hacked at gas drums, splashed the gas over several liaison planes. They threw matches in the gasoline. . . . Two men isolated in the tower telephoned a blow by blow description. The Japs simply didn't make sense; they shot off flares promiscuously, shot holes in wash stands, burned a jeep, overturned a truck, burned several L-5s.[23]

It was called the Battle of the Airstrips. It went on for five days, over a strip of pastureland five miles long. It meant flames and smoke and shooting down the road, sleeping in foxholes, watching for snipers. The land between Dulag and Burauen was flat open country for horses and carabaos. Palm trees shaded the fields and grew thickly behind them. There was one road, of rough gravel. The airstrips were long, narrow strips of gray steel matting awash in brown mud. Across them you could see the bulldozers and jeeps and fueling trucks and above them tall palm trees, fronds splayed out like tattered flags. In that open country, you could see the enemy, and you knew that they could see you. From any one of the palm trees, a sniper's bullet might come in.[24]

At Dulag, Rocky was at one end of the fighting. That first evening, two Japanese transports were shot down: one dropped from the sky above camp, clearing the mess hall by a scant fifty feet. Rocky heard the paratroops shouting "Banzai!" at San Pablo. He would have heard the machine-gun fire and the explosions there—would have seen flames and smoke down the road, as the planes there burned. If he had been drawing up plans for base telephone systems, Rocky would have known the signalmen whom the Japanese overran at Buri, the lieutenant and linemen and radiomen found bayoneted in their tents.

Rocky and his section buckled on their pistols. They had heard that a .45 would knock a man down, no matter where you hit him. They also knew that airmen with pistols would not stop infantrymen with rifles or paratroopers with submachine guns. And it was dark already, and the Japanese had bayonets and grenades, weapons to use in the darkness, and they had none. The members of the 71st Group moved away from their tarmac, out of their tents. They settled in where the palm trees were thick and started digging foxholes, waiting for their own paratroopers to come up.

That first night, the sentries shot at what they could only half-see in the darkness. At dawn it was found they had gunned down two white horses. Next day, Rocky was sent to the nearest hamlet. They would have sentries out again, he told people there, more tonight than last night, and if the sentries saw or heard anything they would shoot it. A man spoke up. He and his wife had a baby, he said. If the baby cried at night and they went to get it, would the sentries shoot? The sentries will shoot at anything they see or hear, Rocky told him, feeling like a heel.

More men from the 11th Airborne arrived, and that night the sentries didn't shoot anyone. The Fifth Photo Squadron shot one paratrooper, and a patrol from 20th Mapping got another. A sniper was shot out of a palm tree by the road. They put up spotter planes and the pilots came back to talk about the A/A fire they had taken. Some P-40s flew in from Tacloban to strafe and bomb, and they watched as one P-40 shot down a Val dive-bomber.

On the ground, both sides were cautious. They had deep mud to slog through already, and the rain never stopped. The airstrip at Buri was a no-man's-land. The Americans attacked across the steel matting in daylight; they met heavy fire and fell back to their own line of foxholes. The next night, the Americans sent out rifle companies looking for the Japanese. The Japanese slipped past them, silently slipped around the tarmac, and fell upon the American perimeter; the headquarters clerks and mortar section drove them off.

After dark on December 10—Sunday evening, five long days after the Japanese had first attacked—a sudden burst of American .50-caliber bullets tore through a plywood wall in Fifth Air Force Bomber Command. It was the commanding general's house, and Ennis Whitehead hit the floor. He ordered a staff officer to make sure the carelessness stopped. The staff officer traced the firing and got a signal battalion lieutenant colonel on the phone.

"Colonel," he said sternly, "you've got to stop that promiscuous firing down there immediately."

"Like to, sir," answered the colonel, "but the Japs . . ."

"Japs," shouted the staff officer, "Can't be Japs. That fire is coming from our fifties."

"That's right . . . and the Japs are doing the shooting."

"Where in hell did the Japs get our machine guns?"

"How in hell should I know, sir? . . . Incidentally, that yelling you hear is a banzai raid on our mess hall."[25]

It had been a year since the promotion party at Moresby—a year since the promiscuous firing at Fifth Bomber Command.

The banzai attack was turned aside. The signal battalion rallied and recaptured its machine guns. The Japanese, that night, melted away along trails in the mountains. Ennis Whitehead worked out the next stage of the campaign, a move that would let the Fifth Air Force build airfields that did not flood. The best place to build those airfields was elsewhere in the Philippine archipelago, south of Manila Bay, the island of Mindoro.

🌀

Rocky came home from the war with three or four medals. He kept them in a round tin box in a drawer in his bureau. (This was the same drawer where he kept the field glasses he bought at a St. Louis pawnshop on a weekend pass from Scott Field—maybe the same trip when the friend with whom he went on pass showed him how to sleep under a newspaper.) I do not know what medals they were or where they are now. But there was another decoration Rocky had, a long sky-blue rectangle framing a silver musket, the Combat Infantryman's Badge. The Combat Infantryman's Badge is earned by soldiers who have engaged with the enemy— been under fire in a combat zone. James Jones said it was the only medal that meant something.

My father never wore that decoration—then again, he never wore any of his medals. But if he earned the Combat Infantryman's Badge, he earned it at Dulag.[26]

18

FIASCO NIGHT
Mindoro

In the middle of the fighting, in the middle of the rain and mud, transfers went forward. Rocky left Wing HQ. He transferred to the 110th Squadron as communications officer.

From Leyte, Douglas MacArthur looked toward Manila. His forces would shift westward now, leapfrogging across the Sibuyan Sea. The next objective was the island of Mindoro, south of Manila. Leyte was facing winter rains and Philippine Sea typhoons; Mindoro was starting its dry season. Tacloban was far from Manila, 350 miles; from San Jose at the tip of Mindoro, it would be only 150 miles. Planes based there could deal with the Japanese planes at Clark Field and give air cover when Krueger's troops went ashore.

The battle for Mindoro would be fierce, as bitter for airmen as Biak had been for the infantry. "Mindoro was a tough little operation from start to finish," Samuel Eliot Morison wrote.[1] The island would be fought for in the air and on the water—by kamikazes who aimed for American ships and by American planes striking at Japanese cruisers.

On December 13, the Japanese drew blood. In mid-afternoon, as the invasion fleet rounded the island of Los Negros, a kamikaze smashed into the cruiser *Nashville*, killing more than 130 men. One was Colonel Murtha, the Wing CO who had talked about how the war was being fought for airfields. On December 15, when the troops went ashore on Mindoro, they met no resistance from Japanese infantry—but the landing ships were targeted by a squadron of kamikazes. Two ships burned and sank that day, the first of dozens.

On Mindoro, the engineers surveyed a new airstrip, Hill Field. The American 1874th Engineer Aviation Battalion worked alongside the Third Airfield Construction Squadron (ACS), RAAF, a hardbitten outfit led by a rogue civil engineer. The Third ACS had acquired so much equipment, inside and outside official channels, that they had been nicknamed "Ali Baba and His Forty Thieves," a sobriquet that pleased them. They also boasted that they had come ashore, dropped their personal gear on the far side of the beach, and begun unloading their equipment within five minutes. Nothing fazed them for long: not the two kamikazes that attacked the ships as they landed, not the kamikaze who next day dived for the open doors of their landing craft. They worked amid a steady howl of sirens—in the first three weeks, there were four hundred Japanese air raids. The engineers were allowed three hours off each day, three night-time hours, which was when the worst air raids came. They worked steadily the other twenty-one hours, taking cover only when bombs actually began to fall.

Hill Field was completed, on schedule, in five days. Japanese pressure had not slackened. When the first P-38s approached for landing, they had to shoot their way in—drive off a swarm of Zeros that were attacking cargo planes on the airstrip. An Australian officer wrote:

> At least 50 fighters involved at once and at least five fights going on simultaneously, Lightnings, Thunderbolts and latest model Zeros. Had a bad scare watching belly tanks falling into camp thinking they were bombs. Watched at least 14 aircraft shot down, and two Lightnings force-landed

on strip. One made a perfect belly landing but caught on fire and the second coming in the opposite end with port engine ablaze had to be waved onto taxiway. He lost speed in [the] swerve and bounced once over one C-47 and then bounced over another C-47. . . . Aircraft destroyed one Zero [which] suicide dived into strip but missed a C-47. . . . Final scores over strip, 12 enemy shot down and six of ours.[2]

When the resupply convoy arrived, kamikazes sank two more landing ships. One was loaded with aviation gasoline and burned for hours. A plume of oily smoke rose, from which a rain of oil fell on the beachhead. Above the convoy, and above Mindoro, the P-38s shot down fifteen Japanese planes. Navy gunners shot down four more Japanese planes that had circled the convoy repeatedly, patiently waiting for an opportunity, until someone realized that the planes were not P-47s.

Reports came in that the Japanese were planning to shift infantrymen to Mindoro, by sea or by air. There were suspicious fires in the mountains above San Jose—beacons for enemy paratroopers, men grimly reasoned. One night the telephone link was cut between the Australian sentries and the American troops on their flank. When another alert sounded, it brought more confusion, more alarm, and a "sincere admonition from Squadron Leader Bouch urging his men to use their bayonets and cut the throat of the bastard."[3]

On Mindoro, Air Corps strength built up. The Eighth Fighter Group with its P-38s was joined by the 58th Fighter Group, which flew P-47s. Two days before Christmas, the first bomber unit arrived: the 17th Squadron, moving up from Biak to Mindoro's newest airstrip, Ellmore Field. On Christmas Day, the 110th Squadron flew in its P-40s from Tacloban, parking them among the revetments at Hill Field.

*In December 1944, the 17th Squadron moved up from Leyte
to Mindoro, south of Manila. Fred Hill photographed B-25
"Charmin' Lady" on the new airstrip at Ellmore Field.*
Courtesy of Eastern Oregon University, Pierce Library,
Fred Hill World War II Photograph Collection. Taken
and donated by Fred Hill.

At the 110th Squadron, there was a new CO, Rubel Archuleta,
a teacher-turned-warrior from northern New Mexico. There was
also a new spirit in the squadron; they had painted a new insignia on their P-40s, a musketeer flexing his rapier. Mindoro would
require all the esprit that they could muster. On Christmas night,
hours after the 110th Squadron arrived on Mindoro, the Japanese
raided in force.

> Great enemy activity after dusk. One shot down imme-
> diately above strip from 200 feet after dropping bombs.
> Twin engine bomber dropped heavy stick immediately
> after. Stream of single engine enemy aircraft operating.
> Amid great cheering red alert given five minutes after action
> joined. Fire blazing merrily on strip is our first and only
> avgas storage tank completed this afternoon and hit by air-
> craft shot down. More aircraft burning on strip as strafing
> continues. Loud cheering from adjacent ack-ack crew who

have got a direct hit at range of two miles. Very nice work. Continue all night. Unfortunately one Black Widow crashed and burnt taking off.[4]

The next day, December 26, the rest of the squadron, the ground echelon, flew into Hill Field. On one of the C-47s was the new communications officer.[5]

Trucks and jeeps were waiting at Hill Field. The ground personnel, five officers and thirty-odd enlisted men, unloaded their gear and drove to the new squadron campsite, on a hilltop two miles east of the runway. They assigned Rocky an empty spot in a six-man officers' tent.

Four other lieutenants from the 110th Squadron, all pilots, had set up their cots already. At twenty-five, Rocky was the old man in the group. Gerald Grandmaison was another Midwesterner, with a baby back home in Michigan. The rest were Southerners. Bill Hilton was from Bristol, Tennessee, only twenty years old. Wilkins Hunt was from Texas, from the coast north of Corpus Christi, where his family ran a duck-hunting lodge for oilmen. Van Kennon was from Texas, too, from Belmena in Milam County, a gravel-road place with a school and a country store. Like Rocky, he had trained at Scott Field—he had been a radioman, but now he flew P-40s.

Rocky might have talked with his tent-mates about farms and radios, if they had time. It is not likely that they did. Before he had settled in, possibly before he had even unpacked, Rocky was in the middle of a sudden, savage battle. George Kenney would call that night's fighting the wildest scramble of the air war. Colonel Sams, not disagreeing, would call it something else. "Fiasco night," the colonel observed. "Bad night and poor orders."[6]

On December 26, at 1700 hours, eight B-25s from the 17th Squadron flew out on a mission, from Ellmore Field.[7] They headed west, where a convoy had been reported, four Japanese freighters and two destroyers. "Rogers," they were still calling their Mitchell bombers. Higher-ups were mindful of what this bravado had cost the squadron in the past. They had specifically ordered the Fighting Seventeenth not to attack destroyers.

At 1740 hours that afternoon, just at sunset, the 17th Squadron spotted the ships. At once they saw that what they faced was not a convoy of freighters: it was a squadron of Japanese warships, a heavy cruiser, a light cruiser, and six destroyers, steaming purposefully toward Mindoro at a fast twenty-five knots. Obeying the order not to attack warships—punctiliously, sarcastically?—they radioed back what they had seen and flew home. By 1900 hours they were back on the ground. On the tarmac at Ellmore Field, they saw a Navy PBY patrol bomber. The Navy plane had sighted the Japanese force in mid-afternoon and raced eastward to Mindoro to report it.[8]

Other reports were coming in. The PBY pilot thought that he had seen the Japanese battleship *Yamato*, with its monster 18-inch guns.[9] Allied intelligence thought there was a larger hostile fleet in Philippine waters: fifteen troopships guarded by two battleships, four cruisers, and seven destroyers. That meant Japanese infantrymen or marines who might come ashore, while paratroopers dropped on the San Jose airfields. From the far side of Leyte, the United States Navy did what it could. It put eight flying boats into the air and set a cruiser force steaming toward Mindoro (knowing, as did the American soldiers and airmen, that the ships could not arrive until the next afternoon). In the meantime, riding off Ilin Island south of San Jose, the Navy had a squadron of PT boats. The naval commander sent four to intercept the Japanese.[10]

The Japanese squadron came from Cam Ranh Bay, a name that Americans would know better in a later war. It had steamed across the South China Sea by night and under a storm front, eluding American submarines. Leading the squadron was Masatome Kimura, an admiral familiar with fast sorties and night dashes. (The year before, in the Aleutians, he had dared to run his destroyers to Kiska and brought home safely the Japanese garrison.) Kimura commanded the heavy cruiser *Ashigara*, with ten 8-inch guns, the light cruiser *Oyodo*, with six 6-inch guns, and three destroyers and three destroyer escorts, all mounting 5-inch guns: the *Kasumi*, *Kiyoshimo*, *Asahimo*, *Kaya*, *Sugi*, and *Kashi*.[11]

Kimura's squadron showed how heavily the Imperial Japanese Navy had suffered. Two years before, at Guadalcanal, the Japanese had bombarded Henderson Field with battleships. But Kimura's fleet had the speed of a raiding party, its salvos could wreck any airfield, the *Ashigara* could handle any American vessel smaller than a battleship—and there were no American warships nearby. If the Americans threw planes at them, the fleet was better armed than the destroyers at Cape Waios. The *Oyodo* mounted fifty-two 25-mm antiaircraft guns, the *Kasumi* and *Kiyoshimo* had twenty-eight 25-mms, and the other small ships mounted twenty apiece.[12] Moreover, the Japanese ships could count on support from their own warplanes. The admiral who had authorized the raid was Vice Admiral Gunichi Mikawa, who at Savo Island had sunk four Allied cruisers. Mikawa was not one to put ships in harm's way without sending naval aircraft to support them.

In the revetments of Mindoro, there were more than a hundred American warplanes. Commanders began to get the aircraft fueled and armed.

> The 310th Wing worked to put every available plane in the air, both fighters and B-25s. Those aircraft which could not carry a bomb load were instructed to create diversions and to strafe the enemy vessels. Participating in the attack were 44 P-38s of the Eighth Fighter Group, 28 P-47s of the 58th Fighter Group, 20 P-40s of the 110th Tactical Reconnaissance Squadron, and 13 B-25s of the 17th Reconnaissance Squadron. A number of P-61s of the 418th Night Fighter Squadron covered the attack.[13]

The squadrons could mount a large air strike, but this was not a force to send out at sunset against an enemy fleet. Only the handful of P-61 Black Widow night fighter crews were trained to fly after dark, and only the thirteen B-25s were likely to do a warship any damage.

Theoretically, the fighter planes on Mindoro were all fighter-bombers, able to carry bombs. That meant little; Mindoro was short on bombs. There were more iron bomb casings than there was tritanol or Explosive D to fill them. On the airfields of Mindoro, it would be hazardous for fighter planes to try nighttime takeoffs when they were carrying high explosives. Hill Field was made of packed clay; Ellmore Field was made of packed gravel, but was still notably soft.[14] The Eighth Fighter Group considered bombing, reconsidered quickly, and sent its three squadrons of P-38s racing north, ready to blast the warships with their 20-mm cannon and .50-caliber machine-guns.[15] But in the 110th Squadron, more than the other fighter units, the pilots had experience; they had dropped plenty of bombs during their strafing runs. For them, it would be worthwhile to give their planes bomb loads: if the ordnance men could find the bombs, if they could find enough fuses, if they could find men to arm the warplanes in the tropical darkness.

The officer in charge of building the airfields on Mindoro—as at Nadzab, Hollandia, and Tacloban—was David Hutchison. He called the 110th Squadron for a briefing. Hutchison spoke tersely:

> The P-40s of the 110th are the only remaining planes on the island and the pilots of these airplanes have not participated in any night flying. You know the capabilities of your pilots and of your planes. I would like the P-40s bombed to attack the task force tonight, or dispersed and take off at first light. Your targets will be the destroyers, either dive-bombing or skip-bombing. If you decide to take off tonight,

I don't want to lose any pilots. Land either at Hill Strip or go to Leyte. If a safe landing doesn't seem possible, bail out and I will see that your planes are replaced. Take your decision and inform me what you are going to do.

Captain Archuleta, Commanding Officer of the Squadron, inquired how critical the situation was and the General informed him, "Either we strike them or they will strike us." It was decided to take off as soon as the planes were bombed up and ready.[16]

They called the camp area. The ground echelon came down to load the P-40s with bombs and .50-caliber rounds. It was after dark, no one was using lights, and the road was new to them, but they made it. Smith "Smitty" T. Charland, the engineering officer, remembered the trip in a 71st Group veterans' newsletter: "I recall riding in a jeep with 'Rocky' Boyer. How he managed to drive totally without lights, over a road we had been over only once before, I'll never know! He, many years later, credited it to an Indiana farm boy upbringing, but who knows?"[17]

Rocky knew radios and his friend Smitty knew engines and aircraft. The only ordnance officer was Glenn Jensen, the one who had called Rocky "a goddam fool." They had 20 planes to arm and 27 500-pound bombs to arm them with, and Jensen had scrounged together enough fuses (16 4–5 second fuses and 11 1/10 second fuses).[18] The fuses were mismatched and not really right for bombing warships, but they would have to serve.

They found the bomb trolleys and pulled a 500-pounder out to each P-40. They hoisted the bombs up under each plane and pushed them into place, until the bomb shackles could hold. An ordnance sergeant felt for the hole in each heavy iron casing and threaded in a fuse and armed the bomb. Out on the wings, men snapped open the long ammo box compartments, reached down to each machine-gun receiver and fed in the first cartridge, then carefully folded and laid in place the long heavy belts of ammunition. For each machine gun (and there were three .50-calibers in each wing), the belt of ammunition weighed more than a hundred pounds.

They had a little light to work by: a fighter plane was burning, and there was a fire down by the 58th Group's bomb dump. There were the runway lights—not much help, but more light they could not risk. The risk was not yet from the ships; it was from Japanese aircraft. Smitty Charland continued: "When we arrived at the airstrip we were under almost constant enemy aircraft bombardment and strafing attacks. Somehow, though, we managed to load a 500-pound bomb under each P-40 along with a load of .50-caliber ammo. As I recall, all of us assisted our armament and ordnance crews in the process. This ordinarily was performed as a routine task conducted in daylight, but became difficult when performed in a total blackout under enemy fire. We did, however, get the job done and our planes were cleared for take-off."[19]

The first plane from the 110th Squadron took off at 2045 hours. One warplane launched, nineteen left. Five minutes later, they began to see ripples of light offshore to the north, the flashes of the Japanese ships' antiaircraft guns.[20]

♋

At Ellmore Field, where the 17th Squadron was arming, Major Wise had gotten his attack flight back into the air. The B-25s were already armed, and they did not wait to refuel. Seven bombers were off the airstrip by 1945 hours, more or less in a group; five others followed by 2030 hours, one plane at a time, every few minutes. "Since there was no longer any daylight, formation attacks were impractical, and the planes were ordered to pick their own targets and attack them singly," the squadron would report. Wise was the first pilot to take off. He was hot to get back to the Japanese fleet, and he snubbed the Navy PBY pilot's request to fly alongside his planes—only if you're ready to go now, he told him, "*now*." Moonrise came at 2030 hours, about the time that the last bomber left the ground.[21]

The P-38s of the Eighth Fighter Group had taken off earliest (starting at 1830 hours) and flown north by squadrons. The planes of the 35th and 36th Fighter Squadrons had been attacking the Japanese ships for an hour already—dozens of large fighters swooping down to strafe in a darkness lit only by antiaircraft fire. They had fired 8,860 rounds of .50-caliber bullets and 1,446 rounds from their 20-mm cannon.[22] The P-47s of the 58th Fighter Group had taken longer to get into the air, starting around 2015 hours. At 2100 hours they saw the phosphorescent wakes of the Japanese warships, followed the ships south until they caught up with them, and then dived to the attack from ten thousand feet. The result was a melee. The *Ashigara* and *Oyodo* steamed straight ahead, while the destroyers began turning violently. To confuse the Japanese gunners, the P-38s attacked from all heights and directions. The P-47s had been ordered to make their strafing runs from west to east, to minimize the chance of collisions, but the destroyers' evasive action played havoc with these plans.[23]

Now the fighters began to break off and head for Tacloban, and it was the bombers' turn. A bomb dropped out of nowhere, off the starboard side of the *Asahimo*. At 2100 hours, the *Oyodo* was hit (probably by the Navy PBY, flying high overhead). Fifteen minutes later, the *Kiyoshimo* was hit. Far down the coast, the airmen on the runway saw a flash of light and a steady glow.[24]

The bombers and the warships saw each other only in flashes. Some B-25s found the Japanese ships only by the muzzle flames of their antiaircraft guns. One pilot wrote that he knew he was over the Japanese ships when he saw a sheet of flame. Another likened the sight to a blast furnace. A PT boat skipper saw a B-25 buzz a Liberty ship. The Navy PBY pilot, flying at nine thousand feet, thought he saw a B-25 crash-dive into a warship (which did not happen). The Japanese, for their part, claimed that they had shot down the PBY and reported that other American warplanes had crashed into the *Ashigara* and the *Kaya*. One of these Yankee kamikazes may have been a reckless P-38 pilot who flew a strafing run so low that his wingtip scraped a destroyer's masthead. (He was also lucky; the PT boats fished him out of the water, alive, the next day.) The other may have been Lieutenant Brown in his B-25, skip-bombing what he thought were Japanese transports—or perhaps Lieutenant Hatcher, who was not so lucky.[25]

Against the night sky, the rippling flares of antiaircraft guns, flaming tracers, and the flames of exploding bombs made some men think of fireworks. Low over the water, Japanese searchlights began swinging across the waves, probing for PT boats, and overhead was a swarm of pinpoint aircraft running lights. The paratroopers in their foxholes thought that the show was spectacular. "Our first indication that there are Japs nearby is a star shell bursting and lighting up the strip. It is followed by high explosive shells, and from that moment on things get bad. . . . We are under orders not to fire at the planes for fear of hitting our own, but

On Mindoro, American engineers worked alongside the Third Airfield Construction Squadron of the Royal Australian Air Force. The Aussies worked twenty-one hours a day, took cover only when enemy bombs actually began to fall, and picked up their rifles and helmets when a Japanese landing threatened. Australian War Museum, Photo No. OG1913

from my position it is quite easy to pick out the Japanese planes from the American. Our planes have red and green lights on the wingtips, while the Japs have an orange and green light on their wingtips."[26]

At Hill Field, Rocky, Smitty, Jensen, and the rest of the 110th Squadron continued to get P-40s armed and into the air. There were still no lights, except for those marking the edge of the strip. There was one wrecked fighter plane at the edge of the airstrip, and worse obstacles facing the pilots: "a soft spot on one side of the strip, and on the runway near the tower, a burning P-47 with exploding ammunition." No one had a good takeoff run, but Lt. Joseph Pritts likely had the worst.

> Lieutenant Pritts with three other planes of his flight had taxied off the end of the strip in order to obtain maximum flying speed to clear the burning and exploding P-47. While waiting for the explosions and fire to die down the tower said the P-47 could not be removed and to take off over it. Pritts led his flight in take-off as a long string of fragmentation bombs walked towards their end of the runway. On take-off he pulled up and over the P-47 so that his fuselage belly was scorched by the flames, at that time his wing man told him to put out his running lights as a Jap plane was firing at him. Pritts switched off his lights and broke to the right. Lacking flying speed he could not chase the Jap, but as he broke to the right, friendly A/A opened up on him mistaking his plane for the strafing Jap.[27]

The bombers from the 17th Squadron were starting to come back now, each B-25 dropping down with a roar and rush of propeller wash—and sometimes a bomber didn't touch down, but dropped a string of bombs and blasted the landing strip with the unfamiliar foreign chattering of Japanese machine guns. "Finally a Jap gets lucky and hits the strip just off center. A B-25 has just touched down as the bomb hits ahead of him, and the aircraft almost looks as if it is kneeling down towards its nose as the pilot applies all the braking he can to pull up before the crater. I am amazed that the nose wheel does not collapse, and stops on the edge of the crater. We rush on to the strip and manage by weight of numbers and adrenalin to push the plane off the runway."[28]

Throughout the evening, from time to time, Rocky and the others would have heard Australian voices out of the darkness, truck drivers hauling bombs to the tarmac and Yank paratroopers to the beach. Half of the Australian engineers had picked up their .303s and Tommy helmets and headed out to the perimeter. The rest stayed at the airfields and did yeoman service.

Major Pat Long, an American who was at Mindoro during this engagement recounted an incident in which an unknown member of the Australian construction squadron distinguished himself by his coolness and devotion to a self-imposed duty during the Japanese naval bombardment. "When the attack commenced," said Long, "an airman walked into the operations room and asked the U.S. officer-in-charge if he could be of any help, adding that he had his bulldozer outside. His offer was readily accepted and the airman, who was hatless, proceeded to fill in the shell holes on the strip and remove crashed aircraft while shells were falling around him."[29]

Thirteen B-25s had headed out. The men at the airstrip watched as twelve came back. No one had seen or heard again from Hatcher's plane. The bombers refueled and sometimes rearmed. They had found the Japanese fleet, most of the pilots reported. The official squadron report acknowledged a problem: "Damage inflicted on the task force could not be assessed too accurately due to darkness." Most of the pilots reported having hit a destroyer. Many reported, with a peculiar consistency, that they had each scored two direct hits. Lieutenant Harold Hilderman, most scrupulous of pilots, admitted that he hadn't found the convoy and salvoed his bombs when he ran low on fuel. Lieutenant Richard Wilson's bomb release hadn't worked. He fueled up his plane and taxied out to try again. As self-effacing as Hilderman, Wilson later reported that he had dropped four bombs and scored "possible near misses."[30]

Major Gilbert, Rocky's compartment-mate on the voyage out, was now operations officer for the 17th Squadron. He watched while the other planes took off and waited for Major Wise to come in. After that, Gilbert took off in his own bomber. He was in the air at 2130 and found the Japanese fleet only thirty miles north, just off Dongon Point—still steaming ahead, now uncomfortably close. As Gilbert circled in, he saw another B-25 attack the ships. The plane flew in low, on a skip-bombing run toward a destroyer. Gilbert's copilot saw two large explosions, and then saw the other B-25 catch fire. Gilbert himself had spotted a cruiser. He bore down on it, ready to skip in his bombs, and then the nose of his own plane exploded in a burst of splintered plexiglass, shredded aluminum, and Japanese flak. Gilbert was hit, his navigator was hit, his turret gunner was hit, the wiring was shot out, and the hydraulics were shot out. The copilot grabbed the controls.[31]

Lieutenant Kluth brought back his B-25, refueled, and rearmed. He was taking off again when he struck a damaged P-40 at the edge of the strip. Kluth's bomber kept going off the end of the strip and cracked up, so badly that the navigator was hurt. They handed the navigator over to the medics. Kluth and his crew rushed into another B-25, found the last of the bombs and nearly the last of the aviation gas, and took off again.[32]

Late in the evening, a bomber came in. It wasn't Hatcher; it was Brown, landing a second time. He had made a second pass at the fleet. This time he saw a cruiser. He banked away from it, but not in time: as the plane banked away, the gunners sprayed them with flak. The electrical system was gone and they could tell that the gas tank was holed. Orders had come in that all B-25s should head for Tacloban. Brown talked the ground crew into fueling up his bomber, and he managed to take off. On the way, the weather front closed in, and they found that the gas tank was leaking more than they had hoped.[33]

At 2310, Lieutenant Vowell brought in his B-25. It had taken them time to find the Japanese ships, Vowell said; he had burned up his fuel. Finally he had found one destroyer, with fires burning aft already, and he had dropped his bombs. And he had more information: the destroyer was just offshore and it was unloading men and equipment into barges.

The airstrip was almost empty. Lt. Bishop Kilgore's bomber was the only other plane on the tarmac. Most of the aviation gas was gone; men said later that fuel tanks had been pushed up on a slant, so that every last drop of fuel could be drained. Kilgore taxied out to the runway, Vowell started fueling—and then the bombardment started.[34]

The star shells exploded first: explosions far overhead, casting down a weird aerial spotlight, lighting up the runway. The sudden glare of a star shell was frightening like a bad dream, scary, embarrassing: you felt naked in the sudden glare, one of the men caught under those shells would recall. After the first blinding blaze of white light, there was something else that was strange and unsettling: while men froze, the landscape seemed to move, as the burning flares above swung on their parachutes. And then after the first star shell, the first high explosive shell hit. The Japanese ships had seen the airstrip and they soon would find the range.[35]

The ground crew blinked in the glare and continued to gas up Vowell's B-25. Another pilot came hurrying in out of the darkness, Van Kennon from the 110th Squadron, one of Rocky's tentmates. He had brought his P-40 back for an emergency landing on Ellmore Strip, and landed hard, so hard that later they wrote off the plane—or perhaps his plane was the one that Kluth hit and completely wrecked. "Lieutenant Vowell's airplane was being serviced with gas when flare shells began bursting over the airstrip. Lieutenant Vowell ordered the ground crew to stop servicing his airplane for he was, quote 'getting out of here in a hurry.' The crew chief states that Lieutenant Vowell did not have adequate fuel to carry him to his destination."[36]

Like Vowell, with the star shells bursting overhead, Kennon wanted to get off the airstrip fast. He climbed into Vowell's B-25. The plane took off at 2335—"into ack-ack being fired over the area by the warships," the squadron reported. Vowell's bomber, "Montana Maid," would not be seen or heard from again.[37]

At Hill Field, at 2310, the last P-40 taxied out to the strip. The base operations officer told them they could go back to their bivouac now. This put no one at ease. The 110th Squadron had loaded all their bombs, sent out all of their warplanes, and still the Japanese ships were steaming south. Their muzzle flashes were two miles off Blue Beach, the closest point to Hill Field, and they had not yet begun to fire their heavy guns. Only a mile away was the beach, flat country that troops could cross quickly from a landing craft. Everyone remembered Dulag, too, the month before, the Japanese paratroops and Japanese infiltrators. On the tarmac at Mindoro that night, Rocky and the other airmen stood on the edge of a world where the Japanese had fleets and squadrons to throw into combat—armies as well, as much as anyone knew. Against that unknown strength, the Allies could put into action a thin line of infantry and a few dozen ground crewmen.

They left Hill Field then, heading for camp. Rocky once more took the wheel of the jeep. As they left the airfield, there was a hopeful sign.

Rocky recalled that they happened upon a general, talking on a radio telephone. "That was the thing that made us feel better," he said. "When we saw that general on the phone, we knew things were going to be all right." (Forty years after Mindoro, as he said that, his face brightened.) The confidence was strong but the feeling was not simple. Rocky meant that the squadron no longer felt forgotten, or alone, or isolated, and that they no longer questioned whether the battle they were fighting was hopeless. The Japanese were an unknown quantity, but the squadron knew generals and knew what generals could do. A general could command resources outside their island. If a general were on the airfield, it meant that the brass thought the situation was safe enough and would improve. If a general were on the radio telephone, help would come. You were glad to see a general on an embattled beachhead, even if this particular general had in the past been a colonel whom you disliked.

> On the way to camp [Smitty Charland wrote on] we came across Headquarters Operations and we stopped to see if anyone could tell us how things were going. We found three kneeling figures looking at a map with a dimmed, shielded flashlight.
>
> As it turned out, one of the figures was General David Hutchison. We told him who we were and that our airplanes had gotten off. He congratulated us and said he hoped that after giving the Japs hell, our planes could make it down to Leyte safely.
>
> He went on to say we should stay encamped where we were, that our position was well located and, even if there would be a naval shelling, we would hardly be affected. As to how successful the operation was going, he said he had no word and that we knew as much he did. We thanked him and left for camp.
>
> With Boyer driving and his radar vision we made it back to camp. Once there we learned that there was a good bit of anxiety over whether to stay at camp or to head "for the hills" in case of a Jap landing.
>
> I told everyone we had been instructed by General Hutchison to stay where we were—our position was relatively safe, and to leave any ground fighting to those trained for it. These words seemed to calm the anxiety and we all went to our tents to wait out the night.[38]

The Japanese began their bombardment. They fired for half an hour or more—mostly high explosives, with an occasional star shell to keep the target illuminated. South of Hill Field, near Mangarin Bay, destroyers fired at PT boats and a Liberty Ship that had been too slow to flee. They missed the PT boats but set the freighter afire.

Off Blue Beach, close to Ellmore Field, the cruisers fired at the airstrip and the town of San Jose. Most of the Japanese shells landed just north of the runway, in the long meandering channel of the Busanga River.[39] The shells that hit the airfield did little damage. Had American planes still been there, it would have been worse: Rocky recalled that the 8-inch shells were wrapped in wire, which would have sliced through aircraft and airmen.

By midnight, the fighting was over. The Japanese fleet had finished the raid and reversed course, heading back for Cam Ranh Bay. The airmen had done better than they knew. The P-38s had killed crewmen at the destroyers' guns and damaged some of the ships' fire control systems. The bombers of the 17th Squadron had hit the *Oyodo*. They had hit the *Kiyoshimo* harder; that damage the airmen had seen in the distant explosion and continuing glow of fire. The strike had slowed the *Kiyoshimo* and inflicted the first of the ship's fatal wounds. For the airmen, what was left was waiting, which was difficult enough. Waiting for paratroopers; waiting for landing craft laden with Japanese marines. Waiting for Zeros on strafing runs, for phosphorous bombs, for kamikazes, for whatever else the Japanese might have.

An hour after midnight, while an endless, weary series of American fighters and bombers were crowding into the taxiways of Tacloban, the end of the naval action came. PT-223 closed with a group of four Japanese warships and at 0105 fired two torpedoes. One torpedo slammed into the *Kiyoshimo* and sent up a tower of flame. The *Asahimo* drew alongside and took off her survivors.[40]

Over Mindoro, the weather had been clear. To the southeast, a weather front had moved in. It began at the island of Cebu and covered Leyte, northward over the mountains, screening Tacloban. As the American warplanes headed east from Mindoro, they struck this front halfway to Leyte. The front rose to 15,000 feet and inside it visibility was zero. The pilots' hope was to fly east by compass until they could get radio bearings from Tacloban.

Rocky's tent-mate Gerald Grandmaison took off at 2045, early in the line of P-40s heading off the airstrip. He was never seen or heard from again.[41]

Another of Rocky's tent-mates, kid pilot Bill Hilton, made a strike at the Japanese ships. Then he headed for Tacloban with another second lieutenant, Warren Twiggs. They flew eastward, lost their way, and circled until they ran out of gas. Twiggs bailed out over Leyte Gulf. Hilton probably did so too, but only Twiggs was found by the search planes.[42]

In the same overcast, also heading eastward, was another of Rocky's tent-mates, Wilkins Hunt. Hunt was flying Morris Washatka's wing. This was odd, for Hunt was a first lieutenant and Washatka was a lowly flight officer, but Hunt's compass was out, and Washatka had two Japanese flags painted beside his cockpit, and Hunt had none.

Washatka took a bearing of 106 degrees and led them toward Tacloban. Three hours after takeoff, they were over Leyte. They had cut back their manifold pressure and slowed their propellers as much as they dared. Washatka had gotten radio bearings from Tacloban; he doubted Hunt had done so. "Lieutenant Hunt apparently did not know where we were," Washatka wrote, "for he asked me, and I told him we were over San Isidro Bay." At that point, they hit the weather front. Washatka had no fuel to spare and bored straight ahead, into the overcast. Very carefully, he slowly climbed, and saw airfield lights through a break in the clouds. Washatka had seen Hunt follow. He never saw Hunt again, and Hunt never answered his radio calls.[43]

ⓢ

That next morning, at Mindoro, in his six-man tent, Rocky was the only man still living. "You knew somebody was going to get killed, and you hoped that it wouldn't be you." I only heard my father say that once. I do not know how often he learned it, but this must have been one of the times.

At Hill Field, the next morning, it was strangely quiet. You would see empty airfields when the outfit was flying a mission, but this was different. The only airplanes were the B-25 that Kluth had abandoned, with its beaten-in nose, and Kennon's wrecked P-40. The P-47 by the control tower had burned to cinders and an engine. There was no gas left. There were no bombs. Clods of dirt and clay dust were everywhere, thrown up when the Japanese cratered the runway. They were finding dud bombs between the tents. Smashed into the wall of a building was a hole shaped like a P-47, as if in a comic strip. The fire by the bomb dump had burned out, too, but you could still smell smoke. Just offshore, a Liberty Ship was beached and still on fire. The smoke was hanging over the water.

At headquarters, they were counting the losses. The total would be nearly thirty planes out of action—most missing, some crashed, some damaged beyond repair. The Eighth Fighter Group had lost seven P-38s and the 58th Fighter Group had lost ten P-47s. Six P-40s had not made it to Tacloban, and the 17th Squadron counted four bombers missing.[44] That was about as many planes as the Fifth Air Force had lost on Black Sunday.

Hatcher's plane, they figured, must have been the bomber that went down on fire. Vowell's plane hadn't been seen again, hadn't been heard from, and hadn't had the fuel to make Tacloban. Kluth had made it to Tacloban. When he was taxiing there, he had banged into two parked P-47s. Captain Sill had ditched off Samar, and his crew were okay. Lieutenant Brown had ditched off Pacijan; some of his crew had drowned. Major Gilbert had made Tacloban—his copilot had flown the plane in. The turret gunner had been wounded himself, but he had given the wounded officers morphine and personally cranked down the landing gear. Probably Gilbert would not lose his leg.[45]

The sirens had shrieked that day already; the Japanese had sent more planes to strafe and bomb. But there was something else that you could hear that morning, of all the sounds in this world the most welcome, next to the voices of your family or sweetheart: the roar of American warplanes. Huge, heavy, loud P-47s were landing, planes bearing the colors of the 58th Fighter Group.[46]

A great general once remarked that a defeat is the only thing sadder than a victory. On that morning, on the patched-up, wreckage-littered runways of Mindoro, they may have considered that they had won a victory.

19

HOME

A year after that, they were home.

On Mindoro, there was more fighting. Some of this Rocky talked about: the night that the Japanese caught the P-38s on the ground, and the day when the kamikaze hit the ammunition ship, and the day when another kamikaze hit another ammunition ship. Never again, however, was there doubt that the Allies would hold the island. More airfields were built on Mindoro, more squadrons of warplanes landed, more fresh regiments shuttled through. Mindoro was a crossroads of war, General Eichelberger wrote. "The airstrips there, like stoves in an all-night diner, never got cold, and the smell of the burn of landing tires hung over the place always."[1]

It was on Mindoro that Rocky was paid the only accolade he ever mentioned. There was an afternoon when he and his section were out on the airfield. He was shirtless in the January dry-season heat and sitting on an airplane wing; so were they all. A jeep drove up, with a major whom they didn't know, who looked them over and asked who the officer in charge was. "He isn't here, sir," said one of the sergeants quickly, before Rocky could say anything. "You know those officers who are never around? He's one of them." A couple of other men chorused, "No, he's never around, no sir." The major glowered and told his driver to head on.

*At the end of the war, on Ie Shima, a small island
off Okinawa, the "Flying Musketeers" of the 110th
Tactical Reconnaissance Squadron, where Rocky was
communications officer, set up a signboard scorecard.*
Collection of the author

That was the highest compliment he had ever been paid, when his men kept him from getting into trouble, my father said. Of course, they were feeling grateful to him that afternoon. Earlier that week, he had stolen a jeep for the outfit.

A few weeks later, the squadron moved to Luzon. Rocky had faced Japanese infantry at Dulag and Japanese shellfire on Mindoro, but it was during this advance that he carried out the only martial exploit to which, not without irony, he ever laid claim. The ground echelon of the 110th Squadron was moving south in trucks. They came to a river, and the convoy stopped. Ahead, someone had blown up the highway bridge. Not far away, there was a railroad trestle.[2] Rocky called for a formal halt. He drove the truck to the rail line and noted that the wheels would just straddle the rails. He walked across the trestle, studying the ends of the railroad ties, looking between the ties to the river (a thirty-foot drop to the water, he thought). He walked back across the trestle, studying again each railroad tie, kicking some of them. He thought they would hold the weight of the truck. Then he picked two sergeants, and found warning flags for them. He sent the sergeants out on the trestle, one to watch each front wheel. Then he edged the truck out onto the trestle. He felt the front wheels settle down between the first and second railroad ties, with the steel rail snug against the inside of his tires and empty air on the outside of each wheel.

A year before, when they were loading the planes to move to Nadzab, Rocky's section had trouble loading the jeeps: *I didn't prove to be a damn good driver*, Rocky had written. That day on Luzon, he was a damn good driver. He eased the truck across the trestle, utterly slowly, utterly carefully, one railroad tie at a time. The sergeants were to signal if the wheels strayed from their straight and narrow path, or if a railroad tie started to shift, but that didn't happen. After Rocky had crossed, the other trucks followed.

The fighting on Luzon never slackened. The 71st Group strafed Japanese infantry columns, or trucks, or railroads. Some of what they did would be remembered.

In January, Captain Shomo of the 82nd Squadron, with Lippy Lipscomb flying his wing, broke off their reconnaissance mission when they spotted a Japanese bomber protected by a dozen enemy fighters. Shomo and Lipscomb turned to attack; they were flying their new F-6 Mustangs, warplanes not seen before in the Philippines, and the Japanese may have been slow to recognize them as hostile. In scant minutes, Shomo shot down seven Japanese planes and earned the Congressional Medal of Honor.[3]

The 110th Squadron gave air cover to the American raiders and Filipino guerrillas who freed the American prisoners at Cabanatuan. On other days, pilots still died—when flak hit them or they didn't pull up out of strafing runs (because they misjudged their speed, perhaps, or because their own gunfire shook loose their controls). Engines still failed and planes still collided in the dust of airstrips.[4]

In the communications section, Rocky had Pfc. Spragg for a clerk again, and a new teletype mechanic. They had a Group newspaper now, the *Group Snoop*, cranked out each day on a mimeograph. There was a jazz band. Lieutenant Zock organized new softball and volleyball teams.

In February 1945, when the 37th Division liberated Valenzuela City, its infantrymen had slaked their thirst by dipping their steel helmets into the vats of beer at the Balintawak brewery. Procuring liquor was no longer so simple and innocent: it now required a man beyond corruption. Not only had Rocky proven himself as a jeep thief and daredevil—he remained the only officer who didn't drink. He thus became the officer whom the squadron sent out to buy beer. When Rocky brought the beer home to the airfield, ground crewmen poured it into a clean drop tank and clipped the drop tank to an F-6 Mustang. A trusted pilot, chosen for his record in making smooth landings, flew the plane into the lower stratosphere and circled half an hour, until the beer was chilled.

꿈

Rocky kept writing letters in the evenings. He had airmail paper and a fountain pen, and he swatted mosquitoes on every thin, rustling onionskin page.

Back in Indiana, Margaret Anne had graduated from Franklin. In the spring of 1945, she was doing her student teaching. Rocky wrote to her often. His letters arrived early enough for her to read them over breakfast; dead mosquitoes fell out of the envelope onto the breakfast table. Once he wrote about a reprimand from his CO; he had given leftover food to a Filipino girl, about five years old, who was standing by the mess-hall garbage cans. She wore a hemp dress, he wrote, "which compares with a good grade of burlap." He had a clean pillowcase to give to the girl, tomorrow, if she came back and the guards did not chase her away. "Pygmalion," he wrote, to comment. Then he wrote something about himself:

Today, many letters (do not know the exact number and I will not walk across the tent to my foot locker to count them for there is approximately two inches of water on the floor. Because the floor is sandy clay, in a few minutes the water will be absorbed and will drain into the rice paddy which is located twenty feet from our tent) arrived from you. Darling, those six weeks of going without mail was forgotten when I saw your first V-Mail placed into my box even though it proved to be a spelling lesson. Darling, I miss you very very much. I miss all of you. I miss loving you in person. I love you.

Rocky wrote again at the end of April 1945. APO 70 was now the place to reach him, the sprawling base at Lingayen: the 110th Squadron and the rest of the Group were camped at the east-side airfield of Binmaley. The first line of his return address now read "Capt. Boyer."

Twenty months have passed and undoubtedly many more will follow before I am with you again. A short time ago there were a few indications that a leave in the States would be possible but that dream has vanished. Perhaps someday I'll be able to remain silent until events actually occur.

Charland, as usual, is visiting me. For the last half hour he has been playing records. We have just completed an argument concerning Christ's last supper. Charland is my only current acquaintance who has a conversational knowledge of the Bible. Last evening we discussed the prostitutes mentioned in the Book.

On May 8, 1945, the airmen at Binmaley heard that the war in Europe had ended. As it happened, George Kenney was also at Lingayen that day, visiting, "up at Photo Hutchison's headquarters."[5]

The Fifth Air Force was making its next jump from island to island. The next objective was Okinawa. Twenty-two airstrips were to be built there, siege-works for the assault on Japan. That assault was scheduled for November, twenty-five weeks away.[6]

> To build so many airfields in so short a time required the largest aviation engineering project ever attempted. There were to be some twenty-five miles of paved airstrips, while the hardstands, taxiways, and service aprons would require a paved area equal to 400 miles of a two-lane high-way. Some five million and a half truckloads of coral and earth would have to be moved.[7]

Ennis Whitehead had a new right-hand man who was equal to this task. In the middle of June, Brig. Gen. David Hutchison set up an Okinawa headquarters for the 308th Bombardment Wing. He had a new title now: commanding general, ADVON, Far East Air Force.[8]

In July the 110th Squadron moved to Okinawa—to Ie Shima, a small volcanic island just off the main island. They were flying missions northward to Kyushu, strafing roads and railyards, when the war ended in August. Rocky kept photos of the white-painted bombers in which the Japanese arrived to arrange the formal surrender.

ⓢ

Rocky reached San Francisco in November and got on an east-bound train. It was an old steam engine; the coaches were full of smoke and cinders, but nobody cared—they were glad to be home. Three days later he got off the train in Tipton, twelve miles from the farm. A farmer gave him a lift along the county road that ran into Pickard, and he carried his duffle bag down the last quarter-mile of gravel road. He had not called or telegraphed his plans, but his family knew to expect him; they had seen his name on a newspaper list of officers landed in San Francisco. When he walked in the front door, his mother was talking on the telephone. "I have to go," she said, hanging up. "Roscoe's home." Anndora

At a bivouac in the Southwest Pacific, sometime in 1944,
First Lieutenant Boyer studies the human condition,
allows himself half a smile, and chews on his pencil.
Collection of the author

was out. She came home later and knew her big brother was back when she saw his hat on the corner of the bureau.

So Rocky Boyer's war ended there—part of it. More of it ended in January, two months later, in New Albany High School downstate, where Margaret Anne was teaching English. She had told him about a job teaching math and Rocky applied without telling her, and when the school superintendent asked Margaret Anne what she thought of her fellow Franklin College graduate, she said that she had been wearing his fraternity pin for three years now. With that recommendation he got the job and a year later he married the girl. And more of the war ended when Rocky sorted out his things. His officer's hat had gone to the attic. In the spring, when he was airing out his uniform, he picked up the hat, turned it upside down, and tapped it against his hand. A legion of dead mites and insects went skittering across the flat-top lining—bugs from the tropics, killed by the clean, cold Indiana winter. He studied the detritus for a moment, then shook out the hat into the sunlight above the yard.

And there is one final scene, one in which they took leave of the Pacific, a scene that Rocky mentioned with a laugh. The troopship was ready, and hundreds of soldiers and airmen had crowded by dockside, ready to board. A health inspection was called for. Rocky was assigned to oversee it. He got behind the wheel of a jeep and put the flight surgeon in the other front seat. He honked and someone blew a whistle to get the men formed in lines. "All right, get ready," he yelled to the mass of servicemen. "Now stick out your tongues!" He let out the clutch and ceremoniously drove the flight surgeon from one end of the crowd to the other, as straight-faced as a young man can be when he is grinning himself.

Epilogue

After the war, Rocky wanted to farm, but he could not afford it, so he went to graduate school in psychology instead. He earned his doctorate from Indiana University. From 1955 to 1989 he taught educational psychology at the University of Mississippi. He tirelessly supported the Mississippi public schools, patented a teaching machine, and published early studies of how computers could be used to design school bus routes. He and Margaret Anne were lifelong members of Oxford-University Methodist Church. He died in April 2008.

David W. Hutchison (1908–82) ran Cold War air operations in Africa, the Arctic, and the United States. He reached the rank of major general.

William Columbus Sams (1906–91) retired as a colonel in the United States Air Force. His honors included the Distinguished Flying Cross and the Legion of Merit.

Charles Frederick Smith (1912–2001), a graduate of Stetson University and Southern Baptist Seminary in Louisville, was called after the war to pulpits in Florida and North Carolina. In 1956 he left the ministry to teach high school in North Carolina.

Earl W. Schafer (1915–91) made a career as an orthopedic surgeon in North Carolina, associated with High Point Memorial Hospital.

William E. Ursprung (1918–2010) returned to the Houston area and worked for Shell Petroleum, retiring in 1985 as the manager of a Shell power plant facility.

In 1955 Brig. Gen. Ralph O. Brownfield (1907–90) was reduced in rank and resigned from the Air Force, following findings of corruption in his dealings with a civilian contractor. Acquitted of criminal charges, he repeatedly filed lawsuits seeking vindication and lost pay, and ran more than once for Congress. The courts and the voters rejected his claims.

Acknowledgments

Thanks for transcribing Rocky's diary, the work of two summers, go to Sarah Marlow of Staten Island.

Katherine Sams Wiley, the daughter of Colonel Sams, merits thanks for her work in collecting and publishing the recollections of officers and men who served with the 71st Tactical Reconnaissance Group, in her book *The Strafin' Saints.*

Thanks for knowledge, help, and service go to the library and special collections staff at the Australian War Memorial, University of Houston, University of North Texas, Wisconsin Veterans Museum, Wisconsin Historical Society, National Personnel Records Center, and the United States Military Academy—and specially to Leeander Morris at the Air Force Historical Research Agency, James Zobel at the Douglas MacArthur Memorial, Katie Townsend at Eastern Oregon University, and Mary Ruwell at the United States Air Force Academy. Jeffrey Nash, at the Peterson Air and Space Museum at Peterson Air Force Base, has amassed and freely shared material on wartime base commander David W. Hutchison. The staff at the High Point Public Library in North Carolina graciously supplied a copy of the *High Point Enterprise* article on Major Tennille. In the Indiana farm country where my father grew up, the

Sheridan Historical Society allowed me access to their microfilm copy of the wartime *Sheridan News*.

The family of pilot Raymond Couk, in particular Michael Couk, shared their father's recollections and his taped interview. Allan Jones of Milwaukee knew SSgt. Ralph Winkle and outlined his later career. Barbara Provin at Providence Baptist Church in Harrisburg, North Carolina, supplied information on the postwar career of Chaplain Smith. Andy Tennille has planned a biography of his grandfather, and that book would be worth reading.

As noted more particularly for each photograph, this book is indebted for its illustrations to the Australian War Memorial; the collection amassed by Lt. Michael Moffitt of the 82nd Squadron and preserved by his son Michael Moffitt Jr.; the collection curated by Gerry Kersey, on and off the web, that focuses on the Third Attack Group of the Fifth Air Force; the San Diego Air and Space Museum; Jeffrey Nash and the Peterson Air and Space Museum; the archives of the Air Force Historical Research Agency at Maxwell Air Force Base; and to Fred Hill's notable photographs of the Pacific War, which he donated to the McDermott Library of the United States Air Force Academy and the Pierce Library of Eastern Oregon University.

Anndora Laflin, Rocky's sister, preserved and shared memories and documents upon which I have drawn. Col. Charles Wesley Borders took time out from writing his own memoirs to discuss, in November 2016, what he saw in New Guinea in the spring of 1944.

This book has benefited from the knowledge and collections of Jean Barbaud, Elizabeth Gilmartin, Gerry Kersey, Michael Moffitt, Robert Rocker, Edward Rogers, Douglas Ruegg, Bill Wynne, and Jason van der Graaff. It has been improved by comments from Terry Dugan of Morgan, Lewis & Bockius; Mark Nicholls of St. John's College, Cambridge; Paul Springer of the Air Command and Staff College; anonymous reader comments from the Naval

Institute Press; and particularly Ronald Sannicandro, a veteran of the New York Stock Exchange Division of Enforcement. To Laura Davulis of the Naval Institute Press goes an author's gratitude to an editor who saw the merits of a manuscript and the ways in which it could be improved. I am also indebted to the Press' production and marketing teams—in particular, Emily Bakely, David Bowman, Judy Heise, Jehanne Moharram, Claire Noble, and Robin Noonan.

My wife Kathleen read drafts of this book, supported its author, and allowed stacks of books and yellowing wartime newspapers to drift up against the wall of more than one room in our house. My sons Declan and Thomas attended patiently to talk of research that did not involve visiting air museums. They merit thanks and praise.

This book was written in the Wertheim Study of the New York Public Library, in the light of windows looking down on 42nd Street, and with the aid of the New York Public Library's collections and knowledgeable, hospitable staff. The author is glad to acknowledge the generosity of the NYPL and the founding patron of the Study, Barbara Tuchman.

To Margaret Anne Boyer, Rocky's wife and the author's mother, go thanks and love and more. This book is dedicated to her.

Notes

Chapter 1. From Sugar Creek to Salinas

1. "It's Army Life for College Graduate," *Franklin (IN) Evening Star*, June 9, 1941, p. 1.
2. "Large Crowds at the Fair," *Tipton (IN) Daily Tribune*, September 4, 1934; "Prize Winners in Livestock Show on Auction Block," *Zanesville (OH) Signal*, December 3, 1931; "Corn Exhibits at Frankfort Break Record," *Kokomo (IN) Tribune*, November 15, 1937.
3. Roscoe A. Boyer, unpublished typescript journal record of basic training in June and July 1941 (entry for June 11, 1941).
4. Ibid.
5. Roscoe A. Boyer, postcard to Margaret Anne Dillard, postmarked June 11, 1941, from Indianapolis.
6. Roscoe A. Boyer, basic training journal (June 16, 1941).
7. Olson, *Those Angry Days*.
8. Roscoe A. Boyer, letter to family, June 15, 1941.
9. Boyer, basic training journal (June 29, 1941).
10. Ibid (June 30, 1941, and June 16, 1941).

Chapter 2. Shipping Out

1. Group History, 71st Tactical Reconnaissance Group, GP-RCN-71-HI (October 1941–December 1944), "Instruction for Security of the Group during the Restricted Period" and "Draft of GI Plans" (both September 1943).
2. Kenney, *General Kenney Reports*, 215–217.
3. Kenney, *Reports*, 214, 216; Craven and Cate, *The Pacific: Guadalcanal to Saipan—August 1942 to July 1944*, 152.

4. Handwritten diary of Roscoe Allen Boyer [hereafter RAB Diary], September 8, 1943.

5. Vail, *Strike! The Story of the Fighting 17th*, 244; War Department, Basic Field Manual FM 30–25, "Military Intelligence/Counterintelligence" (February 1940 ed.), 45; Bryan C. Arnold, "Military Censorship," *Field Artillery Journal* 33/6 (June 1943): 438. Bill Mauldin's wartime cartoon was printed in his book *Up Front* and reprinted in Jones, *WWII*, 131. Diaries and letters of 71st Group men have been collected and edited by Wiley and Nichols in *The Strafin' Saints*.

6. Group history, 71st Tactical Reconnaissance Group, GP-RCN-71-HI (October 1941–December 1944), "Instruction for Security of the Group during the Restricted Period" and "Draft of GI Plans" (both September 1943).

7. RAB Diary, September 9, 1943.

8. Ibid., September 13, 1943.

9. Ibid., September 14, 1943.

10. Raymond A. "Jack" Couk Jr., former pilot with the 17th Tactical Reconnaissance Squadron, interview by William Groniger, graciously supplied by the Couk family.

11. The accident occurred on June 26, 1943. His men made sure that Gordon's upended P-39N, No. 42–18927, was photographed.

12. RAB Diary, September 23, 1943.

13. Ibid., September 24, 1943.

14. Ibid., October 1, 1943.

15. Such headlines, above Associated Press wire reports, ran nationwide that week. Typical of such coverage (whatever newspapers reached Laurel Army Airfield: the *New Orleans (LA) Times-Picayune*, or *Meridian (MS) Star?*) were the stories that ran in the *Jackson (MS) Clarion-Ledger*, *Greenville (MS) Times-Democrat*, and *Dothan (AL) Eagle*, from which these examples are drawn.

16. RAB Diary, October 2, 1943.

17. Ibid., October 28, 1943.

18. Ibid., October 28, 1943.

19. Ibid., October 22, 1943.

20. War Department Technical Manual 16–205, "The Chaplain" (1941), 52.

21. Unit history, 71st Group, GP-RCN-71-HI, 5–1213–52 (October 1941–December 1944).

22. RAB Diary, October 22, 1943.

23. Ibid., October 19, 1943.

24. Ibid., October 20, 1943.

25. Ibid., October 29, 1943.

26. Technical Manual 16–205, 16. These qualities listed were those that a chaplain's assistant should ideally possess. Chaplain Smith, with

his musical training and his typewriter, appears to have handled by himself the practical side of his ministry.

27. RAB Diary, November 3, 1943.
28. Ibid.
29. "Ships with a History," *RIL Post* (magazine of Royal Interocean Lines), October 1974, 190–194.
30. RAB Diary, November 7, 1943.

Chapter 3. An Island North of Australia

1. Kahn, *G. I. Jungle*, 47.
2. Johnston, *The Toughest Fighting in the World*; Allied Geographical Section, *Getting About in New Guinea* (Melbourne: GHQ-SWPA, April 4, 1943), 1.
3. White, *Green Armor*, 11.
4. Kahn, "The Terrible Days of Company E."
5. Milner, *Victory in Papua*, 56–57.
6. McCarthy, *Kokoda to Wau*, 47.
7. Ibid., 40–41.
8. Shaw and Kane, *Isolation of Rabaul*, 442.
9. Waiko, *A Short History of Papua New Guinea*, 74, 97; Bulbeck, *Australian Women in Papua New Guinea*, 168–169.
10. Willis, *Lae*, 80–97; Robinson, *Villagers at War*.
11. McCarthy, *Patrol into Yesterday*, 40, 84, 111–115.
12. Rothgeb, *New Guinea Skies*, 199.
13. McCarthy, *Kokoda to Wau*, 34–107.
14. Willmott, *The Barrier and the Javelin*, 132–133.
15. Ibid., 39–55.
16. The defense of Port Moresby, including the fighting along the Kokoda Track, is well described in Osmar White's *Green Armor*, John Lardner's *Southwest Passage*, Australian and United States Army official histories, principally Samuel Milner's *Victory in Papua* and Ulysses Lee's *The Employment of Negro Troops*, and Bruce Gamble's *Fortress Rabaul: The Battle for the Southwest Pacific*. The story of *Guinea Gold* has been told by Paul Jefferson Wallace.
17. This count of air raids follows the tally in Titus, *Come What Will* (quoted on Pacific Wrecks website, www.pacificwrecks.com). Titus was an American antiaircraft battery officer serving in Moresby.
18. White, *Green Armor*, 58.
19. When the *Shoho* was lost, H. P. Willmott has written, the Japanese immediately "delayed the date of the proposed landings at Port Moresby by two days." Crucially, the Japanese "no longer had the means to counter Allied airpower at Port Moresby and in northern Australia." Willmott, *The Barrier and the Javelin*, 247, 276.

20. Williams, *The Kokoda Campaign*; Zimmerman, *The Guadalcanal Campaign*.
21. Kenney, *Reports*, 41–42, 118.
22. Milner, *Victory in Papua*, 50–55; Williams, *The Kokoda Campaign*, 45.
23. Milner, *Victory in Papua*, 375.
24. Griffith, *MacArthur's Airman*, 85–94.
25. Kenney, *Reports*, 124.
26. Douglas MacArthur had a map of the Pacific Ocean hanging in his headquarters map room, on which the outline of the continental United States had been superimposed. Nothing brings home with greater clarity the challenges of the war. Walter Krueger appropriated the idea for his memoirs, as did Frazier Hunt and William Manchester for their biographies of MacArthur. See, for example, Hunt, *MacArthur and the War against Japan*, 135; Manchester, *American Caesar*, 279.

Chapter 4. The Air Blitz War

1. Official historians have commented: "The war in the Pacific was a naval, air, and engineers' war rather than a land war conducted along orthodox lines." Coakley and Leighton, *Global Logistics and Strategy 1943–1945*, 418.
2. Kenney to Arnold, October 24, 1942, quoted in Craven and Cate, *Guadalcanal to Saipan*, 119. Kenney's strategic vision and tactical innovations are ably discussed in Griffith, *MacArthur's Airman*.
3. Kenney to Arnold, October 24, 1942, quoted in Craven and Cate, *Guadalcanal to Saipan*, 119.
4. The theory of the air base as hidden fortress was propounded by watercolor master and camouflage expert Merrill E. DeLonge in *Modern Airfield Planning and Concealment*, and "How to Baffle a Bombardier."
5. Bartsch, *Every Day a Nightmare*, 90–91.
6. Griffith, *MacArthur's Airman*, 123–124.
7. Ibid., 25–26.
8. Ibid., 83.
9. Dean, "MacArthur's War" in *Australia 1943*, 53–54.
10. Griffith, *MacArthur's Airman*, 104.
11. McAulay, *The Battle of the Bismarck Sea*; Craven and Cate, *Guadalcanal to Saipan*, 135–150; and Griffith, *MacArthur's Airman*, 107–111. The extent of Japanese losses has been intensely debated. Kenney never budged from his wartime claim that his aircraft had sunk twenty-two ships and destroyed a division of 20,000 men, despite evidence showing Japanese losses of twelve ships and 3,500 men. Whatever the extent of Japanese losses, however, Kenney's airmen stopped

the convoy. The undeniable fact is that the air attack prevented reinforcement of the Japanese position in New Guinea and, in shifting the course of the war, supplied a strategic victory very nearly as monumental as MacArthur announced.

12. Letter from Headquarters Advanced Echelon to All Air Force Units, New Guinea, March 5, 1943, quoted in Toll, *The Conquering Tide*, 225.

13. Johnston, *Pacific Partner*, 102–103.

14. Dean, "MacArthur's War," 52–53.

15. Kenney, *Reports*, 276–277; Cortesi, *Valor in the Sky*; Kenney, *Reports*, 251–279; Gamble, *Target Rabaul*, 89–115. Kenney claimed that his bombers had destroyed 90 percent of the Japanese army planes on the four airdromes around Wewak. Postwar analysis indicated that only half as many Japanese planes were destroyed. Nonetheless, whatever the actual extent of Japanese losses, the Fifth Air Force demolished the threat that the Japanese forces represented.

16. Dexter, *The New Guinea Offensives*, 416.

17. Hutchison led from the front, and won medals for it, but he was not the only Allied serviceman to reconnoiter personally the Markham watershed. Other officers scouting and building airfields ahead of Allied lines included Lt. Everette "Tex" Frazier, who wrote that he hoped to do in the Southwest Pacific what Erastus "Deaf" Smith had done in the Texas Revolution, as well as legendary Australian patrol-leader Peter Ryan, and engineer colonel Murray C. Woodbury. Frazier, *Tsili Tsili Sting*.

18. This account draws on Hough and Arnold, *Big Distance*, 95–101, and Dexter, *The New Guinea Offensives*, 423.

19. Kenney, *Reports*, 312–327; Birdsall, *Flying Buccaneers*, 112–134.

20. Gamble, *Target Rabaul*, 263. ("After the second carrier raid on Rabaul [November 11, 1943] . . . the Fifth Air Force would never again return to the stronghold in an offensive capacity.")

21. *Reports of General MacArthur*, 2:251; Craven and Cate, *Guadalcanal to Saipan*, 579–580.

22. Manchester, *American Caesar*, 330–331; Smith, *The Approach to the Philippines*, 1–12.

Chapter 5. Port Moresby

1. Kahn, *G. I. Jungle*, 66; Lardner, *Southwest Passage*, 187.

2. White, *Green Armor*, 43.

3. The 25th Liaison Squadron left Laurel on October 20, traveled to Camp Stoneman, and went via New Zealand to Brisbane and finally Nadzab. "An Historical Account from Activation to December 1944," 71st Tactical Reconnaissance Group, GP-RCN-71-HI (October 1941–December 1944), 14–15.

4. RAB Diary, November 8–9, 1943.
5. Ibid., November 17, 1943.
6. Ibid., November 23, 1943, and November 8, 1943.
7. Ibid., November 17, 1943.
8. Ibid., November 8, 1943.
9. Ibid.
10. RAB Diary, November 9, 1943.
11. Wiley, *The Strafin' Saints*, 23.
12. RAB Diary, November 17, 1943.
13. Ibid.
14. RAB Diary, November 20, 1943
15. Ibid., November 17, 1943.
16. For example, junior officers' failure to observe the "sanctity of mail" by enlisted men generated friction in the 90th Bombardment Group. Pfau, "Postal Censorship and Military Intelligence During World War II," 87.
17. RAB Diary, December 13, 1943.
18. Ibid., November 18, 1943.
19. Ibid., November 19, 1943.
20. The fourth unit belonging to the Group, the 25th Liaison Squadron, flew liaison aircraft, Piper Cubs or Stimson Sentinels painted in olive drab. This squadron usually operated under separate command.
21. RAB Diary, November 20, 1943.
22. Ibid., November 25, 1943.
23. Ibid., November 21, 1943.
24. Ibid., November 25, 1943.
25. Ibid., December 25, 1943.
26. Ibid., November 25, 1943.
27. Ibid., November 27, 1943.
28. *Yank Down Under*, December 31, 1943, 9.
29. RAB Diary, November 29, 1943.
30. Ibid.
31. Wiley, *The Strafin' Saints*, 24.
32. RAB Diary, November 29, 1943.

Chapter 6. Headquarters

1. Kenney, *Reports*, 303–304.
2. The *Lincoln [NB] Star*, August 22, 1941, may have been the only newspaper to spell correctly Major Hutchison's surname.
3. Roosevelt, *As He Saw It*, 8–14, 47–56; Air Force online historical materials for Third Reconnaissance Group and Peterson AFB.
4. This biography draws on the Department of Defense Office of Public Information biography for David W. Hutchison USAF; the Official

Register of the Officers and Cadets, United States Military Academy, 1931; "C. W. Hutchison, Ex-Senator, Dies," *Monroe (WI) Evening Times*, July 10, 1945; an AP wire story, "U.S. Serviceman Decorated by King," *Brownsville (TX) Herald*, December 15, 1944; and "State Native in Charge of Operations for Tactical Air Command," *La Crosse (WI) Tribune*, January 12, 1958. The details of Hutchison's early career in the Southwest Pacific are taken from Stanaway and Rocker, *The Eight Ballers*, 69–82 passim.

5. See, e.g., "9 Wisconsin Airmen Given Flying Awards," *Racine (WI) Journal-Times*, August 4, 1943; "Hutchison's Troop-Moving by Plane Wins Silver Star," *Wisconsin State Journal*, November 23, 1943; "Hutchison Decorated," *Wisconsin State Journal*, July 9, 1944; Lee Van Atta, "Reporter Sees Yank 'Chutists Land Behind Lae Defenses," wire story printed in *Lowell (MA) Sun*, September 7, 1943.

6. RAB Diary, December 1, 1943.

7. Ibid., December 2, 1943.

8. Ibid., December 11, 1943. Other airmen had heard that Hutchison was an in-law of Army Air Force commander Hap Arnold. Bill A. Wynne, letter to author, September 28, 2015.

9. Ibid., December 6, 1943.

10. Ibid., December 10, 1943.

11. Ibid., December 20, 1943.

12. Ibid., December 6, 1943.

13. Ibid., December 1, 1943

14. Ibid., December 8, 1943.

15. Jones, *The Thin Red Line*, 101.

16. RAB Diary, December 9, 1943.

17. 71st Reconnaissance Group, Order of December 6, 1943.

18. RAB Diary, November 30, 1943.

19. Ibid., December 11, 1943.

20. Lardner, *Southwest Passage*, 137–143.

21. RAB Diary, December 11, 1943.

22. Ibid., December 3, 1943.

23. Ibid., December 12, 1943.

Chapter 7. Palace Coup

1. RAB Diary, November 30, 1943.

2. Ibid., December 1, 1943.

3. Ibid.

4. Alcorn, *The Jolly Rogers*, 107–108; Cundiff, *Ten Knights in a Bar Room*, 66–78.

5. Cundiff, *Ten Knights in a Bar Room*, 79.

6. Kenney, *Reports*, 147.

7. Goldstein, "Ennis C. Whitehead: Aerial Tactician," in Leary, *We Shall Return!*, 178–207.

8. Gamble, *Fortress Rabaul*, 273.

9. In one instance, Kenney told Whitehead to use his own judgment in ordering air strikes, no matter what Kenney had promised the Navy. Kenney to Whitehead, November 7, 1943, quoted by Wolk, "George C. Kenney: MacArthur's Premier Airman," in Leary, *We Shall Return!*, 106.

10. Goldstein, "Ennis C. Whitehead: Aerial Tactician," 266n103.

11. The correspondence between Kenney and Whitehead is quoted from letters of December 3, December 5, and December 10, 1943, in the Air Force Historical Research Agency archive at Maxwell AFB. Whitehead/Kenney Correspondence January 1943–December 1943 (IRIS 123916). This includes the original letter sent by Kenney to Whitehead on December 3. The original letter references two enclosures (Chaplain Smith's letter and a radiogram), neither of which is included with this exchange of letters or in the overall file. A carbon copy of Kenney's December 3 letter went into Kenney's wartime log and correspondence record. Another copy went to MacArthur, and has been located in the MacArthur Memorial archive. It does not appear that a copy of Chaplain Smith's letter was filed with either of these copies.

12. Kenney, *The Saga of Pappy Gunn*, and Gunn, *Pappy Gunn*. The most recent biography of Pappy Gunn is *Indestructible: One Man's Rescue Mission That Changed the Course of WWII*, by John R. Bruning.

13. Henebry, *The Grim Reapers*, 35; Cortesi, *Valor in the Sky* 106, 207.

14. Kenney, *The Saga of Pappy Gunn*, 74–76.

15. Gunn, *Pappy Gunn*, 205–206.

16. The explosives may have been stockpiled by Davis for a planned fishing trip. Gunn, *Pappy Gunn*, 285.

17. Willoughby, *MacArthur 1941–1951*, 115–116.

18. Brereton was an airman of long experience, but throughout his career he battled charges of drunkenness and misfeasance. Perry, *"The Most Dangerous Man in America,"* 81–85, and a series of *Air Power History* articles by Roger G. Miller, in particular "'Under the Influence' and 'Acting with Prejudice.'"

19. Ennis Whitehead to George Kenney, December 5, 1943, AFHRA Whitehead/Kenney Correspondence (IRIS 123916).

20. Tunny, *Gateway to Victory*, 9.

21. Whitehead to Kenney, December 5, 1943, AFHRA Whitehead/ Kenney Correspondence (IRIS 123916). Gephardt is *recte* Gephart.

22. Ibid.

23. RAB Diary, December 5, 1943.

24. Ibid., December 6, 1943.
25. Dewitt also demanded, obtained, and exercised the authority to intern Japanese nationals and Japanese Americans on the West Coast—but in 1943, no one in the Southwest Pacific considered this worthy of satire.
26. RAB Diary, December 7, 1943.
27. The mimeograph newspaper of the Eighth Photo Reconnaissance Squadron reported the "new 9 o'clock closing of club bars on this fair Island." *The 8-Ball*, December 12, 1943, posted on the Oz at War website, www.ozatwar.com. See also Stava, *Combat Recon*, 23.
28. RAB Diary, December 9, 1943.
29. George Kenney to Ennis Whitehead, December 10, 1943, AFHRA Whitehead/Kenney Correspondence (IRIS 123916).
30. As Jock Henebry explained: "Surgeons, like chaplains, by virtue of their duties, were privy to delicate data. . . . They could know the make-up of the entire organization better than any other level of officer." Henebry, *The Grim Reapers*, 140.
31. C. P. Markle to Ennis Whitehead, December 22, 1943, with attached handwritten cover note per "Cy Markle" directing a lieutenant colonel to deliver the letter personally to Whitehead ("He does not want it go through the C/S and others of his office"). Ennis Whitehead Correspondence (IRIS 123968).
32. Tunny, *Winning from Downunder*, 68, 248; Kenney, *Reports*, 343. In a January 30, 1944, letter, Whitehead noted that he himself had taken over Fifth Bomber Command duties, "upon Colonel Davies' departure for the United States." Whitehead Correspondence (IRIS 123968).

Chapter 8. First Battles
1. Eichelberger, *Our Jungle Road to Tokyo*, 18–19.
2. RAB Diary, December 14, 1943.
3. Wedemeyer, *Wedemeyer Reports!*, 204–205.
4. Kenney, *Reports*, 332–333, 305.
5. *Guinea Gold*, December 27 and 29, 1943. In other theaters of war, American soldiers read their daily news in *Stars and Stripes*. In the Southwest Pacific, the soldiers' daily paper was *Guinea Gold*, begun by Australian military journalists and later expanded with American editions and staff. Wallace, *Guinea Gold*.
6. Wiley, *The Strafin' Saints*, 17–18.
7. Ibid., 17.
8. *Reports of General MacArthur*, 1:164.
9. RAB Diary, December 16, 1943.
10. Wiley, *The Strafin' Saints*, 17.
11. Ibid., 28, 41.

12. Ibid., 31.

13. Ibid., 27.

14. RAB Diary, November 27, 1943.

15. Ibid., November 29, 1943.

16. Wiley, *The Strafin' Saints*, 24.

17. Ibid., 18–19, 29–30.

18. RAB Diary, December 9, 1943.

19. Wiley, *The Strafin' Saints*, 29; *Ironwood (MI) Daily Globe*, December 26, 1941.

20. Col. Charles Wesley Borders, in discussion with author, November 2016.

21. RAB Diary, December 27, 1943.

22. Ibid., January 17, 1944.

23. Ibid., January 11, 1944.

24. Ibid., December 16, 1943.

25. Ibid., December 18, 1943.

26. Ibid., December 16, 1943.

27. Brinkley, *Washington Goes to War*, 19–20.

28. Link and Coleman, *Medical Support of the Army Air Forces in World War II*, 823.

29. Vail, *Strike! The Story of the Fighting 17th*, 74, 156.

30. Link and Coleman, *Medical Support of the Army Air Forces in World War II*, 822.

31. RAB Diary, November 29, 1943.

32. Ibid., December 5, 1943.

33. Krulak, *First to Fight*, 150–154.

34. Jones, *The Thin Red Line*, 16.

35. "Ernie Pyle's Daily Dispatch," *Des Moines (IA) Register*, May 2, 1943, 2.

36. RAB Diary, November 23, 1943.

37. Field Marshal William Slim, addressing new officers whom he would lead back into Burma.

38. RAB Diary, December 21, 1943.

39. Ibid., December 17, 1943.

40. Ibid., December 19–20, 1943.

41. Ibid.

42. *The Officers' Guide: A Ready Reference on Customs and Correct Procedures Which Pertain to Commissioned Officers of the Army of the United States*, 8th ed. (Harrisburg, Pa.: Military Service Publishing, 1942), 312, 371.

43. Caplow, "Rumors in War"; Shibutani, *Improvised News*.

44. *Yank Down Under*, February 25, 1944 (back-cover cartoon).

45. RAB Diary, December 20, 1943.

46. Wiley, *The Strafin' Saints*, 30.

47. Squadron History, 82nd Reconnaissance Squadron, SQ-RCN-82, August–December 1943 (dated February 19, 1944) (IRIS 66754).
48. Wiley, *The Strafin' Saints*, 44.
49. RAB Diary, December 6, 1943.
50. Ibid., December 22, 1943.
51. Ibid., December 23, 1943.
52. Ibid., December 9, 1943.
53. Ibid., December 6, 1943.
54. Ibid., December 26, 1943.
55. Ibid., December 25, 1943. The censorship regulations in fact prohibited photos "the contents of which are obscene," without further clarification, or which showed military personnel "in familiar poses with native women." Pfau, "Postal Censorship and Military Intelligence During World War II," 84.
56. Wiley, *The Strafin' Saints*, 32–33.
57. Ibid., 30; see *Time*, July 19, 1943; Max Presnell, "The True Spirit of Racing, Forged in Time of Trouble," *Sydney Morning Herald*, April 21, 2006.
58. Wiley, *The Strafin' Saints*, 32, 37.
59. Ibid., 27, 43, 77, 87.
60. Craven and Cate, *Guadalcanal to Saipan*, 269–270. This section of the official history focuses on the difficulties endured by airmen in the South Pacific, but it speaks with equal eloquence to the conditions in which ground crews worked in New Guinea.
61. RAB Diary, December 26, 1944.
62. Stanaway and Rocker, *The Eight Ballers*, 99; "US War Correspondent, 3 Others, Die in Plane Crash," *The Brooklyn (NY) Eagle*, December 28, 1943. Information on R. F. D. Tojo's history with the 19th and 43rd Bomb Groups comes from the Pacific Wrecks website, www.pacific wrecks.com/aircraft/b-17/41-2627.html.
63. RAB Diary, December 28, 1943.
64. These examples are yielded by a short online search and could easily be multiplied. See, e.g., Newell, *Operation Goodtime*, 169; McManus, *The Deadly Brotherhood*, 208; and Kenney, *Reports*, 305–306.
65. RAB Diary, December 31, 1943.
66. Douglas MacArthur, directive, "Return of Personnel to the United States," FEGG 210.68, July 29, 1943, quoted by Craven and Cate, *Guadalcanal to Saipan*, 200.
67. RAB Diary, November 23, 1943.
68. Ibid., November 26–27, 1943.
69. Ibid., November 10, 1943.
70. Pfau, *Miss Yourlovin*, ch 1, ¶ 10.

71. Link and Coleman, *Medical Support of the Army Air Forces in World War II*, 847.

72. *Yank Down Under*, November 26, 1943, 20.

73. Ibid., February 25, 1944, 15.

74. Craven and Cate, *Guadalcanal to Saipan*, 327.

Chapter 9. The New Year

1. RAB Diary, January 1, 1944.

2. Ibid., January 5–11, 1944.

3. Ibid., January 10, 1944.

4. Ibid., December 3, 1943.

5. Ibid., December 20, 1943.

6. Ibid., December 5, 1943.

7. Ibid., December 8, 1943.

8. Ibid., January "18–19–20," 1944.

9. Ibid., December 8, 1943.

10. Ibid., December 9, 1943.

11. Ibid., January 16, 1944.

12. Hill, *Darkroom Soldier*, 49.

13. RAB diary, January 15, 1944 (MacArthur rumor), January 16, 1944 (Wayne and Japanese comfort women rumors), January 24, 1944 (Japanese propaganda).

14. Ibid., January "18–19–20," 1944, January 17, 1944.

15. Ibid., January "18–19–20," 1944.

16. Ibid., January 9, 1944.

17. Ross, *Preparing for Ulysses*, 99–100. The American Legion announced its plans in a news conference on Saturday morning, January 8, in Washington. The planned legislation was reported the next morning in the nation's Sunday newspapers.

18. RAB Diary, January 15, 1944.

19. Pfau, "Postal Censorship and Military Intelligence," 85–87.

20. Clark, "A Comparison of Civil and Court-Martial Procedure," 591.

21. Information learned independently in conversations with Anndora Boyer Laflin and Margaret Anne Boyer.

22. RAB Diary, January 9, 1944.

23. Ibid., February 13, 1944.

24. Ibid., January 13, 1944.

25. Ibid., January 24, 1944.

26. Ibid., January "18–19–20," 1944.

27. Ibid., January 15, 1944.

28. Ibid., December 11, 1943.

29. Ibid., January 17, 1944, November 25, 1943.

30. Ibid., January 24, 1944.

31. Ibid., January 17, 1944.
32. Eyman, *John Wayne*, 133–135; "Benjamin DeLoache, Singer and Teacher, 88," *New York Times* obituary, March 18, 1994.
33. RAB Diary, January 24, 1944.
34. Squadron History, 110th Tactical Reconnaissance Squadron, SQ-RCN-110-HI (January 1944) (statement of Lt. Joe H. Williams, January 24, 1944).
35. Missing Air Crew Report No. 1783 (January 22, 1944).
36. Wiley, *The Strafin' Saints*, 35–36.
37. Ibid., 37.
38. Dougherty, "Flying Fatigue," 37.
39. Greenwood, "The Fight Against Malaria in the Papua and New Guinea Campaigns"; Sheppeck and Wexberg, "Toxic Psychoses Associated with Administration of Quinacrine," 489–510; Ocko, "A Case of Atabrine Psychosis in a Civilian," 833–834.
40. Wiley, *The Strafin' Saints*, 35, 40.
41. RAB Diary, February 4, 1944.
42. Wiley, *The Strafin' Saints*, 37.
43. RAB Diary, January 30, 1944.
44. Ibid., February 4, 1944, January 30, 1944.
45. Ibid., February 4, 1944.
46. Ibid., January "18-19-20," 1944.
47. Ibid., November 18–20, 1943.
48. Ibid., February 4, 1944.
49. Ibid.
50. *Yank Down Under*, January 28, 1944, 14; "Letter Given on 32nd Men," *Milwaukee (WI) Journal*, March 30, 1944.
51. *Sheridan (IN) News*, January 21, 1944–March 4, 1944. The report on Vonnegut's Hardware was carried by *Yank Down Under*, December 24, 1943, 20.
52. "Coed Selected for College Editorship," *Franklin (IN) Evening Star*, March 14, 1943; "College War Council Set," *Franklin Evening Star*, November 19, 1942; "Vandivier Praised on Dr. I. Q. Program," *Franklin Evening Star*, February 15, 1944.
53. RAB Diary, February 8, 1944; *Greeley (CO) Daily Tribune*, February 3, 1944.
54. RAB Diary, February 11, 1944.
55. Ibid., February 16, 1944.
56. Ibid., February 13, 1944.
57. Missing Air Crew Report No. 4504 (February 14, 1944, supplemented May 17, 1944).
58. *Kerrville (TX) Mountain Sun*, March 16, 1944.

59. RAB Diary, February 17, 1944.
60. Missing Air Crew Report No. 3737 (February 16, 1944).
61. RAB Diary, February 16, 1944.
62. "A volcanic dust fell all morning and covered everything." RAB Diary, February 14, 1944. See Johnson, *Fire Mountains of the Islands*, chap. 7.
63. RAB Diary, February 16, 1944.
64. Ibid.
65. Ibid., February 17, 1944.
66. Ibid., February 17, 1944.
67. Ibid., February 18, 1944 (apparently entered February 19, 1944).
68. Ibid.
69. Craven and Cate, *Guadalcanal to Saipan*, 576–580; RAB Diary, February 8, 1944, February 11, 1944, February 14, 1944.

Chapter 10. Nadzab

1. Virgil Sewell, formerly of the 33rd Bombardment Squadron, 22nd Bombardment Group, quoted in Sheehan, *A Missing Plane*, 161–162. Sewell believed that Nadzab was the world's largest airfield complex, "if you don't count England as all one airfield complex."
2. In Wing headquarters, Rocky wrote, "The news that planes will no longer be painted is being discussed and everyone believes it's okay." RAB Diary, February 22, 1944.
3. Yenne, *Aces High*, 172–173.
4. Casey, *Airfield and Base Development*, 170–176; Craven and Cate, *Guadalcanal to Saipan*, 580; Dodd, *The Corps of Engineers*, 254, 258. General Casey praised the river valley where Nadzab was built as one of the best airfield sites in the world.
5. George Kenney Diary, (IRIS 889172), April 20, 1944.
6. *Back Load: February 1943—June 1944: 433rd Troop Carrier Group* (Sydney: Halstead Press, 1945), 49–50.
7. RAB Diary, February 21, 1944. The Navy carrier raid on Truk, on February 17–18, 1944, is discussed in Toll, *The Conquering Tide*, 403–414.
8. RAB Diary, February 25, 1944.
9. Ibid., February 20, 1944.
10. Ibid., April 1, 1944.
11. Ibid., February 22, 1944.
12. Kolln, *The 421st Night Fighter Squadron in World War II*, 26–29.
13. Link and Coleman, *Medical Support of the Army Air Forces in World War II*, 826–827.
14. Vincent Tubbs, the SWPA correspondent for the *Afro-American*, interviewed soldiers from an air base security battalion and a

quartermaster unit at Nadzab, which might have been the 394th Quartermaster Battalion, or Port Battalion ("the unit is really a trucking outfit, but their trucks have not reached the area as yet. They must wait until another colored unit, aviation engineers, completes a roadway up the Markham Valley"). "Engineers Thank Japs For Showing Such Good Taste," *The Afro-American* (Baltimore, Md.), December 11, 1943. See also Ulysses Lee, *United States Army in World War II: Special Studies*, 8:598–610; Hall, *Love, War, and the 96th Engineers (Colored)*; and Frazier, *Tsili Tsili Sting*, 3–4, 16, 21.

15. RAB Diary, February 22, 1944.
16. Wiley, *The Strafin' Saints*, 41.
17. Missing Air Crew Report No. 12464 (and/or MACR No. 2549) (initially filed February 23, 1944).
18. Special Service Division, Army Service Forces, *A Pocket Guide to New Guinea*, 29.
19. White, *Green Armor*, 176.
20. Interview of Charles Whitlock, of the 90th Bomb Group (later dean of Harvard College), Rutgers Oral History Project, http://oralhistory.rutgers.edu/interviewees/30-interview-html-text/70-whitlock-charles-p.
21. Whitehead to George Kenney, May 7, 1943, quoted in Gamble, *Target Rabaul*, 84.
22. Fortier, *An Ace of the Eighth*, 19.
23. Craven and Cate, *Plans and Early Operations—January 1939 to August 1942*, 113–114.
24. RAB Diary, February 24, 1944.
25. *Back Load*, 161.
26. The story of Guerry's escape was told by White, "They Fight with Cameras." The story ran the same month in *Reader's Digest*, as "Flyers Who Fight without Guns." Post's long, eventful stay behind Japanese lines, eventually in the company of three Australian coastwatchers who welcomed a fourth hand at bridge, is summarized by Bruce Gamble in *Target Rabaul*, 238–239.
27. RAB Diary, March 15, 1944.
28. Ibid., February 29, 1944.
29. Ibid., February 23,1944.
30. Ibid., February 28, 1944.
31. Ibid., February 29 1944.
32. Ibid., February 29, 1944.
33. Ibid., March 1, 1944.
34. During the last week of February 1944, front-page headlines in *Guinea Gold* screamed of "19 Enemy Ships Sunk, 201 Destroyed in First Two Days of Assault on Truk," "Offensive Against Japs Rages in All

Pacific Zones," "New Heights Reached in Terrific Anglo-U.S. Battering of Nazi Aircraft Factories," "Germans Routed in Russia; Red Army Captures Three Great Cities," and "U.S. Sea Bombardment of Rabaul & Kavieng Sinks 4 Ships."

35. RAB Diary, February 26, 1944.

36. Ibid., February 27, 1944.

37. Ibid., February 28, 1944.

38. Squadron History, 110th Tactical Reconnaissance Squadron, March 1944, SQ-RCN-110-HI (IRIS 66913).

39. RAB Diary, March 1, 1944, March 9, 1944.

40. Ibid., March 15, 1944,

41. Ibid., March 21, 1944.

42. Ibid.

43. Ibid., March 9, 12, and 21, 1944.

44. Ibid., March 28, 1944.

45. Ibid., March 12, 1944.

46. Squadron History, 82nd Tactical Reconnaissance Squadron, February 1944, SQ-RCN-82-HI, 4.

47. RAB Diary, March 21, 1944.

48. "1ST LT LAWRENCE O. ANDERSON, Signal Corps, announced as Signal Officer vice 1ST LT ROSCOE A. BOYER, Air Corps, Acting Signal Officer relieved"; "Major George H. MacBride is announced as Communications Officer," Wing History, 5212th Photographic Reconnaissance Wing, March 1944, WG-5212- HI (IRIS 110005) (orders of March 18 and March 29, 1944, respectively).

49. RAB Diary, March 21, 1944.

50. Ibid., March 26, 1944.

51. Ibid., March 28, 1944.

52. Ibid., March 26, 1944.

53. Ibid., March 9, 1944.

54. Pfau, *Miss Yourlovin*, ch. 1, 48.

55. Nyles C. Christensen to M. C. Whitehead [*sic*], January 21, 1944, Ennis Whitehead Correspondence (IRIS 123968); Ennis Whitehead to Nyles Christianson [*sic*], January 17, 1944; Memo, Recent Correspondence Regarding American Red Cross Recreation Program for Air Force Units in New Guinea, with handwritten addendum, January 29, 1944, Ennis Whitehead Correspondence (IRIS 123968).

56. Mitchell, "Those 'Y' Blokes."

57. RAB Diary, March 27, 1944.

58. Ibid., March 29, 1944.

59. Ibid., March 27, 1944.

60. Ibid., March 30, 1944.
61. Ibid., March 28, 1944.
62. Ibid., March 30, 1944.

Chapter 11. From Minimum Altitude

1. Squadron History, 17th Tactical Reconnaissance Squadron, January 1944 (dated February 28, 1944).
2. Squadron History, 17th Tactical Reconnaissance Squadron, Narrative Report on Mission 34-H-1 (February 4, 1944).
3. Squadron History, 17th Tactical Reconnaissance Squadron, Narrative Report on Mission 36-J-1 (February 7, 1944).
4. Wiley, *The Strafin' Saints*, 40.
5. Squadron History, 17th Tactical Reconnaissance Squadron, Narrative Report on Mission 37-I (February 7, 1944).
6. RAB Diary, February 8, 1944. Rocky also noted a death in the 110th Squadron. This was Carl H. Gilpatrick, from Dover, New Hampshire, who died on February 6, 1944, when his P-39 crashed on the Number Two strip at Gusap when returning from a combat mission. Squadron History, 110th Tactical Reconnaissance Squadron, SQ-RCN-110-HI (dated February 29, 1944).
7. Wiley, *The Strafin' Saints*, 40–41.
8. Cappy Pellaux, "Airmen Attack Naval Task Force," *Wing-ding*, June 24, 1944, 1, 4.
9. Tennille, "A Special Mission," at F-1.
10. RAB Diary, February 27, 1944.
11. Tennille, "A Special Mission." The identity of the 17th Squadron officer of whose sense Sams thought little is narrowed down by the fact that Sams' account, as edited, supplies the names for other officers with whom he conferred, but does not mention Tennille.
12. Tennille, "A Special Mission." Bert Smiley recalled that after Tennille's wingman had been shot down—which has to be the loss of Brown's plane at Bunabun—Tennille's copilot and navigator brought this request to him as squadron operations officer. Smiley scoffed at the complaints, but these officers seem to have gotten what they asked for; they are not listed subsequently among Tennille's plane's crew.
13. Vail, *Strike! The Story of the Fighting 17th*, 160.
14. Ibid., 173–174.
15. Anderson, "Suicide at Cape Waios," 6, 13.
16. Vail, *Strike! The Story of the Fighting 17th*, 163, 125.
17. Taaffe, *MacArthur's Jungle War*, 57.
18. Miller, *CARTWHEEL—The Reduction of Rabaul*, 320; Kenney, *Reports*, 359–360.

19. Taaffe, *MacArthur's Jungle War*, 56–76; Craven and Cate, *Guadalcanal to Saipan*, 559; Miller, *CARTWHEEL—The Reduction of Rabaul*, 320; Kenney Papers, February 25, 1944. AFHRA Microfilm 2713 (IRIS 889172); Drea, *MacArthur's Ultra*, 99.

20. The final pass at twenty feet is confirmed by the squadron historian in Vail's *Strike! The Story of the Fighting 17th*, 124.

21. Squadron History, 17th Tactical Reconnaissance Squadron, February 1944 (dated March 1, 1944).

22. Squadron History, 82nd Tactical Reconnaissance Squadron, SQ-RCN-82-HI, March 1944 (IRIS 66759).

23. Squadron History, 82nd Tactical Reconnaissance Squadron, SQ-RCN-82-HI, February 1944, Part 1 (IRIS 66757). The same report said that "rest leaves and furloughs are scheduled during the month of March."

24. Wiley, *The Strafin' Saints*, 43.

25. Squadron History, 82nd Tactical Reconnaissance Squadron, SQ-RCN-82-HI, March 1944 (IRIS 66759) (Air Medals earned by Graham and Zaleski), and February 1944 (IRIS 66757) (Zaleski receives Distinguished Flying Cross).

26. Wiley, *The Strafin' Saints*, 43, 47–48.

27. Ibid., 45.

28. Ibid., 47.

29. Squadron History, 110th Tactical Reconnaissance Squadron, April 1944, SQ-RCN-110-HI; Squadron History, 82nd Tactical Reconnaissance Squadron, March 1944, SQ-RCN-82-HI (IRIS 66759).

30. Kenney, *Reports*, 43.

31. Ennis Whitehead Correspondence, March 9, 1944 (IRIS 123970).

32. Wiley, *The Strafin' Saints*, 48.

33. Ibid., 47.

34. The story is told in Sheehan, *A Missing Plane*.

35. Robert Rocker, e-mail message to author, March 10, 2016.

36. Squadron History, 110th Tactical Reconnaissance Squadron, May 1944, SQ-RCN-110-HI (IRIS 66915); Wiley, *The Strafin' Saints*, 53.

Chapter 12. Quakes and Tremors

1. Palau was seven hundred miles northeast of Hollandia. The Navy's fast carrier forces arrived offshore on March 30. Over the next two days, Navy aviators cratered the Japanese airstrips on Palau, shot down fighters that attacked them from the Japanese fields on Yap and Peleliu, and finished by mining the harbors. Morison, *History of United States Naval Operations in World War II*, vol. 8, *New Guinea and the Marianas*, 32–33.

2. Kenney, *Reports*, 377.

3. Birdsall, *Flying Buccaneers*, 158–164.

4. RAB Diary, April 3, 1944.
5. Ibid., April 7, 1944.
6. Descriptions, biographical details, and activities for Major Chenery and other 91st Wing HQ personnel are taken from a staff directory done in or about June 1944, "Military History and Duties of the Personnel of Headquarters and Headquarters Squadron, 91st Photo Wing, Reconnaissance," in the AFHRA 91st Wing files.
7. RAB Diary, April 7, 1944.
8. Kolln, *The 421st Night Fighter Squadron*, 37.
9. Squadron History, 82nd Tactical Reconnaissance Squadron, March 1944, SQ-RCN-82-HI (IRIS 66759); Squadron History, 82nd Tactical Reconnaissance Squadron, April 1944, SQ-RCN-82-HI (IRIS No. 66760); Wiley, *The Strafin' Saints*, 51–52, 53.
10. Kenney, *Reports*, 387–388; Craven and Cate, *Guadalcanal to Saipan*, 597.
11. RAB Diary, April 16, 1944.
12. Yoshino, *Lightning Strikes*, 68–69.
13. Wiley, *The Strafin' Saints*, 54–55.
14. Kupferer, *No Glamour . . . No Glory*, 129.
15. Wiley, *The Strafin' Saints*, 54.
16. A harrowing account of the debacle is given by Claringbould, *Black Sunday*.
17. A correspondent noted that Bong had two upsetting talents, one for playing poker, the other for "buzzing this camp so low that palm trees bend and tents flap." Frank J. Kluckhohn, "Ace Is An Ace At Poker Or In The Air, Bong Teaches Griping Newsmen," *New York Times*, April 19, 1944, 10. Kluckhohn also noted that Bong began his poker game by laying a .32 revolver on the card table. A group photograph preserved in the AFHRA archive at Maxwell AFB, No. 80008AC, shows Captain Bong frowning while the newsmen scribble down his comments, and dates the press conference to April 16.
18. RAB Diary, April 17, 1944, April 29, 1944.
19. Ibid., April 16, 1944.
20. Ibid.
21. Ibid., Wiley, *The Strafin' Saints*, 51.
22. RAB Diary, April 16, 1944.
23. Ibid., April 16–20, 1944.
24. Ibid., April 20, 1944.
25. Ibid., May 3, 1944.
26. Ibid., April 29, 1944.
27. Ibid., April 23, 1944.
28. Ibid., April 17, 1944.

29. Ibid., April 27, 1944.

30. "Wolf Howls Greet Camp Show Singer," *Wing-ding*, April 29, 1944, 1.

31. RAB Diary, April 19, 1944.

32. Ibid., April 27, 1944.

33. Ibid., April 16, 1944.

34. Ibid., April 20, 1944, April 16, 1944.

35. Ibid., April 14, 1944.

36. Ibid., April 1, 1944.

37. Ibid., April 21, 1944.

38. Ibid., April 2, 1944, April 22, 1944.

39. Ibid., April 20, 1944.

40. "Seismological Notes," *Bulletin of the Seismological Society of America* 34 (July 1944), 175. Over the next several days, short news items reporting the earthquake ran in American newspapers, often as sidebar stories to reports on the Allied landings.

41. RAB Diary, April 22, 1944.

42. Eichelberger, *Our Jungle Road to Tokyo*, 114.

43. Manchester, *American Caesar*, 344, 347.

44. RAB Diary, April 22, 1944.

45. A short biography of Brownfield is given by the website for Davis-Monthan Airfield, the air base outside Tucson where he served early in his career. See http://dmairfield.com/people/brownfield_ro/index.html.

46. George Kenney to R. O. Brownfield, November 28, 1943, Kenney Papers, AFHRA Microfilm 27132 (IRIS 889171).

47. RAB Diary, April 26, 1944.

48. Ibid., April 29, 1944.

49. Ibid., April 22, 1944.

50. "Military History and Duties of the Personnel of Headquarters and Headquarters Squadron, 91st Photo Wing, Reconnaissance."

51. RAB Diary, May 3, 1944, May 7, 1944.

52. Ibid., April 30, 1944.

53. Ibid., May 3, 1944.

54. Missing Air Crew Report No. 16528, "Status of Crew of a B-25 Aircraft Missing in Action in the SWPA Since 18 August 1943" (August 19, 1944, later supplemented); Gamble, *Target Rabaul*, 251–261, 363–365.

55. RAB Diary, May 1, 1944, May 6, 1944.

56. Ibid., May 6, 1944.

57. Wiley, *The Strafin' Saints*, 52–53.

58. Kenney, *Reports*, 55; Griffith, *MacArthur's Airman*, 131.

59. Heller, *Catch-22*, 49.

60. Squadron History, 82nd Tactical Reconnaissance Squadron, May 1944, SQ-RCN-17-HI (IRIS 66562); Wiley, *The Strafin' Saints*, 58.

61. Missing Air Crew Report No. 5063 (May 28, 1944).

62. Griffith, *MacArthur's Airman*, 116.

63. Ibid., 175.

64. Robert Eichelberger to Ennis Whitehead, May 21, 1944, Ennis Whitehead Correspondence (IRIS 123970).

65. Eichelberger, *Our Jungle Road to Tokyo*, 113.

66. Manchester, *American Caesar*, 347–348.

67. Kenney, *Reports*, 394–395.

68. Wiley, *The Strafin' Saints*, 58.

Chapter 13. Cape Waios

1. On the Biak landings and the Japanese naval response, see Taaffe, *MacArthur's Jungle War*, 152–154; Griffith, *MacArthur's Airman*, 171–172; and Morison, vol. 8, *New Guinea and the Marianas*, 124–125.

2. RAB Diary, June 4, 1944.

3. Kolln, *The 421st Night Fighter Squadron*, 51–52.

4. Birdsall, *Flying Buccaneers*, 177.

5. RAB Diary, June 10, 1944.

6. Wiley, *The Strafin' Saints*, 63.

7. Charles Andrew Willoughby delivered this assessment the next day. Taaffe, *MacArthur's Jungle War*, 154–155, 275n41, and Morison, vol. 8, *New Guinea and the Marianas*, 124–125. The Sixth Army report and official figures collected by Taaffe consistently reflect a devastating blow. Taaffe, *MacArthur's Jungle War*, 275n40.

8. Kenney, *Reports*, 403–404.

9. Wiley, *The Strafin' Saints*, 69.

10. Ennis Whitehead Personal File Letter to 17th Tactical Reconnaissance Squadron, May 20, 1944 (IRIS 123968).

11. Squadron History, 17th Tactical Reconnaissance Squadron, May and June 1944, SQ-RCN-17-HI (IRIS 66562, 66563).

12. Tennille, "A Special Mission" (recollection of Bert Smiley).

13. Squadron History, 17th Tactical Reconnaissance Squadron, June 1944, SQ-RCN-17-HI (IRIS 66563).

14. The sources relied on for the 17th Tactical Reconnaissance Squadron's attack on the Japanese destroyer convoy at Cape Waios are the squadron history of the 17th Squadron for June 1944, SQ-RCN-17-HI (IRIS 66563) and the following: Individual Combat Report of Perry J. Dahl, Mission No. 2-300, 8 June 1944, attached to Squadron History, 432nd Fighter Squadron, June 1944, SQ-FI-432-HI (IRIS 660421); the Associated Press wire story by Spencer Davis, which

ran in different versions in newspapers including the *Fresno Bee*, *Emporia Gazette*, and Benton Harbor *News-Palladium*, on or after June 13, 1944; Cappy Pellaux, "Airmen Attack Naval Task Force," *Wing-ding*, June 24, 1944, 1, 4; Hough and Arnold, *Big Distance*, 145–148; Vail, *Strike! The Story of the Fighting 17th*, 119–121; Morison, vol. 8, *New Guinea and the Marianas*, 123–130; Anderson, "Suicide at Cape Waios"; Baumgardner, *Fifth Air Force*; Tennille, "A Special Mission"; Kelly, *Voices of My Comrades*, 278–280; Hara, *Japanese Destroyer Captain*; Watts and Gordon, *The Imperial Japanese Navy*; and Stille and Wright, *Imperial Japanese Navy Destroyers 1919–1945*, 1:40–42.

15. RAB Diary, September 13, 1943.
16. Hough and Arnold, *Big Distance*, 146
17. Pellaux, "Airmen Attack Naval Task Force," 1, 4.
18. Tennille, "A Special Mission."
19. Hough and Arnold, *Big Distance*, 147.
20. Tennille, "A Special Mission."
21. Keegan, *Six Armies in Normandy*, 108.
22. Baumgardner, *Fifth Air Force*, 64; Anderson, "Suicide at Cape Waios," 13. These ultimately draw on the pre-mission breakfast scene from Vail, *Strike! The Story of the Fighting 17th*, 119–121.
23. Anderson, "Suicide at Cape Waios," 56.
24. Davis, "Fresnan Has Part in 'One of Finest Feats of War,'" *Fresno (CA) Bee*, June 13, 1944, 1; Anderson, "Suicide at Cape Waios," 56–58.
25. Narrative Report on Mission 160 B-310, Squadron History, 17th Tactical Reconnaissance Squadron, June 1944 (IRIS 66563).
26. Anderson, "Suicide at Cape Waios," 58.
27. Narrative Report on Mission 160 B-310.
28. According to Samuel Eliot Morison, the *Harusame*, *Shiratsuyu*, and *Samidare* were each towing a large landing barge. Morison, vol. 8, *New Guinea and the Marianas*, 125.
29. Watts and Gordon, *The Imperial Japanese Navy*, 270; Stille and Wright, *Imperial Japanese Navy Destroyers*, 1:40–42.
30. McAulay, *Battle of the Bismarck Sea*, 69.
31. Hara, *Japanese Destroyer Captain*, 240–241; Craven and Cate, *Guadalcanal to Saipan*, 326.
32. Mission Report, 432nd Fighter Squadron; Davis, "Fresnan Has Part," *Fresno Bee*, 4.
33. Davis, "Fresnan Has Part," *Fresno Bee*, 1, 4; Anderson, "Suicide at Cape Waios," 62–64; Narrative Report on Mission 160 B-310.
34. Pellaux, "Airmen Attack Naval Task Force," 4; Anderson, "Suicide at Cape Waios," 62–64; Narrative Report on Mission 160 B-310.

35. RAB Diary, June 10, 1944.
36. Morison, vol. 8, *New Guinea and the Marianas*, 125–130.
37. Hara, *Japanese Destroyer Captain*, 210–211.
38. Wiley, *The Strafin' Saints*, 64.
39. RAB Diary, June 6, 1944, and June 10, 1944. Nadzab standard time is ten hours ahead of Greenwich. News of the Normandy landings was announced in Nadzab at 5:30 p.m. local time on June 6, 1944, according to the *Wing-ding*, which immediately rushed out a two-page extra edition. "Allied Invasion of Europe Begins," *Wing-ding*, June 6, 1944, 1. Servicemen with radios could have pulled in news of the landings as early as mid-afternoon.

Chapter 14. Summer

1. Between June 10 and July 11, Rocky made no diary entries. He gave no explanation, and although the ink changes from blue to black, there is no break in the text; the same manuscript page goes from the Japanese attack on Wakde and the anticipated liberation of Paris, *i.e.,* the second week of June, directly to the gossip about Colonel Brownfield. The next identifiable event mentioned is the rescue of Capt. Jowell Wise and his bomber crew, who ditched their B-25 on July 13.
2. RAB Diary, July 15, 1944.
3. Ibid., July 17, 1944.
4. Manchester, *American Caesar*, 348.
5. RAB Diary, July 20, 1944.
6. Ibid., July 18, 1944.
7. The following section draws on Rogers, *MacArthur and Sutherland*, 65–71, 80–85, and Thompson and Macklin, "MacArthur's Kingdom," chap. 7 in *The Battle of Brisbane*.
8. RAB Diary, July 11, 1944.
9. Ibid., July 12, 1944.
10. See, *e.g.*, Eichelberger, *Dear Miss Em*, 93 ("a screened Chic Sale").
11. Link and Coleman, *Medical Support of the Army Air Forces in World War II*, 826–827.
12. RAB Diary, July 15, 1944.
13. Whyte, *A Time of War*, at 29.
14. RAB Diary, July 12, 1944.
15. Ibid., July 15, 1944.
16. See the following *Wing-ding* articles and items: "Good Photo Joe," July 24, 1944, 6; "Lt. Col Geurry [sic] Hits '100 Mark,'" June 24, 1944, 1; "Stork Clubbers," May 6, 1944, 1; "Play Ball," May 20, 1944, 4; "Willful Winnie," May 13, 1944, 4; and "Strafer Group Poop," June 24, 1944, 5.

17. *Wing-ding*, June 24, 1944, 7; May 13, 1944, 1; July 7, 1944, 1.

18. RAB Diary, July 20, 1944.

19. Kenney, *Reports*, 242. Ennis Whitehead's correspondence for mid-1944 contains a letter, not necessarily related to this but otherwise unexplained, in which General Whitehead identifies several individuals with traditional Chinese names as persons who will be moved forward as his headquarters advances.

20. George Kenney Papers, March 4, 1944. AFHRA Microfilm 27132 (IRIS 889172).

21. RAB Diary, July 20, 1944.

22. Ibid., July 21, 1944.

23. Ibid., July 29, 1944.

24. Ibid., July 11, 1944.

25. Ibid.

26. RAB Diary, July 20, 1944.

27. Ibid., July 13–14, 1944.

28. "L. I. Flier Survives 'Suicide Blow' at Japs," *Brooklyn (NY) Eagle*, December 28, 1944, 1, 9; Stava, *Combat Recon*, 57.

29. Wiley, *The Strafin' Saints*, 65.

30. Craven and Cate, *The Pacific: Matterhorn to Nagasaki— June 1944 to August 1945*, 330; Wiley, *The Strafin' Saints*, 74.

31. Wiley, *The Strafin' Saints*, 65–69, 74.

32. Ibid., 62–63.

33. Ibid., 74.

34. Squadron History, 110th Tactical Reconnaissance Squadron, July 1944, SQ-RCN-110-HI; Wiley, *The Strafin' Saints*, 74.

35. Wiley, *The Strafin' Saints*, 63.

36. Kolln, *The 421st Night Fighter Squadron*, 35.

37. Wiley, *The Strafin' Saints*, 69, 72, 75, 77.

38. Conrad, "The Combat Man Presents Himself," 25 (emphasis in original).

39. Missing Air Crew Report No. 6690 (July 6, 1944).

40. Wiley, *The Strafin' Saints*, 65.

41. Ibid., 70; Squadron History, 82nd Tactical Reconnaissance Squadron, June 1944, SQ-RCN-82-HI (IRIS 66753). Grenda died on June 26, 1944.

42. RAB Diary, February 29, 1944; Wiley, *The Strafin' Saints*, 26.

43. "Mrs Bessemer Clarke Captain in American WAC," *Melbourne Argus*, March 27, 1944; Rogers, *MacArthur and Sutherland*, 65–71, 80–85.

44. RAB Diary, July 21, 1944.

45. Ibid., July 22, 1944.

46. DePastino, *Bill Mauldin*, 186–188. For this, Mauldin was called on the carpet by Lt. Gen. George S. Patton, who charged that the cartoon showed disrespect for officers.

47. "Kepler said he heard from a captain that when the Jack Benny show was at Port Moresby, one soldier got up on the stage to dance with Carole Landis and he started to wrestle with her. Several men had to pull him off of Miss Landis after he had thrown her to the floor." RAB Diary, July 25, 1944.
48. Kolln, *The 421st Night Fighter Squadron*, 26–29.
49. RAB Diary, July 13, 1944. Rocky and Bristowe may have been discussing military justice because Rocky had been named to two officer panels for special court-martials during this period. 91st Photo Wing Special Orders Nos. 75, 94 (June 3, 1944, and June 23, 1944, respectively), WG-91-HI, June 1944 (IRIS 106851).
50. Luszki, *A Rape of Justice*, ix and passim.
51. RAB Diary, July 31, 1944.
52. *Wing-ding*, July 7, 1944, 3, 7; and May 20, 1944, 1; Sturzebecker, *The Roarin' 20s*, 62, 83; RAB Diary, July 11, 1944.
53. RAB Diary, August 1, 1944.
54. Lt. Richard Blend, wire officer of the Wing signal company. *Wing-ding*, May 20, 1944, 1.
55. RAB Diary, July 20, 1944.
56. Ibid., July 25, 1944.
57. Ibid., July 29, 1944.
58. Ibid., July 29, 1944.
59. Compare *Yank Down Under*, November 12, 1943, 8, with "Guinea Like Waukegan, Comments Jack Benny," *Wing-ding*, August 1, 1944, 3.
60. "Guinea Like Waukegan."
61. "Demand for Pix Explains Issue," *Wing-ding*, August 1, 1944, 1. A newsreel clip preserved at the Australian War Memorial, Film F01437, captures the vision of Miss Landis whirling in a white gown, utterly graceful, energetic, and enticing, https://www.awm.gov.au/collection/F01437/.
62. RAB Diary, July 29, 1944.

Chapter 15. Moving Up
1. 91st Photo Wing Special Orders No. 132, WG 91-HI, July 1944 (IRIS 00106852) (August 2, 1944).
2. Discussions of the Biak campaign rely on the U.S. Army official history; Smith, *The Approach to the Philippines*; Eichelberger, *Our Jungle Road to Tokyo*; and Riegelman, *Caves of Biak*, 152–153.
3. Kamma, *Koreri*, 166–207; Rutherford, *Raiding the Land of the Foreigners*, 76–78, 172–203; Penders, *The West New Guinea Debacle*, 115–131; and *Report on Investigation of Illegal Firing By Native Policemen at Anggop, Biak Island, 29 March 1943*, Enemy Publications No. 340, Australian War Memorial shelfmark AWM55-30 EP-340.

4. Smith, *The Approach to the Philippines*, 287.
5. Hough and Arnold, *Big Distance*, 137.
6. Ibid., 140–141.
7. Ibid., 144–145.
8. RAB Diary, August 1, 1944.
9. Ibid.
10. Ibid., August 9, 1944.
11. Wiley, *The Strafin' Saints*, 66–69.
12. RAB Diary, August 16, 1944.
13. Wiley, *The Strafin' Saints*, 76.
14. Ibid., 84.
15. Ibid., 83.
16. Hill, *Darkroom Soldier*, 105–107.
17. Ibid., 108.
18. Squadron History, 17th Tactical Reconnaissance Squadron, May 1944, SQ-RCN-17-HI.
19. Smith, *The Approach to the Philippines*, 297.
20. RAB Diary, August 16, 1944.
21. Ibid., August 10, 1944.
22. Ibid., August 13, 1944.
23. Ibid., August 13, 1944 (but including logistical misadventures on August 14).
24. Ibid., August 15, 1944.
25. Ibid.
26. Riegelman, *Caves of Biak*, 152–153.
27. RAB Diary, August 16, 1944.
28. Ibid., August 10, 1944.
29. Ibid., August 13, 1944.
30. Ibid., August 23, 1944.
31. Ibid., August 17, 1944, August 16, 1944.
32. Ibid., August 20, 1944.
33. Ibid., August 16, 1944.
34. Rosenfeld and Gross, *Air National Guard at Sixty*, 5–6.
35. Lindbergh, *Wartime Journals*, 869, 877.
36. Lindbergh, *Wartime Journals*, 856; Eichelberger, *Our Jungle Road to Tokyo*, 155.
37. RAB Diary, August 16, 1944.
38. Ibid., August 17, 1944.
39. Kenney, *Reports*, 400–401.
40. RAB Diary, August 23, 1944.
41. Ibid., August 21, 1944.
42. Wiley, *The Strafin' Saints*, 72–73.
43. RAB Diary, August 16, 1944.

44. Ibid., August 21, 1944.
45. Ibid., July 29, 1944.
46. Ibid., August 23, 1944.
47. Ibid., August 24, 1944.
48. Ibid., August 25, 1944.
49. *Yank Down Under*, September 15, 1944, back cover.
50. Wiley, *The Strafin' Saints*, 75, 82.
51. RAB Diary, August 17, 1944, August 23, 1944, August 10, 1944.
52. White, *Green Armor*, 130, 136; Wiley, *The Strafin' Saints*, 73.
53. Wiley, *The Strafin' Saints*, 83.

Chapter 16. Biak

1. Craven and Cate, *The Pacific: Matterhorn to Nagasaki—June 1944 to August 1945*, 301–302; RAB Diary, August 31–September 1, 1944.
2. Wing History, 91st Reconnaissance Wing unit history, July 1944, WG-91-HI (IRIS 106825), 4.
3. RAB Diary, September 2, 1944.
4. Ibid., August 25, 1944.
5. Ibid., August 26, 1944.
6. Ibid., September 16, 1944.
7. Wiley, *The Strafin' Saints*, 80, 81, 82, 84, 91.
8. Wing History, 91st Photo Reconnaissance Wing, July 1944, WG-91-HI, (IRIS 106825), 5.
9. Ibid.
10. RAB Diary, September 12, 1944.
11. Ibid., September 10, 1944.
12. Wing History, 91st Reconnaissance Wing, July 1944, WG-91-HI (IRIS 106825), 6.
13. RAB Diary, September 5, 1944.
14. Ibid., October 12, 1944.
15. Wiley, *The Strafin' Saints*, 85-86.
16. Ibid., 91-92.
17. Missing Air Crew Report No. 8634 (September 3, 1944); Wiley, *The Strafin' Saints*, 89–90, 94.
18. Wiley, *The Strafin' Saints*, 102.
19. Ibid., 97.
20. RAB Diary, September 2, 1944.
21. Ibid., September 3, 1944.
22. RAB Diary, September 3, 1944. Compare the official citation, for a flight that won a Distinguished Flying Cross apiece for Brownfield and Darnell and a third Oak Leaf Cluster (i.e., a fourth DFC) for Guerry, Wing History, 91st Reconnaissance Wing, July 1944, WG 91-HI (IRIS 106852), 2.

> The three officers, flying unarmed F-5 airplanes, took off on 7 May 1944 on the longest over-water flight which had ever been attempted by single-place aircraft in this theater. Extremely adverse weather conditions obscured a small island which was to have been the only navigational checkpoint throughout the flight. Flying part of the time in formation entirely by instruments, the pilots reached their destination, but clouds prevented their taking photographs, and only a visual reconnaissance could be made. . . . [T]he officers repeated the record flight on 9 May 1944, but again low clouds were encountered over the area. However, the two missions proved the feasibility of extended over-water navigation in this type of aircraft.

The close relation of the official citation to Lieutenant Bristowe's paraphrase, as reported by Rocky's diary entry, testifies to the accuracy of Rocky's reporting, whether he recorded it directly from Bristowe's recitation or confirmed it against the text of the citation.

23. Wiley, *The Strafin' Saints*, 75, 82, 85, 95.
24. Ibid., 94–96.
25. Ibid., 92–93, 95.
26. RAB Diary, October 9–10, 1944.
27. "WACs at Work," *Yank Down Under*, September 8, 1944, 6–7; "Patience, Patients, Here Come the Nurses," *Wing-ding*, July 24, 1944, 4–5; "Mail Call," *Yank Down Under*, September 15, 1944, 18; RAB Diary, September 10, 1944.
28. RAB Diary, September 13, 1944.
29. Wiley, *The Strafin' Saints*, 84.
30. RAB Diary, September 14, 1944.
31. *Yank Down Under*, September 8, 1944, 18.
32. RAB Diary, September 15, 1944.
33. RAB Diary, September 17, 1944; Missing Air Crew Report No. 7012 (August 5, 1944). The draft controversy had been noted in the *Wing-ding*, May 13, 1944, 1; "Deferment Ban for Religion Students Hit," *Brooklyn (NY) Eagle*, May 8, 1944, 9.
34. Link and Coleman, *Medical Support of the Army Air Forces in World War II*, 849–850.
35. Ibid., 850; Stouffer, *The American Soldier* 1:278.
36. RAB Diary, October 1, 1944.
37. Ibid., September 15, 1944.
38. Ibid., September 6, 1944.
39. Ibid., September 19–20, 1944.
40. Goldstein, "Ennis C. Whitehead: Aerial Tactician," 196.

41. RAB Diary, September 23, 1944.

42. Stouffer, *The American Soldier*, 1:235; Craven and Cate, *The Pacific: Matterhorn to Nagasaki—June 1944 to August 1945*, 328–329.

43. RAB Diary, September 26–29, 1944.

44. Wiley, *The Strafin' Saints*, 89–91, 96.

45. RAB Diary, August 26, 1944.

46. Ibid., October 1, 1944.

47. Ibid.

48. Ibid., October 2, 1944.

49. RAB Diary, August 29, 1944.

50. Ibid., August 29, 1944, September 26, 1944.

51. Ibid., October 12, 1944.

52. Penders, *The West New Guinea Debacle*, 92. These figures are for the period ending at year-end 1944.

53. RAB Diary, October 3–4, 1944.

54. Wiley, *The Strafin' Saints*, 79–80, 135.

55. Ibid., 82–83, 95. See Schafer, "Investigation of Japanese Medical Depot at an Evacuated Air Strip in New Guinea," and "Investigation of Japanese Medical Depots on Biak Island."

56. Ibid., 106.

57. RAB Diary, August 21, 1944.

58. Ibid., September 15, 1944.

59. Ibid., October 8, 1944.

Chapter 17. Leyte

1. Craven and Cate, *Guadalcanal to Saipan*, 615.

2. Kenney, *Reports*, 447–450; Morison, *History of United States Naval Operations in World War II*, vol. 12, *Leyte*, 148.

3. RAB Diary, October 14, 1944.

4. Wiley, *The Strafin' Saints*, 105.

5. RAB Diary, October 22, 1944.

6. Ibid., October 26, 1944.

7. Craven and Cate, *The Pacific—Matterhorn to Nagasaki—June 1944 to August 1945*, 357–358; Kenney, *Reports*, 453–467; Cannon, *Leyte: The Return to the Philippines*, 85–88, 187; Hubbard, "Scrub Team at Tacloban," 8; Morison, vol. 12, *Leyte*, 151; Kolln, *The 41st Night Fighter Squadron*, 62.

8. Birdsall, *Flying Buccaneers*, 223; Kenney, *Reports*, 464–465; Kenney, *Pappy Gunn*, 101. In the latter book, Kenney dates this attack to October 30, 1944.

9. Craven and Cate, *The Pacific—Matterhorn to Nagasaki—June 1944 to August 1945*, 369.

10. RAB Diary, October 28, 1944.

11. Ibid., October 31, 1944.

12. Ibid., November 4, 1944.

13. Ibid., November 6, 1944.

14. Ibid.

15. Cannon, *Leyte: Return to the Philippines*, 190.

16. Valtin, *Children of Yesterday*, 187. Quoted in Cannon, *Leyte: Return to the Philippines*, 214.

17. Dodd, *The Corps of Engineers—The War Against Japan*, 583; Cannon, *Leyte: Return to the Philippines*, 187.

18. RAB Diary, November 16, 1944.

19. Wiley, *The Strafin' Saints*, 119. Lieutenant Stoegbauer, Lieutenant Thompson, and Sergeant Rocco, a waist gunner, were later rescued. Squadron History, 17th Tactical Reconnaissance Squadron, December 1944, SQ-RCN-17-HI.

20. Wiley, *The Strafin' Saints*, 109.

21. Ibid., 119–120, 135–136. Another pilot died in a P-51 accident: Lt. Jim Richards, a tall flyer from Wyoming, who was caught in bad weather while ferrying a plane and ran out of gas. His orders home had already reached the operations tent. Ibid., 123.

22. Monthly Report, 1094th Signal Service Company, 63rd Service Group, December 1944; Supplemental Report, 1804th Ordnance Supply and Maintenance Company, 46th Service Group (AVN) December 6, 1944; Organizational History, 46th Service Squadron, 308th Bomb Wing, December 1944 (IRIS 100454); Johansen, "Banzai at Burauen," 4.

23. Johansen, "Banzai at Burauen," 6.

24. The following account of the Battle of the Airstrips draws on Cannon, *Leyte: Return to the Philippines*, 294–305; Organizational History, 46th Service Squadron, 308th Bomb Wing, December 1944 (IRIS 100454); Johansen, "Banzai at Burauen," 4–8; Wiley, *The Strafin' Saints*, 133–134 (account by Colonel Sams); Boggs, "Marine Ground Troops in Leyte Action"; and Spencer Davis, "Heroic Yanks Battle Sky Troops Raid," *Fresno (CA) Bee*, December 11, 1944.

25. Johansen, "Banzai at Burauen," 7.

26. In or prior to August 1978, my father was informed by the National Personnel Records Center that his military service records, including those relating to his Second World War service, had been destroyed by fire. His military service and decorations were initially researched using his AGO Form 66 Officer Qualification Record (dated October 11, 1950) and various family and university records. The decorations listed on the Form 66 do not include the Combat Infantryman's Badge. Nor do they include the Presidential Unit Citation for the night action at Mindoro, in which he is among the officers mentioned

by name. Other records were obtained following a diligent search by archivists at the National Personnel Records Center (representing materials relating to his continuing career in the Air Force Reserve, from the Korean War to the date on which he retired). The records confirm that Rocky did indeed qualify, as he said once, as an expert with the Thompson gun. More significantly, the records indicate that the decorations that my father earned include the American Defense Service Medal, American Campaign Service Medal, Asiatic-Pacific Service Medal (with four Bronze Stars for campaign service), and the Philippine Liberation Medal (with a Bronze Star), as well as the ribbon for the Presidential Unit Citation. I do not believe that the badge in his drawer was or that my father qualified for the Expert Infantryman Badge, which is similar in appearance.

Intriguingly, the Army Human Resources Command has found it necessary to state, as a FAQ answer on its website, that Army Air Corps members who "engaged in ground combat in defense of the Philippines" are not eligible to wear the Combat Infantry Badge, which suggests that other airmen have frequently found reason to ask this question. https://www.hrc.army.mil/content/Combat%20 Infantry%20Badge%20CIB. Clarification of whether any airmen earned this badge during the war, or were awarded it in any other circumstances, will be welcomed.

Chapter 18. Fiasco Night

1. Morison, *History of United States Naval Operations in World War II*, vol. 13, *The Liberation of the Philippines*, 50.
2. Journal of RAAF Squadron Leader A. Overland (December 20, 1944), quoted in Wilson, *Always First*, 77–78.
3. Wilson, *Always First*, 79.
4. Journal of RAAF Squadron Leader A. Overland (December 25, 1944), quoted in Wilson, *Always First*, 79.
5. Rocky had also been assigned the duties of a temporary paymaster and entrusted with $40,000 to pay the squadron. 71st Tactical Reconnaissance Group, 72, Special Orders 191 (December 18, 1944).
6. Kenney, *Reports*, 499; Wiley, *The Strafin' Saints*, 134. For the night battle at Mindoro, this chapter draws on the following sources: Morison, vol. 13, *The Liberation of the Philippines*; Kenney, *Reports*; Wilson, *Always First*; Kupferer, *No Glamour . . . No Glory*; Stanaway and Hickey, *Attack and Conquer*; Odgers, *Air War Against Japan*; Bulkley, *At Close Quarters*; Dull, *A Battle History of the Imperial Japanese Navy 1941–1945*, 332; Prados, "Mindoro's Desperate Hours," 90–101; Charland, "The Mailbag," 3–5 (71st Tactical Reconnaissance Group

association newsletter article); Nycum, "How I Remember It" (memoir published on website maintained for 503rd Airborne Battalion); Abbott, "Remembering Mindoro" (published on website maintained for the 503rd Airborne Battalion); Veatch, *Jungle, Sea, and Occupation;* 71st Tactical Reconnaissance Group, Special Orders 184, 191 (December 4, 1944 and December 18, 1944); 110th Tactical Reconnaissance Squadron, "Summary of the Strike against the Jap Naval Task Force the Night of 26 December 1944," SQ-RCN-110-HI, December 1944 (dated January 18, 1945); 17th Tactical Reconnaissance Squadron, Historical Record and Report, SQ-RCN-17-HI, December 1944 (dated March 9, 1945); Eighth Fighter Group, "Mission of the Night of 26 December 1944," GP-8-HI (December 1944) (dated December 30, 1944); "Brief Account of the Attack on Mindoro by a Japanese Naval Task Force, 26–27 December 1944," Special Projects File, shelf-mark R110.7011–15, December 26–27, 1944 (IRIS 467888); and the following Missing Air Crew Reports: MACR No. 12604 (January 12, 1945) (for crew of B-25 flown by Burwell Vowell, including Van Kennon); MACR No. 12603 (January 12, 1945) (for B-25 flown by William N. Hatcher); MACR No. 15017 (December 29, 1944) (for William R. Hilton); MACR No. 15018 (December 29, 1944) (for Wilkins Hunt); MACR No. 15019 (December 30, 1944) (for Gerald Grandmaison); and MACR No. 12199 (January 15, 1945) (for Robert K. Foulkes). Also of value are the facts set forth and participants identified in the Presidential Unit Citation honoring the 110th Tactical Reconnaissance Squadron for its actions at Mindoro on December 26–27, 1944.

7. 17th Tactical Reconnaissance Squadron, Historical Record and Report, December 1944, SQ-RCN-17-HI, 4–5.

8. The role played by this Navy warplane has been well told by John Prados in "Mindoro's Desperate Hours," 90–101.

9. Prados, "Mindoro's Desperate Hours," 95.

10. Odgers, *Air War against Japan 1943–1945*, 378; Morison, vol. 13, *The Liberation of the Philippines*, 38–40. Admiral Morison minimized that night's report of Japanese troopship convoys in his history of naval operations. In MacArthur's army, most of the men who actually listened to Japanese radio transmissions were Australian. Few Australian soldiers came north to the Philippines, but the radio eavesdroppers, with the RAAF airdrome construction squadrons, were there. The Australian official history appears to reflect the original decrypts of December 1944.

11. Morison, vol. 13, *The Liberation of the Philippines*, 37–38; Dull, *Battle History of the Imperial Japanese Navy*, 332.

12. Stille and Wright, *Imperial Japanese Navy Destroyers 1919–1945*; Stille, *The Imperial Japanese Navy in the Pacific War*.
13. "Brief Account of the Attack on Mindoro," 1.
14. Kupferer, *No Glamour*, 194–195.
15. Eighth Fighter Group, "Mission of the Night of 26 December 1944," GP-8-HI (December 1944).
16. 110th Tactical Reconnaissance Squadron, "Summary of the Strike against the Jap Naval Task Force the Night of 26 December 1944," 1.
17. Charland, "The Mailbag," 3–5.
18. 110th Tactical Reconnaissance Squadron, "Summary of the Strike against the Jap Naval Task Force," 1.
19. Charland, "The Mailbag," 4.
20. 110th Tactical Reconnaissance Squadron, "Summary of the Strike against the Jap Naval Task Force," 1; Bulkley, *At Close Quarters*, 407.
21. 17th Tactical Reconnaissance Squadron, Historical Record and Report, 5–9; Prados, "Mindoro's Desperate Hours," 96–97.
22. Eighth Fighter Group, "Mission of the Night of 26 December 1944," 1; Stanaway and Hickey, *Attack and Conquer*, 226–227.
23. Stanaway and Hickey, *Attack and Conquer*, 227; Kupferer, *No Glamour*, 194–203.
24. Prados, "Mindoro's Desperate Hours," 98; Bulkley, *At Close Quarters*, 407.
25. 17th Tactical Reconnaissance Squadron, Historical Record and Report, 5–9; Prados, "Mindoro's Desperate Hours," 97–99; Stanaway and Hickey, *Attack and Conquer*, 227.
26. Nycum, "How I Remember It."
27. 110th Tactical Reconnaissance Squadron, "Summary of the Strike against the Jap Naval Task Force," 2.
28. Nycum, "How I Remember It."
29. Odgers, *Air War Against Japan*, 378.
30. 17th Tactical Reconnaissance Squadron, Historical Record and Report, 9, 5–9.
31. Ibid., 9.
32. Ibid., 7.
33. Ibid., 6.
34. Ibid., 5; Missing Air Crew Report No. 12604 (January 12, 1945).
35. Abbott, "Remembering Mindoro"; Veatch, *Jungle, Sea, and Occupation*, 89–92.
36. Missing Air Crew Report No. 12604. In late 1945, the wreck of Montana Maid was discovered on a mountainside on the island of Panay, between Mindoro and Leyte. The remains of the bomber's crew and Lieutenant Kennon were reinterred after the war at Zachary Taylor National Cemetery, in Louisville.

37. 17th Tactical Reconnaissance Squadron, Historical Record and Report, 5.

38. Charland, "The Mailbag," 4–5.

39. Abbott, "Remembering Mindoro."

40. Morison, vol. 13, *The Liberation of the Philippines*, 41–42; Prados, "Mindoro's Desperate Hours," 99.

41. Missing Air Crew Report No. 15019 (December 30, 1944).

42. Missing Air Crew Report No. 15017 (December 29, 1944).

43. Missing Air Crew Report No. 15018 (December 29, 1944).

44. "Brief Account of the Attack on Mindoro," 2.

45. 17th Tactical Reconnaissance Squadron, Historical Record and Report, 5–8.

46. Kupferer, *No Glamour*, 203.

Chapter 19. Home

1. Eichelberger, *Our Jungle Road to Tokyo*, 204.

2. John Dos Passos, on assignment in Luzon for *Life* magazine, traveled the same route from Lingayen to Manila. Along the way, he reported crossing "a series of temporary bridges across a broad dry riverbed with intermittent channels of slimy green water. Beside us was a railroad bridge. Every other span was blown up." Dos Passos, *Tour of Duty*, 134.

3. Kenney, *Reports*, 510–511.

4. Craven and Cate, *Matterhorn to Nagasaki*, June 1944 to August 1945, 421, 413–414.

5. Kenney, *Reports*, 544.

6. Casey. *Airfield and Base Development*, 389.

7. Craven and Cate, *Matterhorn to Nagasaki*, June 1944 to August 1945, 691–692.

8. Ibid., 693.

Bibliography

Unpublished Materials
Handwritten diary of Roscoe Allen Boyer, Serial Number 0-856663, begun September 8, 1943, and continued through November 16, 1944, with related journal entries (including separate typescript journal entries relating to basic training), letters, and photographs. All in the author's possession.

Borders, Charles Wesley. Discussions with author, November 2016.

Military Records
Archival records of the following Army Air Force units and individuals, maintained in the nonclassified archive of the Air Force Historical Research Agency (AFHRA), Maxwell Air Force Base, Montgomery, Alabama.
    Sixth Photo Reconnaissance Group
    Eighth Fighter Group
    Eighth Photo Reconnaissance Squadron
    17th Tactical Reconnaissance Squadron
    58th Fighter Group
    71st Tactical Reconnaissance Group
    82nd Tactical Reconnaissance Squadron
    91st Photo Reconnaissance Wing
    110th Tactical Reconnaissance Squadron
    5212th Photo Reconnaissance Wing (Provisional)

Eighth Fighter Group, "Mission of the Night of 26 December 1944," GP-8-HI (December 1944) (December 30, 1944).

110th Tactical Reconnaissance Squadron, "Summary of the Strike against the Jap Naval Task Force the Night of 26 December 1944," SQ-RCN-110-HI, December 1944 (January 18, 1945).

"Brief Account of the Attack on Mindoro by a Japanese Naval Task Force, 26–27 December 1944," Special Projects File, AFHRA shelf-mark R110.7011–15, December 26–27, 1944.

Correspondence of George C. Kenney.

General George C. Kenney Diary and Papers.

Correspondence of Ennis Whitehead.

Missing Air Crew Reports.

Published Materials

Newspapers cited have generally been accessed online, via the News papers.com (http://www.newspapers.com/) and NewspaperARCHIVE .com (http://newspaperarchive.com/) websites, or by sites maintained by the newspapers. Military, census, and similar records have generally been accessed online via fold3.com (http://www.fold3.com) or Ancestry .com (http://www.ancestry.com/) websites.

Two newspapers and one magazine served the Southwest Pacific and warrant further note. *Guinea Gold* was an Australian serviceman's daily newspaper, published from November 19, 1942, to June 30, 1946, initially at Port Moresby. After American troops arrived, Americans contributed and a second daily edition was published from Dobodura. It was published in Northern, Southern, American, and Australian editions. *Yank Down Under* was published from Sydney, beginning in August 1943, under the distant authority of the general *Yank* organization. The *Wingding* was the newspaper of the 91st Photo Reconnaissance Wing. It began publishing in Nadzab in April 1944 and moved on with the offensive. These journals have been consulted from original publications.

Abbott, Don. "Remembering Mindoro." The Heritage Battalion: Official Website of the 503rd P.R.C.T. http://corregidor.org/heritage_battalion /abbott/ mindoro.html (accessed March 25, 2016).

Alcorn, John S. *The Jolly Rogers: History of the 90th Bomb Group during the Second World War.* Temple City, Calif.: Historical Aviation Album, 1987.

Allied Geographical Section. *Getting About in New Guinea.* Melbourne: GHQ-SWPA, April 4, 1943.

Anderson, Carrol. "Suicide at Cape Waios." *Air Classics* 6 (October 1969): 6 et seq.

Arnold, Bryan C. "Military Censorship." *Field Artillery Journal* 33/6 (June 1943): 438.

Back Load: February 1943–June 1944: 433rd Troop Carrier Group (Sydney: Halstead Press, 1945).

Bartsch, William H. *Every Day a Nightmare: American Pursuit Pilots in the Defense of Java.* College Station, Tex.: Texas A&M University Press, 2010.

Baumgardner, Randy. *Fifth Air Force.* Paducah, Ky.: Turner Publishing, 1998.

Birdsall, Steve. *Flying Buccaneers: The Illustrated History of Kenney's Fifth Air Force.* Garden City, N.Y.: Doubleday, 1977.

Boggs, Charles W., Jr. "Marine Ground Troops in Leyte Action." Appendix V in *Marine Aviation in the Philippines.* Washington, D.C.: U.S. Marine Corps, 1951.

Brinkley, Douglas. *Washington Goes to War: The Extraordinary Transformation of a City and a Nation.* New York: Random House, 1988.

Bruning, John R. *Indestructible: One Man's Rescue Mission That Changed the Course of WWII.* New York: Hachette, 2016.

Bulbeck, Chilla. *Australian Women in Papua New Guinea: Colonial Passages, 1920–1960.* Cambridge: Cambridge University Press, 1992.

Bulkley, Robert J. *At Close Quarters: PT Boats in the US Navy.* Washington, D.C.: Department of the Navy, 1962.

Cannon, M. Hamlin. *United States Army in World War II: The War in the Pacific.* Vol. 9, *Leyte: The Return to the Philippines.* Washington, D.C.: Department of the Army, 1954.

Caplow, Theodore. "Rumors in War." *Social Forces* 25 (1947): 298.

Casey, Hugh. *Engineers of the Southwest Pacific.* Vol. 6, *Airfield and Base Development.* Washington, D.C.: U.S. Government Printing Office, 1951.

Charland, Smith T. "The Mailbag." *The Reconnnoiterer* 2, no. 5 (Oct. 1997): 3–5.

Claringbould, Michael John. *Black Sunday: When the U.S. Fifth Air Force Lost to New Guinea's Weather.* Brisbane: privately printed, 1995.

Clark, Howard. "A Comparison of Civil and Court-Martial Procedure." *Indiana Law Journal* 4 (1929): 589–599.

Coakley, Robert W., and Leighton, Richard M. *United States Army in World War II: The War Department.* Vol. 2, *Global Logistics and Strategy 1943–1945.* Washington, D.C.: Department of the Army, 1968.

Conrad, Cecil D. "The Combat Man Presents Himself." In *Observations on Combat Flying Personnel,* edited by David G. Wright, 23–32. New York: Josiah Macy Jr. Foundation, 1945.

Cortesi, Lawrence. *Valor in the Sky.* New York: Zebra Press, 1985.

Craven, W. F., and J. L. Cate. *The Army Air Forces in World War II.* Vol. 1, *Plans and Early Operations—January 1939 to August 1942.* Chicago: University of Chicago Press, 1948.

———. *The Army Air Forces in World War II*. Vol. 4, *The Pacific: Guadalcanal to Saipan—August 1942 to July 1944*. Chicago: University of Chicago Press, 1950.

———. *The Army Air Forces in World War II*. Vol. 5, *The Pacific: Matterhorn to Nagasaki—June 1944 to August 1945*. Chicago: University of Chicago Press, 1953.

Cundiff, Michael J. *Ten Knights in a Bar Room: Missing in Action in the Southwest Pacific, 1943*. Ames, Iowa: Iowa State University Press, 1990.

Dean, Peter J. "MacArthur's War: Strategy, Command and Plans for the 1943 Offensive." In *Australia 1943: The Liberation of New Guinea*, edited by Peter J. Dean. Cambridge: Cambridge University Press, 2013.

DeLonge, Merrill E. "How to Baffle a Bombardier." *Saturday Evening Post*, July 11, 1942, 18–19.

———. *Modern Airfield Planning and Concealment*. New York: Pitman, 1943.

DePastino, Todd. *Bill Mauldin: A Life Up Front*. New York: Norton, 2008.

Dexter, David St.-A. *Australia in the War of 1939–1945: Series 1; Army*. Vol. 6, *The New Guinea Offensives*. Canberra: Australian War Memorial, 1961.

Dodd, Karl C. *The Corps of Engineers: The War Against Japan*. Washington, D.C.: U.S. Government Printing Office, 1966.

Dos Passos, John. *Tour of Duty*. Boston: Houghton Mifflin, 1946.

Dougherty, John E. "Flying Fatigue—The Effects of Four Months Combat Flying in a Tropical Combat Zone on Fighter Pilots." In *Observations on Combat Flying Personnel*, edited by David C. Wright, 33–39. New York: Josiah Macy Jr. Foundation, 1945.

Drea, Edward J. *MacArthur's Ultra: Codebreaking and the War against Japan, 1942–1945*. Lawrence, Kans.: University Press of Kansas, 1992.

Dull, Paul S. *A Battle History of the Imperial Japanese Navy 1941–1945*. Annapolis: Naval Institute Press, 1978.

Eichelberger, Robert. *Dear Miss Em: General Eichelberger's War in the Pacific*. Westport, Conn.: Greenwood Press, 1972.

———. *Our Jungle Road to Tokyo*. New York: Viking, 1950. Reprint edition, Nashville: Battery Press, 1989.

Eyman, Scott. *John Wayne: The Life and Legend*. New York: Simon & Schuster, 2014.

Fortier, Norman J. *An Ace of the Eighth: An American Fighter Pilot's War in Europe*. New York: Random House, 2003.

Frazier, Everette E. *Tsili Tsili Sting*. San Antonio: privately printed, Kinko's Copy Center, 1992.

Gamble, Bruce. *Fortress Rabaul: The Battle for the Southwest Pacific, January 1942–April 1943*. Minneapolis: Zenith, 2010.

———. *Target Rabaul: The Allied Siege of Japan's Most Infamous Stronghold, March 1943–August 1945*. Minneapolis: Zenith, 2013.

Gann, Timothy. "Fifth Air Force Light and Medium Bomber Operations during 1942 and 1943: Building Doctrine and Forces that Triumphed in the Battle of the Bismarck Sea and the Wewak Raid." Thesis, School of Advanced Air Power Studies, Air University, 1992. http://permanent.access.gpo.gov/websites/dodandmilitaryejournals/www.maxwell.af.mil/au/aul/aupress/SAAS_Theses/SAASS_Out/gann/gann.pdf.

Goldstein, Donald M. "Ennis C. Whitehead: Aerial Tactician." In *We Shall Return! MacArthur's Commanders and the Defeat of Japan 1942–1945*, edited by William M. Leary, 178–207. Lexington, Ky.: University Press of Kentucky, 1988.

Greenwood, John T. "The Fight against Malaria in the Papua and New Guinea Campaigns." Lecture presented at the U.S. Army—Japanese Ground Self-Defense Force Military History Exchange, Tokyo, 2001. http://history.amedd.army.mil/booksdocs/wwii/Malaria2.pdf.

Griffith, Thomas E. *MacArthur's Airman: General George C. Kenney and the War in the Southwest Pacific*. Lawrence, Kans.: University Press of Kansas, 1998.

Gunn, Nathaniel. *Pappy Gunn*. Bloomington, Ind.: Authorhouse, 2004.

Hall, Gwendolyn Midlo. *Love, War, and the 96th Engineers (Colored): The World War II New Guinea Diaries of Captain Hyman Samuelson*. Urbana, Ill.: University of Illinois Press, 1995.

Hara, Tameichi. *Japanese Destroyer Captain*. New York: Ballantine Books, 1961.

Heller, Joseph. *Catch-22*. New York: Charles Scribner's Sons, 1962.

Henebry, John P. *The Grim Reapers at Work in the Pacific Theatre: The Third Attack Group of the U.S. Fifth Air Force*. Missoula, Mont.: Pictorial Histories, 2002.

Hill, Fred. *Darkroom Soldier*. La Grande, Oreg.: Photosmith Books, 2007.

Hough, Donald, and Elliott Arnold. *Big Distance*. New York: Duell, Sloan and Pearce, 1945.

Hubbard, Lucien. "Scrub Team at Tacloban." *Reader's Digest*, February 1945, 8.

Hunt, Frazier. *MacArthur and the War against Japan*. New York: Charles Scribner's Sons, 1944.

Johansen, Herbert O. "Banzai at Burauen." *Air Force* 28 (March 1945): 4–8.

———. *WW II*. New York: Grosset & Dunlap, 1975.

Johnson, R. Wally. *Fire Mountains of the Islands*. Canberra: Australian National University Press, 2013.

Johnston, George H. *Pacific Partner*. New York: Duell, Sloan and Pearce, 1944.

——. *The Toughest Fighting in the World*. New York: Duell, Sloan and Pearce, 1943.

Jones, James. *The Thin Red Line*. New York: Charles Scribner's Sons, 1962.

Kahn, E. J. *G. I. Jungle*. New York: Simon & Schuster, 1943.

——. "The Terrible Days of Company E." *Saturday Evening Post*, January 8, 1944, 43–44.

Kamma, Freerk Ch. *Koreri: Messianic Movements in the Biak-Numfor Culture Area*. The Hague: Martinus Nijhoff, 1972.

Keegan, John. *Six Armies in Normandy*. London: Jonathan Cape, 1982.

Kelly, Carol Adele. *Voices of My Comrades: America's Reserve Officers Remember World War II*. New York: Fordham University Press, 2007.

Kenney, George C. *General Kenney Reports*. New York: Duell, Sloan and Pearce, 1949.

——. *The Saga of Pappy Gunn*. New York: Duell, Sloan and Pearce, 1960.

Kolln, Jeff. *The 421st Night Fighter Squadron in World War II*. Atglen, Pa.: Schiffer Publishing, 2004.

Krulak, Victor. *First to Fight: An Inside View of the U.S. Marine Corps*. Annapolis, Md.: Naval Institute Press, 1984.

Kupferer, Anthony J. *No Glamour . . . No Glory: The Story of the 58th Fighter Group of World War II*. Dallas: Taylor Publishing, 1989.

Lardner, John. *Southwest Passage: The Yanks in the Pacific*. Philadelphia: J. B. Lippincott, 1943. Reprint edition, Lincoln, Nebr.: University of Nebraska Press, 2012.

Lee, Ulysses. *United States Army in World War II: Special Studies*. Vol. 8, *The Employment of Negro Troops*. Washington, D.C.: Department of the Army, 1966.

Lindbergh, Charles. *The Wartime Journals of Charles A. Lindbergh*. New York: Harcourt Brace Jovanovich, 1970.

Link, Mae Mills, and Hubert A. Coleman. *Medical Support of the Army Air Forces in World War II*. Washington, D.C.: Office of the Surgeon General, United States Air Force, 1955.

Luszki, Walter A. *A Rape of Justice: MacArthur and the New Guinea Hangings*. New York: Madison Books, 1991.

MacArthur, Douglas. *Reminiscences*. New York: McGraw-Hill Book Company, 1964.

McAulay, Lex. *The Battle of the Bismarck Sea*. New York: St. Martin's Press, 1991.

McCarthy, Dudley. *Australia in the War of 1939–1945: Series 1; Army*. Vol. 5, *Southwest Pacific Area—The First Year: Kokoda to Wau*. Canberra: Australian War Memorial, 1959.

McCarthy, J. K. *Patrol into Yesterday: My New Guinea Years*. Melbourne: F. W. Cheshire, 1963.

McManus, John. *The Deadly Brotherhood: The American Combat Soldier in World War II*. New York: Random House/Presidio Press, 2003.

Manchester, William. *American Caesar: Douglas MacArthur 1880–1964*. Boston: Little, Brown, 1978.

Mauldin, Bill. *Up Front*. New York: Holt, 1945.

Miller, John. *United States Army in World War II: The War in the Pacific*. Vol. 3, *Guadalcanal—The First Offensive*. Washington, D.C.: Department of the Army, 1949.

———. *United States Army in World War II: The War in the Pacific*. Vol. 5, *CARTWHEEL—The Reduction of Rabaul*. Washington, D.C.: U.S. Army Center of Military History, 1959.

Miller, Roger G. "'Under the Influence' and 'Acting with Prejudice': Allegations against Maj. Lewis H. Brereton at Fort Sill, Oklahoma, 1929–1930," *Air Power History* 57, no. 2 (2010): 4–13.

Milner, Samuel. *United States Army in World War II: The War in the Pacific*. Vol. 4, *Victory in Papua*. Washington, D.C.: Department of the Army, 1957.

Mitchell, Angus S. "Those 'Y' Blokes." *The Rotarian*, June 1944, 32–33.

Morison, Samuel Eliot. *History of United States Naval Operations in World War II*. 15 vols. Boston: Little, Brown, 1947–1962.

Newell, Reg. *Operation Goodtime and the Battle of the Treasury Islands, 1943*. Jefferson, N.C.: McFarland, 2012.

Nycum, Chet. "How I Remember It: My Private War." The Heritage Battalion: Official Website of the 503rd P.R.C.T. http://corregidor.org/Heritage_Battalion/nycum/ch7.html (accessed March 25, 2016).

Ocko, Felix H. "A Case of Atabrine Psychosis in a Civilian." *American Journal of Psychiatry* 103 (1947): 833–834.

Odgers, George James. *Australia in the War of 1939–1945: Series 3: Air*. Vol. 2, *Air War Against Japan*. Canberra: Australian War Memorial, 1957.

The Officers' Guide: A Ready Reference on Customs and Correct Procedures Which Pertain to Commissioned Officers of the Army of the United States. 8th ed. Harrisburg, Pa.: Military Service Publishing, 1942.

Olson, Lynne. *Those Angry Days: Roosevelt, Lindbergh, and America's Fight over World War II, 1939–1941*. New York: Random House, 2013.

Penders, C. L. M. *The West New Guinea Debacle: Dutch Decolonisation and Indonesia 1945–1962*. Honolulu: University of Hawai'i Press, 2002.

Perry, Mark. *"The Most Dangerous Man in America": The Making of Douglas MacArthur*. New York: Basic Books, 2014.

Pfau, Ann Elizabeth. *Miss Yourlovin: GIs, Gender, and Domesticity During World War II*. New York: Gutenberg-e, Columbia University Press, 2008. http://www.gutenberg-e.org/pfau/chapter1.html.

———. "Postal Censorship and Military Intelligence During World War II." In *The Winton M. Blount Postal History Symposia: Select Papers 2006–2009—Smithsonian Contributions to History and Technology 55*, edited by Thomas Lera, 81–90. Washington, D.C.: Smithsonian Institution Press, 2010. http://postalmuseum.si.edu/symposium2008/pfau-postal_censorship.pdf.

Prados, John. "Mindoro's Desperate Hours," *MHQ: The Quarterly Journal of Military History* 8 (Autumn 1995): 90–101.

Reports of General MacArthur. 2 vols. Washington, D.C.: Department of the Army, 1966.

Riegelman, Harold. *Caves of Biak: An American Officer's Experiences in the Southwest Pacific.* New York: Dial Press, 1955.

Robinson, Neville K. *Villagers at War: Some Papuan New Guinean Experiences in World War II.* Canberra: Australian National University Press, 1979.

Rogers, Paul P. *MacArthur and Sutherland: The Bitter Years.* New York: Praeger, 1991.

Roosevelt, Elliott. *As He Saw It.* New York: Duell, Sloan and Pearce, 1946.

Rosenfeld, Susan, and Charles Gross. *Air National Guard at Sixty: A History.* Washington, D.C.: Government Printing Office for the Air National Guard, 2007.

Ross, Davis R. B. *Preparing for Ulysses: Politics and Veterans During World War II.* New York: Columbia University Press, 1969.

Rothgeb, Wayne. *New Guinea Skies: A Fighter Pilot's View of World War II.* Ames, Iowa: Iowa State University Press, 1992.

Rutherford, Danilyn. *Raiding the Land of the Foreigners: The Limits of the Nation on an Indonesian Frontier.* Princeton: Princeton University Press, 2002.

Schafer, Earl W. "Investigation of Japanese Medical Depot at an Evacuated Air Strip in New Guinea," *Journal of the American Medical Association* 125/6 (1944): 435.

———. "Investigation of Japanese Medical Depots on Biak Island," *Journal of the American Medical Association* 126/2 (1944): 34.

Shaw, Henry I., and Douglas T. Kane. *History of United States Marine Corps Operations in World War II.* Vol. 2, *Isolation of Rabaul.* Washington, D.C.: United States Marine Corps, 1963.

Sheehan, Susan. *A Missing Plane.* New York: Putnam, 1986.

Sheppeck, M. L., and L. E. Wexberg. "Toxic Psychoses Associated with Administration of Quinacrine." *Archives of Neurology and Psychiatry* 5 (1946): 489–510.

Shibutani, Tamotsu. *Improvised News: A Sociological Study of Rumor.* Indianapolis: Bobbs Merrill, 1966.

"Ships with a History." *RIL Post* (magazine of Royal Interocean Lines), October 1974, 190–194.

Smith, Robert Ross. *United States Army in World War II: The War in the Pacific.* Vol. 8, *The Approach to the Philippines.* Washington, D.C.: Department of the Army, 1953.

Special Service Division, Army Service Forces. *A Pocket Guide to New Guinea.* Washington, D.C.: War and Navy Departments, 1944.

Stanaway, John, and Lawrence J. Hickey. *Attack and Conquer: The 8th Fighter Group in World War II.* Atglen, Pa.: Schiffer Publishing, 1995.

Stanaway, John, and Bob Rocker. *The Eight Ballers: Eyes of the Fifth Air Force.* Atglen, Pa.: Schiffer Publishing, 1999.

Stava, Robert. *Combat Recon: Images from the Southwest Pacific 1943–45.* Atglen, Pa.: Schiffer Publishing, 2007.

Stille, Mark E. *The Imperial Japanese Navy in the Pacific War.* Oxford: Osprey Publishing, 2014.

Stille, Mark, and Paul Wright. *Imperial Japanese Navy Destroyers 1919–1945.* 2 vols. Oxford: Osprey Publishing, 2013.

Stouffer, Samuel A. *The American Soldier: Adjustment during Army Life.* Princeton: Princeton University Press, 1949.

Sturzebecker, Russell L. *The Roarin' 20s: A History of the 312th Bombardment Group.* Kennett Square, Pa.: KNA Press, 1976.

Taaffe, Stephen R. *MacArthur's Jungle War: The 1944 New Guinea Campaign.* Lawrence: University Press of Kansas, 1998.

Tennille, Andy. "A Special Mission: Reporter Discovers Grandfather's War Record." *High Point Enterprise* (High Point, North Carolina), June 16, 2002, F-1.

Thompson, Peter A., and Robert Macklin. *The Battle of Brisbane.* Brisbane: Australian Broadcasting Company, 2000.

Titus, Richard W. *Come What Will: A Chronicle of Georgia's 101st Separate Coast Artillery Battalion.* Georgia: privately printed, 1994.

Toll, Ian W. *The Conquering Tide: War in the Pacific Islands 1942–1944.* New York: Norton, 2015.

Tunny, Noel. *Gateway to Victory: The Establishment of the First U.S. Armed Forces in Australia 1941–42.* Brisbane: privately printed, 1991.

——. *Winning from Downunder.* Brisbane: Boolarong Press, 2010.

Vail, Richard M., ed. *Strike! The Story of the Fighting 17th.* Melbourne: Jackson & O'Sullivan, 1944.

Valtin, Jan [Richard J. Krebs]. *Children of Yesterday.* New York: Readers' Press, 1946.

Veatch, Paul D. *Jungle, Sea, and Occupation: A World War II Soldier's Memoir of the Pacific Theater.* Jefferson, N.C.: McFarland Publishing, 2000.

Waiko, John Dademo. *A Short History of Papua New Guinea.* Melbourne: Oxford University Press Australia and New Zealand, 1993.

Wallace, Paul Jefferson *Guinea Gold: History, 1942–1946*. Sydney: F. Cunninghame, 1971.

War Department. Basic Field Manual FM 30-25. "Military Intelligence/Counterintelligence." February 1940 ed., 45.

War Department Technical Manual 16-205. "The Chaplain." 1941, 52.

Watts, Anthony G., and Brian G. Gordon. *The Imperial Japanese Navy*. New York: Doubleday, 1971.

Wedemeyer, Albert C. *Wedemeyer Reports!* New York: Devin-Adair, 1958.

White, Osmar. *Green Armor*. New York: Norton, 1945.

White, W. L. "They Fight with Cameras." *American Mercury*, November 1943, 537–542.

Whitlock, Charles. Interview, Rutgers Oral History Archives. oralhistory.rutgers.edu/interviewees/30-interview-html-text/70-whitlock-charles-p (accessed March 25, 2016).

Whyte, William H. *A Time of War: Remembering Guadalcanal, A Battle Without Maps*. New York: Fordham University Press, 2000.

Wiley, Katherine Sams, and Robert Nichols, eds. *The Strafin' Saints: The 71st Tactical Reconnaissance Group: Memories of Their Service in the Pacific Theater 1943 through 1945*. Houston: privately printed, 1994.

Williams, Peter. *The Kokoda Campaign 1942—Myth and Reality*. Cambridge: Cambridge University Press, 2012.

Willis, Ian. *Lae: Village and City*. Melbourne: University of Melbourne Press, 1974.

Willmott, H. P. *The Barrier and the Javelin: Japanese and Allied Pacific Strategies, February to June 1942*. Annapolis: Naval Institute Press, 2008.

Willoughby, Charles A. *MacArthur 1941–1951*. New York: McGraw-Hill, 1954.

Wilson, David. *Always First: The RAAF Airfield Construction Squadrons 1942–1974*. Fairbarn, Australia: Air Power Studies Centre, 1998.

Wolk, Herman S. "George C. Kenney: MacArthur's Premier Airman." In *We Shall Return! MacArthur's Commanders and the Defeat of Japan 1942–1945*, edited by William M. Leary, 88–114. Lexington: University Press of Kentucky, 1988.

Yenne, Bill. *Aces High: The Heroic Saga of the Two Top-Scoring American Aces of World War II*. New York: Berkley Caliber, 2009.

Yoshino, Ronald W. *Lightning Strikes: The 475th Fighter Group in the Pacific War, 1943–1945*. Manhattan, Kans.: Sunflower University Press, 1988.

Zimmerman, John L. *The Guadalcanal Campaign*. Washington, D.C.: Historical Division, Headquarters United States Marine Corps, 1949.

Index

About the Authors

Allen D. Boyer studied at Vanderbilt University and the University of Virginia and received his doctorate from the University of St. Andrews. This is his fifth book. His longtime day job was senior appellate counsel at the New York Stock Exchange Enforcement Division. He lives on the North Shore of Staten Island with his wife and sons.

Rocky Boyer, on whose diary this book draws, was born in 1919 on a farm in Indiana. He kept the diary while serving with the 5th Air Force in New Guinea and the Philippines. After the war, he wanted to farm but could not afford to, so he earned a graduate degree in psychology instead. He taught at the University of Mississippi, training a generation of teachers and tirelessly supporting the public schools. He died in 2008.

The **Naval Institute Press** is the book-publishing arm of the U.S. Naval Institute, a private, nonprofit, membership society for sea service professionals and others who share an interest in naval and maritime affairs. Established in 1873 at the U.S. Naval Academy in Annapolis, Maryland, where its offices remain today, the Naval Institute has members worldwide.

Members of the Naval Institute support the education programs of the society and receive the influential monthly magazine *Proceedings* or the colorful bimonthly magazine *Naval History* and discounts on fine nautical prints and on ship and aircraft photos. They also have access to the transcripts of the Institute's Oral History Program and get discounted admission to any of the Institute-sponsored seminars offered around the country.

The Naval Institute's book-publishing program, begun in 1898 with basic guides to naval practices, has broadened its scope to include books of more general interest. Now the Naval Institute Press publishes about seventy titles each year, ranging from how-to books on boating and navigation to battle histories, biographies, ship and aircraft guides, and novels. Institute members receive significant discounts on the Press' more than eight hundred books in print.

Full-time students are eligible for special half-price membership rates. Life memberships are also available.

For a free catalog describing Naval Institute Press books currently available, and for further information about joining the U.S. Naval Institute, please write to:

Member Services
U.S. NAVAL INSTITUTE
291 Wood Road
Annapolis, MD 21402-5034
Telephone: (800) 233-8764
Fax: (410) 571-1703
Web address: www.usni.org